BUSINESS AND
GENERAL
REFERENCE
BOOK SERIES
FROM IDG

Dogs For Dummies®

Quick Reference Card

W9-AUT-294

Puppy gear

These are the things you probably need if you have (or are planning to get) a new puppy. Chapter 4 offers more information.

- ❏ Baby gates (for keeping puppy in bounds)
- ❏ Brush and comb
- ❏ Chew toys
- ❏ Dishwasher-safe, non-chewable bowls (one for water, one for food)
- ❏ Enzyme cleaner for pet stains
- ❏ Flat or rolled collar, buckle or snap-together — *not* a slip-collar — with an ID tag
- ❏ High-quality puppy food, as recommended by a breeder or veterinarian
- ❏ Lightweight leash, six feet long
- ❏ Nail trimmer and Kwik Stop powder
- ❏ Pooper scooper
- ❏ Properly sized shipping crate (for house-training)
- ❏ Puppy shampoo

Keys to dog-training success

The right attitude is every bit as important in dog training as the right equipment — a properly fitted collar and leash. Chapter 11 offers step-by-step training tips, but here are a few basics to keep in mind:

- ❏ Be prepared to dedicate time on a regular basis.
- ❏ Be consistent in your approach.
- ❏ Be on the same team: Work with your dog, not against him.
- ❏ Be positive about training.
- ❏ Be fair when correcting your dog.

Preventive-health checklist

The following are some preventive-care guidelines. Talk to your veterinarian about what is best for your pet.

Puppy veterinary care

- ❏ Initial exam within 48 hours of adoption.
- ❏ Four or five combination vaccinations at three-week intervals, starting at the age of 6 to 8 weeks. Rabies vaccination at 16 weeks.
- ❏ Wormings as prescribed by your veterinarian, at two- to three-week intervals or until fecal test comes up clear.
- ❏ Heartworm preventive. No heartworm test required if puppy's mother was on preventive and puppy is started by the age of 12 weeks.
- ❏ Follow-up exam at time of final vaccinations to spot congenital problems, retained baby teeth, etc.
- ❏ Spaying or neutering, as early as 8 weeks, as recommended by your veterinarian.

Adult veterinary care

- ❏ Annual examination, which may include periodic chemistry profile and urinalysis, especially for older pets and prior to procedures requiring anesthesia.
- ❏ Combination vaccination, annually. Rabies vaccination, once every three years or as required by law.
- ❏ Heartworm testing.
- ❏ Dental cleaning and scaling under anesthesia, annually or as recommended by your veterinarian.

Adult home care

- ❏ Heartworm preventive, daily or monthly
- ❏ Nail trim, weekly
- ❏ Regular bathing and grooming
- ❏ Home exam, including checking for lumps and bumps, weekly
- ❏ Tooth-brushing, two or three times a week
- ❏ Regular flea-control program

...For Dummies: Bestselling Book Series for Beginners

...FOR DUMMIES
BUSINESS AND
GENERAL
REFERENCE
BOOK SERIES
FROM IDG

Dogs For Dummies®

Quick Reference Card

Signs that your dog needs immediate veterinary attention

Following is a list of some symptoms that require your dog to see a vet. Remember that when in doubt, day or night, don't wait: Call your veterinarian!

- ✔ Allergic reactions, such as swelling around the face, or hives, most easily seen on the belly

- ✔ Any eye injury, no matter how mild

- ✔ Any respiratory problem: Chronic coughing, trouble breathing, or near drowning

- ✔ Any signs of pain: Panting, labored breathing, increased body temperature, lethargy, restlessness, or loss of appetite

- ✔ Any suspected poisoning, including ingestion of antifreeze, rodent or snail bait, or human medication

- ✔ Any wound or laceration that's open and bleeding, or any animal bite

- ✔ Seizure, fainting, or collapse

- ✔ Snake bite

- ✔ Thermal stress, either too cold or too hot, even if the dog seems to have recovered

- ✔ Trauma, such as being hit by a car, even if the dog seems fine

- ✔ Vomiting or diarrhea, anything more than two or three times within an hour or so

Items to keep in your canine medicine chest

Following is a list of the items you should include in your canine medicine chest. Refer to Chapter 10 for more information.

- ❏ Adhesive tape

- ❏ Benadryl antihistamine

- ❏ Betadine antiseptic

- ❏ Buffered aspirin

- ❏ Cotton swabs, balls, and rolls

- ❏ Eye wash

- ❏ Forceps or tweezers

- ❏ Hydrogen peroxide

- ❏ Kwik Stop powder

- ❏ Scissors

- ❏ Sterile gauze, both rolls and pads

- ❏ Syringe with the needle removed (for giving liquid medication)

- ❏ Syrup of Ipecac

- ❏ Thermometer

- ❏ Tranquilizers (as prescribed by your veterinarian)

- ❏ Triple antibiotic cream or ointment

- ❏ Vet Wrap padded bandages

- ❏ Water-based lubricating jelly, such as K-Y

IDG
BOOKS
WORLDWIDE

...For Dummies: Bestselling Book Series for Beginners

Praise, Praise, Praise for Dogs For Dummies!

"Despite the title of the book, living with dogs and not owning a copy of this book might become a new definition for 'Dummy'."
— Paul D. Pion, D.V.M., President & CEO, Veterinary Information Network, Inc.

"Dogs For Dummies is anything but. It's an intelligent, thorough, and humorous reference that should be on any dog-lover's list of must-haves."
— Duncan C. Ferguson, V.M.D., Ph.D., DACVIM, DACVCP, Professor,
    University of Georgia College of Veterinary Medicine

"If you had to pass a test to be a dog owner, this is all the book you'd need to get your license. Your dog will be glad you read this. So will you."
— Gene Lock, Reigning Cats and Dogs Store, Sacramento

"This kind of owner's manual for dogs is indispensable, and I can think of no one more qualified to write it."
— Beth Adelman, former managing editor of the *American Kennel Gazette,*
    the official magazine of the American Kennel Club

"Owning a copy of this delightful book is one of the best things you can do for your dog."
— Maria Goodavage, author, *The California Dog Lover's Companion*

"Gina Spadafori is one of the most knowledgeable dog writers I know. Her talents as a journalist combined with her passion for all things canine make her uniquely qualified to educate and motivate new dog owners."
— Audrey Pavia, former managing editor of *Dog Fancy* magazine and
    former senior editor of *American Kennel Gazette*

"Gina is extremely perceptive when it comes to dogs and people, and is able to communicate ideas in a clear, insightful, and humorous manner."
— Mary Young, top dog trainer, Texas

"I am really excited about Gina's book! This is a book I will recommend to all my clients, and to anyone who has a dog. Gina's enthusiasm, knowledge, and compassion show on every page."
— Linda Randall, D.V.M., Dipl. American Board of Veterinary Practitioners

"An intriguing book filled with a wealth of practical information for dog owners that stands tails above the rest — two paws up!"
— Darris O. Hercs, Executive Assistant Director, Oakland SPCA

Praise, Praise, Praise for Gina's Columns

"Gina's Pet Connection column comes from the mind of a journalist who knows pets and from the heart of a pet owner who loves them. And her readers benefit greatly."
— Gregory Favre, executive editor, *The Sacramento Bee* newspaper

"THE PET CONNECTION: pet protection, pet reflection, pet selection, pet perfection, pet correction, pet direction, pet affection, pet inspection, pet collection and pet retrospection. Where else can you find all this but in Gina Spadafori's entertaining and indispensable column, The Pet Connection. I love it."
— Mordecai Siegal, editor of *The UC Davis Book of Dogs* and president of the Dog Writers Association of America

"I am impressed by the breadth of Gina Spadafori's knowledge, the extent of her research, and the depth of her sincerity. Her columns are a labor of love and anyone who has known, and loved, a dog, should never miss them."
— Margaret Gavel, Georgia

"Gina Spadafori captured the attention of the online world when her Pet Connection appeared in the Pet Care Forum on America Online. Her personable writing style and great knowledge of dogs make her column a regular favorite with AOL members."
— Mike Richards, D.V.M., former head of the America Online Pet Care Forum

TM

References for the Rest of Us!^{TM}

by Gina Spadafori

Foreword by
Marty Becker, DVM
Coauthor of *Chicken Soup for the Pet Lover's Soul*

IDG Books Worldwide, Inc.
An International Data Group Company

Foster City, CA ♦ Chicago, IL ♦ Indianapolis, IN ♦ New York, NY

Dogs For Dummies®

Published by
IDG Books Worldwide, Inc.
An International Data Group Company
919 E. Hillsdale Blvd.
Suite 400
Foster City, CA 94404
www.idgbooks.com (IDG Books Worldwide Web site)
www.dummies.com (Dummies Press Web site)

Library of Congress Catalog Card No.: 96-77267

ISBN: 1-56884-861-7

Printed in the United States of America

10 9 8 7 6

1O/RU/RQ/ZY/IN

Distributed in the United States by IDG Books Worldwide, Inc.

Distributed by Macmillan Canada for Canada; by Transworld Publishers Limited in the United Kingdom; by IDG Norge Books for Norway; by IDG Sweden Books for Sweden; by Woodslane Pty. Ltd. for Australia; by Woodslane (NZ) Ltd. for New Zealand; by Addison Wesley Longman Singapore Pte Ltd. for Singapore, Malaysia, Thailand, Indonesia and Korea; by Norma Comunicaciones S.A. for Colombia; by Intersoft for South Africa; by International Thomson Publishing for Germany, Austria and Switzerland; by Toppan Company Ltd. for Japan; by Distribuidora Cuspide for Argentina; by Livraria Cultura for Brazil; by Ediciencia S.A. for Ecuador; by Ediciones ZETA S.C.R. Ltda. for Peru; by WS Computer Publishing Corporation, Inc., for the Philippines; by Unalis Corporation for Taiwan; by Contemporanea de Ediciones for Venezuela; by Computer Book & Magazine Store for Puerto Rico; by Express Computer Distributors for the Caribbean and West Indies. Authorized Sales Agent: Anthony Rudkin Associates for the Middle East and North Africa.

For general information on IDG Books Worldwide's books in the U.S., please call our Consumer Customer Service department at 800-762-2974. For reseller information, including discounts and premium sales, please call our Reseller Customer Service department at 800-434-3422.

For information on where to purchase IDG Books Worldwide's books outside the U.S., please contact our International Sales department at 650-655-3200 or fax 650-655-3297.

For information on foreign language translations, please contact our Foreign & Subsidiary Rights department at 650-655-3021 or fax 650-655-3281.

For sales inquiries and special prices for bulk quantities, please contact our Sales department at 650-655-3200 or write to the address above.

For information on using IDG Books Worldwide's books in the classroom or for ordering examination copies, please contact our Educational Sales department at 800-434-2086 or fax 317-596-5499.

For press review copies, author interviews, or other publicity information, please contact our Public Relations department at 650-655-3000 or fax 650-655-3299.

For authorization to photocopy items for corporate, personal, or educational use, please contact Copyright Clearance Center, 222 Rosewood Drive, Danvers, MA 01923, or fax 978-750-4470.

is a trademark under exclusive license to IDG Books Worldwide, Inc., from International Data Group, Inc.

About the Author

Gina Spadafori writes an award-winning column on pets and their care for the Universal Press Syndicate, which distributes it to newspapers across the United States and in the pets area of America Online, the world's largest commercial online service. She is affiliated with the Veterinary Information Network, Inc., an international online service for veterinarians and the content provider for AOL's Pet Care Forum.

Gina has served on the Board of Directors of both the Cat Writers Association and the Dog Writers Association of America. She is a three-time recipient of the DWAA's Maxwell Medallion for Best Newspaper Column, and she has been awarded the Geraldine R. Dodge award for her pet writing. She has also been honored with the Pedigree Dog Food Outstanding Journalist Pet Care award.

Dogs For Dummies received the DWAA award for Best General Reference as well as the DWAA President's Award for outstanding entry in the association's writing competition, topping 1,000 entries in more than 50 categories.

She lives in Sacramento, California, where she is an editor at *The Sacramento Bee* newspaper and shares her home with two dogs: Andy, a Shetland sheepdog, and Benjamin, a flat-coated retriever adopted by way of the Internet.

ABOUT IDG BOOKS WORLDWIDE

Welcome to the world of IDG Books Worldwide.

IDG Books Worldwide, Inc., is a subsidiary of International Data Group, the world's largest publisher of computer-related information and the leading global provider of information services on information technology. IDG was founded more than 25 years ago and now employs more than 8,500 people worldwide. IDG publishes more than 275 computer publications in over 75 countries (see listing below). More than 90 million people read one or more IDG publications each month.

Launched in 1990, IDG Books Worldwide is today the #1 publisher of best-selling computer books in the United States. We are proud to have received eight awards from the Computer Press Association in recognition of editorial excellence and three from *Computer Currents'* First Annual Readers' Choice Awards. Our best-selling *...For Dummies®* series has more than 50 million copies in print with translations in 38 languages. IDG Books Worldwide, through a joint venture with IDG's Hi-Tech Beijing, became the first U.S. publisher to publish a computer book in the People's Republic of China. In record time, IDG Books Worldwide has become the first choice for millions of readers around the world who want to learn how to better manage their businesses.

Our mission is simple: Every one of our books is designed to bring extra value and skill-building instructions to the reader. Our books are written by experts who understand and care about our readers. The knowledge base of our editorial staff comes from years of experience in publishing, education, and journalism — experience we use to produce books for the '90s. In short, we care about books, so we attract the best people. We devote special attention to details such as audience, interior design, use of icons, and illustrations. And because we use an efficient process of authoring, editing, and desktop publishing our books electronically, we can spend more time ensuring superior content and spend less time on the technicalities of making books.

You can count on our commitment to deliver high-quality books at competitive prices on topics you want to read about. At IDG Books Worldwide, we continue in the IDG tradition of delivering quality for more than 25 years. You'll find no better book on a subject than one from IDG Books Worldwide.

John Kilcullen
CEO
IDG Books Worldwide, Inc.

Steven Berkowitz
President and Publisher
IDG Books Worldwide, Inc.

Eighth Annual Computer Press Awards ≥1992

Ninth Annual Computer Press Awards ≥1993

Tenth Annual Computer Press Awards ≥1994

Eleventh Annual Computer Press Awards ≥1995

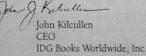

IDG Books Worldwide, Inc., is a subsidiary of International Data Group, the world's largest publisher of computer-related information and the leading global provider of information services on information technology. International Data Group publishes over 275 computer publications in over 75 countries. More than 90 million people read one or more International Data Group publications each month. International Data Group's publications include: ARGENTINA: Buyer's Guide, Computerworld Argentina, PC World Argentina; AUSTRALIA: Australian Macworld, Australian PC World, Australian Reseller News, Computerworld, IT Casebook, Network World, Publish, Webmaster; AUSTRIA: Computerwelt Osterreich, Networks Austria, PC Tip Austria; BANGLADESH: PC World Bangladesh; BELARUS: PC World Belarus; BELGIUM: Data News; BRAZIL: Annuario de Informática, Computerworld, Connections, Macworld, PC Player, PC World, Publish, Reseller News, Supergamepower; BULGARIA: Computerworld Bulgaria, Network World Bulgaria, PC & MacWorld Bulgaria; CANADA: CIO Canada, Client/Server World, ComputerWorld Canada, InfoWorld Canada, NetworkWorld Canada, WebWorld; CHILE: Computerworld Chile, PC World Chile; COLOMBIA: Computerworld Colombia, PC World Colombia; COSTA RICA: PC World Centro America; THE CZECH AND SLOVAK REPUBLICS: Computerworld Czechoslovakia, Macworld Czech Republic, PC World Czechoslovakia; DENMARK: Communications World Danmark, Computerworld Danmark, Macworld Danmark, PC World Danmark, Techworld Danmark; DOMINICAN REPUBLIC: PC World Republica Dominicana; ECUADOR: PC World Ecuador; EGYPT: Computerworld Middle East, PC World Middle East; EL SALVADOR: PC World Centro America; FINLAND: MikroPC, Tietoverkko, Tietoviikko; FRANCE: Distributique, Hebdo, Info PC, Le Monde Informatique, Macworld, Reseaux & Telecoms, WebMaster France; GERMANY: Computer Partner, Computerwoche, Computerwoche Extra, Computerwoche FOCUS, Global Online, Macwelt, PC Welt; GREECE: Amiga Computing, GamePro Greece, Multimedia World; GUATEMALA: PC World Centro America; HONDURAS: PC World Centro America; HONG KONG: Computerworld Hong Kong, PC World Hong Kong, Publish in Asia; HUNGARY: ABCD CD-ROM, Computerworld Szamitastechnika, Internetto online Magazine, PC World Hungary, PC-X Magazin Hungary; ICELAND: Tolvuheimur PC World Island; INDIA: Information Communications World, Information Systems Computerworld, PC World India, Publish in Asia; INDONESIA: InfoKomputer PC World, Komputek Computerworld, Publish in Asia; IRELAND: ComputerScope, PC Live!; ISRAEL: Macworld Israel, People & Computers/Computerworld; ITALY: Computerworld Italia, Macworld Italia, Networking Italia, PC World Italia; JAPAN: DTP World, Macworld Japan, Nikkei Personal Computing, OS/2 World Japan, SunWorld Japan, Windows NT World, Windows World Japan; KENYA: PC World East African; KOREA: Hi-Tech Information, Macworld Korea, PC World Korea; MACEDONIA: PC World Macedonia; MALAYSIA: Computerworld Malaysia, PC World Malaysia, Publish in Asia; MALTA: PC World Malta; MEXICO: Computerworld Mexico, PC World Mexico; MYANMAR: PC World Myanmar; NETHERLANDS: Computer! Totaal, LAN Internetworking Magazine, LAN World Buyers Guide, Macworld Netherlands, Net, WebWereld; NEW ZEALAND: Absolute Beginners Guide and Plain & Simple Series, Computer Buyer, Computer Industry Directory, Computerworld New Zealand, MTB, Network World, PC World New Zealand; NICARAGUA: PC World Centro America; NORWAY: Computerworld Norge, CW Rapport, Datamagasinet, Financial Rapport, Kursguide Norge, Macworld Norge, Multimediaworld Norge, PC World Ekspress Norge, PC World Nettverk, PC World Norge, PC World ProduktGuide Norge; PAKISTAN: Computerworld Pakistan; PANAMA: PC World Panama; PEOPLE'S REPUBLIC OF CHINA: China Computer Users, China Computerworld, China InfoWorld, China Telecom World Weekly, Computer & Communication, Electronic Design China, Electronics Today/ Electronics Weekly, Game Software, PC World China, Popular Computer Week, Software Weekly, Software World, Telecom World; PERU: Computerworld Peru, PC World Profesional Peru, PC World SoHo Peru; PHILIPPINES: Click!, Computerworld Philippines, PC World Philippines, Publish in Asia; POLAND: Computerworld Poland, Computerworld Special Report Poland, Cyber, Macworld Poland, Networld Poland, PC World Komputer; PORTUGAL: Cerebro/PC World, Computerworld/Correio Informático, Dealer World Portugal, Mac*In/PC*In Portugal, Multimedia World; PUERTO RICO: PC World Puerto Rico; ROMANIA: Computerworld Romania, PC World Romania, Telecom Romania; RUSSIA: Computerworld Russia, Mir PK, Publish, Seti; SINGAPORE: Computerworld Singapore, PC World Singapore, Publish in Asia; SLOVENIA: Monitor; SOUTH AFRICA: Computing SA, Network World SA, Software World SA; SPAIN: Communicaciones World España, Computerworld España, Dealer World España, Macworld España, PC World España; SRI LANKA: Infolink PC World; SWEDEN: CAP&Design, Computer Sweden, Corporate Computing Sweden, Internetworld Sweden, it.branschen, Macworld Sweden, MaxiData Sweden, MikroDatorn, Nätverk & Kommunikation, PC World Sweden, PCaktiv, Windows World Sweden; SWITZERLAND: Computerworld Schweiz, Macworld Schweiz, PCtip; TAIWAN: Computerworld Taiwan, Macworld Taiwan, NEW ViSiON/Publish, PC World Taiwan, Windows World Taiwan; THAILAND: Publish in Asia, Thai Computerworld; TURKEY: Computerworld Turkiye, Macworld Turkiye, Network World Turkiye, PC World Turkiye; UKRAINE: Computerworld Kiev, Multimedia World Ukraine, PC World Ukraine; UNITED KINGDOM: Acorn User UK, Amiga Action UK, Amiga Computing UK, Apple Talk UK, Computing, Macworld, Parents and Computers UK, PC Advisor, PC Home, PSX Pro, The WEB; UNITED STATES: Cable in the Classroom, CIO Magazine, Computerworld, DOS World, Federal Computer Week, GamePro Magazine, InfoWorld, I-Way, Macworld, Network World, PC Games, PC World, Publish, Video Event, THE WEB Magazine, and WebMaster; online webzines: JavaWorld, NetscapeWorld, and SunWorld Online; URUGUAY: InfoWorld Uruguay; VENEZUELA: Computerworld Venezuela, PC World Venezuela; and VIETNAM: PC World Vietnam. 5/7/98

Dedication

For Bruce Rubin, who makes things happen, and for Jan Haag and Carol Lea Benjamin, who always knew I could.

Publisher's Acknowledgments

We're proud of this book; please register your comments through our IDG Books Worldwide Online Registration Form located at: http://my2cents.dummies.com.

Some of the people who helped bring this book to market include the following:

Acquisitions, Development, and Editorial

Project Editor: Jennifer Ehrlich

Acquisitions Editor: Kathleen A. Welton

Copy Editor: Tamara S. Castleman

Technical Editor:
Dr. William G. Porte, M.B.A., D.V.M.

Editorial Manager: Mary C. Corder

Editorial Assistant: Ann Miller

Special Help

Jay Gavron, Illustrator; Constance Carlisle, Editorial Assistant; Photography by the following: Gay Currier, Kerry Drager, Randy Pench, Richard D. Schmidt, HSUS

Production

Project Coordinator: Valery Bourke

Layout and Graphics: E. Shawn Aylsworth, Brett Black, Cameron Booker, Linda M. Boyer, Maridee V. Ennis, Angela F. Hunckler, Todd Klemme, Jane E. Martin, Mark C. Owens, Tricia R. Reynolds, Anna Rohrer, Brent Savage, Gina Scott, Deirdre Smith

Proofreaders: Kathy McGuinnes, Michael Bolinger, Kelli Botta, Joel K. Draper, Rachel Garvey, Nancy Price, Dwight Ramsey, Robert Springer, Carrie Voorhis, Ethel M. Winslow, Karen York

Indexer: Sherry Massey

General and Administrative

IDG Books Worldwide, Inc.: John Kilcullen, CEO; Steven Berkowitz, President and Publisher

IDG Books Technology Publishing: Brenda McLaughlin, Senior Vice President and Group Publisher

Dummies Technology Press and Dummies Editorial: Diane Graves Steele, Vice President and Associate Publisher; Mary Bednarek, Director of Acquisitions and Product Development; Kristin A. Cocks, Editorial Director

Dummies Trade Press: Kathleen A. Welton, Vice President and Publisher; Kevin Thornton, Acquisitions Manager

IDG Books Production for Dummies Press: Michael R. Britton, Vice President of Production and Creative Services; Cindy L. Phipps, Manager of Project Coordination, Production Proofreading, and Indexing; Kathie S. Schutte, Supervisor of Page Layout; Shelley Lea, Supervisor of Graphics and Design; Debbie J. Gates, Production Systems Specialist; Robert Springer, Supervisor of Proofreading; Debbie Stailey, Special Projects Coordinator; Tony Augsburger, Supervisor of Reprints and Bluelines

Dummies Packaging and Book Design: Robin Seaman, Creative Director; Kavish + Kavish, Cover Design

♦

The publisher would like to give special thanks to Patrick J. McGovern, without whom this book would not have been possible.

♦

Author's Acknowledgments

There are so many people involved in the making of a book it doesn't seem fair only one name goes on the cover. My first wish would be to thank the readers who have let me know they enjoyed my columns, both in newspapers and on America Online.

The staff at IDG Books is amazing. In particular, I'd like to thank Kathy Welton, who had the idea for this book and asked me to write it, and Jennifer Ehrlich, who shepherded the project through with the grace and dedication of a border collie. Others who deserve mention are Tammy Castleman, Sarah Kennedy, Stacy Collins, Ann Miller, Michelle Vukas, Jamie Klobuchar, Valery Bourke, and Maridee Ennis. The contributions of illustrator Jay Gavron are positively first-rate, and I'm grateful, too, for his calmness at deadline times. Rich Tennant's swell "The 5th Wave" cartoons prove he has a good handle on the sweet quirkiness of the canine soul. Photographers Gay Currier (who's also a fine dog trainer), Kerry Drager, Randy Pench, and Dick Schmidt brought their unique vision to this book. My thanks, too, to the Humane Society of the United States for the use of their photographs. Dr. William G. Porte, M.B.A., D.V.M., of Sacramento Veterinary Surgical Services has my thanks for reviewing the text for medical accuracy.

My family — parents Nino and Louise Spatafore, brothers Joe and Pete, sister-in-law Sally, and Pete and Sally's children, Kate and Steven (and Max, the Lab) — have in general looked kindly upon my "dog-centric" life, and for that, I'm grateful.

The following friends — and their dogs — deserve thanks for their help: Sue Ballenger (and her dogs, Major and Scooter); Ann Cony; Tami Collier and the Skylark Shelties; Peggy Conway (Shanna and Toastie); Terry Dvorak (Molly); Audrey Fitzgerald (Maggie); Joan Frazzini (Ali and Gator); Peg Gavel (Sunny, Cali, and Mark Spitz); Robin Glass (Whitney Jane); Gene and Susan Lock (Sydney); Ellen O'Connor and Darryl Young (Sarah, Harold, and Cap); Morgan Ong; Tonya Machen (Moose and Sierra); Carrie Peyton; Sue and Bob Priest (Muffin Marie); Maggie Roth (Katie and Ebenezer); and Eleanor Shaw (Murphy and O'Neal). A special thanks to Robin Shapiro, who let me send him backups of my work for safe-keeping on his hard drive and e-mailed me lovely pictures of his first child, Marissa, in return.

My colleagues at the Veterinary Information Network are all funny and brilliant, a pleasure to work with, especially Dr. Paul Pion, D.V.M., DACVIM, and Dr. Stuart Turner, D.V.M. Dr. Carl Pfeil, D.V.M., is another outstanding veterinarian who deserves a note of thanks. The Dog Writers Association of America has long been a source of support, especially from Beth Adelman, Ranny Green, Audrey Pavia, Mordecai Siegal, and the late Job Michael Evans. Likewise helpful over the years have been the folks at my home newspaper, *The Sacramento Bee,* especially Mike Mattis, who came to me years ago and said: "You know something about animals. Want to write a column?" I also want to thank *The Bee's* Executive Editor, Gregory Favre, for his support.

I cannot close without acknowledging the dogs who have shared my life, especially Lance, the Original Demo Dog, whose spirit will always be with me. Andy and Benjamin, who share my life now, could not be more perfect. That's my story and I'm sticking to it.

Andy and Ben would like to thank Al's Fish Poultry & Meats in Sacramento, source of many fine, fresh, and meaty bones during the course of this project.

Contents at a Glance

Table of Contents

Foreword

*T*hese days, people's pets have become bona fide members of the family. Moving from the kennel to the couch, they share our beds, family rooms, and holidays and are recipients of our kindest impulses and utmost concern.

Yet pet owners know that a pet is also a big responsibility because they are dependent on us for almost all of their basic needs, including food, water, shelter, and love. A pet is a living being whose life your human family will shape, share, and nurture. A pet partnership is a lifetime commitment. Do it right, and your pet will become an important and valuable part of the family for years to come. Do it wrong, and you've broken a sacred covenant between mankind and man's best friend.

As a veterinarian who's done thousands of new puppy and kitten visits, and as someone who works with the leading veterinary experts at most of the major veterinary schools in the United States, I've had the good fortune to see firsthand what steps you can take to begin your pet ownership the right way. Luckily, they are all found in the wonderfully written, comprehensive book that you hold in your hands: *Dogs For Dummies* written by Gina Spadafori.

Many veterinarians recommend this award-winning book to new pet owners because it so quickly and easily delivers the information that clients want — and pets need. It's a proven "in-the-trenches" look at the simple steps you can and must take to make your pet an "ideal" pet — one that is well-behaved, content, and perfectly integrated within the human family.

I enthusiastically recommend *Dogs For Dummies* to all of my clients and to millions of pet lovers through my work on television, radio, and in print because the book is both a comprehensive manual and a quick reference, is easily understandable yet authoritative, and is inspirational as well as instructional. Complete this educational book and you'll have an honorary "Dogtorate" degree in *The Bond*.

Buying this book is most certainly one of the greatest gifts you can give a beloved pet. By following the principles, plans, and proven positive approaches described in *Dogs For Dummies*, you'll be the owner every pet wants and deserves — informed, responsible, and loving.

Marty Becker, DVM

Introduction

Welcome to *Dogs For Dummies,* the canine reference for those who want all the basics covered in one easy-to-use book.

Well, you've found it. Dog health. Dog training. Not to mention dog gear, dog grooming, dog breeding, and dog sports. All in one place with a cover so vivid you'll be able to spot the book even if your dog eats the last two chapters and leaves it for dead in the yard — and if *that* happens, you can easily locate the chapter with the information you need to keep it from happening again. (Look in Chapter 12, in case you can't wait.)

Whether you're looking to adopt a dog, trying to improve your relationship with the one you have, or attempting to come up with fun things to do with your furry pal, this book contains something for you.

So make yourself comfortable and enjoy this comprehensive and easy-to-follow book *for* dog lovers *from* dog lovers. The dog you get — or the dog you have — will thank you, believe me.

We Love Dogs!

If you didn't love dogs, you probably wouldn't have picked up this book. Guess what? You're in great company: The United States and Canada are two of the most dog-crazy countries in the world.

How else would you account for an American Animal Hospital Association survey of U.S. and Canadian pet owners — four-fifths of whom own dogs — where more than half say they prefer an animal companion over a human one if stuck on an island? Where 55 percent consider themselves to be their dog's "mom" or "dad"? Where one-third say they call their dogs on the phone when they're away, and two-thirds travel with them on vacation? Four-fifths give them gifts, and six in ten send cards in their dogs' names. More than one-fifth admit to dressing their dogs on occasion — but I'm guessing that the actual figure is really higher, because I bet a number of people don't admit on a survey to doing so.

My big dog wears a bow tie on special occasions; I admit that up front. The little one has sunglasses, although, in my own defense, let me add that they were a gift — from my neighbor's poodle mix!

We Love Dogs . . . to Death, Sometimes

Some other numbers suggest we don't love dogs all that much. How can anyone explain a society where doggy birthday parties and doggy day care aren't all that rare, but millions of dogs are put to death every year in humane society shelters and municipal animal-control facilities?

Undoubtedly, some of these dogs are semiwild strays, some are psycho, some incurably ill, and some are ancient. But many are none of those things: They're healthy, young, beautiful dogs — mixes and purebred both — who will die because the people who took them in don't want them anymore, for reasons as frivolous as redecorating and as serious as biting.

And what about the puppies who won't make it? Where did they come from? Some end up in shelters as part of "oops" litters, others are leftovers from litters planned by people who overestimated the demand for golden retrievers or poodles or Rottweilers and got tired of the extra mouths to feed.

Because no one wants to imagine the worst, everyone who has ever dropped a dog at a shelter imagines that he ends up in a perfect home.

For many, that home is in heaven. Such is the dark side of a dog-crazy society.

How Do Dog Disasters Happen?

Too many decisions about dogs are made because of emotions, not facts. The truth is, most of us are suckers for a puppy face.

Few things are more adorable than a puppy, no matter the breeding. They are endowed with noses like licorice jelly beans, big eyes that sparkle with curiosity and affection, big paws and gangly legs that give them an adorably bouncy gait, and soft, fluffy fur that's better for snuggling than any teddy bear ever made.

Like human babies, puppies even smell special.

My own theory is that they are made this way as some kind of ingenious natural defense, to keep the humans they rely on from seeking revenge for every carpet soiled, every finger nipped, and every couch corner chewed during what can seem at times a very long babyhood and adolescence. You come upon your wondrous puppy in possession of your new and very expensive running shoes, the upper of the left one neatly severed from its sole by sharp puppy teeth. You feel the blood rush to your face. The puppy stops, a piece of fine leather dangling from an eye tooth.

Before you can snap his little neck, he's running toward you, stumbling over those big paws of his, every inch of his body happy to see you. And before you know it, you're smiling.

See what I mean? Do you think a wild dog would fall for cuteness? Think again. He'd nail him if they had been *his* running shoes. Or his tasty leg of rabbit. Cuteness counts for nothing in the wild.

The awwwwww factor

It's a shame we aren't a little less impressionable where puppies are concerned. Every year hundreds of thousands of people bring puppies into their homes, many after little more than a moment or two of thought.

If you take away only one thing from this book, it's that getting a dog on impulse offers probably the lowest odds for a successful relationship. Still, it's easy to see how it happens.

Maybe you see a puppy at the mall, in a pet-store window that's emblazoned with the symbols of every credit card in your wallet. Or maybe you get waylaid by a couple of kids outside the grocery store, hawking a box of "free" puppies.

"And you say the amount of shedding isn't really that bad?" you ask the nice people at the pet store while cuddling a collie pup, thinking of your navy-blue couch and your closet full of basic black. The puppy sighs and snuggles against your chest. Soon you're adding a lint brush to the growing pile of supplies on the counter and, lest you start to worry about the cost, the sales clerk quickly points out that you can always breed your dog and get your money back with puppy sales. You look at that wonderful puppy face and imagine seven more just like her, and then seven times the purchase price in your pocket. A beautiful pet *and* a return on your investment? Sold.

Or maybe you're moved by pure altruism.

"Say, mister, that one really seems to like you!" says the kid in front of the market, as you stop just long enough to cuddle the pup with that amazingly adorable patch over his eye. The puppy is licking your fingers while your brain struggles to work this dilemma out. You know you ought to call your spouse. But hadn't you talked about getting a dog someday, now that you've bought a house? How much effort can a little puppy be? You always had dogs when you were a child; how can you deny *your* children that pleasure?

"Dad says if we don't get rid of 'em today he's going to drown 'em," says the kid, urgently.

"Not Patch!" you yell and, a little while later, you're driving home with a puppy in your lap and ten pounds of puppy food in the trunk of your car.

Puppy love is fleeting

When it comes to puppies, love at first sight is a disaster in the making. A year later, Patch and the collie touch noses at the shelter. Timmy never seemed to care about Lassie's fur on his jeans, but you can't stand it on your clothes anymore. As for Patch, who'd have thought he'd turn out so large? You have neither the kind of space nor the time for the exercise he needs. And you're tired of yelling at the kids over whose turn it is to clean up the yard. One dog's not house-trained, the other never seemed to understand that chewing wasn't OK. Not surprising, because neither dog was ever trained as a puppy.

They're still nice dogs, though. Young, and apparently healthy. A country home, a little training, and they'd be perfect — for someone else.

Problem is, they aren't so cute anymore. Maybe they both make it, maybe neither does. It's not your fault, is it?

A Preventive Approach

Nobody adopts a dog guessing that they'll be dropping him off at the shelter later. Just thinking about doing so is heartbreaking. You get a dog because you want a loving, well-mannered companion. A playmate for the children. A crime deterrent, perhaps.

The most important factors in determining whether you end up with your dream dog or an ill-mannered and possibly dangerous beast is how well you educate yourself before you buy and how well you educate your dog thereafter.

That's part of what this book is all about. Preparing you to make the right selection when you're ready to adopt a dog and giving you the information you need to make good on the bright promise of that first meeting.

Improving the Dog You Have

Of course, many people wouldn't dream of giving up on their dogs, although the infatuation stage is long past and the relationship is strained. They endure "bad" dogs the way they do bad marriages — and for many of the same reasons. Because the children would be heartbroken or because friends and relatives would be disappointed. Because it's the right thing to do, or because they don't want to admit they made a mistake. Because if they wish hard enough, maybe the situation will get better. Because maybe the problem is their fault, and they're sure that they still love him (or her).

Is this you? You may get points for being a good sport, but admit it: This isn't any fun, either. You want a *good* dog.

I can help you with that. Your marriage? You've got the wrong book.

Why You Need This Book

A saying in dog-training circles — "Every handler gets the dog he deserves" — refers to the fact that your chances at success are directly related to your abilities to choose, raise, and live with your dog properly. What you put in determines what you get out.

In the more than ten years that I've been advising people about dog problems, I've discovered that, more often than not, the lack of accurate information — *not* the lack of effort or concern — is the No. 1 reason for doomed people-pet pairings.

What kind of dog do *you* deserve? I think you deserve a healthy, happy, and well-mannered canine companion, and I'm going to show you how to get one — or turn yours into one. And then I show you how to have a great time sharing your life with your wonder dog.

Becoming an Informed Consumer

Think about what you did before you bought your last car or television set. You probably comparison-shopped, trying to figure out which manufacturer made the product that was best for you in terms of its specifications, its reputation for reliability, and its cost to purchase and maintain.

If you're young, single, and in an entry-level job, I'm guessing you didn't buy a minivan. Likewise, if you spend a lot of time ferrying your daughter's soccer team to the pizza parlor on Saturday afternoons or buying plywood sheets for the latest home-improvement project, your choice wasn't a sporty economy car.

As for the TV, you probably took a tape measure with you to make sure that it fit in your entertainment cabinet.

Now, consider the following: If things go right, you'll have a dog longer than you'll keep a new car and probably longer than a TV will work.

So why should it come as a surprise that you need to shop carefully for a dog? Take your time, study the specifications. Determine the rate of defects, consider the cost of maintenance. Even do your homework on the person from whom you get a dog, because if you have a warranty, you want to deal with people who'll be there when you need them.

You need to be a savvy shopper — before you get a dog and every day after.

With that attitude and the information that follows in this book, you're well on your way to becoming a dog expert — and better still, a satisfied dog owner.

How This Book Is Organized

Dogs For Dummies is divided into five sections. If you're looking for a dog, you may want to start at the beginning. If you already have a dog, you can skip around, checking out the chapters that address your most urgent dog problems. If you want to impress your coworkers by explaining the difference between the two kinds of terriers, you probably want to read the whole book.

No matter the order you choose, here's what you'll find:

Part I: Starting to Think Dog

Mixed breed or purebred? What size? What breed type? Puppy or adult? Male or female? Breeder, humane society, or pet store? Which collar? Which brush? Complicated as these decisions may be, they're also some of the most enjoyable ones you'll ever make. This section walks you through them, step by step.

Part II: Bringing a Puppy or an Adult Dog into Your Life

More decisions — which puppy? which dog? — and the information you need to get through them. And once you get your new puppy or dog home, there's everything you need to get the relationship off on the right paw, including house-training tips for little pups or big dogs.

Part III: Living with Your Dog

Problem-solving and basic care for all stages and ages are outlined here, along with tips on choosing animal-care professionals. Planning puppies? Educate yourself on why you probably shouldn't be, and find out how to handle it if you go ahead anyway, from finding a mate to screening good homes for the puppies.

Part IV: Finding Cool Things to Do with Your Dog

Have some fun! Take a trip or train for competition. You can do more things with your dog than walk her to the park, and here's a whole section of them, just to get you thinking.

Part V: The Part of Tens

From protecting your landscaping to teaching your dog tricks, some of the best has been saved for last. Read them with your dog in your lap — you'll both enjoy them more.

Icons Used in This Book

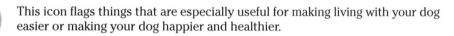

 Maybe you want to know a little more *why* some house-training strategies work better than others. This icon is the place to look to find that sort of information. If you just want to catch the basic concepts, give this guy a pass.

 This icon flags things that are especially useful for making living with your dog easier or making your dog happier and healthier.

This icon highlights some of the best products or services for dog lovers.

 This icon is used to point out special information that's interesting and fun to know, although not essential.

This icon is used to remind you of related information elsewhere in the book, or to steer you to a more detailed discussion of a subject in another chapter.

 This icon reminds you of information so important that you should read it more than once, just to make sure it stays with you.

This icon marks some of the most common mistakes dog owners make along with tips for avoiding them.

This icon flags things that dog lovers ignore at their peril — situations that can be dangerous to people or pets.

Some Additional Notes

In addition to advising people about their pets, I make my living as an editor, so I'm pretty fussy about the "correct" use of language. In one little area, however, the experts and I disagree: The use of the pronoun "it" when referring to animals. I don't like it.

A chair is an "it." A CD is an "it." A laser printer is an "it," even though mine's named "Lance" — after a very special dog, of course. Animals are living, thinking, loving beings, "hims" and "hers." And so will they be described in this book, alternately.

The use of "him" or "her" in any given reference applies to both genders, unless specifically noted otherwise.

While this book has been checked for accuracy by other canine experts, including a team of veterinarians, if you have any questions regarding your dog, don't delay in finding help from a veterinarian, trainer, behaviorist, or other pet-care professional. No book, this one included, can substitute for their hands-on expertise.

Finally, I invite you to let me know about *your* dog and your tales of living with a canine companion. You can read the exploits of my two — Andy, a Sheltie, and Benjamin, a flat-coated retriever — as part of my weekly column, Pet Connection, which is syndicated through the Universal Press Syndicate and also carried every week in the Pet Care Forum of America Online (keyword PETS takes you there). My e-mail address is `Giori@aol.com`, but "snail mail" is just as nice to get at:

Gina Spadafori
Pet Connection
5714 Folsom Blvd., No. 211
Sacramento, CA 95819

Part I
Starting to Think Dog

In this part . . .

This part explains where to look for your new puppy or dog and what equipment you need to get the relationship off to a good start. I also tell you how best to evaluate whether a male or female, puppy or grown dog is a better fit with your family. If you want a purebred puppy, you get the facts you need to find a good breeder — and find out why you should avoid any other kind. Considering a grown dog? Good for you! I give you plenty of information in this part to help you find a good source.

Chapter 1

Considering Canine Possibilities

You don't have to go to a dog show to realize dogs may have started out as wolves, but we've meddled some since then with amazing results. No matter how many steps or how many hundreds of years passed between them, imagining the ancestor of a Maltese or toy poodle as a wolf is difficult at best. A malamute, sure, a German shepherd and maybe even a collie — you can see the wolf in them. But a Maltese? Fluffy, sweet-natured, small enough to fit in an oversized purse . . . it's hard to imagine such an animal chasing deer through a frozen forest or lifting a muzzle to howl at the moon.

But if you observe even the smallest dogs closely for awhile, you see the wolf. The same is true of every dog that has set foot on this earth since dogs began, generations of hounds and herding dogs, lap dogs and sled dogs. Despite the best efforts of our species to change theirs, they are at heart still the animal they came from. Pack animals with a language that's in many ways close to our own, making them a close fit in our own families.

That means Maltese or malamute, toy poodle or Tibetan mastiff, every dog is going to understand the meaning of a smile, both human and canine. Every dog is going to enjoy a good sniff of, and probably a roll on, the most disgusting, smelly object available. And every dog, no matter the mix or breed, wants to be part of a family, a *pack.*

Considering Canine Packaging

Every dog may be a wolf at heart, but we've certainly done plenty to change the rest of the package, to soften some traits and strengthen others. No species on earth shows such diversity of size, shape, and purpose.

In my own home, I have one dog who'd crawl on his belly for miles, skip meals, and forgo sleep on the off chance that someone, somewhere, will throw something into a body of water for him to retrieve, again and again and again until he falls over from exhaustion, still dripping the water that is as much his element as the air he breathes. My other dog walks around puddles but has a tendency to herd children. One's a retriever, the other a herding dog. The behavior of one comes from the instinct to fetch prey, the other is motivated by an age-old desire to drive prey. Along the way, these hunting behaviors were separated — one to the retriever, one to the sheep dog — and bred to be selectively stronger to give the animals a function in the human community.

Dog breeds and breed types differ in size, activity level, shedding levels, and trainability. That means that becoming a canine expert is a good idea less for the opportunity to impress the family when you see a dog show on TV — "the Schipperke, a Belgian breed, first became popular as a watch dog for use on canal boats" — and more for the ability to analyze how any particular breed or breed type will work as a member of your family.

Choosing the right dog for you, your family, and your lives is the first step in acquiring the dog of your dreams.

Go back in time again to the wolf. Remember many of those desirable breed traits — chasing game, herding sheep, and protecting the pack — are wolf traits that have been strengthened or adjusted over time to make dogs a better fit in the human community. Other vestiges of other wolf traits live on in today's dogs, including the desire to know exactly where one stands in the pack, whether it's a canine or human family — and the accompanying desire to better one's status. (See how like us they are?)

Dogs in general are a little more easy-going than wolves, thanks to thousands of years of domestication. But you have to look no farther than dog-bite statistics to see that some problems still exist in this area.

The common victim of these power struggles are children, the smallest, most vulnerable members of the "pack." When I read stories of a family dog — commonly an unneutered male from one of the currently popular tough breeds — that has attacked a child "without warning," I know that's not the whole story. While you may find some psycho dogs, in most cases the humans had more to do with the outcome than the dog did. They got a breed that was too much for them, compounded the problem by not socializing and training the animal, and then didn't recognize the warning signs of a dog looking to be leader. The result was a tragedy for both the child, who must live with the repercussions of an attack for the rest of his life, and for the dog, who usually loses his life in the aftermath.

CAUTION

Call of the wild: wolf-dog hybrids

We never seem to get the balance right when it comes to wolves. First we hated them, almost to extinction. Now we love them — and their close relatives, wolf-hybrids — with a devotion that is for many wolfdogs as lethal as the hatred it replaced.

The result of a breeding between a wolf and a dog — most commonly a husky, malamute or German shepherd — the wolf-hybrid is a beautiful, intelligent animal and a potentially dangerous companion that few people can handle or adequately care for. They are often destructive and can rarely be house-trained. Determined and resourceful escape artists, they can be chillingly efficient predators.

On these points, virtually everyone agrees.

On the point of whether they should be allowed a place in human society at all, widespread and often heated disagreement exists.

The intelligence that fanciers adore, combined with size and strength, causes problems at maturity, when wolf-hybrids do what comes naturally: Try for a higher place in their social order, challenging the authority of their human "packmates." A high rate of human deaths and injuries is associated with the animals, as compared to domesticated dogs as a whole, and you hear many anecdotal accounts of vicious attacks — especially on children — by seemingly docile pets.

Because of these problems, some communities have tried to ban the wolfdogs, many humane and animal control shelters will not put them up for adoption, and the few groups that do give permanent sanctuary to unwanted hybrids are always at capacity. As a result, many a wolf-hybrid has paid for the surge in popularity with its life.

All of which means the wolf-hybrid is a pet most people should avoid.

Statistics show the dogs involved in attacks are most commonly unneutered males, especially young adults coming into their prime — just another reason why neutering is so important. For more reasons to neuter your pet, see Chapter 13.

Always look at the history of your particular breed. A large, powerful dog developed to protect land or property, working on his own and making his own judgments, is not likely to accept your input graciously. He may be highly intelligent, and even biddable in the hands of experienced dog handlers, but in an average family, he's all too often a time bomb.

For most people and most families, the best dog is one from a breed or mix of breeds that have been developed to be responsive to training and human guidance and isn't too hung up on being in charge. Dogs specially developed as companions, such as the toy breeds, fill that role, and so do some hunting and herding breeds, such as the golden retriever or the collie.

Letting Go of "Love at First Sight"

In dogs as in humans, the one you're immediately and most powerfully attracted to may not be the best bet for a long-term companion. You may have grown up with collies in a suburban home with a large yard, and your mother home all day, and you may still consider the collie your "favorite breed." But a collie may not be the best choice for you today if you live alone in an apartment and are fond of expensive clothes in dark colors.

So start fresh, with a fair appraisal of your life and of the dogs who offer the best fit.

I grew up in a home where the undisputed best breed of all time was considered to be a boxer. While I'm still fond of them, I haven't lived with one since I left home. The reason? Dog spit gives me hives, and while boxers aren't the drooliest breed around — the Newfoundland would probably win that prize — they are proficient enough to make me limit my exposure to them.

My mother, on the other hand, thinks nothing of carrying a towel to wipe off a dog, but the little "fur mice" that congregate in the corners of my house — my dogs shed so much I'm thinking of having sweaters made from the fur — would make her scream. I keep the hand-held vacuum close by but otherwise pay little attention to the fact that my medium-coated dog drops black fur, hair by hair, every day, and the long-haired one produces enough gray, white, and tan fuzz during his twice-yearly "big shed" to fill a grocery bag a week.

Fur or drool. Sometimes choosing a dog that suits you comes down to something as simple as that.

Starting from Scratch

Choosing a breed or breed type is one of the most enjoyable aspects of adopting a dog. You have a chance to window-shop on a grand scale, to discover dogs you've never heard of and imagine life with breeds you've never seen before.

Start with an open mind, and be honest about your own life, your own preferences, your own expectations. Keep these factors in mind:

 ✔ Size and space requirements

 ✔ Activity level

 ✔ Fur factor

 ✔ Trainability and dominance

Remember the dog is only one side of the equation; *you* are the other. Be honest about yourself, and about the changes you're willing to make to accommodate a dog, whether that means vacuuming more frequently, keeping his training up, or working some form of daily exercise for the dog into your life.

Sizing up a breed type

The range of size in dogs is truly remarkable, so broad that even though they are the same species, it would be unthinkable for a dog from one end of the spectrum — say, a St. Bernard — to mate with one from the other, like a toy poodle. (Although never underestimate the desire of any dog to try to make such a coupling possible!)

Some people who adore small dogs are scared of large ones. Some who adore large ones speak derisively of small ones, considering them less than "real dogs," and calling them "powder puffs," "dust mops," or "rats." Size doesn't seem to matter as much to the dogs themselves as to the people who own them; many small dogs have the pugnacious attitude that would be downright dangerous in a large dog, and many large dogs want nothing more than to curl up in their owners' laps.

But for practicality, size is the first factor you should look at when choosing a dog, if for no other reason than figuring out the cost difference between keeping a dog that eats one-quarter cup of food a day versus one that eats seven cups.

Dogs come in all sizes, from the giant Irish wolfhound to the delicate papillon.

My, that's a big dog!

For some people, only a large dog will do. Large dogs are the perfect choice for active people: joggers, hikers, and cross-country skiers. Even the friendliest large dog is a bigger crime deterrent than the surliest small dog (although crime experts say that even small dogs do a good job of alerting owners to the presence of strangers and letting the bad guys know that their approach has not gone unnoticed).

Should you consider protection training for your dog? See Chapter 12.

Large dogs can pull a wagon, walk for miles, chase a ball for hours. They are usually not so sensitive to the ear-pulls and tail-grabs of children, and a solid pat on the ribs will not send them flying across the room. Although a small dog may seem like a hot-water bottle if you let him share your bed, a large one may seem like a hot-water heater — as reassuring a presence and as loud (many large dogs snore) as another human.

Still, there are trade-offs. The bigger a dog gets, the more food she eats and the more waste she produces. Big dogs are harder to handle, more likely to knock over your toddler or your grandmother, more capable of destroying your home, more likely to inflict a serious injury should they decide to bite. A pushy small dog is amusing; a pushy large one is dangerous. Large dogs are harder to travel with and more expensive to kennel. If you don't own your own home, you may find securing housing that accepts a large dog nearly impossible.

Larger breeds generally need more exercise and are more likely to find other ways to shed nervous energy — like digging, barking, or chewing — if they don't get enough to keep them happy.

Even the largest dogs are not impossible to keep in apartments, townhouses, and homes with small yards — if you doubt me, visit any doggy play group in Manhattan — but you have to work doubly hard to meet their exercise needs under those circumstances. Another thing to consider if you are an urban dog-owner is that a small dog can use a couple sheets of newspaper for relief on those blizzard days, while with a large dog the Sunday *New York Times* won't suffice.

In some breeds, the size difference between males and females is large — as much as three to six inches and up to 40 pounds or more. If you're attracted to the looks of giant breeds such as the Bernese mountain dog or mastiff — or even more reasonably sized breeds such as the boxer — but want something toward the lighter end of the standard, choose a female.

Little things mean a lot

They may get their share of snickers, but little dogs don't care. They live a life big dogs can only dream about. Only a small dog can sneak into a department store hidden in an oversized purse. This kind of portability, the go-anywhere functionality, combined with adorable faces and shoe-button eyes, makes the small dog a whole lot more fun to own than a lot of "real dog" people can imagine.

Some practical advantages exist, too.

You can give a small dog a bath in the kitchen sink, without straining your back lifting the animal. A small dog can sit in your lap while you watch TV. They're no trouble to walk, even for small children. Food costs are low. Your walk is a rapid trot for them, so exercise is easy.

On the negative side, toy breeds can be yappy, and they are definitely fragile, which makes them unsuitable for homes with boisterous children. They have to be protected, too, from large dogs, some of which may consider a powder-puff dog as an appetizer.

Keeping up with your pup

Activity level isn't tied to size, except at the extremes. Some of the largest dogs seem barely interested in getting out of bed in the morning, while some of the smallest are on the go practically 24 hours a day. In between are dogs of all sizes and various activity levels.

You can sometimes gauge a breed's activity level by looking at the work it was bred to perform but, still, all you're getting is an overall impression. Each individual varies by breeding, age, and health, although the general rule holds true: Bred to go all day long, a sporting breed, for example, is going to be more consistently "up" than a large, heavy guarding breed that only worked when intruders arrived. Dogs such as Dalmatians, bred to run for miles alongside carriages or horse-drawn fire-trucks, aren't likely to take a laid-back attitude toward life. Terriers, developed to keep vermin at bay, are always on the alert and ready to rumble.

Puppy-testing can also give you an idea about activity level and is especially useful when evaluating a pup whose parents are of different breeds. See Chapter 6 for more information.

Some breed types tend to be selectively active — "on" outside, "off" indoors. Many hunting dogs and their mixes are active in the fresh air and fields, but are fairly content to curl up in front of the fire in the house after their exercise requirements have been met. The world's fastest dog, the racing greyhound, is so fond of lounging that one rescue group calls the animal "a 40 mph couch potato."

You can take the edge off the problems high activity can trigger — destructive-ness and barking, for example — by giving active dogs enough aerobic daily exercise to keep them happy. When my young retriever doesn't get his 40 minutes on an almost daily basis, he paces, brings me toys nonstop, and tries to get the older dog to chase him. One good run, or a fast-paced game of fetch settles him down for the day.

Activity level means more than exercise requirements, of course. Some breeds like not only to be moving constantly, but also to be keeping the world informed of their activities. "Hyperactivity" and "yappiness" are also a matter of indi-vidual preference: One person's watchdog is another's yappy pest. For others, the playful liveliness of such breeds is ample trade-off for a little — or a lot — of extra barking. Again, be aware of what your tolerances are. Training can take the edge off the most undesirable of temperament traits, but nothing in this world can turn a peppy, barky Sheltie into a calm, quiet bulldog.

Some active breeds are so yappy that even their fanciers can't stand the noise and routinely have their dogs debarked. While the surgical removal of the vocal cords is sometimes the last chance for an otherwise good dog's survival (a discussion of barking problems is in Chapter 12), a breeder whose own dogs are debarked ought to give you pause. At the very least, debarked parents suggest that your puppy may grow into a dog who is unlikely to let a leaf fall without barking at it.

Facing up to fur

Let me settle one thing up front: *There's no such thing as a dog with fur that doesn't shed.* (The slight hedge is for such breeds as the hairless variety of the Chinese crested, a tiny little dog that can't shed what it doesn't have.) The corollary is that there's no such thing as a dog that's hypoallergenic. Some dogs do shed less and some may be manageable for some asthmatics and allergy sufferers, but if you're not prepared for or capable of handling some fur, you're better off with goldfish (not a cat and not a bird, because those can be even worse for many allergy sufferers).

The long and short of it

All dogs are covered with fur, except for the aforementioned Chinese crested and a couple of other hairless breeds. But there the similarity ends, for the variety of coat lengths, colors, patterns, and texture is nearly endless.

Length? Think short fur like the boxer to start with; then a little longer, like a golden retriever; then longer still, like a collie; to the long-as-they-can-grow preferred locks of the show Komondor, a Rottweiler-sized dog covered with floor-length "cords" of twisted fur that looks like nothing so much as a cotton mop when set in motion.

Color? Think sparkling white like the Samoyed to glossy black like the Schipperke. Then think of everything in between, all kinds of colors with more words describing them than the marketing division of a fashion house could think up in a year. How about mouse-gray, fawn, wild boar, badger, and red stag? Wheaten and deadgrass, mahogany and chestnut? Medium brown? Too dull. Call the color *Isabella;* Doberman fanciers do.

Patterns? Spots, like the Dalmatian. Black with tan accents, like the Doberman, Rottweiler, Gordon setter, or Manchester terrier. Patches like some Great Danes and Akitas. The tiger-stripes of the *brindles,* like boxers or pit-bull terriers. The mottled mishmash of color known as *merle* in some Australian shepherds, collies, and Shelties. And don't forget the importance of accessories: white paws, white chests, white chest ruffs, and white head blazes.

And what about texture? Velvety short, long and silky, or wiry — and that's just in dachshunds! Those coats exists elsewhere in the dog world, too, along with curly coats, wavy coats, rough coats, and smooth coats.

Can you say lint brush? All dogs shed. The short white hairs of a Dalmatian or the pale ones of a yellow Lab turn up on everything and are notoriously hard to get off. The Keeshond and the collie, with luxurious coats so long and thick you can lose things in them, shed in clumps the size of hamsters in spring and in fall — as do most of the breeds with a long, thick overcoat and a downy undercoat — more on this in the grooming section in Chapter 10. The rest of the year, these fur factories shed "normally," as in "a lot." Some breeds shed so much long, silky fur that a small industry has sprung up to spin the hair into material for knitting, so dog-loving crafters can fashion their pets' fur into garments — for some, a season's shedding is all they need for a nice warm sweater.

You can handle some of the fur preemptively by frequently combing and brushing your pet — what you pull out on a comb doesn't end up on your sofa — but you're still going to have plenty of hair with many breeds. If the hair is going to drive you crazy, think short-haired dog in darker color so the fur won't show as much.

Shedding isn't the only issue. Some dogs, such as poodles, have coats that need clipping every six weeks or so. You can learn to do the grooming yourself — your dog will probably survive the embarrassment — or you can take him to a groomer. If you choose the latter, that means money. Everything factors in.

Dog-supply catalogs — a list is in the "Additional Resources" appendix at the back of this book — sell lint rollers in bulk at greatly reduced prices, as do pet-supply stores. You can also find a rubber squeegee-like tool that does a great job of pulling shed fur from carpets and upholstery, and vacuum cleaner attachments specially designed for dealing with pet hair.

When I bought my first long-haired dog, I left the breeder's home with pages of instructions — what to feed, what shots he'd had, how to get him registered, the names of trainers, the names of veterinarians, and the names of kennels. My head was spinning, and I paused on the porch, a puppy in my arms, and asked the breeder if I needed to know anything else.

She thought about it. "Yes," she said. "Never wear black."

Fashion dictates otherwise, so I became adept at lint brushes. Four years after Lance, the Original Demo Dog, died, I was going through some financial records, looking for a receipt. In the file folder was dog hair. His. I almost cried.

I have a high tolerance for dog hair, but at least one of my dogs now is in sync with the trends: jet black. What he throws doesn't show, but the hair is still there.

Factoring in intelligence

People are always asking about how smart a particular dog is, as if that's good for anything more than bragging rights. Intelligence is fairly irrelevant when predicting how well a dog is going to work as a member of your family. What's more important is *trainability* or *biddability,* qualities that describe how much — or how little — a dog concerns herself with what you want her to do.

Part of the puzzle again goes back to looking at the job a breed was developed to perform. Some dogs — such as hounds — were developed to work alone or with other dogs but, in any case, independently of human control. The scent hounds — beagles, bloodhounds, and basset hounds — are more likely to follow their nose than your directions. Sight hounds — Afghan hounds, greyhounds, and salukis — aren't going to hear you at all once they get up to speed after something that's running. That doesn't mean that they won't wag their tail in rapt devotion after you get them back on a leash, but it does mean that in the heat of the chase, their instincts take over. Just as with a tendency to bark, training can take the edge off the tendency to ignore your wishes. Getting your dog to mind is just going to be easier with some breeds than with others.

Consider three of the breeds most often touted as highly intelligent — the border collie, golden retriever, and the Doberman pinscher. These dogs do extremely well in obedience competitions. Does that mean they're smart? Undoubtedly. According to dog-intelligence expert Stanley Coren, these three breeds start to understand a command after they've had the command demonstrated less than five times. But something else is at work here, and if you think about how and why these dogs were developed, you can see what these breeds — a herding dog, a hunting dog, and a protection dog — have in common: They were all developed to work closely with a human handler. The successful performance of their work function — moving sheep around, retrieving downed game, and patrolling with a police officer or soldier — relied on teamwork between human and animal. They come prewired to look to a human for guidance, and if the human knows enough to provide that guidance, these breeds will gladly serve. That's their job, after all.

As with activity levels, intelligence and biddability is a little hard to predict in mixed-breed puppies. Puppy testing can help. See Chapter 5 for more information.

Surfing Canine Cyberspace

A great place to research dogs is cyberspace. Dog lovers have taken to the Internet and commercial online services with a fever matched by few other enthusiasts. There are hundreds of dog-related e-mail lists, newsgroups, and Web sites on the Internet, and active online communities on commercial services such as America Online (where my weekly column runs in my own section of the Pet Care Forum, "Gina Spadafori's Pet Connection").

You can have a lot of fun looking for dog-related Web sites, chatting with other dog lovers or sharing your opinions on which breed, training method, or dog bed is the best, but if you're thinking about getting a dog, the information available is incredible in its scope and is, for the most part, accurate and honest. For that you can thank a woman named Cindy Tittle Moore of Irvine, California, who has written, collected, and organized the best electronic guides to dog information imaginable.

You can get information about dogs in many ways; I use all of them when researching or trying to come up with more ways to better enjoy life with my dogs. Here's the rundown:

- **FAQs:** Short for *Frequently Asked Questions,* these dog-related documents on the Net range from such broad topics as dog sports to specific descriptions of particular breeds to suggestions for solving common behavior problems. Some FAQs are lists of other Internet resources, such as e-mail lists, Web pages, online publications, and pet products suppliers. To find The Mother Of All Dog FAQs, thank Cindy Tittle Moore and point your Web-browsing software to

  ```
  http://www.zmall.com/pet/dog-faqs/
  ```

- **E-mail lists:** For those who like a full mailbox, you won't find anything like joining an e-mail list. Some are overwhelming, with hundreds of pieces of mail collected every day from members and distributed to everyone on the list, which may range from a couple of dozen people to several hundred. The best e-mail lists develop a sense of community, with people united by a common interest — such as a particular breed of dog or dog sport — sharing helpful tips and warm stories of their canine companions. If you have a particular breed in mind but aren't sure what they're like to live with, a couple of months on an e-mail list will paint you as accurate a picture as can be imagined.

  You can subscribe to lists in several ways. For some, you only need to send a note to a host computer. In other lists, subscriptions are handled manually by the list owner. Some lists have numerical limits — usually around 400 members, — while others, such as the list for dog obedience instructors — ask for your credentials up front.

  To check out the list of e-mail groups and the rules for subscribing, point your Web browser to

  ```
  http://www.zmall.com/pet/dog-faqs/lists/email-list.html
  ```

- **Newsgroups:** Sort of like an e-mail list, except anyone in the whole world can post to it, and the information doesn't come to your mailbox — you have to go get it.

  Because newsgroups are open to anyone — including anonymous twits who like to cause trouble — you have less of a sense of community than with an e-mail list and less reason to be civil because the threat of being thrown off the subscriber list doesn't exist. The wide-open nature of newsgroups means that some people are more likely to post outrageous items — and engage in annoying *flame wars* similar to the squabbles of children and just as entertaining.

I like e-mail lists better, but for more general information, newsgroups are worth exploring — just take them with a grain of salt. The `rec.pet.dogs` family includes seven newsgroups: `rec.pet.dogs.activities`, `rec.pet.dogs.behavior`, `rec.pet.dogs.breeds`, `rec.pet.dogs.health`, `rec.pet.dogs.info`, `rec.pet.dogs.misc`, and `rec.pet.dogs.rescue`.

For the history and charters of these newsgroups, point your Web browser to

`http://www.zmall.com/pet/dog-faqs/introduction.html`

✔ **Web sites:** Like newsgroups, but with the added excitement of graphics and pictures. Scores of dog-related Web sites exist, from ones dedicated to individual breeds to ones devoted to dog sports and dog gear. The American Kennel Club has its own home page (`http://www.akc.org/akc/`), as do a few national breed clubs.

Most Web sites are either an individual's labor of love or a profit-minded commercial venture, so content and quality vary widely.

For a list of dog-related Web sites, point your Web browser to

`http://www.zmall.com/pet/dog-faqs/lists/www-list.html`

You can also check out the Yahoo! Web directory's list of dog-related sites at

`http://www.yahoo.com/Entertainment/`
`Animals__Insects__and_Pets/Dogs/`

✔ **Chatting:** While possibilities for real-time discussions with other like-minded dog nuts exist on other commercial services and on the Net, America Online and CompuServe offer the easiest way to communicate "live" with other dog-lovers. Regularly scheduled "chats" are part of the CompuServe Dogs Forum (GO: `DOGS`) as they are in the AOL Pet Care Forum (Keyword: `PETS`).

I've not only used online services and the Internet to collect information and communicate with other pet-lovers for a few years now, but I've also used them to find a dog. I wasn't looking for a dog, but when news of a sweet-natured young retriever who needed a new home was posted to one of the e-mail lists I subscribe to, I was taken enough to write for more information. Many e-mails, faxes, and phone calls later, my cyberpup, Benjamin, flew from Cleveland to Sacramento. I've seen lots of stories of people falling in love with other *people* online, but with a *dog?* What can I say? I'm a sucker for a sad story and big brown eyes.

There's more to canine cyberspace than cold hard facts — there's plenty of dog-related silliness out there, too. From thousands of contenders I've selected Ten Must-See Dog Sites on the World Wide Web, and put them all in Chapter 22. Enjoy!

Two products are custom-made for dog-loving computer nerds like . . . well, me! The first is Dogz, a software package that produces an interactive pet to live in your computer. You choose a puppy to adopt from a handful of contenders and give him a name. You can pet him, feed him, play fetch or take his picture. It's all great fun, and it's $19.95 from PF.magic. To order, call 1-800-48-ADOPT, or visit the company's Web site at http://www.pfmagic.com/dogz.

A good deal and a good deed is the outcome when you order the second product, the "Digital Dog" poster from the San Francisco SPCA. Originally designed to promote adoptions, the work — designed and written by Paul Glassner — is a clever homage to computer advertising. An adorable dog is in the middle of the poster, surrounded by "product description" such as this one, for the dog brain: "Totally Random-Access Memory." "Dual floppies" describe the ears, and the nose is advertised as "DOGS (Double-barreled Olfactory Guidance System) — super-cooled, ultra-sophisticated and very wet. The best!" And it is, too. The "Digital Dog" poster is $12 plus $4 shipping and handling from the SF SPCA, 2500 16th Street, San Francisco, CA 94103. Proceeds go to the society's programs for helping animals and people.

Chapter 2

Narrowing the Field

- -

- -

*I*f I ask you to choose a subject you feel certain everyone has an opinion on, what would you pick? Politics? Religion? Sports?

I've never met a person who couldn't answer this question: What's your favorite (or least favorite) breed of dog?

Even people who'd never own a dog, wouldn't think of petting one, and cross the street when one approaches are interested enough in dogs to know — or be misinformed about — the breed they'd least like to be confronted by. As for dog lovers, the topic of breed favorites can keep conversation going — civilly, one hopes — for hours. Even people who prefer all-Americans — the politically correct term for "mutt," — show a definite affinity for *breed type*: curly-headed little poodle mixes, strapping Lab crosses, or scrappy terrier crosses.

What exactly *is* a breed? Do papers make the dog? Does popularity? Some crosses such as the cockapoo — one parent a cocker, the other a poodle — are so common that people start to think of them as a breed in their own right. And while purebred registries aren't in the business of recognizing such dogs, groups are springing up all the time to acknowledge their popularity.

Simply put, a *purebred dog* is one that when bred with another of its kind produces more of the same. Breed a poodle to a poodle and you get a litter of smart, curly-coated wonders. Breed a cocker to a cocker and you get long-eared, sweet natured pups with eyes you can get lost in.

Breed a cockapoo to a cockapoo, though, and you won't necessarily get more of the same. Some pups may look like the parents, some like poodles, and some like cockers.

The ability to produce predictable traits when bred is what defines a purebred. Which makes the cocker spaniel a breed, and so, too, the poodle, but not cockapoos — or terra-poos, peke-a-poos, or Labradoodles.

Playing Favorites

I became convinced of breed craziness years ago when I realized that the dog show is the only sporting event where 90 percent of the spectators couldn't care less about the winner. People come for a variety of reasons, the following being only a few:

- For the pure and simple pleasure of looking at the dogs
- To talk about the dogs
- To look at breed-related merchandise — key chains, books, and "I love my Doberman!" bumper stickers
- To celebrate their last dog acquisition — "that Akita looks *just* like Kiro!" — or their next
- To debate the relative merits of the three kinds of setters — English, Irish, and Gordon
- To argue if taller, like an Irish Wolfhound, or heavier, like the Newfound-land, is the criterion for "biggest," and which one eats more
- To marvel at the contrasts between long-legged and short-legged, between slender and stocky, between big and little
- To celebrate the dog, in all its many incredible variations

But mark my words: No matter how many breeds they study, how many they talk about, how many they touch, the people leaving a dog show take with them the sure knowledge that *their* favorite breed — or favorite breed type — is best. Everyone believes that everyone else is slightly daft, or sorely misguided, not to share this point of view.

Reputable breeders strive to produce dogs that closely conform to a document called the *breed standard,* a blueprint that lays out the rules for things as major as size and as relatively minor as the distribution of dots on a Dalmatian. The breed clubs decide the rules, and organizations such as the American Kennel Club serve as the keeper of the standard. Dog show judges follow these standards to make their choices. American breed standards — along with official breed histories — are collected in *The Complete Dog Book* (Howell Book House/ Macmillan General Reference), the AKC bible now in its 18th edition. (Other registries will share their breed standards if you write to them — see this book's "Additional Resources" appendix for more information.) Reading the standard is worth a trip to the library, if for no other reason than to keep from paying extra for a "rare" dog such as a white boxer, only to find out later that the reason the animal is so uncommon is because it's disqualified under the breed standard. That doesn't mean the dog won't be a fine pet, though!

To find out more about what those judges are actually looking for and how a dog becomes a champion, see Chapter 16.

Mixed Breeds

Mixed breeds, mongrels, or mutts. Call them anything you want, but millions of them are out there, each and every one of them a true original.

The roll of the genetic dice has produced some of the best dogs.

Some people tell you that getting a mixed breed is a huge gamble. You don't know how big your puppy will get, or what she will look like when she's grown. You don't know if her father is a purebred dog with bad hips and a roving eye. You don't know if the circumstances of her birth and lack of early socialization by owners who wanted neither her nor her littermates and could not dump them fast enough will have long-term consequences that make her unsuitable as a family pet.

All of these statements are true. But let me clue you in: It's all a crapshoot at the end, even with purebred dogs. You do the most you can to better the odds in your favor, close your eyes, say a prayer, and throw the dice.

And you *can* do things to improve your odds with mixed-breed dogs. Work with shelters and rescue groups that test the temperament and check out the health of the animals they put up for adoption. The best ones take the concept of "adoptability" a step further, putting dogs with problems through training and working with new owners after placement to smooth over the rough spots. You can find more on dealing with shelters and rescue groups in Chapter 3.

What you should *not* do is encourage irresponsibility by taking a mixed-breed puppy from the kids outside the supermarket, or the woman selling them for $5 at the flea market. Nor should you buy a mixed-breed dog from a pet store or from someone who breeds them intentionally.

Why? Do you really think people who just want to "dump" puppies have taken care of the mother during pregnancy? Do you think they've given the puppies proper food and medical care, shots, and worming on schedule? Do you think someone who produces mixed-breed puppies intentionally — cockapoos, peke-a-poos, or super-sized pit-bull mixes — is concerned with how many unwanted dogs die every year? When you realize that almost every breed club in the country has in its code of ethics a pledge not to sell to pet shops, what does that leave you with?

I'll tell you. People who shouldn't be breeding dogs. People who are contributing to the millions of dogs put to sleep as *surplus* or *unwanted* every year. People who haven't educated themselves enough to care, or have chosen to ignore the consequences of their actions.

Don't encourage this behavior. Do consider a mixed-breed dog, and look for one in a shelter or from a rescue group.

You can do more things with mixed-breed dogs than ever before. You can get them certified as a Canine Good Citizen (see Chapter 15 for more on this program). You can train them and take them to the highest levels of national obedience competitions. You can train for the sport of agility. (More on these in Chapter 16.)

And you can love the heck out of them and be loved in return, which is, after all, the highest calling any dog can follow.

Evaluating Breeds

The rest of this chapter is a broad overview of the more than 150 breeds available in the United States and Canada today. I've divided them into eight groups, the first seven of which are American Kennel Club classifications. For information on purebred dogs in other countries, see the list of canine registries in this book's "Additional Resources" appendix.

- ✔ Sporting
- ✔ Hounds
- ✔ Working
- ✔ Terriers
- ✔ Toys
- ✔ Non-sporting
- ✔ Herding
- ✔ Non-AKC breeds

Why go with the American Kennel Club groupings? Because the venerable AKC is the Microsoft of the dog world, omnipresent and dominant, with an impact on all things dog. Only the Kennel Club, in Great Britain, can touch the AKC's clout. Other registries exist, including the Canadian Kennel Club, and, in the United States, the United Kennel Club and the American Rare Breed Association. But no canine organization, and there are thousands all over the world, is better known than the American Kennel Club, for better or for worse. I've used AKC rankings and groupings for examples in this chapter, but the popularity and availability of a breed in any particular country varies. For more information, contact one of the registries listed in the "Additional Resources" appendix of this book.

Most purebred dogs in the United States are registered with the AKC, which also awards titles for show championships and other dog sports. Although the organization has assumed investigative and educational responsibilities over the years, the AKC is primarily in the business of processing paperwork. "AKC" is not a brand name, like Sony or Chevrolet. The organization, which is actually a federation of breed and kennel clubs, neither breeds dogs nor certifies breeders.

Your chances of getting a Labrador or chow chow or French bulldog with the qualities associated with the breed rely on your ability to find a reputable breeder. So bear in mind as you study breeds that the wonderful qualities associated with, say, the golden retriever, are much more likely to be found in a dog purchased from a knowledgeable and reputable breeder. Chapter 3 offers information on choosing a breeder.

Remember — no dog is perfect

Every breed is perfect for someone, but *no* breed is suitable for everyone. Some breeds or breed types — because of reasonable size and activity levels, low-maintenance coats, high trainability, and low dominance — fit in a majority of dog-loving homes. Many of these breeds are not as well-known as others, and I've singled these and some others out for special consideration if you're looking to add a furry bundle to your home.

Still, no matter what any expert says, you're the one who has to live with your choice. So do your homework, be realistic, and proceed with caution.

I provide the background of the dogs in each of these groupings so that you can get a sense of what the breed was developed to do, which is an important step in determining how it will fit into your life. ***Note:*** When I mention breeds that are *good* or *bad,* the terms are not used to denigrate the breed itself, but rather to evaluate its suitability as a pet in an "average" family with neither the background nor the time to work with a less-suitable breed.

Genetic defects are common in purebred dogs, thanks to unscrupulous or ignorant breeders. In addition to being a poor choice for a family pet, a sick dog can cost you lots of money. Among the most common inherited defects is *hip dysplasia,* a malformation of the hip joint. While hip dysplasia is widespread in medium- and large-sized dogs, other common congenital defects are more breed-specific, such as deafness in Dalmatians. You *must* become aware of which defects are common in whatever breed you choose so that you know to find a puppy whose parents are have been checked out by a registry such as the Orthopedic Foundation of America or the Canine Eye Registry Foundation.

CD-ROMs are another great resource for choosing and living with a dog. Two that I like are *Microsoft Dogs* (Microsoft Home, for PCs; $34.95) and *Multimedia Dogs: The Complete Interactive Guide to Dogs* (Inroads Interactive, for PCs and Macintosh; $29.95.). Both offer good basic information on dozens of breeds, as well as tips on care and quizzes to test your "Dog IQ."

The sporting group

Some of the best dogs for families are in this group, so you shouldn't be surprised that some of the most popular breeds, including the No. 1 breed, the Labrador retriever, also call the sporting group home. Two other sporting dogs — the golden retriever and the cocker spaniel — routinely claim spots in the AKC's top 10.

Sporting dogs such as the Labrador retriever and English setter are a good match for active people.

Like the hounds, these are hunting dogs. Unlike the hounds, sporting dogs cannot trace an ancestry to the earliest stages of human/dog companionship. Their development is more recent and is tied to the invention of the device that changed the world in so many other respects: the gun.

Sporting dogs — setters, pointers, retrievers, and spaniels — were developed not to chase and to kill game, but to help firearms-equipped hunters locate game birds, to flush the birds from hiding places so that they could be shot and, finally, to bring back the dead and injured to the hunter's hand without further damage. While the traditional work of many breeds — such as the bulldog, bred to fight a bull for the bloody amusement of the masses — is thankfully no longer available, many sporting dogs still practice their craft. Thousands are dual-purpose animals: Family pets who roll around with children by day and sleep on the beds by night, they are also working dogs who spend fall weekends joyously slogging through half-frozen fields with the hunter of the family.

Nor is their work confined to hunting. Within this group are two breeds — golden and Labrador retrievers — most commonly trained to serve as helpers for people who are blind or use wheelchairs. In addition, the keen noses of sporting dogs have been put to good use detecting drugs or explosives.

Most of these dogs are large, but not overly so, for a massive breed would possess neither the agility nor the stamina to survive a day in the field. Some smaller breeds are in this group, too — most notably the cocker spaniel, a happy little dog that doesn't do much hunting but has taken a couple of turns at the top of the popularity charts.

Coats are pretty reasonable in this group, as befits any class of dogs bred to spend time amongst the brambles — short, medium, and wiry coats are the rule. The exception is the cocker spaniel and, to some extent, the golden retriever, breeds that rarely hunt anymore and have more coat than would make sense for a field dog to bear.

Sporting breeds in brief

History: The first dog registered with the American Kennel Club in 1886 was from the sporting group, the English setter Adonis. The sporting group, which once included hounds, was one of two original groups — the other was non-sporting — and sporting dogs have been important in every imaginable canine endeavor ever since.

Most popular: Labrador retriever, No. 1 in AKC ranking.

Least popular: Sussex spaniel, No. 138 in AKC ranking.

Small- to medium-sized breeds (24 to 50 pounds): American water spaniel, Brittany, cocker spaniel, English cocker spaniel, English springer spaniel, field spaniel, Sussex spaniel, Welsh springer spaniel.

Large breeds (50 to 80 pounds): Chesapeake Bay retriever, Clumber spaniel, curly-coated retriever, English setter, flat-coated retriever, German shorthaired pointer, German wirehaired pointer, golden retriever, Gordon setter, Irish setter, Irish water spaniel, Labrador retriever, pointer, Vizsla, Weimaraner, wirehaired pointing griffon.

Activity level: Most sporting breeds have energy to burn, but the heavy, low-slung Clumber and Sussex spaniels are relatively calm.

Some lesser-known breeds worth a good look:

- **Flat-coated retriever.** This friendly, high-energy dog is considered to be similar to goldens before popularity "ruined" that breed.

- **American water spaniel.** A good-natured, easily trained, and adaptable dog, this smaller breed developed by hunters in Wisconsin is covered in short curls.

- **English setter.** Overshadowed by the flashy Irish setter, the English is just as good-natured but less flighty.

Popularity often breeds disaster, and that's certainly true of some breeds in this group. The cocker spaniel, in fact, could be the poster dog for the problems of popularity. What could be a near-perfect family dog should be sold with a warning label today because of health and temperament problems caused by bad breeders. Some cockers are so unstable they cannot be trusted around children; others are made miserable by no fewer than a half-dozen common congenital problems. You have to be very careful when dealing with this breed, and find a reputable breeder. The same is true of others in this group, most notably the Labrador and golden retrievers. For more on finding a dog that typifies what these breeds *should* be, see Chapter 3.

In many sporting breeds, some dogs differ enough in body structure and temperament that they could almost be separate breeds. In most of these breeds the split is between *show* and *field;* that is, dogs bred with lots of coat and a more laid-back attitude for the show ring versus dogs bred for hunting instinct, a more practical amount of coat, and an intensity for work that is a must in field competitions. Unless you intend to hunt with your pet, a dog from a reputable show breeder is probably a better bet, because the energy and intensity of a field-trial dog is a poor fit with all but the most active households.

The hound group

The hound group consists of *scent hounds* (dogs who hunt by scent), *sight hounds* (dogs who hunt by sight), and one breed, the dachshund that, based on its development to "go to ground" after vermin, arguably belongs with the terriers. Some of the oldest known of the world's breeds, such as the saluki and greyhound, are in this group, as well as breeds that have been in the United States since before the Revolutionary War. (George Washington kept foxhounds at Mount Vernon; he kept records on his dogs back to 1758.)

The size range is dramatic in this group, from miniature dachshunds, about five inches tall at the shoulder with a weight of less than 10 pounds, to the tallest dog of all, the Irish wolfhound, more than 30 inches tall and weighing more than 100 pounds.

For many of these breeds, you need look no further than their names to find the key to their origin: Otterhounds were developed in England to hunt otters; rabbits were the prey of harriers. For other breeds this naming trend doesn't hold true; the Pharaoh in Pharaoh hound is a reference not to the dog's pre-ferred game, but to his antiquity. The petit basset griffon Vendeen was bred to hunt rabbits in France, but you wouldn't know that from the name, which means "small, low-slung, wire-coated dog of Vendee," (*Vendee* being a French province).

Two of the most recognizable breeds in the world are in this group — the basset hound and the dachshund. So, too, is one of the world's most unusual breeds, the Basenji, which is incapable of barking and communicates pleasure by chortling or yodeling.

The hounds are a varied group made up of dogs who hunt by scent, such as the beagle and petit basset griffon Vendeen, and those who hunt by sight, such as the borzoi.

Some wonderful potential pets are in this group, most notably the beagle, a happy, sturdy dog considered to be an outstanding companion for children. Highly recommended, too, is the basset hound. With the growth of rescue organizations, greyhounds are becoming an increasingly popular pet as word has gotten out on the sweet nature of former racers.

Do not expect hound breeds to watch your every step out of doors, however: They've got better things to do, following their nose and their eyes as their heritage demands. "Come" can be a difficult concept for many hounds.

Coats are generally low-maintenance: Most, but not all, of these are short- or wire-haired. The most notable exception is the Afghan hound, whose long silky coat tangles and mats quickly without constant attention.

As with the sporting breeds, some hounds are divided into show and field types. The energy and intensity of field hounds makes them less suited for the job of pet, so stick with reputable show breeders for a temperament that's easier to get along with.

TECHNICAL STUFF

Hound breeds in brief

History: The most ancient of all known breeds can be found in this group; the first hounds — a basset hound, beagle, bloodhound, dachshund, greyhound, and harrier — were registered with the AKC in 1885. The hound breeds were originally classified with the sporting breeds but got their own group in the late 1920s.

Most popular: Beagle, No. 5 in AKC ranking.

Least popular: Otterhound, No. 137 in AKC ranking.

Tiny breeds (less than 20 pounds): Dachshunds, standard and miniature.

Small- to medium-sized breeds (20 to 50 pounds): Basenji, basset hound, beagle, harrier, Norwegian elkhound, petit basset griffon Vendeen, whippet.

Large breeds (50 to 80 pounds): Afghan hound, American foxhound, black and tan Coonhound, English foxhound, greyhound, Ibizan hound, Pharaoh hound, Rhodesian ridgeback, saluki.

Giant breeds (more than 80 pounds): bloodhound, borzoi, Irish wolfhound, otterhound, Scottish deerhound.

Activity level: Most hounds have energy to burn, but many breeds are fairly calm in the house.

Some lesser-known breeds worth a good look:

- ✔ **Petit basset griffon Vendeen.** Contrary to popular impression, this happy hound is *not* a wire-haired basset hound. The breed is considerably more agile than the basset, a good choice for an active family. Plus, that fuzzy face melts your heart.

- ✔ **Whippet.** "The poor man's race horse," according to the breed standard, the whippet is a lot tougher than his delicate looks suggest, yet gentle and quiet. He loves to snuggle, and his smooth coat is as close to low-maintenance as you could wish for.

- ✔ **Scottish deerhound.** A gentle, good-natured giant with wiry coat that needs little maintenance and gives his face a look of charming dignity. If you're thinking of a manageable dog in a jumbo-sized package, this breed should be one you consider.

The working group

No doubt about it: Some pretty tough customers are in the working group, made up of no-nonsense dogs who earned their keep as protectors and load-pullers.

Some dogs here relied on their size and untrusting attitude to keep the belongings of their employers safe. A couple of these — the Rottweiler and Akita — are among the trendiest breeds around, their popularity fueled by fear of crime and the desire of some to own a formidable animal, whether they can control him or not.

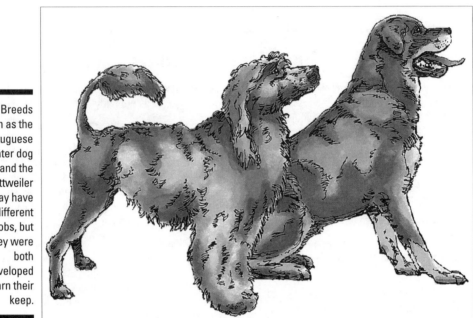

Breeds such as the Portuguese water dog and the Rottweiler may have had different jobs, but they were both developed to earn their keep.

Some of dogdom's gentlest of giants — the Great Dane and Newfoundland — are in this group, along with versatile smaller breeds developed for other work but who, today, excel in obedience and other dog sports. Modernity seems to have eluded the Nordic breeds, whose appearance and tendency to howl in the night are eerily reminiscent of the wolf.

If you like the look of the wolf but have wisely chosen to avoid the wolf-dog hybrid, (see Chapter 1), consider the Siberian husky or Alaskan malamute. They're still a lot of dog — and too much for many novices — but at least they're domesticated. In the right situation, both are good pets.

With a few exceptions, the working group offers little for beginners. These breeds are powerful, intelligent, and prefer making their own decisions unless you have the training skills and leadership ability to convince them otherwise. Despite their popularity, many of these breeds are best left in the hands of experienced dog handlers able to give these breeds the training and exercise they need to reach their full potential.

Also adding to the challenge, some of the more prolific shedders can be found in this group, along with one of the most high-maintenance coats found in any dog: the corded coat of the flock-protecting Hungarian breed, the Komondor. (Keeping this coat in condition is so time-consuming that most pet Komondors — or, as the fanciers say, Komondorok — and retired show dogs are kept shorn of their trademark locks.) Other working dogs, however, are no problem in the coat-care department. One more caveat: This group includes more than a couple of droolers.

If you simply cannot live without some of the more dominant members of this group, you must be sure to socialize them early and often. Doing so will *not* hurt their protective instincts, but it *will* make them more discriminating in their uncharitable outlook on "strangers," a category that for an unsocialized, untrained dog may include your friends and relatives — or the neighbor's children. Early and constant obedience training is another must, not only to allow you to control these strong dogs, but also to keep them reminded of the chain of command. For more information, see "Early Puppy Training," Chapter 6.

Working breeds in brief

History: As long as humans have had property and goods, they've had dogs to protect them, so some of these breed are quite old. The first members of this group, the St. Bernard and mastiff, were registered with the AKC in 1885. The working breeds were part of the non-sporting group until the early 1920s and, then, for decades remained the AKC's largest group. That distinction ended in 1983 when the herding breeds were separated from the balance of the working breeds and moved into their own group.

Most popular: Rottweiler, No. 2 in AKC ranking.

Least popular: Komondor, No. 122 in AKC ranking.

Small- to medium-sized breeds (20 to 50 pounds): Portuguese water dog, standard schnauzer.

Large breeds (50 to 80 pounds): Boxer, Doberman pinscher, giant schnauzer, Samoyed, Siberian husky.

Giant breeds (more than 80 pounds): Akita, Alaskan malamute, Bernese mountain dog, bullmastiff, Great Dane, Great Pyrenees, Komondor, Kuvasz, mastiff, Newfoundland, Rottweiler, St. Bernard, and greater Swiss mountain dog.

Activity level: Many of these strong, powerful dogs are fairly laid-back, although exercise is still a must.

Some breeds worth a good look:

- **Portuguese water dog.** Sometimes mistaken for a poodle (to the horror of Portie fanciers) this curly- or wavy-coated rare breed was developed to help fishermen by retrieving objects, carrying messages, and other tasks that required swimming, which Porties still love. His fanciers tout his calmness and intelligence.

- **Great Dane.** You want a really big dog, you have room for a really big dog, but you aren't sure that you can handle a dog that's both big and dominant? Consider the Dane. Like all giant breeds, obedience training is a must to keep him from pulling you down the street or knocking you over but, aside from that, the Dane's generally a mild-mannered dog who enjoys children.

The terrier group

Talk about moxie! These dogs, developed to go *mano a mano* with all manner of vermin, have the qualities commonly associated with New Yorkers: They know what they want, they're not shy about going for it, and they don't look charitably on those who get in their way.

Terrier fanciers call it *fire,* but most terrier owners would call the traits unmanageable if these breeds weren't almost all small, and also possessed as good a sense of humor as you'll find in any dog, especially if the joke's on you.

The terriers include both feisty wire-haired breeds such as the soft-coated wheaten terrier and miniature schnauzer, as well as thick-set breeds such as the Staffordshire bull terrier.

The terriers should be looked at as two separate groups:

- ✔ The first contains what most think of when they think "terrier": Mostly small, wire-coated breeds such as the Cairn terrier and miniature schnauzer, dogs developed to dispatch rats, foxes, badgers, weasels, otters, and anything else landowners decided they could better do without.

- ✔ The second group contains those breeds that resulted from crossings of bulldogs and terriers to produce animals such as the bull terrier that were as solidly built and heavily muscled as the bulldog, but with the terrier's classic tenacity and boldness. These breeds, commonly — but incorrectly — lumped under the name "pit bull," were developed to fight other dogs in cruel contests that have been illegal for decades (but unfortunately continue, in inner cities and backwoods alike).

Pet potential exists in both groups, but you do have to be especially cautious with the latter.

Classic terriers first. These dogs are tireless, plucky, and stylish, equally comfortable in city, suburban, or rural homes. Even small terriers are sturdy enough to be a child's pet, but their take-charge attitude can be a problem if they are not socialized and trained. If allowed to rule the roost, some of these little dynamos can become little despots, a dangerous role for any dog to assume, especially in homes with children.

Other common behavior problems come straight from the terrier's background: They dig, and they bark. Key tools for a dog trying to out-burrow a badger or drive out a fox from the den, but not so appreciated in a suburban backyard. Some terriers may get a little glassy-eyed and drooly over the presence of rodents in the house — you may call hamsters, gerbils, rats, and mice "pets," but you'll never convince a terrier they belong. Terriers may also be less than civil to other dogs.

While you will find short-haired and silky, long-haired terriers, most have a wiry coat that needs *stripping* (plucking of the dead hairs) to keep them in show-ring condition. The owners of pet terriers usually skip this tedious task and use electric trimmers on their dogs instead or have a professional groomer do the job every couple of months. Aside from this factor, these stylish breeds are pretty easy keepers in the coat department, and they don't shed much.

The bull-and-terrier breeds — the American Staffordshire terrier, bull terrier, miniature bull terrier, and Staffordshire bull terrier are the AKC versions — have come in for some bad press in recent years, and that's a shame, because these dogs were considered to be stable pets for generations. What prompted the change is they became popular with an element that broadened their traditional aggression toward other dogs, producing animals that would like as not bite people. Couple this trait with these dogs' awesome physical power and you've got an animal that justifiably should be feared.

If you buy from a reputable breeder, however, and socialize and train your puppy, you end up with a calm, sensible dog with an easy-care coat who provides good companionship for a human family — though he's still unlikely to be overly fond of other dogs, and people will be a little tentative because you own a "pit bull."

As important as finding a reputable breeder is for any dog you choose — Chapter 3 tells you just how important — it's absolutely crucial with these bull-and-terrier breeds. Dogs from show lines are a better bet as pets. Good temperament is always on the mind of reputable breeders, who are anxious to

Terrier breeds in brief

History: Terriers were developed from hounds to get into the places larger dogs could not when pursuing prey. The first members of this group, the Scottish terrier, bull terrier, fox terrier and Irish terrier, were registered with the AKC in 1885. The terriers were part of the non-sporting group until they got their own group as part of the AKC's reorganization in the early 1920s.

Most popular: Miniature schnauzer, No. 14 in AKC ranking.

Least popular: Sealyham terrier, No. 129 in AKC ranking.

Small- to medium-sized breeds (15 to 50 pounds): Australian terrier, Bedlington terrier, border terrier, bull terrier, Cairn terrier, Dandie Dinmont terrier, Irish terrier, Kerry blue terrier, Lakeland terrier, standard manchester terrier, miniature bull terrier, miniature schnauzer, Norfolk terrier, Norwich terrier, Scottish terrier, Sealyham terrier, soft coated wheaten terrier, smooth fox terrier, Staffordshire bull terrier, Welsh terrier, West Highland white terrier, wire fox terrier.

Large breeds (50 to 80 pounds): Airedale terrier, American Staffordshire terrier.

Activity level: The bull-and-terrier breeds can be quiet and calm. The classic terriers have energy to burn.

Some breeds worth a good look:

- **Border terrier.** One of the "softer" terriers as far as temperament goes, this rough-coated charmer packs a lot of personality in less than 20 pounds. Some borders do well in competitive obedience work, which marks them as a cut above the pack in biddability.

- **Soft coated wheaten terrier.** Another of the more mild-mannered terriers, this time in a medium package. *Soft-coated* refers to his trademark coat, which is silky and wavy, and *wheaten* notes the only allowable color, an eye-pleasing golden-brown that lightens as the dog matures. Unlike the border terrier, the soft coated wheaten has the trademark terrier look: a long, fuzzy face with whiskers.

- **Staffordshire bull terrier.** The smallest of the bull-and-terrier breeds, this easy-care dog is a solid, go-anywhere companion. Deal with only a reputable show breeder, and be aware that you'll hear a lot of negative reactions when you're out with your pet. Socialize and train your dog; as the owner of the bull-and-terrier breed you have a responsibility to help improve the public's bad impression of any dog who resembles a "pit bull."

prove their dogs deserve a chance in the face of legislative attempts in many cities and towns to ban these breeds. Buy from anyone other than a show breeder, and you may well end up with exactly the kind of dog these laws are aiming at. Make sure, too, you socialize these dogs. More on that in Chapter 6.

The toy group

They're cute. They're feisty. They're often quite long-lived. Some places with "No Dogs Allowed" signs don't enforce the rules when it comes to these charming little dogs.

Toy breeds such as the pug and Pomeranian were developed to be companions — and they're good at what they do!

Toy dogs are the only ones who can routinely travel in the cabins of airliners because generally, they are the only dogs whose carriers can fit under the seat.

They're special. Just ask them.

You can give them ironic names like Spike, Ripper, and Killer, and people will think you're amusing. You can give them names like Daddy's Itsy-Bitsy Little Cutesy-Poo and people won't think you too addle-brained. You can dress them in sweaters. You can have their toenails painted bright red. You can laugh at their furious displays of territoriality when a large dog passes in front of your house, and you can pick them up to keep them out of trouble when that large dog decides he's not about to tolerate insults from a scrap of fur no bigger than his head.

Mostly what you can do with a toy breed is enjoy. Heaven knows they've enjoyed us. Most toy breeds haven't had to work for a living. While larger dogs were out pulling sleds, chasing deer, retrieving birds, herding sheep, or killing rats, these breeds spent their days being pampered and wondering when dinner would be served.

Smart dogs, no? Indeed, they've got brains inside those little heads, and they're anxious to use them. Toys are some of the brightest breeds around, and more than a few of them excel in obedience competitions. Better still, they love to be the center of attention and so are naturals when it comes to learning tricks.

Many of these breeds have luxurious coats that need either to be kept clipped short or groomed frequently to keep tangles and mats at bay. Some real shedders are in here, too, but because the dogs are small, so too, is the problem of dealing with the fur.

Toys breeds in brief

History: While toy dogs have been kept as pampered pets for centuries, the popularity of these breeds started to climb in the late nineteenth century. Although the AKC first registered a Yorkshire terrier and a pug in 1885, most early shows did not include classes for toy breeds. That changed in 1928 with the creation of the toy group.

Most popular: Pomeranian, No. 9 in AKC ranking, although toy poodles are counted together with the two larger varieties; as a single breed poodles stand at No. 6.

Least popular: English toy spaniel, No. 120 in AKC ranking.

Size: All small, ranging from two pounds for some Chihuahuas to just under 20 for the stocky pug. The group includes the affenpinscher, Brussels griffon, Cavalier King Charles spaniel, Chihuahua, Chinese crested, English toy spaniels, Italian greyhound, Japanese chin, Maltese, miniature pinscher, papillon, Pekinese, Pomeranian, pug, shih tzu, silky terrier, toy poodle, toy manchester terrier and Yorkshire terrier.

Activity level: Most toys are lively and energetic.

Some lesser-known breeds worth a good look:

✔ **Papillon.** This French breed was named for her large ears, which resemble the spread wings of a butterfly. Papillons do well in competitive obedience work, are happy to learn, and easy to teach.

✔ **Chinese crested.** Looking for something a little out of the ordinary? The hairless version of this charming breed may fit the bill. With hair on their head, lower legs, and tail, these dogs resemble a prancing little pony. The crested also comes in a fully coated variety, called the *powderpuff*.

✔ **English toy spaniel.** Quiet, calm, and affectionate, this breed ought to be a little higher in the popularity parade. Pamper him all you want: He's unlikely to get an attitude.

These dogs are among the best for inexperienced dog owners, but some problems exist where children are concerned. Tiny dogs are fragile and not up to the rough handling that some children can dish out. You know your own children best: If they are gentle and thoughtful, a toy breed will do fine in your home. Otherwise, you may want to consider a larger breed or wait until your children are old enough to handle these breeds properly.

The non-sporting group

The only thing these dogs have in common is they don't have enough in common with the breeds of any other group. This is the catchall group, and has been since the AKC had just two groups — Sporting and Non-Sporting.

The poodle and Boston terrier have little in common except a reputation for being great pets and a place in the non-sporting group.

You find dogs here like the bichon frise who were bred to be pampered but are bigger than toys. A bird dog, the Finnish spitz, is prized in his native land for his ability to bark his fool head off. (Go figure. At least he's cute, resembling a red fox.) You see the poodle, a multipurpose breed that today is primarily a companion, but has worked as a retriever, truffle hunter, and circus performer. Then you have two bulldog breeds that have been without work for so long — bull-baiting long gone out of fashion — they didn't really count as working dogs any more. And although his official AKC history mentions nothing of it, dog experts say the chow chow was prized as much for his meat as for any other feature in his native China.

You can say one thing for sure about this group: Some top-notch companions are in it.

Primary among them in terms of numbers is the poodle, a highly intelligent dog who has been the butt of more jokes than any other breed. Fortunately the poodle enjoys laughter as well as any other dog, and if he knows he's the one being laughed at, he doesn't let on.

The No. 1 reason poodles are picked on is probably the way they are groomed for the show ring. While based on a theoretically useful clip that protected the chest and joints of a water dog, this style has been taken to the limit by fanciers. The hairstyle may be a plot to keep this popular breed out of even more hands, for underneath all this foppishness is a dog that even the most avid poodle bashers would admire if they'd allow themselves to, especially if they considered the "real dog"-sized standard poodle.

Coats run the gamut in this group, from the profuse shedding of the chow chow and Keeshond to the easy-care glamour of the dog who wears a tuxedo to even the most casual of occasions, the Boston terrier.

This group seems to have more than its share of congenital problems, some caused by irresponsible breeding, others a result of breeding for a body shape that, while distinctive, isn't really conducive to the normal patterns of canine life. Many Dalmatians are deaf; bulldogs are prone to heatstroke and breathing difficulties; and a half-dozen congenital problems frequently show up in poodles. The sometimes difficult chow chow has a reputation as the breed veterinarians like to work with least. As with all groups, the larger breeds here are candidates for hip dysplasia.

Non-sporting breeds in brief

History: The AKC's class for dogs that don't fit anywhere else, this group has been around since the AKC began. The first member of this group to be registered was a bulldog, in 1886.

Most popular: Poodle, No. 6 in AKC ranking, although the ranking includes toy poodles as well as the miniature and standard varieties seen in this group.

Least popular: Finnish spitz, No. 131 in AKC ranking.

Tiny breeds (less than 15 pounds): Tibetan spaniel, Schipperke.

Small- to medium-sized breeds (15 to 50 pounds): American Eskimo dog, bichon frise, Boston terrier, bulldog, shar-pei, Finnish spitz, French bulldog, Keeshond, Lhasa apso, miniature poodle, shiba inu, Tibetan terrier.

Large breeds (50 to 80 pounds): Chow chow, Dalmatian, standard poodle.

Activity level: All across the board. Poodles at the high end, bulldogs at the low end.

Some breeds worth a good look:

- ✔ **Boston terrier.** They got it half-right. This smart-looking dog was developed in Boston, but he isn't a terrier. Sometimes called a Boston bull terrier, which makes a little more sense, because he does have bulldog in his background. A playful, lively breed, if you don't mind a little wheezing.

- ✔ **Keeshond.** Yes, they have a lot of fur. Are you going to hold that against a breed that actually pulls his lips back and smiles? This medium-sized breed is amiable, reasonably trainable, and gets along well with most everyone, including other pets.

- ✔ **French bulldog.** Another wheezer who may steal your heart. He's playful and sweet, an outgoing character who has no idea a lot of people think him homely, with his squat body, pushed-in face, and bat ears.

The herding group

Not many people keep sheep and cattle these days, but that doesn't bother the herding breeds much. These versatile and intelligent dogs have made their mark in the modern-day world as police dogs, drug-detection dogs, search-and-rescue dogs, and even movie stars.

Most of them, however, will serve as pets, and some wonderful breeds can fill that role in this group.

Some of the most versatile and personable breeds, such as the German shepherd and bearded collie, are in the herding group.

The work of the sheep dog is older than the Bible and almost as widespread. While many countries have native sheep dogs — including the United States, where the Australian shepherd was developed — most of the commonly known herding dogs come from the United Kingdom and France. Some of these breeds are now counted among the glamour-pusses of dogdom, but for generations they were just plain and humble working dogs whose ability to do what humans could not — control large herds of animals — was essential in the development of civilization.

The herding breeds are among the most intelligent and biddable of all dogs, developed to work in partnership with a human handler as the sporting breeds were. The nature of their work, however, demands a dog a little more aggressive than the setters, retrievers, and spaniels who serve hunters. Herding dogs work through intimidation and harassment to control animals larger than they are. This job is not for wimps and, indeed, the herding instinct is a toned-down version of techniques used by wolves working a herd of prey animals, looking for a weakling to kill. Sometimes a hard-driving herding dog gets so seriously annoyed at an animal who isn't moving where he wants that he takes a hunk out of him, although this technique is frowned on.

This combination makes for a great working dog, but should raise a flag of caution if you're looking for a pet. The herding breeds that still work today — as herding or protection dogs — may be a little much for novices to handle. What's arguably the dog world's whiz kid and best sheep dog ever made, the border collie, doesn't take well to the confines of a suburban backyard and a life without challenges. The same goes for the German shepherd and the three Belgian shepherds, the tervuren, malinois, and sheepdog, breeds with so much potential that denying them a chance to fulfill it ought to be a crime.

Herding breeds in brief

History: Herding was the first new AKC group in more than 50 years when these breeds were pulled out of the oversized working group in 1983. The collie was the first breed in this group to be registered with the AKC, in 1885.

Most popular: German shepherd, No. 3 in AKC ranking.

Least popular: Puli, No. 117 in AKC ranking.

Small- to medium-sized breeds (15 to 50 pounds): Australian cattle dog, bearded collie, border collie, Cardigan Welsh corgi, Pembroke Welsh corgi, puli, Shetland sheepdog,

Large breeds (50 to 80 pounds): Australian shepherd, Belgian malinois, Belgian sheepdog, Belgian tervuren, bouvier des Flandres, Briard, German shepherd, Old English sheepdog, rough collie, smooth collie.

Activity level: These agile breeds have energy to burn.

Some breeds worth a good look:

✔ **Bearded collie.** The bright, sweet-natured breed with the fuzzy face is occasionally mistaken for an Old English sheepdog. A beardie fancier will probably put the record straight by pointing out that this herding dog is one of the U.K.'s oldest breeds, older than the Old English, which isn't very old at all. The only thing bad about this breed is that their silky coats — especially profuse on their legs — means hours of dematting should you be foolish enough to take your dog into the fields.

✔ **Smooth collie.** Call it the collie-with-a-haircut if you like, these short-haired dogs should be more popular. They still shed, but nothing like their rough-coated relatives. Although you shouldn't expect your collie to pull children out of wells Lassie-style, the generous collie temperament is in the smooth. However, some say smooths are a little more *reserved*, which is breederspeak for a little timid.

✔ **Welsh corgis.** Cardigans have tails, Pembrokes don't, but all Corgis have attitude, and you got to love them for it. These dogs are smart and highly trainable, but they're as likely to train you as the other way around if you're not careful. The short-legged dynamos are sturdy enough for children. Get two, because few things will make you smile faster than seeing a pack of corgis run.

Other dogs in this group, although plenty smart, have not nearly as much drive. Some of them have been cultivated primarily as pets for generations. Long before Lassie came home, Queen Victoria took a liking to the collie, and the smaller herding dogs are well-loved companions in many homes.

Almost every one of the large breeds in this group is prone to hip dysplasia, and the German shepherd is susceptible to a half-dozen additional congenital defects.

Coats vary in this group, including many profuse shedders, such as the collie (which many don't realize comes in a short-haired variety, called *smooth* by fanciers) and the Shetland sheepdog (which is, please note, a notorious barker). You do find some easy-care coats here, as well as the second of the AKC's two Hungarian "corded" breeds, the puli. (The other, the Komondor, is found in the working group.)

Many of these breeds still demonstrate a strong desire to keep things in a nice, tight herd. They do so with toys, other pets, children, and even party guests. An acquaintance of mine's Australian shepherd once demonstrated this trait at a backyard party. The dog spent the early part of the events nudging guests, slowly and oh-so subtly working around the group until they moved unwittingly toward the center of the yard, realized what the dog had done, and had a good laugh. Then they spread out again — much to the shepherd's frustration, no doubt!

A world of other breeds

Just slightly more than 150 breeds in the seven different groups are allowed to compete for American Kennel Club championships; at least twice that many breeds are in the world. That leaves a whole lot of purebred dogs unaccounted for, a couple of them popular on the AKC's home turf.

Information on non-AKC breeds is a little harder to find, but you must make an effort if considering one of these breeds. Your library may have the AKC's book of breed standards, *The Complete Dog Book,* but it is considerably less likely to have standards from the Canadian Kennel Club, the United Kennel Club, or the American Rare Breed Association, much less those from breed clubs themselves or the kennel clubs in other countries. A reputable breeder will have those standards, so ask. Ask, too, about congenital defects, dominance and trainability, activity levels, shedding, and grooming requirements.

TECHNICAL STUFF

Some non-AKC breeds worth a good look

- **The Jack Russell terrier.** Probably the most popular of all non-AKC breeds, thanks to his starring roles in numerous commercials, on the TV show *Frasier,* and in the movie *The Mask.* But just as you shouldn't expect a collie to act like Lassie, you shouldn't expect a JRT to act like Eddie: It takes a lot of effort for any Jack Russell to sit still. A true terrier, this small dog is a barker and a digger, but his roguish charm makes up for it in the eyes of his devotees. Just make sure that you know what you're getting before you commit.

- **Nova Scotia duck tolling retriever.** This Canadian Kennel Club breed has a loyal following in the United States as well. And it's easy to see why: The medium-sized toller resembles the golden retriever not only in looks but in temperament: He's good-natured, easy to train, and his tail never stops wagging. How can you miss?

There are a world of wonderful breeds beyond the grasp of the American Kennel Club, including the Nova Scotia duck tolling retriever and the Jack Russell terrier.

Decisions, Decisions

You've probably got a breed or two in mind, or an idea of the characteristics you want in a dog — large, small, long-haired, or short-haired. Before you start looking for your pet, though, you should give a little bit of thought to some other details. What age of dog is right for you? What gender? And how much money is this going to cost, anyway?

As with the people who want a Labrador retriever because "we've always had Labs in our family," those who automatically choose a puppy, or always choose a male (or female), and aren't willing to be flexible on costs may be denying themselves the chance for a good dog.

Keep an open mind to the possibility that some things about the mental image of your dream dog should be left vague until you consider absolutely everything.

Puppy or grown dog?

The advantages of a puppy are obvious: Puppies are adorable, sweet, and cuddly. To look at them is to smile. A puppy is yours to work with, an almost-clean slate you can mold to fit perfectly into your life. Yours will be the only family she knows, as long as you keep up your part of the deal. That said, there are some real advantages to choosing a grown dog. They're often less expensive to acquire, and certainly less expensive to maintain, since their puppy shots and wormings are behind them. If you choose carefully, you can find one who's already house-trained, and maybe knows a little basic obedience, too.

So why don't more people consider a grown dog? The No. 1 reason I hear is that most people believe that a "recycled rover" doesn't bond as well with their family as a puppy does. That's true if you intend to keep your dog in a barren backyard with little human contact. But if you welcome your dog fully into your life, she's yours just as much as the puppy you took from her mother at seven weeks. Some people say the bond is tighter because the dog has seen the world and knows how lucky she is.

I'm not sure about that, but I've seen plenty of both kinds of dogs. (And have one of each now.) The quality of love they show for their owners — and vice versa — is the same.

A puppy is a good choice for you if you have the time, patience, and flexibility — not to mention the sense of humor — to deal with canine babyhood and adolescence. You won't find any short-cuts to the delightful business of puppy-raising. It's 3 a.m. walks and chewed loafers, endless hours of play and just as many in training. You don't really know what you're going to end up with until you do — this is especially true of mixed-breed puppies, many of whom end up bigger or smaller than anyone at the shelter could have guessed.

Puppyhood is a wonderful trip, full of surprises and delights, but one you shouldn't take if you haven't the time. If you don't put in the effort, you may end up with a dog who drives you crazy — or one you'll drive to the shelter when you can't stand it anymore.

Grown dogs have a bad reputation, one that's often undeserved. Aren't grown dogs that are up for adoption usually pets that *other* people couldn't stand? Is adopting one really such a good idea? It depends on the dog, of course. The real plus is this: While an adjustment period is inevitable with any canine relationship, it's a lot shorter with a grown dog.

An adult dog is past crazy adolescence and settled, for good or for bad, into her adult personality. That *doesn't* mean that she can't be trained — all dogs, young and old, benefit from training — but it *does* mean that you aren't able to influence her personality as much. If you've got a puppy with shy or aggressive tendencies, you can do things to help her before a problem arises (more on this in Chapter 6). If you have a shy or aggressive grown dog, change is a lot more difficult, and maybe not possible at all. Which is why you shouldn't be influenced by a sad story and big brown eyes when you're considering a grown dog.

A grown dog is an excellent choice for situations where no one is home during the day. For retirees who love the companionship of a dog, but haven't the energy for a puppy. For someone who wants to feel good about giving a decent dog a second chance.

There are so many mature dogs who deserve that second chance — mixed-breeds and purebreds both, retired racing dogs, service dogs, and show dogs. Dogs whose owners have died, divorced, or moved. Dogs who want nothing more than the chance to belong to someone.

In all the time I've been writing about dogs, I've watched lots of puppies grow up and disappear because the people who bought them did so because of emotion, not common sense. Consider your situation carefully, and if you honestly aren't up for a year of puppy antics, adopt a grown dog instead.

Male or female?

Does a male or female dog make a better pet? There's no way of settling that question for sure, so for most people the choice comes down to personal preference. You should consider *some* differences, however, because even spaying and neutering does not make males and females the same.

If you do not plan to spay or neuter your pet (more about that in Chapter 13) the differences are more distinct. Females are generally moodier and males, although more constant in temperament, can be constantly annoying in the pursuit of such male-dog activities as sex, leg-lifting, and territory protection.

Unspayed females usually come into season for a couple weeks twice a year, during which you need to deal with a varying amount of mess and the constant attention of canine suitors. Unneutered males may be less than attentive when such attractions beckon. They can also be more likely to challenge your leadership — or anyone else's. Studies have shown, for example, that young unneutered males are the most likely to be involved in attacks on children. Spaying or neutering generally evens things out a bit. It makes females more emotionally constant and males less likely to fight or roam. But differences remain.

In some breeds, for example, males are considerably larger than females — as much as 20 or 30 pounds and two or three inches. *The Complete Dog Book,* available in most libraries and bookstores, contains the official AKC breed standards, the "blueprint" of each breed in all areas, including size. This should give you an idea of the size difference to expect, as in this citation regarding the Newfoundland: "Average height for adult dogs [males] is 28 inches, for adult bitches, 26 inches. Approximate weight of adult dogs ranges from 130 to 150 pounds, adult bitches from 100 to 120 pounds."

Other differences aren't so easily defined. In the more dominant breeds, such as the Rottweiler, a female may be sweeter and more anxious to please. In the more shy and standoffish breeds, such as the Shetland sheepdog, a male may be more outgoing and friendly. In some breeds, such a golden retriever, you might not notice much difference at all.

It's a better idea to concentrate on the breed or breed type rather than the gender, since the toughest male of an easy-going breed is probably a bigger cupcake than the mildest female of a breed with dominant tendencies. Talking to reputable breeders gives you a clear picture how the sexes differ not only in the breed as a whole, but also in particular breeding lines.

For some people, the choice comes down to matter of landscaping: Males often kill shrubs by lifting their legs on them, females often kill lawns by squatting. Although some males squat and some females lift (at least some of the time), the generalization is pretty much on the mark. For more on dogs and landscaping, see Chapter 18.

Cost considerations

How much should a puppy or dog cost? Prices vary so widely that you can pay anything from "free," to the (generally) less than $50 that shelters charge, to the deal-of-the-century price that breed-rescue groups charge for purebreds, to several hundred for an "ordinary" purebred, to several thousand dollars for a "show-quality" dog of a rare or red-hot breed.

In general, however, a purebred "pet-quality" puppy from a reputable breeder costs between $300 and $600, depending on several factors:

✔ Breeds that have small litters, such as many of the toy dogs, may cost more because there are fewer puppies to divide the costs of screening the dam for congenital defects, transporting her to the stud dog, paying the stud fee, caring for the mother during her pregnancy, and caring for the mother and puppies in the weeks that follow.

✔ Breeds such as the bulldog require high levels of veterinary care in the breeding process, including cesarean sections, and that, too, boosts the price of puppies.

✔ Puppies with the potential to be successful in such canine endeavors as dog shows, field trials, or protection competition are more expensive, because these features are "add-ons" in the same way that a bigger engine or better options package is in a new car.

Bear in mind that a reputable breeder produces dogs hoping to improve her lines and, by extension, her breed, but she raises *all* her pups to be healthy companions first. More puppies end up in pet homes than in show homes, and a good breeder wants them all to be happy and well-cared for. If you want to lower your cost, consider this: Those things that distinguish the *pick* puppies — which can be something as unidentifiable to the majority of people as the correct placement of dots on a Dalmatian — are not really very significant to those who are looking for a companion animal. A knowledgeable breeder can explain those differences, most of which you can pick up by studying the breed standard.

Paying . . . and paying . . . and paying

The true cost of a dog, of course, is in the up-keep, but at least you get to make payments on that. The most cost-conscious proper care — food, basic gear, preventive veterinary care, boarding or pet-sitting while you're on vacation — will cost you hundreds of dollars a year, up to a thousand or more for a 100-pound-plus dog who can consume 6 or 7 cups of high-quality kibble a day. Add in occasional veterinary emergencies and the strictly optional, but enjoyable, collecting of such tempting canine merchandise as a wardrobe of fancy collars, softer, more decor-conscious bed, pictures with Santa, and breed wind chimes, and the cost of keeping a dog can consume a significant percentage of your budget.

As a result, you should keep the cost of acquiring a dog in perspective. A $500 purebred puppy from a reputable breeder costs less than $50 a year if you figure the cost over a ten-year lifespan. And $50 is about what it costs to keep my two in kibble for a month.

In the end, it's what you feel comfortable with, purebred or mixed, shelter dog or show dog, the price you pay has no bearing on the love a dog can offer.

Chapter 3

Finding Out about Breeders, Shelters, and Other Sources

*Y*ou've done your homework. You've evaluated your likes and dislikes, and you've taken a good hard look at which breeds or breed types mesh with your lifestyle. (And if you haven't, you might want to take a look at Chapters 1 and 2 to help you.) You're ready to move from picking the kind of dog you like to picking the individual dog you want to share your life with.

Where do you find that dog?

You can find puppies and dogs through many sources — examples include breeders, shelters, and pet stores. Although locating the perfect pet is at times trying and difficult, someone, somewhere has a wonderful pet to prove that any source can be the "right" one in some cases. You *can* get a good pet from a less-than-ideal source. But *possible* and *probable* are often two different things, and as an informed consumer you want to work to narrow your risk so that you increase the chance of coming up with a healthy and temperamentally sound puppy or dog.

Welcome to the '90s

Finding a family pet used to be so easy. Did your parents go through much when they chose a family dog? Probably not. Your mother noticed a classified ad in the paper, or your father's coworker talked up the litter of puppies he was selling or giving away. Until fairly recently, few dogs were spayed and almost none were neutered, so puppies were everywhere.

When your folks decided it was time to get a dog, they probably rounded you and your siblings up and went to take a look at a litter they'd heard about. The puppy that came home that day was your closest pal until you went off to college, a perfect dog and stalwart companion for years. Things worked out great.

You may be wondering whether you really have to go to all the pet-purchasing efforts I advocate later in this chapter, (carefully selecting a breeder, for example). You know the breed you want, you should be able to open the classifieds, call a number or two, and have a pet by the weekend. Or if you're not quite sure about a breed, but probably have it narrowed down to two or three breeds, why not go to a pet store where you can see different breeds at the same time?

Before you do either, think about how much the world has changed — how different the home you can offer a dog is compared with the one your parents offered. Dogs are different, too, especially purebreds, as I discuss in the section "Different dogs" later in this chapter.

A different world

For many people, caring for a dog is more difficult today. Twenty or thirty years ago, dual-income couples were rare, whereas today, both parents (or the only parent in the home, in the case of so many families) often work outside the home to make ends meet. More people, too, are delaying marriage and family — or are choosing to skip them entirely. All these changes mean that more homes than ever before are empty for hours, except for a pet. The stay-at-home mom of the *Leave It to Beaver* era was ready with milk and cookies when the children came home from school — and she was also home for the family dog. Even as today's parents struggle to provide quality time for their children, today's pet owners have to do the same for their "fur children."

Work patterns aren't the only things that have changed. Land is more valuable (read: expensive), making homes on immense suburban lots less common than apartments, townhouses, condominiums, duplexes, and single-family homes with drastically reduced lot sizes to increase affordability. The yard of the suburban house my grandparents bought new in 1954 was so deep I couldn't throw a tennis ball to the back fence when playing fetch with their spaniel. The house I live in now has a yard so small that when we play fetch, the dogs play the back fence as outfielders do, waiting for the ball to bounce before catching it — which means we go to the lake or the dog park several times a week for my big dog to get the exercise he needs. The outings are rewarding for all, but they do take time.

My mom posed for a picture with her dog Pelo in the 1930s, when getting a dog wasn't as complicated as it is today.

Photo courtesy of Irene McMullin.

DUMMIES APPROVED

Rex-ercise

In a few urban areas, businesses have sprung up offering *doggy day care,* which isn't as preposterous or indulgent as it sounds. For those people who cannot — or can no longer — meet the exercise and social needs of their dogs, or who are away from home for periods longer than a dog can reasonably be expected to "hold it," these facilities offer an option. Look under "Dog" or "Pet" in the Yellow Pages to see if your area has such facilities, or ask your veterinarian, groomer, or trainer if he knows of such a service.

Other dog owners in big cities address the same problem by hiring a *dog walker* for their pet's midday outing, a service that was once the province of the society class, but no longer. Of course, you can deal with walking your dog in other ways: Get a responsible neighborhood kid or a retired person to exercise your pet, or trade the task with another dog lover who works different hours. Today's dog lovers are nothing if not resourceful! For more on the importance of exercise, see Chapter 12.

Different dogs

The growing number of two-career couples and hard-working singles aren't the only things that have changed since your first dog was a pup. Dogs have, too.

In 1955, when my parents got their first boxer ("our oldest child," my father called him, because the dog came along two years before I did), the AKC registered 359,900 individual dogs. In 1981, when my parents bought their last dog (now retired, they prefer freedom and travel to pets), the number had jumped to 1,033,248.

In the years before the World War II, purebred dogs belonged primarily to people with names like Rockefeller and Belmont. In the years after, when U.S. government mortgage programs and well-paying jobs expanded the home-owning middle class, young families wanted a dog in their new backyard, and they wanted the same kind of dog as the rich had: a purebred.

The number of AKC-registered purebred dogs grew in the timespan from the '50s into the '70s, mirroring the growth and the prosperity of the American and Canadian middle class. The purebred dog boom finally leveled off not too long after the baby boom did. Since then about a million purebred dogs a year have been registered with the American Kennel Club — in 1994 the figure was 1,345,941. Any way you count 'em, that's a lot of dogs.

The boom caused purebred dogs to become a commodity. Instead of a hobby the wealthy indulged in, the breeding of dogs became big business. Commercial breeders and casual ones started producing puppies, often without regard for health and temperament. The quality of purebred dogs fell as a result, to the point in the '90s where "puppy lemon laws" started showing up on the books to give consumers some warning and rights.

But you don't need laws to protect you if you inform yourself before buying a puppy. While some advantages to pet stores and casual breeders exist — convenience among them — your odds of getting a healthy, happy purebred puppy improve when you seek out a more reputable and knowledgeable breeder. And I'm going to tell you how to find them.

The work of the reputable breeder hasn't changed much over the years: They're in it to preserve and improve the breed they love. When they breed, their goal is to end up with animals who more closely conform to the ideal for their chosen breed or who demonstrate working ability that can be proven in competitive events — for winning is a part of the appeal, too. The pet puppies who come out of these litters are a by-product of these competitive endeavors, in a way, but the animals benefit from the knowledge and expertise of their breeder. And so do you, when you buy a puppy from this source.

If you choose a purebred puppy from another source, you're more likely to end up with a dog who's sick, or whose temperament is undesirable — either too shy or too aggressive. A dog like that will cost you money — in veterinary bills or even lawsuits — but he will also break your heart.

The bottom line is this: Meeting the challenge of keeping a dog has never been more difficult, and you can make the wrong choice in more ways than ever before — which is why *where* you get your dog is every bit as important as *what kind* of dog you get. You need all the help you can to make this work. You need someone who can decide whether what someone is offering is what you need and is someone who will always be there, in one month, one year, or ten years, when you need advice.

For now, though, you've got me, and I want to help you find that person, or, in the case of mixed-breeds, a good shelter or rescue group.

Being informed is the best guarantee that you'll adopt a happy, healthy pet.

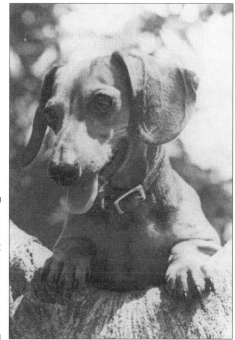

Photo courtesy of the HSUS/Tolle.

Purebred Puppies: Going to the Source

The time to start looking at puppies and dogs has finally arrived. And suddenly everyone has a dog for you to look at — "my neighbor's moving and can't take her dog" — or a litter of puppies, any one of whom would be perfect for you, even though they're not the breed or breed type you've chosen.

Listen politely, smile, and thank them for thinking about you. Who knows? The dog your coworker's neighbor is leaving behind may be exactly the dog you have in mind.

But don't count on it. It's time to go . . . dog shopping!

Breeders: The good, the ignorant, the unscrupulous

The words *champion lines* and *AKC-registered* sell a lot of puppies. So does the word *extra* as in *extra-large Rotties* or *extra-small teacup poodles*. And so do the words *rare,* as in *rare white boxers,* as well as *see both parents, home-raised, must go now!,* and *will deliver.*

Reputable breeders don't consider most of these incentives a selling point. "AKC-registered" (or another registry, such as the Canadian Kennel Club) is a given, as is proven show-quality or working lines. But then, a lot of reputable breeders don't have to advertise at all: Their reputation, secured by years of producing healthy, temperamentally sound puppies for show, work, and home, is such that business comes to them. They breed few litters, and they often have waiting lists for the puppies they produce.

A *reputable breeder* is the kind you want to find.

So what are the differences between a good breeder and the others? Look at the words you may find in a classified ad or flyer on the bulletin board at work and see why they mark the seller as someone with little real experience with purebred dogs or the breed they're producing:

- ✔ **Champion lines.** The only thing it takes to get a "champion" on a pedigree is to buy a poor-quality dog whose great-grandfather earned that title. Less than two or three champions on a pedigree — and on only one side of the pedigree, either the mother's side or the father's — indicates a seller who isn't taking her dogs into the show ring to see how judges think they compare to the breed standard. She's breeding dogs who haven't been judged to be good examples of their breed. So ignore *champion line;* look for *champion-sired* or *champion parents.*

- ✔ **AKC-registered.** Big deal. Any breeder will sell you a purebred who's eligible for registration with the American Kennel Club or other registry, although a good breeder may hold back that registration until certain conditions — such as spaying or neutering — are met.

✔ **Extra.** You see this a lot with the protection breeds, with people trying to produce super-sized Rottweilers and other dogs with a scary reputation. The aim is to produce the biggest, baddest dog around, but the result is likely a dog who's not going to move as well as he should, or a dog with bad hips or other problems. Size limits in the breed standard exist for reasons; deal with people who do not know about them or do not care, and you've got to wonder what else is wrong with the dog.

✔ **Rare.** Puh-lease. I recently saw this in a classified ad for shar-peis. These dogs may have been the rarest in the world when they were first introduced in the U.S. in the early '70s, but the breed's in the AKC's top 25 now. This seller has been either asleep for two decades or is hoping to make a little extra money off someone who has been.

✔ **See both parents.** What could possibly be wrong with this statement? Maybe nothing. You should *always* be able to see the mother, but many times reputable breeders *don't* have the father on hand. That's because they research and scour the country for the male they consider to be the *best* mate for their female, a dog they hope will enhance her strong points and reduce her weak ones. That dog may be across town, across the state, or across the country; wherever he is, they send their female — or they arrange for artificial insemination.

If both parents are on hand, you may be dealing with a seller for whom the only qualities important in a stud dog are proximity and price: He was there. He was free.

✔ **Must go now! and Will deliver.** These are people who want to get rid of these puppies *now.* Where will they be when you have questions or when problems pop up? Not available, or trying to move the next litter just as fast. And how are you going to see the conditions under which your puppy was raised or meet your puppy's mother or siblings if the seller arrives on your doorstep as if she's delivering a pizza? A reputable breeder wants you to come over. She's proud of her dogs. She wants you to take your time, come over a couple of times, ask all the questions you need to — not just now, but six months or six years from now.

You're probably getting the idea. The thing I like to tell prospective puppy buyers is you're probably on the right track if the breeder asks *you* more questions than you can think of to ask her. She knows her breed, and she knows what sort of homes work best for it. She knows which puppies are better in a quiet family, and which ones in a rambunctious one. She wants to make sure you know what you're getting into because she feels personally responsible for the dogs she has brought into the world.

Thinking of breeding your dog? In Chapter 13, I show you why breeding dogs is both less profitable and more effort than you realize, how it puts your own pet at risk, and how it contributes to the problems of surplus pets — even if you're thinking of breeding purebreds.

When you should avoid show breeders

You ought to beware of some show breeders as well, no matter how long they've been turning out champions. For puppies to be proper companions, they must be around people from the day they are born. They must be handled by children and by adults of both sexes. They need to hear the ordinary sounds of life among the two-legged. This is true of all breeds, but it's especially true of those dogs who tend to be shy or aggressive — extra socialization is especially important in their upbringing.

Ask your questions about screening for genetic defects, about whether the breeder shows or otherwise competes with her dogs, about papers, contracts, and guarantees. But don't forget to ask where and how the puppies were raised.

If the breeder says "in my kitchen" and stresses how much they've been handled, you're on the right track.

If she says "in my kennels outdoors," you can do better.

If you still want to breed dogs, that same chapter includes a basic primer on canine matchmaking, puppy raising, and placement — the "good breeder" way.

Chapter 21 in the Part of Tens tells you the top ten questions you should ask a seller of purebred puppies.

Finding a good breeder

A reputable breeder can be very hard to find and may not have a puppy available when you want one, like now. Those facts alone send many puppy buyers to other, less-than-ideal sources.

If everything goes well, you'll have your dog for more than a decade. Doesn't taking a little time to find the right breeder seem reasonable? To make a few phone calls, take a few field trips? To ask more questions of a person who has lived for years with the breed you want, so you can get more answers than a book provides? To see for yourself how some dogs shed hamsters, and others drool rivers? To get a sense of what it's like to live with a canine dynamo, a dog who's always on the go, go, go?

A pet store with a selection of puppies won't be able to provide this information because their staff, no matter how well-meaning, can usually offer only cursory information about the breeds they stock. A backyard breeder with one "let the kids watch" litter can tell you what it's like living with their golden retriever but hasn't the expertise to talk about the breed as a whole. And neither, of course, is offering dogs bred expressly for the top-quality health and temperament you should demand.

The serious breeder, on the other hand, can tell you more than you possibly imagined about the breed. Their commitment to the puppy you buy doesn't end when the sale is final. You get a healthy, well-socialized puppy and technical support that would be the envy of any software company. A serious breeder is just too good a deal to pass up, believe me.

Maybe you still think one AKC Labrador retriever puppy is about the same as another. Maybe you think I'm putting too much emphasis on tracking down the elusive "reputable breeder." The fact is, I can't emphasize it enough. In more than a decade of writing a syndicated newspaper column on pets, I've talked to thousands of people about their pet problems, enough to know that what breed or breed type you choose and where you get the puppy or dog has a great deal to do with how happy you'll be with the dog later — and even if the dog will be with you later.

I'm just trying to save a little heartbreak all around.

Shopping at the dog show

A dog show, especially a *benched* one where the dogs are on display all day, is the ultimate in window-shopping for a dog lover and prospective dog buyer. You want to find good breeders? Go where they turn up to show off their canine pride-and-joys. A dog show is the place.

If all you want to do is see dogs and shop for dog supplies — including that "I love my Papillon" bumper sticker — when you go doesn't matter. If you're at a dog show to track down a breeder, go early. Shows start at 8 a.m., sometimes 9 a.m. and, at most shows, the exhibitors aren't required to stay around after they've competed. (The exception I get to in a minute.) That means if you're hoping to see a curly-coated retriever and they go in the ring at 8:30 a.m., if you don't drag in until noon, you're lucky to spot so much as a ringlet.

Benched shows best for pup-shoppers

The absolute best kind of show for researching a breed is a *benched* show. These events require exhibitors to display their dogs on raised platforms called "benches,' except when they're in the ring or brief respites for exercise or grooming. Before World War II, benched shows were the norm, but now not many are left because they're expensive and more complicated to produce and because exhibitors don't like them — they'd rather show and go. Tradition and prestige keeps the last six benched shows going —

in Detroit, San Francisco, Philadelphia, two in Chicago, and at the U.S.'s most prestigious canine event: The Westminster Kennel Club dog show, held the second Monday and Tuesday of February in New York City's Madison Square Garden.

If you are within a half-day's drive to a benched show, go! The people sitting with their dogs in the benching area can't leave, so they may as well talk.

The best situation is for you to know when the breed you're checking out is competing, but that's not always possible. Some show-sponsoring clubs advertise ring times in the local newspaper, but most don't. It's a fact of life in the dog-show world that these events are put on not with the general — and ticket-buying — public in mind, but with the exhibitor first and foremost. So don't expect the sponsors to make it any easier for you.

So go early, and prepare to be treated with indifference. Don't worry: I tell you everything you need to know to talk dog with the breeders, handlers, and owners that make up the cliquish and sometimes confusing sport of showing dogs.

Dog shows are sometimes hard to find, because advertising and publicity seems to be a hit-and-miss affair with many sponsoring clubs. The general circulation magazines *Dog Fancy* and *Dog World,* available at newsstands, offer listings, as does the AKC Events Calendar, which is provided to subscribers of its official magazine, the *AKC Gazette. Dogs in Canada* magazine lists Canadian Kennel Club events. Listings are also available on the AKC's home page on the World Wide Web, at `http://www.akc.org./akc/`. For more information on canine publications, see the "Additional Resources" appendix.

The first thing you need on this mission is a show catalog. It'll set you back a few bucks, but it's full of the names and addresses of the owners of every dog there, plus some advertisements, plus some coupons. Plus it makes you look serious when you start asking questions.

OK, say you've found the right ring, you're there on time, and you've got your nose buried in the catalog. Now you need to pick out a couple of people to talk to. Look at your catalog for owner-handlers and, especially, for owner-handlers who the catalog also reveals as being the breeder of the dog they're showing. Next, look for a name in your area or region. Then make a beeline for that person and introduce yourself. Before the dogs go in the ring is fine, but be brief and don't pet the perfectly groomed dog — or even worse, spill your soda on a fresh canine coif, a capital offense if there ever was one in the dog-show world. Tell the person you're interested in talking about the breed, and ask if they have a few minutes after the judging. If they don't — they have to take another dog somewhere else, for example — get a business card or a phone number and ask when is a good time to call.

Do that a couple of times, until you've got someone buttonholed. And then ask your questions. Get names. Get numbers. You are, after all, on a fact-finding mission. You'll have more questions later.

A *dog* is a boy dog; a girl dog's a *bitch.* Some dogs are getting points, and some don't need them. Everyone seems to know who the judges pick for the winner except you and why are the handlers teasing those dogs. The answers are in Chapter 16.

Dealing with dog-show snobs

I don't know why some dog-show people have to be so snooty, but they are. Things will go more smoothly if you've done basic research before you go to the show looking for that reputable breeder. You won't get very far by complimenting a proud breeder of Shetland sheepdogs on her "adorable miniature collie." For a couple of years I wrote a column for the AKC's own magazine on public relations, and as far as I can tell, it hasn't helped much among some rank-and-file dog people.

The good news is once you show you have basic knowledge and you're seriously interested in learning more about the dogs they adore, show people can be just as hard to get to stop as they are to get started. What can I say? The dog-show's world is a small club. You don't have to join, but you're better off if you know the secret handshake going in. And you do want to get in, because these are the people with the goods.

Check out the free educational materials that may be available at the show site, usually at an informational table set up by the sponsoring club. You can often find fliers for upcoming shows and canine events, along with informational material provided to the club by the AKC. The "Dog Buyers Education Packet" is one such worthwhile freebie; ask for it. If it's not available, you can order a single copy directly from the AKC; the address is in the "Additional Resources" appendix in the back of this book.

Perusing the periodicals

Attending a dog show is probably the most enjoyable way to start tracking down a breeder, but other ways exist.

The canine magazines — *Dog Fancy, Dog World, the AKC Gazette* and *Dogs In Canada* — have breeder advertisements, as do a couple of notable annuals: *Dogs USA* (put out by the *Dog Fancy* folks) and the *Dogs In Canada* annual.

These magazines do not screen breeders, however, so proceed with caution. If you can't find anyone locally for the dog you want, call the nearest breeder. If he's a reputable breeder, he likely belongs to a national or regional breed club and can give you a referral to a breeder nearer to you — if there is one. If he asks for your Visa card number and says your puppy will be on the next flight, thank him politely and move on to the next ad.

Finding a breed club

Joining a breed club is another way to come in contact with reputable breeders — or find out more about your chosen breed while you wait for your puppy. National clubs for AKC-recognized breeds are members of the American

Kennel Club, which is a club made up of smaller breed and activity clubs, run by delegates from its member clubs. (The Canadian Kennel Club offers memberships to individuals; the AKC does not.)

How much assistance you get from a national club varies widely by breed. The corresponding secretaries of clubs overseeing the standards of popular breeds may send out little more than an information sheet. The clubs for less popular breeds may send you a list of club members actively breeding. Joining the club gets you a subscription to the newsletter, which is a wonderful resource for finding a breeder. Many breeds have local or regional clubs as well; the national club should be able to point you in their direction. If nothing else, belonging to a breed club gives you a built-in circle of acquaintances who think your breed is every bit as perfect as you do!

The American Kennel Club maintains a list of contacts for its breed clubs, as do other registries; write to them or visit their Web site at `http://www.akc.org/akc/` for a particular listing.

Surfin' for a dog

A more recent way to connect with reputable breeders is though the use of Internet *e-mail lists*. An e-mail list is like an ongoing group discussion, except that it's carried out over the Internet and shared among those who have joined the list electronically. Many e-mail lists have sprung up to focus on a single breed, such as Dobermans, or breed group, such as spaniels. Procedures for subscribing vary; check out the canine e-mail FAQ at `http://www.zmall.com/pet/dog-faqs/lists/email-list.html`. Chapter 22 has more great dog-related online sites.

TIP

Should you buy a puppy sight unseen?

While you'll likely find a reputable breeder in your area, or within a few hours drive, that's not always going to be the case, especially if you've your heart set on a puppy of a less popular breed. In such cases you'll have to decide if you want to buy a puppy you've never met and have him shipped, probably by air.

Buying a puppy unseen may seem a risky business, but it's perhaps not so much as you may think. Before you consider this option, you'll have checked out the breeder thoroughly and talked to references. The breeder considers it a big

jump, too, so she'll have had plenty of conversations with you. Pictures of the parents will have changed hands, along with the array of documentation and contracts good breeders provide.

Experienced breeders are used to dealing with airlines and will work to minimize the risk of air travel. (Shipping tips are also in Chapter 15.)

So if everything seems in order, go for it. It's likely better to deal with a reputable breeder a time zone or two away than a clueless one in your home town.

Some warning flags

A very few breeders are downright evil and fail to provide for even the basics of their animals' needs. A few more are mentally ill, living in filthy homes packed to the rafters with freely mating dogs. These people are fairly easy to spot and avoid — unless their pups are cleaned up and sold elsewhere.

Maybe I believe too much in the essential goodness of human nature — or the goodness of those who love dogs — but I think the majority of "bad" breeders — "backyard breeders," they're commonly called — are not uncaring. They're uninformed. They don't know that many of the dogs they produce can end up in shelters or spend their lives in pain from a congenital illness. They just want a litter "so the kids can see," or because "puppies are fun," or because they heard breeding dogs is an easy way to make a little money. They aren't bad people, but they're still not good breeders.

Following are a few things that should give you pause when dealing with a breeder:

- ✔ **Lack of knowledge about the breed.** Someone who doesn't know about the history of the breed or how suitable it is for different homes probably isn't someone who's too concerned about producing puppies that are fine examples of the breed.

- ✔ **Ignorance or denial of genetic defects.** Every breed has some problems, and some of the most common ones — such as hip dysplasia — can cause great pain and cost big bucks. A person who isn't aware of congenital defects almost certainly isn't screening breeding stock to avoid them.

- ✔ **No involvement in dog sports.** Every dog doesn't have to be a champion before he's bred, but you improve the odds of getting a high-quality purebred if you buy from someone involved in showing or otherwise competing with their dog. The point of a dog show, in fact, is to evaluate breeding stock.

- ✔ **Not letting you observe the litter, meet the mother or other dogs, or see where the puppies were raised.** Healthy, well-mannered adults and a clean, well-run kennel are a breeder's best testimonial. If a person doesn't want you to see anything except the puppy she's trying to sell, you ought to be wondering why.

- ✔ **No documentation.** If the purebred puppy's represented as "AKC-registered" then registration papers should be available. (This goes for other registries, too.) So, too, should papers backing up health claims. A sales contract spelling out the rights and responsibilities of both parties is highly desirable. Such a document provides you with recourse should the puppy not turn out as promised — if he has congenital health problems or isn't suitable for showing, if that was part of your intent in buying him.

> ✔ **Doesn't seem to understand the importance of socialization.** Puppies need to be nurtured, loved, and handled to make good pets. Someone who can't explain what they've done in this area, or who tries to sell a puppy less than seven weeks old, probably doesn't understand enough about puppy-raising to be breeding dogs.

Again, it's all about increasing the odds of success. Can you find a good puppy from a backyard breeder advertising in your local newspaper? Sure. My own brother has just such a dog, the most wonderful lump of a yellow Labrador two kids could ever pester. A fantastic temperament, this dog. But I also know of other people whose backyard-bred Labs are so crippled by hip dysplasia that their activities are limited and their days filled with painkillers. Which is why I think it's important, when shopping for a purebred puppy, to do everything you can to make sure you're getting the best in health and temperament.

Pet stores: Proceed with caution

You don't have to put much effort into buying purebred puppies at pet stores. They have a wide selection. You don't have to wait for a puppy. They may offer some health guarantees. They take credit cards. What could be better or more convenient?

Based on the what you already know, you should realize that you increase your odds dramatically of getting a healthier, more stable puppy by dealing with a knowledgeable, reputable breeder. But that's not the only reason to avoid retail puppy outlets: *Puppy mills* are an even more compelling one.

In the farming regions across the U.S. — but most commonly in the Midwest and in Pennsylvania — the wholesale breeding of dogs is the stuff of nightmares. In these puppy mills, breeding stock spend their whole miserable lives knee-deep in their own filth in tiny, makeshift cages exposed to the elements. Medical problems go untreated, and worn out or critically ill dogs have, in some cases, been killed and fed back to the survivors. It is cruelty on a most appalling scale, well-documented over the last two decades by humane groups and continuing under the noses of overburdened federal investigators.

When you buy a purebred puppy from a pet store, you may well be supporting just such an operation with your money, and don't let anyone tell you otherwise.

Stung by public horror over the media exposés of puppy mills, the pet industry, the U.S. Department of Agriculture, and the AKC — which penalizes breeders for registration fraud — have beefed-up efforts to clean up this problem. Their efforts are to be commended and encouraged but humane investigators say puppy mills still exist.

But even if — and that's a mighty big "if" — every commercial breeder kept their kennels scrupulously clean and properly cared for every animal on site, you're still more likely to do better with a home-raised puppy from a small, reputable breeder. Puppies are not well-suited to be mass-produced "merchandise," and that's what you get when you buy from a pet store. (Also, consider the life of the "breeding stock," who will never know what it's like to be a beloved pet!)

Remember, finding a good puppy is about being an informed consumer. There are people who have ended up with a pet they truly love from a retail pet store. Still, your best chance at finding a healthy, temperamentally sound, properly socialized purebred puppy is not at a pet store. On this point, veterinarians, trainers, humane societies, and breed registries agree.

The bottom line when it comes to purebred puppies is this: More sick or psycho dogs are out there than you can possibly imagine, and to buy from those producing such animals because they don't know better or don't care is not smart on your part. Take your time. Educate yourself. You are better off for the effort you put in up front — and you'll sleep better at night afterward knowing you've done a good deed by not supporting a bad breeder.

The Poop on Papers

A purebred dog's "papers" consist, at the very least, of two elements: a pedigree and slip that allows you to register the dog as yours with an entity such as the American Kennel Club or Canadian Kennel Club. A reputable breeder likely sends you home with far more. Here's a rundown of what you may get:

- **Pedigree.** A diagram of your dog's ancestors for three or more generations, listing the registered names of these dogs, as well as the titles they earned. You want to see a lot of titles, and you want to see them in recent generations, on both the mother's and the father's sides. You want to see *Ch.*, for *champion*, a "looks" award, and you want to see working titles, for obedience or such breed-specific endeavors as herding or hunting. A reputable breeder is able to explain any abbreviations on a pedigree; her dogs are likely to have plenty for her to explain, and she's happy you asked.

- **Registration application or certificate.** A pedigree is a tremendously useful source of information for a buyer, but it doesn't mean a thing at the AKC, which is looking for a different piece of paper to do its job. The registration slip is one of two kinds: Either an application to name and record a puppy for the first time, or a certificate that is used to transfer the ownership of an already named and registered dog. (AKC rules say once a dog has been given a registered name, there's no changing it. What you actually *call* him, of course, they don't care about.)

If you're buying a puppy, you'll probably get a form commonly called a *blue slip*. A grown dog should come with an official registration certificate, white with a purple border. The transfer of ownership form is on the back. Other registries have rules of their own and can assist you with their paperwork.

✔ **Health records.** This sheet shows when your puppy was vaccinated and wormed. (Many breeders take care of this themselves, so don't be surprised if a veterinarian is not mentioned on the records.) Certificates clearing the puppy itself of a particular defect, such as deafness in the case of Dalmatians, should be included.

Your puppy's parents' health clearances may show on the registration application; if not, ask to see the documents. You're looking for letters such as *OFA* (Orthopedic Foundation for Animals) or *PennHIP* (another kind of certification developed at the University of Pennsylvania's School of Veterinary Medicine) in breeds prone to hip dysplasia; *CERF* (Canine Eye Registration Foundation) in breeds with congenital eye problems; or *BAER* (Brainstem Auditory Evoked Response) in breeds where deafness is common.

✔ **Sales contract.** This document defines your responsibilities — such as to spay or neuter your pet, or to inform the breeder if you can no longer keep the dog. The breeder spells out her role in the transaction, too: health and temperament guarantees and the remedies the breeder will offer if the puppy or dog falls short, such as replacing the puppy. The contract for a companion-quality dog sold on a spay-neuter contract is pretty basic, and grants you full ownership of the animal. If you intend to buy the dog to show and, ultimately, hope to breed her, the contract is considerably more complicated.

A breeder's reputation is on the line when an animal capable of reproducing leaves her place, and she wants to ensure her kennel name doesn't end up on the pedigree of a puppy-mill dog. She may refuse to give you full title to the dog — a situation known as a *co-ownership* — and she may additionally stipulate that she has a major role in deciding when and to whom the dog is bred. If you've never shown before, co-ownership may be the only way to acquire a dog of a quality capable of earning a championship. If you can work within the confines of co-ownership and feel a rapport with the breeder, you can learn the ropes under the tutelage of someone who knows the breed and the sport. (Often when the dog's show career is over and the animal is spayed or neutered, the breeder will "sign off" on the dog and leave you as sole owner.)

✔ **Care instructions.** Finally, the breeder often sends you home with directions on what to feed and how often, when to visit the veterinarian, and so on. Some breeders even provide booklets on puppy raising and basic obedience.

Perhaps you think this is a lot of paperwork, but paperwork, it seems, is one of the hallmarks of modern life. You never have to look at any of it ever again if you don't intend to exhibit or breed your dog. You don't even have to register your dog with a registry — many people never bother.

But that thick file you take home with your puppy is important because its very existence speaks volumes about the quality of the breeder you've just done business with. She's done her job, and you have the paperwork to prove it.

The rest is up to you.

Expanding the Possibilities

Please don't think because I go to such great lengths explaining how to buy a purebred puppy, I think purebred puppies are the only way to go when looking for a dog.

Nothing could be further from the truth.

But from my experience, when most people start thinking about a dog, they think about a purebred puppy. There are so many ways to mess up this purchase I wanted to cover these folks thoroughly. Now it's your turn. If you're willing to open your heart a little wider, a whole new world of wonderful dogs suddenly opens to you. Want to talk about the appeal of a rare breed? How about taking that extra step and going for "unique," that 100 percent original, one-of-a-kind, never-seen-anything-like-it canine companion: the *mixed breed*.

But you have even more to consider. Depending on your lifestyle, what respected dog trainer and author Carol Lea Benjamin calls a "second-hand dog" may be a much better choice for you than a puppy. And these come in both purebred and mixed-breed varieties.

Chosen carefully, your second-hand dog can become just as cherished a family member.

Also, I personally believe you get bonus points in the afterlife by adopting a pet who needs you from a shelter or rescue group. Are you so perfect that you couldn't use the help? I thought not.

Dog trainer Carol Lea Benjamin has written two wonderful — and inexpensive — paperback books that are must-haves for anyone thinking of adopting from a shelter or rescue groups: *The Chosen Puppy: How To Select and Raise a Great Puppy from an Animal Shelter* and *Second-Hand Dog: How To Turn Yours into a First-Rate Pet*. Both are endorsed by shelters and breed-rescue volunteers across the country, some of whom sell them or give them out with their dogs. I myself buy *Second-Hand Dog* five copies at a time and hand it out when placing the strays that always seem to find their way to my door. (How do they do that?)

Shelters: A good choice and a good deed

The word that often links "mixed-breed puppies," "older dogs," and "depressing" is *shelter,* but if you haven't been to a shelter lately, you find traditions are changing fast.

Creative outreach programs working in partnership with the media and with businesses such as pet-supply superstores take pets where the people are to increase the volume of adoptions. And shelters themselves are changing — after years of listening to people talk about avoiding the gloomy surroundings, progressive organizations are giving their buildings a face-lift to make them light, bright, and inviting. One such shelter belongs to the SPCA of Oakland, CA which, in 1994, opened their PeopleSoft Adoption Center, a place so decidedly upbeat that schoolchildren go there on field trips to enjoy the interactive educational displays. The best shelters have well-trained, caring staffs, and a healthy core of volunteers to keep dogs socialized and counsel potential adopters as to the animal that will provide the best match with their circumstances.

In short, today's shelter pets are more adoptable than ever before, thanks to programs that temperament test and perform basic health services — and some extraordinary ones — before animals are made available to the public.

However, all shelters are not the same. Some shelters are run by municipal animal-control facilities, and some are run by nonprofit humane organizations. Some of the latter have widely different policies that affect the kind of dogs they have available for adoption, which means that doing a little checking first pays.

Still, good puppies and dogs are in any shelter, no matter how rundown the facilities and uncaring the staff. After all, a dog cannot help where he's dumped, sometimes for the most capricious of reasons. But just as you can improve your odds of buying a healthy, happy puppy by choosing a reputable breeder, you can better the chance of a successful adoption by choosing a progressive shelter.

Making a decision about a shelter dog is often difficult. You want to take them all, and the realization that some of these dogs aren't going to find a new home softens even the hardest heart. But you aren't doing anyone any favors if you let your heart make your decisions here. If you pass over a dog who suits you better because of one you felt sorrier for, the dog you should have taken — the one that would have worked — may not make it. And you may end up miserable with your choice to the point where you take him back and don't try again. So instead of one happy ending, you've got at least three sad ones — yours and the two dogs'.

Take a friend to keep you from making a foolish decision. And take your time. Go back a few times if you have to. Play it cool. After your new dog settles in you can make up for it by spoiling her like crazy.

Be aware of some potential problems with going to a shelter. Shelter puppies are at risk for contracting highly contagious diseases such as *parvovirus,* and the considerably less serious *kennel cough* — a short-term illness — is common among shelter dogs. (More on these in Chapters 10 and 15.)

In addition, you probably won't be offered the choice of not spaying or neutering your dog, since most shelters either do it for you or require it done as a condition of adoption. Some also screen you as thoroughly as an adoption agency might, to make sure you're "qualified" to have a dog — and turn you down if they decide not! Like them or not, these are understandable policies for organizations in the front lines of fighting pet overpopulation. These should not dissuade you from considering a shelter when choosing a puppy or dog. Shelters are a good source for puppies and dogs — and a reasonably priced one when compared to the cost of a purebred puppy.

Shelters are not just for mixed breeds. While most young puppies in a shelter are mixes, the supply of grown dogs in any given shelter includes plenty of purebreds — up to 25 percent in some areas. And not just common breeds such as Labrador retrievers, German shepherds, and poodles. Shelter workers have dealt with breeds so rare they had to look in books to ID them. Said one shelter director, whose family ended up with a fairly rare but nonetheless unwanted Schipperke, "Everything shows up eventually."

Animal-control shelters

Municipal animal-control facilities are perhaps the easiest to figure out. Finding homes for pets was not the reason they were founded and is not their primary purpose to this day — although many of them do a good job of it, nonetheless.

Animal-control departments were formed to protect people from animal menaces — primarily rabies. They remove dead animals and enforce animal regulations, such as those regarding licensing — a rabies-control measure — and how many animals (and what kinds) people can keep. They respond to calls on vicious animals, as well as calls involving animals disturbing a neighborhood because of noise or odor. They also serve as a "convenience," disposing of unwanted animals through adoption, euthanasia, or, in some locales, through sales to biomedical research.

Animal-control shelters have never been well-funded operations, and this situation has not improved in recent years. With so much required of them and so few resources, readying animals for adoption and counseling prospective adopters cannot be number-one on the animal-control director's list of priorities. And yet, because of caring people in many of these departments and in the communities they serve, some decent volunteer programs are in place to fill the gap.

Because of these programs, municipal animal-control shelters can be good places to adopt. But many of the nonprofit humane societies shelters have the potential to be better, because their mandate has always put helping animals at the top of the list.

Private nonprofit shelters

Nonprofit shelter groups run the gamut from squalid outfits that serve as little more than a fund-raising gimmick for the people in charge of them to organizations with well-funded endowments and programs that not only help homeless animals but also work to improve conditions for all animals — and animal-lovers — in their communities.

Most shelters fall somewhere in the middle: Their buildings could use some work, their budgets are always tight, and they do the best with what they have to provide for the animals in their community.

New buildings don't necessarily a good shelter make, but you certainly want to work with a shelter that clearly cares enough for its charges to make sure they are kept in areas that are clean and don't facilitate the spread of disease.

"He followed me home"

It must be fate. Here you are, thinking about getting a dog and one follows your daughter home from school (with the aid of half a bologna sandwich). Or a dog is in the parking lot at the supermarket. Or your neighbor found one on his front porch.

Before you start picking out names, consider two possibilities: 1) He may not be the right dog for you (check out Chapters 1 and 2); and 2) He may already belong to someone.

You may not think the second possibility could possibly be the case with a dog who isn't wearing a collar and looks as if he is malnourished and, possibly, maltreated. But a lot of people — promise me you won't be one of them — never bother to put collars on their dogs, much less an ID tag or license. And it only takes a few days on the loose to make even a previously well-cared-for dog look dirty, tired, and sick.

If you find a stray and want to do what's best, try everything you can to find the owner first. Put up fliers in the neighborhood — most dogs stay within a couple miles of home when they get out — take out a classified ad in the newspaper and post "found" notices at local shelters and animal-related businesses such as groomers and veterinary hospitals.

Give it your best shot for a week or two and then if your decide to keep him, feel free. If by then you've decided he's not the pet for you, however, guidelines for finding a dog a new home are in Chapter 13.

Shelter work is difficult and stressful, and employees and volunteers can suffer burnout quickly. A well-run shelter is as compassionate to its staff as it is to the animals, because one has a lot to bear on the treatment of the other. Look for a shelter where employees are helpful and knowledgeable and clearly interested in helping the shelter's animals find responsible new homes.

The best shelters have a good handle on a dog's history, health, and temperament before putting her up for adoption and have done what they can to enhance her chances of success in a new home, through socialization and screening for the right home. They provide not only preadoption counseling but follow-up help, with behavioral advice or reduced-cost training classes.

These are the shelters you should seek out when looking for a dog or puppy. If you want to go one step better, look for ways to help the shelters that don't measure up. Usually it's a question of money and volunteers, and you can do a lot to contribute in these categories. Contact your local shelter to find out how.

"Humane Society" and "Society for the Prevention of Cruelty to Animals" ("SPCA") are generic terms freely used in the United States and Canada by animal organizations that have no connection to one another or to national organizations such as the Washington, D.C.-based Humane Society of the United States or the ASPCA in New York City. And yet, local shelters are often stymied in their fund-raising efforts by people who have "given to the national organization" and consider their charitable efforts complete — even though money given to the HSUS and ASPCA is used to fund their own programs, not the local shelters'.

Which is why it's important not to forget your local animal shelter when giving. For an overview of how the national groups spend their money, check out the annual report from the newspaper *Animal People,* which is itself a nonprofit organization. To get the "Where the Money Goes" issue, send $3 to Animal People, P.O. Box 960, Clinton, WA 98236-0960.

A bit of a war in the animal-welfare community occurs over those organizations that call themselves "no kill" shelters. There are more pets than there are suitable homes, which sets up a grim game of "musical homes" resulting in the death of millions of animals every year. "No kill" shelters get that way by refusing to accept animals that are not adoptable or by refusing all animals when they are full. The turn-aways often end up at another shelter, one whose staff often very much resents having to be the bad guy.

To be fair, some "no kill" shelters — such as the San Francisco SPCA — have a fairly broad definition of "adoptable" that includes those animals that can be made adoptable through medical care or training.

As someone who's looking to adopt an animal, you shouldn't get distracted by policy debates. Look for a shelter offering healthy, well-socialized animals and adoption counseling to help you pick out the right one for you. These shelters, with well-trained staffs and a solid volunteer corps, are your best bets for a successful adoption, no matter their policy on euthanasia.

Breed-rescue groups: A first-rate source for purebreds

One very positive change in the handling of homeless animals in the last decade or so has been the growth of the volunteer, grass-roots breed-rescue movement. If you're looking for a purebred, and are willing to accept a grown dog instead of a puppy, then choosing a breed-rescue group is a good deal, and a good deed.

Breed-rescue groups work with a single breed, such as the basset hound, or a couple of related breeds, such as one group I know of specializing in collies and Shetland sheepdogs. (In some areas, all-volunteer groups also foster and place mixed breeds.)

These groups range from one-person operations placing a few dogs a year to a few massive nonprofits with their own sheltering facilities, boards of directors, and a well-organized volunteer network all dedicated to stepping in when one of their particular breed needs a hand. Some breed-rescue groups work by referral only, keeping lists of dogs in private homes and shelters that need homes and referring potential adopters. Others take in dogs from shelters and private individuals and foster the dogs, a policy that allows them to get a good feel for an individual animal's personality.

While such diversity of policies makes it impossible to describe a "typical" breed-rescue effort, probably the closest description of one would be a group consisting of two to four volunteers who work together to foster and place dogs of their chosen breeds and are both affiliated with a local breed club and loosely tied to a national network of rescuers for that particular breed. They typically offer dogs who have been vet-checked, vaccinated, and spayed or neutered, and the adoption fees they charge cover these veterinary expenses. Transportation and foster care costs often come out of the volunteers' pockets.

The nature of breed rescue lends itself to both advantages and disadvantages for a potential adopter.

The advantages include getting a vet-checked, altered purebred at a very reasonable price — commonly, just the cost of the veterinary care. You also get more personal service with a breed-rescue group than with a shelter. A breed-rescue group puts you on their waiting list if they haven't a dog who suits you, and also works with other rescuers in the region to find what you want. Breed-rescue volunteers have often lived with the dogs they're trying to place, and so they are more keenly aware of how each dog handles a home situation — such as how she gets along with cats.

Difficult aspects of breed rescue exist, too. Breed-rescue groups rely on volunteers, and volunteers can easily get in over their heads and burn out quickly. Breed-rescue groups start up and stop and regroup and drop out at a surprising rate, which makes tracking down a current breed-rescue contact in your area a little difficult, as well as dealing with the same person you worked with if you have problems a year or two down the line, or need to give the dog up.

But don't let these problems dissuade you if you're looking for an adult purebred. Shelters, veterinarians, and reputable breeders often can provide you with a referral to a breed-rescue group and, if not, you can start at the national level and work your way down. Many AKC and CKC breed clubs have national rescue coordinators who maintain a current list of local and regional efforts. To find the national coordinator, write to the breed registries or visit the AKC's home page on the World Wide Web.

If you are looking for a purebred dog, exploring the breed-rescue option is worth the effort, if for no other reason than to support thousands of dedicated volunteers coast to coast.

You may be lucky to live in an area with a well-organized umbrella group of breed-rescue volunteers. One such area is greater Seattle, where Seattle Purebred Dog Rescue (SPDR) has for years served as a model organization for other communities. For more information on SPDR, contact P.O. Box 3523, Redmond, WA 98073-3523; or call the SPDR message line at 206-654-1117.

Other Possibilities

You should consider a couple of other sources for healthy adult dogs before you make your final decision.

"Career change" dogs

Groups that train service dogs to work with people who are sight- or hearing-impaired or who use wheelchairs demand a great deal from their dogs and, so, have a high rate of *washouts,* or animals who didn't quite make the cut.

Service-dog organizations often maintain their own breeding programs, producing animals of exemplary health, intelligence, and temperaments. These dogs, mostly Labrador retrievers, golden retrievers, or German shepherds, have such wonderful potential for pets that there is often a waiting list for those animals who for one reason or another didn't make it through the rigorous selection and training process.

Placement procedures vary from group to group. Contact the service-dog training organizations in your area for details.

Another excellent source of pets: Groups that rescue and place former racing greyhounds. These groups — both industry-sponsored and independent — have sprung up in response to increased public awareness of the fate of greyhounds who don't cut the mustard on the track. These gentle and elegant creatures used to be killed by the thousands every year, but more and more retired racers are finding happiness as treasured pets.

A few dozen organizations in the United States rescue, foster, and place former racing greyhounds; one with affiliations nationwide is Greyhound Pets of America, (800) FON 1 GPA (366-1472). Cynthia Branigan's *Adopting the Racing Greyhound* is a nice little paperback book that helps potential adopters decide if a greyhound is for them and helps smooth the transition afterward.

Private parties

Finally, you can't rule out dogs offered by private parties, some of them people trying to find homes for a stray, or help out a friend or neighbor in a pinch who has to place a dog. Some good dogs have turned up this way, too, but remember to let you head, not your heart, be your guide. Ask your questions, and if you don't get the answers you want, don't consider the dog, no matter how sad the story.

Chapter 4

All the Right Stuff

. . . .

In This Chapter

▶ Choosing basic dog gear

▶ Sniffing out the coolest things

▶ Avoiding dangerous products

▶ Finding fun dog stuff for you

. . . .

A dog can get by without much in the way of material belongings and a great many of them do. A collar. A leash. A container for water, and one for food. A warm, dry place to sleep. Food. Something to chew on.

Add love and attention to the list and, in truth, a dog doesn't need much more. But oh, how we love to spend on our dogs! Pet food and supplies is a multi-billion-dollar industry, with so much money spent on dog-related furniture, food, and toys I often joke the only difference between having a kid and having a dog is you don't need a college fund for the latter. That, and no matter how many things you buy your dog, she never gets spoiled.

Your dog, in fact, could not care less if the collar you buy her is jeweled. A crystal bowl or a stainless steel one, it really doesn't matter to her, as long as you put food in it. Color-coordinate her leash to match her collar and to complement the interior of your sport-utility vehicle; it won't impress her. Most of the dog-accessories decisions you face you make to please *yourself*. And that's fine, as long as your dog's needs are met with gear that is well-made, practical, and appropriate for her size and temperament.

At the most basic level, your dog needs food and shelter. That's about the most any dog could ever have hoped for during the thousands of years humans and dogs have worked and lived together as companions and workmates. Everything you add to those basics is designed to make your dog's life — and your own — safer, more convenient, and more enjoyable.

I know you want that, so you'll be doing some shopping.

Your dog needs more than you can buy her at a pet-supply store. She needs a healthy relationship with a veterinarian, and she needs socialization and training. Everything you need to know about dog health care and training, as well as explanations of how to *use* some of the gear described in this chapter, is in Part III: "Living With Your Dog."

Canine Cuisine

Up until this century, the feeding of dogs wasn't that carefully thought-out an affair. They ate what we gave them. They ate what we left behind, They ate what other animals left behind. They killed things to eat, and they ate the remains of what other animals killed.

Dogs are not the pickiest of creatures, as anyone who has ever watched one wolf down rotting fish on a beach knows.

The hit-or-miss approach to feeding worked well enough for generations, especially when most dogs lived in rural areas, with access to rodents in the barn, rabbits in the fields, or leftovers in the farmer's kitchen. But then things changed, and more dogs assumed the role of companions in a more urban environment where living off the land wasn't such an easy thing to accomplish. At the same time, the burgeoning interest in animal husbandry had the men and women who were developing and refining breeds wanting their prize animals treated appropriately, with the best food that could be provided.

"There is no doubt that a great deal of a dog's goodness goes in at the mouth," says Vero Shaw's *The Illustrated Book of the Dog,* first published in 1879 and re-issued as a novelty more than a century later as *The Classic Encyclopedia of the Dog.* "We do not, certainly, advocate the feeding of dogs wholly upon meat . . . [But] we do recommend meat to be given, in addition to the meal or biscuits which form the staple portion of the daily meal."

The book describes the ingredients and preparation of a dog's diet, the careful and considered mixing of grains such as rice and barley with vegetables such as cabbage, broccoli, and turnip-tops, and, finally, with the different kinds of meat available. "Horses suitable for slaughtering can usually be bought for from one pound to thirty shillings," notes the author.

Decades later, after untold hours of research by thousands of universities and pet-food manufacturers, Shaw's advice holds true: Modern dog foods are still a combination of grains and meat products.

The daily diet

Today's pet-owner, thankfully, doesn't have to mix ingredients. And even better — doesn't have to kill the occasional horse to provide the meat!

With the demand growing at the end of the century, the emerging food-processing industry, so busy providing more convenient foods for an increasingly urban human population, adapted the same methods to manufacturing food for pets. This, too, has not changed too much in decades: The commercially available choices for your dog's main diet are still the following:

- ✔ Dry, bagged rations, commonly called *kibble*
- ✔ Canned foods, ranging from meat-and-meal diets to preparations meant to be mixed with kibble
- ✔ Semi-moist foods, a more recent development, often designed to look like "people food" such as hamburger patties or sausage

What *has* changed in the last decade or so is the number of choices within these classifications. What once was an industry dominated by one or two manufacturers is now considerably more diverse, with many small- and medium-sized manufacturers. The biggest growth area has been in "premium" foods and in special diets targeted to a particular subgroup of dogs: Puppies, older dogs, or animals under stress, such as pregnant dogs or canine athletes.

Still, the competition has improved the quality of most lines to the point where you can probably choose a product from any reputable company and your dog will be fine. This is a big difference from a decade ago, when I was advising people to avoid grocery-store food. You can find good food anywhere now, in grocery stores, pet-supply stores, and veterinary hospitals, from manufacturers big and small.

While there are more good foods out there than ever before, there is one category of food that you should be a little careful with, though: "generic" foods.

In a 1986 study by the University of Georgia School of Veterinary Medicine, puppies fed on various discount no-label foods showed nutritional deficiencies not evident in their better-fed cousins — a situation that changed when the puppies were switched to a brand-name food.

The problem, experts say, is that ingredients such as protein may come from poor-quality sources that are difficult to digest. You might be fine with these foods, but with so many high-quality and reasonably priced alternatives, why take a chance?

What to feed your dog

As to choosing between dry, canned or semi-moist, you'll probably do OK whatever you decide on those, too. Dry foods offer economy and convenience, but some dogs don't like them. Canned and semi-moist foods are very pleasing to the canine palate, but they are more expensive — and some have sugars and dyes that aren't the least bit necessary for your dog's nutrition. Even though pets prefer canned food, if you start your puppy on dry food, you shouldn't have a problem with finicky eating, which is a behavior that's mostly *taught* by humans.

Dry foods help keep your dog's teeth cleaner, but if you're brushing them and having them cleaned regularly — more information on this is in Chapter 10 — your pet's teeth should be OK on other diets.

If you're house-training a puppy or dog, you may want to feed kibble only, at least until the task is accomplished. The water content of canned foods can make a dog need to urinate more frequently. This consideration is especially important if your dog is left home alone for several hours at a time, like while you're at work.

If you prefer canned food, you can always change after the puppy's a little older and able to "hold it" longer, or your adult dog understands completely what the house rules are.

My own preference is to feed an appropriate, premium kibble from a reputable manufacturer, and nothing else. By "appropriate," I mean puppy food for puppies, food with lower fat and protein for older or overweight dogs, and performance food for highly active dogs.

Why a *premium* kibble? It's a little more expensive than some other dry foods, but still competitive when compared to canned or semi-moist. Premium kibble also results in a lower volume of stools than is produced by many other foods. Both of these concerns are not major if you've got a Chihuahua, but they may be if you've got a Great Dane.

Ask your veterinarian or other animal-care professional — groomer, trainer, or reputable breeder — for a recommendation, and stick to it after you're satisfied it's working well for your dog and that he likes it. Dogs don't need variety, and they don't get bored with the same ration day after day. When a healthy dog is a picky eater, it's usually because the owners taught him to be that way, by adding tempting tidbits at the least sign of reluctance to eat.

Dog-sports enthusiasts are often much more up on trends in nutrition than many veterinarians. That's because they demand more of their dogs than do most of the clients a veterinarian will see. They want glossy coats on their show dogs, and energy to burn from their field, agility, or obedience dogs. They are always looking for an edge, and that makes them good people to talk to when it comes to choosing a food. Another reason: They usually aren't dealing with the conflict of interest many veterinarians have: Recommending a food sold in the veterinary hospital or clinic.

Bear in mind, however, that dog-sport competitors can be a little *too* trendy when it comes to food. They're often big on supplementing, prepared formulas as well as vitamins, vegetables, raw meat, or herbal concoctions. And that's just flat-out not necessary for the normal nutritional demands of a dog whose primary job is companion. Some supplements may even be dangerous, depending on what's being added. So here's my advice: If you don't know what you're doing, don't do it. Buy a top-quality food and leave it at that. And if you have questions, ask your veterinarian.

Don't think it's too dull if your pet's food is just plain brown: Fancy shapes and chunks of meat or cheese — or bits made to *look* like meat or cheese — are put there for *your* benefit. As long as it smells good, your dog doesn't care what it looks like. (There's even a saying, "looks like the dog's dinner," that pretty much sums up the fact that our idea of unappetizing is *not* the same as our dogs.) There's no evidence these people-pleasing touches will hurt your pet — unless they're too high in sugar, fat, or salt for your dog — but they're nothing you need to seek out, and you certainly shouldn't pay extra for them.

Some people just can't believe a dog can be happy with plain kibble, even of a top-quality variety. If it makes you happy, add some canned food, maybe a little water and microwave it briefly. You'll likely get the enthusiastic response you're looking for. (Don't forget to cover the leftover canned food and refrigerate.)

Before you start feeding this way, however, consider this: Should you ever want to travel with your dog, or need to leave him with your veterinarian, at a boarding kennel, or with a house-sitter or friend, he'll do better if he's used to eating kibble.

How much food, and when?

The label provides a guideline on the amount of food recommended for your dog. It's just a start, though. Dogs who are highly active, pregnant, or are nursing puppies have higher energy requirements than the average couch-potato canine. In the wintertime, indoor dogs often need less food because they're less active, while outdoor dogs need more because staying warm requires more energy.

Do dogs really need meat?

Can a dog be a vegetarian? Although many may be surprised, the answer is "yes." Unlike cats, who are true carnivores, dogs can thrive on a carefully balanced vegetarian diet. Even their needs for protein can be met this way.

A dog would probably not *choose* to live without meat, however. The choice is made for them by owners, usually those who for ethical reasons are against the killing of other animals for food. (For some dogs, though, vegetarian diets are a way to fight food allergies.) Vegetarian diets are popular enough that some companies include no-meat dog foods as part of their product line.

A good rule of thumb is to feed two-thirds of the daily ration in the morning, and the remaining one-third in the evening. Since dogs have a tendency to sleep after meals, this is especially useful for animals who have to stay alone all day — a sleepy dog is less likely to chew or bark. (Obviously, if you're working a night shift you want to turn this around and feed the larger portion at night, before you head for work.)

Another reason to feed smaller, more frequent meals is that doing so helps your dog avoid *gastric torsion*, otherwise known as *bloat*. This potentially lethal medical emergency can hit many larger breeds and can be triggered when a dog wolfs down a huge meal. (More about veterinary emergencies in Chapter 10.)

You need to feed puppies more frequently than older dogs — three or four times a day, depending on their age. For a feeding schedule for puppies, see Chapter 8.

Some people can get away with letting the dog decide when and how much he eats. Keeping a constant supply of dry food available (known as *free-feeding*) works in some cases, usually in single-dog households where there's no competition for kibble.

If you find your pet can maintain his own weight and you aren't having related behavioral problems like house-soiling, then free-feeding is fine. But realize that you will not be able to pick up on some subtle changes in your pet's eating habits that may be an earlier indicator of health problems. You also won't be able to use giving your dog food — after he sits — as an effortless way to reinforce your role as "pack leader." (For more on this and other strategies for dealing with problem dogs, see Chapter 12.)

Also, it's hard to keep kibble fresh when free-feeding, and the constant availability of food may attract other animals, such as the raccoon who used to pop through a friend of mine's cat door at night for his evening snack. When a rat started visiting, too, she put up the food for good.

Concerns over preservatives

In the last few years, a lot of controversy has been generated over the use of preservatives in dog foods, primarily BHT, BHA, and ethoxyquin. The latter has been blamed for just about everything that can happen to a dog, not to mention the increase in violence on our streets and the perceived decline in traditional values.

Many manufacturers have adopted the "if you can't beat 'em, join 'em" approach, which is why some products are labeled ethoxyquin "free" or "naturally preserved," with vitamins C and E, usually. And some canned products boast of being completely free of preservatives of any kind.

Still, the highly respected *UC Davis School of Veterinary Medicine Book of Dogs* (Harper Collins) sums up the situation this way: "…[W]ell-controlled studies have failed to show any detrimental effects of chemical preservatives."

Which will, of course, do nothing to end the controversy. But at least when you look at a bag of dog food, you don't have to say to yourself, "What the heck's 'ethoxyquin' and why should I care?" If it worries you, choose a food that doesn't have these ingredients. But be aware no good scientific evidence supports that decision.

Treat 'em good

We humans often express our love through food. Special family times have food in the center of activities, no less than on the mother of all pig-outs: Thanksgiving. Food plays an important role on Passover and Easter (forget the yams; give me those yellow marshmallow chicks!) and even Halloween is an excuse to treat yourself a little. Meals prepared and shared loom large in our memories.

The way to a man's heart is said to be through his stomach, but is it the way to a dog's heart, too? We certainly seem to think so.

Treats fill whole aisles of pet superstores and whole pages of catalogs. They come in all shapes and sizes and dogs certainly love to get them as much as people love to give them. Every dog deserves a few, so put them on your shopping list.

Treats don't have to meet the same stringent nutritional requirements dog foods do; in fact, they don't have to meet any requirements at all. So if you're giving your pet too many — some sources say anything more than 10 percent of his diet — you may be throwing "complete and balanced nutrition" out the door.

Another problem: Treats add calories, and calories add weight. Obesity is the No. 1 food-caused health risk veterinarians see in the United States.

So treat your dog, but remember: A little goes a long way.

Biscuits and cookies

As with dog food, the marketplace for biscuits and cookies has changed dramatically in recent years. You used to be able to sum up your choices pretty much this way: Milk Bones, small, medium, or large. My grandmother kept a box of the small, multi-colored Milk Bones in her cupboard for decades, for her dog and, later, for mine when we dropped in to visit. (She always thought they liked the liver-colored ones best, the green ones least, but I don't think they were anywhere near that picky. And I always suspected they all tasted the same, although I never personally tested my theory.)

Milk Bones are still around, of course, and doing well. You still find them in my cupboard, a gift from a friend's dog on the occasion of my oldest dog's tenth birthday. But you find a lot more in my cupboard, too. Like peanut-butter flavored gourmet cookies, a "dog-warming" gift from a reader when my younger dog appeared in print for the first time. I also have organic treats with a list of ingredients so healthy I could probably stand to gnaw on them a little.

At least one manufacturer offers a line of treats to complement dogs' regular diets, with formulas designed for puppies, active and older, or overweight dogs.

Experiment all you want. Your pet will help you, that's for sure!

In my house one of the dogs, Andy, has a tendency toward a condition I call "biscuit butt," so I'm a little stingy with the cookies and biscuits, even the reduced-calorie variety.

There are, however, a couple of alternatives I've been using and recommending for years: carrot sticks and mini rice cakes. Dogs love them, honest. Andy doesn't pay any attention to me while I work unless I start nibbling on carrot sticks, and from that moment on, you've never seen such devotion!

If you don't have enough to do in your busy life, you can always make cookies for your dog. A handful of books offering treat recipes exist, and you can find more with a little digging. Dog-treat recipes turn up in newsgroups and e-mail lists on the Internet, and chances are your groomer, trainer, or veterinarian's receptionist has squirreled one away. The classifieds of dog-magazines offer them, too, for a small price.

Not being much of a cook — I lived in my current house for six weeks before I noticed the oven didn't work! — I haven't baked homemade dog cookies often. But they're a fun project to do with children and a great way to come up with holiday gifts for the pets of your friends.

One treat you should not share with your pet is chocolate. Although your pet would have to eat a lot of chocolate to get into the toxic range — more than10 ounces of milk chocolate, but considerably less of baking chocolate — even a nibble can make a small dog mighty sick. If your pet gets into chocolate, call your veterinarian right away.

Animal-based chews

While rawhide — made from the skins of cattle — has been a popular dog treat for a long time, in recent years there doesn't seem to be any part of any animal intended for human consumption that hasn't ended up being marketed as a dog treat.

I think the trend started with beef hooves, discovered, as the story goes, by some savvy dog lover who noticed that dogs enthusiastically devour the pieces farriers trim off horses. (If I were a horse, this would have made me a little nervous around dogs, but many people are into both horses and dogs, and everyone gets along just fine!)

Horse-hoof parings weren't easy to find, but beef hooves were. The product was a smash, and manufacturers started looking for opportunities to duplicate the success. Next up: Pig ears, another hit.

No matter how unappetizing some of these products look to *us,* they're certainly a hit with our dogs. As a result, there seem to be plenty of takers, not only for pig ears but also dried beef neck muscles, lamb ears, beef ears, and sterilized bones.

Fresh bones are available, too, from your local butcher or grocery store.

All of these treats are fine for your dog, but you have to take into consideration your dog's size and chewing style. The bigger and stronger your dog is, the bigger and sturdier you want these treats to be.

 Rawhide, hooves, and bones can cause problems with aggressive chewers. Some large dogs are capable of chewing off and swallowing big chunks of rawhide, and pulverizing bones and hooves. This can cause internal problems, like when bone bits reform as a blockage that may even have to be surgically removed.

So know your dog's chewing style. Pressed rawhide and large knots are best for these chewers, as are plastic alternatives, covered later in this chapter. Watch to see that big chunks aren't being swallowed, and discard these treats when they become worn enough to be swallowed in one big gulp.

Them bones, them bones, them fresh bones

Poultry bones are a ticket to the veterinary emergency room and should be avoided at all costs. There are some other fresh bones out there, though, that are real special treats for your dog.

Beef bones, big and sturdy, are your best choice. Oxtails are good for small- or medium-sized dogs, but don't hold up too well to big, aggressive chewers. Beef knuckle or leg bones are good for all dogs. Leave them whole for big dogs, or have them cut to a more manageable size for smaller ones.

While grocery stores often have these bones — if you don't see them, ask! — I've had the best luck with small butcher shops. One in my area saves a huge piece for me with a leg bone in the middle and knuckles on both ends, and cuts it into five smaller pieces — two half-knuckles and a leg bone — for my dogs.

Some people like to cook them first, but I don't bother. I let them chew on them for a day or so and then out they go.

A couple more cautions about bones: If you've got a multi-dog household, you may want to forget fresh bones entirely because they can cause fights. Likewise, unless you're 100 percent sure of your dog's gentleness, I wouldn't give bones to your dog if children are around — a snap could result. For your dog's safety, trim the fat off the bones first or it could end up triggering diarrhea or worse.

On a less serious note, remember that bones are *messy!* This treat is best left outside or in the kitchen, and if you don't believe me, I've got a stained carpet to prove it.

Give 'Em Shelter

You have a responsibility to provide a safe, dry place for your dog, one that's cool in the summer and warm in the winter. One that keeps him from roaming the neighborhood, and protects him from cars, thieves, and assorted sickos like poisoners. That's the basic requirement, but again, you'll have a much better relationship with your dog — and he'll be much happier — if you take him out of the dog house and into your house.

I'm going to be blunt here: What's the point of keeping a completely outdoor dog as a pet? Protection? Fat lot of good that big dog will do you outside when burglars are inside your house. Companionship? You work all day, you come home, feed the outdoor dog, and maybe play with him a little. Then you go in and watch TV and he sits outside alone.

While some dogs handle the outdoors better than others, they still can cause a lot of problems. They bark, day and night, out of boredom and loneliness. They dig. They chew the siding off your house. They can teach themselves to be overzealously protective to the point of dangerousness.

A lot of people with outdoor dogs didn't start out intending them to be that way. The dog never was fully house-trained, perhaps, or was never taught not to jump up on guests or behave himself around children. Perhaps he's destructive and you figure better that he eat the picnic table than the coffee table. Perhaps he flat-out smells horribly rank.

Look, these things are *fixable*. The behavior problems can be solved by training, and the smell — well, did you ever hear of a bath? Grooming tips are in Chapter 10; behavior problems in Chapter 12. You owe it to your dog, your family, and your neighbors to do what you can to avoid leaving your dog outside all the time.

It's still necessary to do your best to bring a little joy into your lonely dog's life with time and outings to strengthen the bond between you.

Barriers

Still, unless you're an apartment-dweller, your dog spends a certain amount of time in your back yard, ranging from a few minutes a day to do his business to the hours while you're at work. You want to make his time outdoors as pleasant and safe as possible.

The dangers of chains

In many parts of the country fenced yards are uncommon, so many people keep their dogs on chains. Tethering a dog for a short while is OK in a pinch — *never* with a choke collar, though — but should never become an existence. And a chained dog should *never* be left unattended.

Dogs who spend their lives on chains are more likely to become dangerous, biting anyone who comes onto their turf. The profile of the average dog in a vicious bite incident, in fact, is a young, unneutered male on a chain.

And chaining is dangerous for the dog, too: I know of a handful of cases where a dog tried to jump a fence, didn't have enough chain to clear and ended up hanging himself from his collar on the other side of the fence. Dogs have also wrapped their chains around trees and died because they were unable to get to water on hot days.

If you don't have a fenced yard, walking your dog or buying a kennel run for him is better than chaining him out.

The best setup is a fenced yard away from the street. Solid six-foot fencing is best to protect your pet from the view of people who might tease or steal him and to give him fewer reasons to bark. If you're a gardener, consider breaking off part of the yard for your dog and keeping the rest of it off-limits unless you're with him. My favorite example of this comes from a coworker and her architect husband, who designed their yard with a U-shaped area around the outside for their Airedale, and an interior courtyard that was kept safe from his big paws. (More on dogs and gardens in Chapter 18).

Kennel runs are fine, too, for keeping dogs out of trouble when you're not with them, as long as the area is well-protected from heat, cold, and wind, fresh water and toys are always available, and the time in the run is kept to a minimum. A 10-foot-by-6-foot run is a safe place to spend a few hours, but it's no place to spend a life.

Electronic boundary systems that use shock collars to teach dogs the property lines can be useful in some situations, but they have some serious limitations. First, some dogs choose to be shocked if the temptation is great enough on the other side, and once out, avoid taking another hit to get home. Second, an electronic boundary system does not protect your pet from animals or people who enter your property — so your dog can be easily attacked, poisoned, or stolen.

Two products that make the ins and outs a little easier to handle are dog doors and baby gates:

- Most *dog doors* consist of a flap of metal or plastic a pet can push with nose or paws to open. They are great for anyone who doesn't want to get up every time the dog scratches at the door, and even better for people who leave a dog alone all day and want to provide access to the outdoors while they're gone. They can be set up between house and yard, or between a garage and yard. Some people build "chutes" with dog doors at both ends to cut down on drafts.

  For the sake of security, have your door installed where your pet's comings and goings aren't so noticeable, and close and lock it when it's not needed.

- *Baby gates* — available in pet-supply catalogs or anywhere children's things are sold — can be used to limit a pet's access to certain parts of the house.

  I use the two in combination to provide a safe and secure place for my pets when I'm away from home: Baby gates to keep them in the kitchen, a dog door to allow them to go to the part of the yard they're allowed in when I'm not with them.

Dog houses

If your dog spends much time outside — while you're at work, perhaps — he needs shelter from heat or cold. One of the easiest ways to provide this is a dog house. Your choices here: wood or high-impact plastic.

No matter the material you choose, a dog house should fit your pet snugly — he should be able to stand up and turn around, but not much more. Providing your dog with a house that's too large makes staying warm inside difficult for him. It should have an entrance that's off-center so the dog can curl up in one end for warmth. A removable roof is a must for easy cleaning, and the doorway should have a flap over it to keep drafts out.

Building a dog house is an easy weekend project for anyone with basic carpentry skills; you can find plans can be found at libraries or building-supplies stores. You can also buy wooden dog houses, including some that are extremely fancy and designed to match your home's architecture — Cape Cod, Georgian, ranch, and so on.

Several manufacturers offer dog houses of molded, high-impact plastic that are in some ways superior to traditional wooden ones. They clean easily, do not retain smells and offer no place for fleas to breed — as long as the bedding is kept fresh. (More on bedding in the next section.)

Where you place the dog house has a lot to do with how comfortable your dog is when in it. In winter, it should be in a spot that's protected from the wind. And in summer, it should be in the shade.

Crates and beds

Indoor dogs need a place to sleep, too. Unless your dog has impeccable manners and respects your authority, it shouldn't be on your bed — it gives him the wrong idea concerning who's the Top Dog in your family. (More on this in Chapter 12.) Don't feel sorry for him, though: More beautiful and comfortable beds are available today than ever before, beds to fit every dog, every budget, and every decor.

One possibility for a bed is a *crate,* probably the most versatile piece of dog gear every made. Once used primarily for transporting dogs on airlines, the crate in all its varieties — open mesh, solid metal, or high-impact plastic — is now widely used and recognized as one of the best tools for making living with your pet easier. The crate is the easiest and fastest way to house-train a puppy or dog — for more on that, see Chapter 8 — and it's also a decent whelping box, should you ever breed your pet. With some modifications to cut down on the drafts, it even makes a decent doghouse.

If your dog misbehaves, it's a good place to put him for a "time out." For any reason you don't want him underfoot — a guest with allergies, a contractor marching in and out — the crate is a godsend.

The crate is also perfect for its original purpose: transporting your pet. A loose dog in the car can be an annoyance, even a danger. Everyone is safer when crates are used. And talk about safety! In an automobile accident a loose dog is as vulnerable as an unbelted human. But some crates are so tough it's not unheard of for a crated dog to survive an airline crash with near-total human casualties. When traveling with your pet, you'll find showing up with a crate will endear you to hotel owners, some of whom can be sweet-talked into lifting "no dog" rules if they know your dog will be crated in the room — as opposed to chewing up the bedspread.

Dogs who are used to crates love them. It's a "room of their own," cozy and secure, so much so that many dogs seek out their crates voluntarily. In my house, where an always-open, retriever-sized crate serves as an unconventional end table in the den, a dog is always snoozing inside, by choice. To increase comfort, you can buy pads to fit the floor of crates, make your own without too much difficulty, tuck a washable blanket inside — or you can just leave them empty, especially in warmer weather.

Crates are both a comfortable place to sleep and an invaluable training tool.

Need another reason to buy a crate? In times of disaster — floods, earthquakes, hurricanes — a crate can save your pet's life by keeping him secure and providing you with alternatives should you have to evacuate your home. The cages of veterinary hospitals and animal shelters adjacent to a disaster area fill up quickly, but there's always room for the pet that brings his own shelter. More on disaster planning in Chapter 19.

Consider what you'll be using a crate for before you buy one. If you ever intend to ship your dog by air, be aware that not all crates are intended for this purpose. Some are designed for light use — house-training puppies in the home, for example — while others are designed for car travel, a medium-grade use. If you intend to use a crate for house-training, a bed, travel, occasional confinement and, possibly, a whelping box, you're better off buying a top-quality crate of high-impact molded plastic, such as the Vari-Kennel or Furrarri.

Buy a crate to fit the size your puppy will be. A grown dog should be able to stand, turn around and lay down comfortably. When house-training a puppy, make the crate smaller by using a panel. An alternative: Borrow a puppy-sized crate from a friend or the puppy's breeder.

A crate is a big-ticket item, so shop aggressively. One important source: Garage sales and classified ads. When I was fostering dogs as a breed-rescue volunteer, I owned close to a dozen Vari-Kennels, many of them constantly on loan to adopting families. I picked up most of them second-hand at less than two-thirds of the best retail price I could find.

The use of a crate in solving house-training problems is in Chapter 8; other training uses for the crate are in Chapters 5 through 8, for puppies, and Chapters 8, 11, and 15, for adult dogs.

While a crate can be used for almost anything, it's not the only choice when it comes to a bed. Beds keep floors and carpets cleaner, provide a cushion that makes all dogs more comfortable, but especially older or arthritic ones, and allow you to live without guilt for keeping your dog off *your* bed.

Every dog needs a bed, even if it's just an old blanket. Two of the most popular varieties: Oval "cuddlers" designed for dogs to curl up in and lined with plush or polyester "sheepskin"; and stuffed cushions that resemble '60s bean-bag chairs, albeit in more muted colors than those popular then. The most important thing to remember when picking out a bed is that it must be *washable,* or at the very least have a removable, washable cover. You'll almost certainly have a problem with fur, smells, and fleas if you don't wash pet bedding on a regular basis — weekly is ideal.

Dogs love having their own bed, and this plush cuddler is easy on an older dog's joints.

Photo courtesy of Gina Spadafori.

Washability is why I don't recommend carpet remnants. You just can't keep them fresh and clean-smelling, and they're like a welcome mat for fleas.

Some of the handsomest and sturdiest beds are available by mail order, in a wider range of colors and sizes than you may be able to find locally. Doctors Foster and Smith, a mail-order pet-supply firm in Wisconsin, has some of the nicest. (Mail-order addresses and phone numbers are in the "Additional Resources" appendix in the back of this book.)

Dog shows are another good source for pet beds — two of the half-dozen dog beds in my home were handmade and sold only at dog shows. Those two — one a platform bed made of PVC pipe and the material found on outdoor furniture, the other a pellet-filled cushion in a handsome houndstooth cover — have outlived two dogs, hundreds of washings, and more than a half-dozen beds of lesser quality.

Bowls and Waterers

In dog dishes, too, you have a lot of options, from using an old pot to buying a hand-thrown ceramic bowl with your dog's name painted on it. Dishes designed to store up to a couple of days' worth of food or water are available, as are paper bowls good for one meal only (the latter most commonly used at boarding kennels and veterinary hospitals).

I prefer sturdy dishes of molded plastic or stainless steel that resist chewing or scratching and can be sterilized in the dishwasher. These dishes — stainless steel especially — retain their good looks, handle any abuse a dog can dish out, and last forever. Dishes that damage easily are hard to keep clean and invite the buildup of food and bacteria in the dents and scratches. Some dogs also have a sensitivity to plastic bowls.

For tall dogs, consider an elevated unit that brings the bowl up to the dog's level, an especially nice product for older dogs. For dogs with long, silky ears — like cocker spaniels — look for bowls with a narrow opening and high sloped sides to keep that fur out of the muck. If your dog is a ravenous eater, a bowl with a nonskid base will help keep the dish from ending up in the next county.

Some people are a little squeamish about putting dog dishes in the dishwasher, but, honestly, if your dishwasher's doing its job right, the water will be hot enough to render everything in it clean enough for *you* to eat out of.

One of my favorite dogs and dishwasher stories involves my brother's in-law, who swear the "Labrador Pre-Wash" extended the life of their dishwasher. Although not allowed to beg while people were eating, their chocolate Lab helped with after-meal clean-up by licking the plates clean before they were loaded in the dishwasher. During California's drought years, they argued it was a real water-saver, too.

While food dishes should be picked up, washed, and put away after meals, water dishes need to be kept full and available at all times. Here, too, stainless steel is your best choice. Dishes with reservoirs are fine, but I find they're hard to keep clean. And, unless your dog needs a lot of water, these products get mucky before the water needs to be refilled.

For outside water, the "Lixit," available in any pet-supply store or catalog, has long been a popular device. Attached to a faucet, it releases fresh water when the dog licks or nuzzles the trigger — and stops the flow when the dog is through. They need to be installed in a protected area, however, for the metal can become frying-pan hot if exposed to full summer sun.

All water sources need to be sheltered from both heat and freezing cold, or they won't be available to your dog — a potentially deadly situation in extreme weather.

A couple blocks of ice — you can make them by putting water-filled margarine tubs in your freezer — will keep a shaded water supply cool for hours.

As for keeping water warm, there are heated bowls available to keep water from freezing, as well as special devices designed to fit into buckets to do the same thing.

If you and your dog are constantly on the go, look into a more portable water source. Several different kinds of traveling bowls are designed to reduce splashing, and some collapsible products can be put away in a space as small as a fanny pack. I especially like the Wad'R Buck-it, a vinyl dish that folds up small enough to fit in a glove box — which is where you'll find mine. It's available through J-B Wholesale Pet Supplies (information on how to reach them is in this book's appendix).

You can also use a squeeze-type bottle like bicyclists use — your dog will quickly learn to catch the flow. A tip, though: You may want to mark it with indelible ink so everyone knows it's "dog water."

A friend of mine had her dogs in mind when she remodeled her kitchen. The three bottom drawers of the center island pull out to reveal recessed dog dishes — stainless steel pop-outs, for easy cleaning — and secure storage for 40 pounds of kibble. On the other side of the kitchen another stainless steel bowl in a recessed bay provides the dogs with fresh water and keeps most of the drip off the floor.

It's one of the best ideas I've ever seen, and it keeps things neater in her lovely kitchen.

Collars and Leashes

A confession: Collars and leashes are the things I most like to buy for my dogs, even though it has only been recently when I got a dog who shows off a nice collar to its best advantage. My retriever, Benjamin, has medium-length glossy black fur. Every collar and every color looks nice on this dog, and so he has a couple, plus some bandanas for special occasions. Leashes simply *must* coordinate, of course, so he has a couple of those. My current favorite collar on him — his, too, I think — bright red with silhouettes of black Labradors. Stunning, simply stunning.

My older dog, Andy, a Sheltie, has a ruff so thick it's hard to find his collar, much less see it. He has a couple of very handsome leashes, though.

Fashion aside, collars, harnesses, halters, and leashes perform a very vital function: They help you to train your dog and allow you to keep him out of trouble in public. Collars also protect your dog when you can't, by carrying identification that will get him home should he ever slip away from you.

The everyday collar

A collar is an essential purchase for your dog, but if he's wearing the wrong collar at the wrong time, your dog could end up hurt or even dead. Which is why learning a little is important before you go shopping.

Your pet's everyday collar, the one you put her tags on, should be a buckled collar, either flat or rolled, made of nylon web or leather. Either a flat collar or a rolled collar will work fine on dogs with short or medium fur, but rolled collars are preferable on dogs with thick, long fur at the neck, such as collies.

I like nylon web collars because of the incredible variety of colors and patterns, and because some dogs are more apt to chew off a leather collar. Other dogs may find a nylon collar irritating, and do better with leather. As long as the collar is well-made, both nylon and leather will last for years.

In recent years, quick-snap closures have become popular, especially on flat nylon web collars. And it's easy to see why: Press in at the edges and the collar's off easily for baths and changing tags. Press the tips together and *snap!* it's on again. For most dogs, these collars present no problems. Because they are so simply adjusted, they're ideal for growing puppies. Some trainers think buckled collars are more secure for large, strong and impulsive dogs, but a high-quality quick-snap collar should be just as sturdy.

How big should that collar be?

When ordering a collar — buckled or quick-snap — for regular wear, measure a couple of inches down the neck from your dog's head, and then add two inches. For tiny dogs, add an inch. When trying on collars, you should be able to fit two fingers snugly between collar and neck; one finger on a small dog. The goal is to have a collar snug enough so your dog back can't back up and out of the collar, but loose enough for comfort.

A slip collar — commonly called a "choke" collar — should fit a little more loosely because it fits over a dog's head instead of being wrapped around the neck. Add an inch-and-a-half for small dogs and up to three inches for large ones — you should just be able to slip it over your pet's head and no more. (Some slip collars use a snap connection to allow them to be wrapped around and more closely fitted, riding behind the dog's ears. If you're working with a trainer who uses this type of collar, ask to make sure it's fitted properly.)

The goal of a slip collar is for you to have enough slack to manage the "snap-and-release" action essential to training with this equipment. (More on training with this collar is in Chapter 11.)

Match the width of the nylon or leather — or the heaviness of the links — to the size of your dog: Narrower measures and lighter lengths are for smaller dogs. Too light a link on a slip collar can dig in to a large pet's neck, plus the chain may not be strong enough to hold him should he lunge.

While some people may think that elegant canine collars are a recent development, it's simply not true. Those who can afford it have always put ritzy collars around the necks of their prized canine companions — gold and silver, pearls and other gems have been part of the society dog's wardrobe for centuries.

Today's dogs don't have it so ruff, either. Some of the loveliest collars around are available from a Dover, DE, mail order firm, The Company of Dogs. (Information on them is in this book's "Additional Resources" appendix.) Italian crocodile embossed calfskin at $32 may be acceptable for running errands, but for evening wear, who would consider going out in anything less than pearls? Four rows of them, to be precise, and such a buy at $40!

Oh, why not? Just make sure that you make a matching donation to your local shelter so the guilt doesn't get you down.

Training collars

A properly-fitted buckle or quick-snap collar — with tags and a license! — is all a puppy needs for the first few months of his life and may be all that he ever needs. But most dogs need a collar for training, or for you to be able to control yours better on leash.

The most commonly used — and misused — training collar is the *slip*. This collar is a length of chain — and sometimes nylon — with rings at both ends. To use, you drop the length of chain or nylon through one of the rings and then slip the resulting loop over your dog's head. The leash is attached to the moving ring, not the stationery one.

The most important thing you need to know about a slip collar is that it *never, ever* should be your dog's everyday collar and *must always* be removed when you're through training or walking your dog.

That's because the moving ring of the collar can get caught on just about anything — even the eye-tooth of another dog in play. Once caught, a dog's natural reaction is to pull away, a move that tightens the collar, which panics the dog into pulling away more. Even if you're there, you may not have the strength to rescue a terrified dog in this situation — and if you *do* have the strength, you may be badly bitten while trying.

A great many dogs have died because of the misuse of this common piece of training equipment, and the near-misses are even more common.

This risk to your dog's well-being is one of the easiest in the world to avoid.

You can call it a choke collar if you want, but know this: If you're choking your dog, you're using it wrong. That's not training, that's cruelty, however unintentional. More than half the time this happens because pet-owners put the collar on upside-down.

Lassie come home!

Your young daughter leaves the front door open, the wind blows down the fence: A lost dog can happen to the most conscientious of families.

For this reason, your dog's collar should *always* have tags. An ID tag with your phone number. A license. Getting a new tag should be the *first* thing you do when you move. Checking the tags frequently is important to ensure that the information is still readable.

There are other ways to ID your dog, of course. *Tattooing,* with your driver's license number or another traceable number, like a registry number from the American or Canadian Kennel Clubs, has been popular for years, and *microchipping* has come on strong in the last decade.

The microchip is permanent identification no bigger than a grain of rice, which your veterinarian imbeds under the skin over your pet's shoulder blades using a large needle (but don't worry: One yip is about all you'll hear at most, and then it's done!). Microchips have been of dubious value for returning lost pets because one company's chips couldn't be read by another company's scanner, and shelters couldn't and wouldn't cope with competing systems.

That's changed recently, with moves by manufacturers toward one industry standard and with the entry of the American Kennel Club as a registry of microchipped animals in the United States and Canada — any animals, not just AKC registered purebred dogs. It'll cost anything from $20 to $50 to have your pet chipped by your veterinarian, but it's a good investment in his safety.

If you're going to have your dog microchipped — and I highly recommend it — find out what, if any, chip scanners are in use at the shelters in your area, and make sure your pet is implanted with a chip that can be read using that brand of scanner. You also should register your pet with AKC Companion Animal Recovery — (800) 252-7894 — which offers 24-hour match-up service 365 days a year. The cost to register is $9, and although the service was set-up in conjunction with one manufacturer, you can register the number of whatever chip — or tattoo — you use. If someone calls to report they have your pet, the service will release your number so you can be reunited quickly.

The moving part of the training collar should go *over* the dog's head, not under it. When positioned properly, the collar tightens when you pull on the leash, and releases when you slack off. Done properly, this motion take a split-second: *snap!,* release, and *praise!* (More on this in Chapter 11.)

If the moving part of the collar is *under* the dog's head, when you tighten, the collar tightens, but it doesn't release when the pressure's off.

How to get it right? With the dog sitting on your left — in "heel" position — hold the collar in a "P" position, with the loop away from you and the "back" of the "P" on top (see the following figure). Slip it over your dog's head, and it will be in perfect position.

A slip collar must be fitted properly and put on correctly to be effective.

The slip collar's by far the most common for training and control, but there are a few others you should know about:

- ✔ **Partial slip collars** can be a hybrid between a flat collar and a slip collar, part flat nylon, part chain, or all chain. They are designed to limit the "choking" action of a slip collar — they tighten, but only so much. Some trainers use them all the time, others recommend them for people who have an exceptionally difficult time with the "release" of the slip collar's "snap and release" motion.

- ✔ **"Pinch" or "prong" collars** are more popular than ever before, because they are an efficient way of dealing with large dogs with especially well-muscled necks, like the Rottweiler. Like a partial slip, they can only be tightened so far but, unlike the partial, they have blunt metal prongs evenly spaced along the inside of the length of the collar. When tightening, these prongs press into the flesh of the dog's neck.

    These collars are very controversial, in part because of their "cruel" appearance — which is probably why some people like them: they look "macho." They should not be a "first choice" training collar, but in the hands of a knowledgeable trainer, they can help with a powerful dog.

- **Head halters** are another device with a public-relations problem; this time completely unwarranted. The problem: They look like muzzles. In fact, they operate on the same principle that has worked for years with horses: Where the head goes, the body follows. The leash is attached to a ring under the jaw, and when pulled, pressure is placed around the muzzle and around the neck — both important in canine body language.

  Properly fitted and used, a head halter can make even a large, powerful dog controllable enough to be walked by a child — but then, so can a proper course of training!

- **Electric collars** give a shock either automatically, such as when a dog barks, or manually at the trainer's discretion. They are widely used in training dogs for hunting and field work and for correcting some serious behavior problems, such as predation. Although widely available in pet-supply stores and catalogs, they should *not* be used by pet owners except under the guidance of experienced trainers. Without a thorough knowledge of training theory and a perfect sense of timing, this training tool is more cruel than effective.

- **Harnesses** for walking a dog are best left on little dogs, since they offer nothing in the way of control and give up a great deal in the way of leverage. Some small breeds — such as poodles — have a tendency toward "collapsing tracheas," where the rings of cartilage in the neck collapse temporarily when the dog's excited. These dogs are ideal candidates for harnesses to relieve the pressure on their necks from pulling. (Again, you can train your dog *not* to pull, but people with tiny breeds don't really have to, so they rarely do.)

  Your veterinarian may suggest a harness if your dog is of a breed known for neck or back problems, or if your dog has had a neck trauma or surgery.

  A couple of harnesses are on the market that *do* offer some control, tightening around the dog's chest as he pulls. These are an option even for larger dogs.

  Some harnesses are made for dog sports — tracking, or pulling sleds or wagons. For more information on these sports — and others — see Chapter 16.

Leashes

The choices aren't as varied in leashes as in collars. There are a lot more colors and designs than there used to be, but the same basic choices remain: leather, nylon, or chain.

You can use anything you want when your dog is trained, but for before you reach that point, the standard six-foot leather leash is your best choice. Nylon is a very close second — it's what I use on my trained dogs, because I like the colors — but it's not so easy to grip as leather and can give you burns if your dog takes off suddenly and whips the leash through your hands. Chain is a horrible thing to train with: It'll cut your hands to pieces, and your dog will confuse the noise of the leash with the noise of the collar.

Other lengths are available, from a one-foot "traffic" lead that's useful for moving a large dog quickly from one place to another, to long leads for training or to give a dog a little more room to roam without unleashing him. For walking or training, the six-foot is still best: It lets you give your dog some freedom while leaving you with plenty of control. (It's also the length spelled out in most leash laws.)

Leashes are sold in $1/4$-inch, $3/8$-inch, $1/2$-inch, $5/8$-inch, $3/4$-inch and 1-inch widths, with the two middle sizes the most commonly used in obedience training because they're easier to grip than the other sizes. The weakest parts of a leash is where the snap's attached and the handle is formed. Look for sturdy stitching or, in leather leads, one-piece construction.

One of the most popular pieces of equipment introduced in recent years is the a reel-type Flexi lead that offers a dog up to 32 feet of freedom and yet can be shortened with the touch of a button on the plastic handle/line reel. While it's not meant to help you teach dogs to walk without pulling, it is commonly used to help teach them to come when called. It's great for travel, too.

These leads, widely available in different sizes and lengths, are wonderful for letting a dog sniff around in areas where it's not safe or where you're not allowed to let him off-leash.

Lookin' Good

Your dog may have a trophy for winning an ugly dog contest, but he's still beautiful. And nothing shows off that beauty more than good grooming.

Grooming is more than for looks, however. It's an important part of preventive health care and an essential part of building a closer bond between you. Fleas, ticks, lumps, and bumps and injuries of all sorts turn up when you're grooming your pet, and the time you spend doing it is of the highest quality — talking to your dog, stroking your dog, telling your dog what an amazing beasty he really is.

Grooming tools can be an expensive investment, especially if you decide to show your dog. Show people travel with boxes of combs, brushes, scissors, shears, nail clippers, nail files, forceps, and other tools of the trade. At this level, scissors alone can represent hundreds of dollars — up to $75 a pair for some specialty shears.

Although you don't need to spend *that* kind of money, investing in top-quality equipment is best: a few well-chosen pieces that do the job well and last forever. Choose metal combs and brushes with sturdy bristles set into a comfortable wooden handle.

Everything you need to know to groom you dog — including trimming nails — is in Chapter 10.

Two of the best mail-order sources for dog-grooming supplies are the J-B Wholesale Pet Supplies and Cherrybrook catalogs. These two companies are popular sources for those in the dog-show game and have an outstanding selection of top-quality grooming equipment. Information on how to reach them is in this book's "Additional Resources" appendix.

Combs and brushes

For most dogs, the grooming kit starts with a comb and a brush. The ones you choose depends on your pet's coat type. If you bought your puppy or dog from a reputable breeder, you should be able to ask for equipment recommendations and grooming advice (you may even have gotten it on a sheet when you picked up your puppy). If not, here are the basic coat types and the comb or brush best suited. Remember, these are recommendations to keep coat in "pet shape"; show grooming is considerably more involved and requires a lot more equipment.

- ✔ **Short, smooth coats. (Labs, pugs, Rottweilers)** You get off easy. You can either run a comb through to catch the shedding hairs or use a grooming glove, a tool you slip your hand into and run over your dog. It's like petting, and dogs love it!

- ✔ **Curly coats. (poodles, Portuguese water dogs, the softer terriers)** Clipping is part of the regimen for these breeds. If you want to do the clipping yourself, you need an instruction book and a basic clipper set with a couple of blades. For daily grooming, a medium metal brush keeps tangles at bay. Follow by brushing with a slicker brush.

- ✔ **Medium coats. (golden retrievers, Australian shepherds)** A medium steel comb and a natural-bristle brush keeps these coats in fine shape.

- ✔ **Long and silky coats. (Afghan hound, Yorkshire terrier, Maltese)** Use a medium steel comb and a natural bristle brush — gently — to keep these glamorous coats from breaking.

- ✔ **Wiry coats. (Most terriers, schnauzers, wire-haired hunting dogs)** A medium comb and a slicker brush gets the dirt out. Terriers need to be clipped every two months to get rid of dead hairs and maintain their smart appearance, and if you're going to do this yourself, you'll need clippers. (For show, terriers are *stripped,* a laborious task involving plucking out dead and dying hairs.)

- ✔ **Long and double-coated. (Shetland sheepdogs, collies, Keeshonden, Alaskan malamutes, Pomeranians).** Wide toothed steel "collie comb," natural bristle brush, dematting tool. Bred to thrive in coldest weather, these breeds shed plenty and require a lot of grooming. A thorough brushing against the grain and down to the skin keeps the downy under-coat from matting into a block of felt.

While daily coat care — combing and brushing — is the owner's responsibility, a groomer can help keep your dog's coat in good shape, especially if you've got a terrier- or poodle-type dog. For help in choosing a groomer, see Chapter 10.

Nail trimmers

Because some — OK, most — dogs don't like to have their nails trimmed, this is the most often neglected piece of a regular grooming regimen. A lot of people leave it to their veterinarian or groomer, sometimes waiting until the dog must be anesthetized for another reason.

Better you should trim a little bit every week than let your dog struggle with long nails. If left unattended, overgrown nails can cause lameness. And no, a daily walk isn't enough to keep them worn down.

Three kinds of nail trimmers are widely available — guillotine style, scissors style, and an electric nail grinder. The latter is the most expensive — around $50 — but is a good way to keep nails short without nicking the quick, a common problem with nail cutters. A nail grinder may be more acceptable to dogs who don't like their nails trimmed — unless they're put off by the noise and the vibration.

Nail clippers are the most common, however, and which of the two kinds you use are a matter of personal preference — both do a good, fast job. Since I have a tendency to misplace nail clippers, I have at least one of both kinds and use whichever kind's handiest.

You will, however, need a small jar of blood-stopping powder on hand when you trim nails to stop bleeding should you cut too far. There are a couple of brands on the market; Kwik Stop is probably the best known. Another good buy: A metal file, for cleaning up the rough edges.

Instructions for nail trimming are in Chapter 11.

Shampoos and conditioners

Remember that old saw about only washing a dog once or twice a year? Forget it! Who'd want to live with a dirty, stinky dog?

It's true dogs don't need to wash as often as we do — because they don't sweat — but they are natural filth magnets. Frequent bathing — as often as once a week — can make living with a dog manageable for many allergy sufferers, and a clean dog is just more pleasant for everyone to be around.

Maybe you've heard that frequent bathing strips the coats of its natural oils. To some extent, that's true, although as a person who lives with a retriever, I can tell you in some breeds there's plenty of oil to spare. Good nutrition has a bigger impact on a glossy coat than bathing does, but you can put back in some of what you take out by following shampoo with a conditioner, just as, probably, you do when you wash your own hair.

There are oodles of shampoos — some to keep dark coats dark, others to make white coats brighter. Shampoos with every imaginable scent, shampoos for fleas, shampoos for itchiness.

If your pet has a skin problem, ask your veterinarian for a recommendation. Otherwise, experiment a little to you find products you like working with.

Regular shampoos are almost as effective as flea shampoos at controlling the pests: they aren't very. When you wash your dog — with regular or flea shampoos — the result is the same: The fleas go down the drain. After that the last effect of a flea shampoo is short-lived. If you're figuring to fight fleas by treating only your pet, you won't get anywhere. Instead, check out the flea-fighting guide in Chapter 10.

Toys

Every dog need toys. They keep your pet occupied and amused when you cannot, and they provide you with another avenue for interacting and bond-building. Toys give your pet something to chew on besides your toys (or shoes, furniture, or books), and they are absolutely essential to puppy-raising, making puppies feel better when their teeth are cutting through.

Not only that, but they are great fun to choose and buy. A couple of cautions in the toy area exist, but not many. Enjoy!

Chewies

The kind of chewie you buy has everything to do with the size of your dog and how aggressive a chewer he is. Some of the toughest chew-toys on the market are made by Nylabone, in a variety of sizes, shapes, and colors.

The king of chew toys is, arguably, the Kong, a hard rubber toy that looks a little like the Michelin Tire man. Not only are Kongs almost impossible to destroy, they bounce in a sprightly manner, in unpredictable directions.

Chewies designed to remove plaque and stimulate gums are a popular recent development. They have nubs along their length, or indentations designed to be filled with canine toothpaste.

Rope chews — some of them adorned with hooves at the ends or rubber balls in the middle — are popular, but some trainers think they're too much like things you *don't* want your pet to chew on, like carpet fringes.

Monitor your pet's chew toys. When they are worn or chewed to the point where they can be swallowed, replace them.

Squeakies

Puppies and dogs alike love toys of either plush or vinyl that make noise when squeezed. These can be a very expensive proposition if you own a dog who isn't happy until the squeaker is "dead." My older dog once with surgical precision removed the squeakers from four green vinyl frogs in under 20 minutes — at $8 each, and the younger one, who adores stuffed toys, will treat one like a cherished love for days and then shred it looking for that squeaker. (His beloved hedgehog, which roared rather than squeaked, lasted two whole weeks, a record.)

It pays to be cautious with these toys. If your dog is inclined to leave them intact, then indulge him with the wonderful variety of shapes and sizes — a liberal friend of mine has a dog whose best pal is a Ronald Reagan squeaky toy, which I think he hoped his dog would destroy rather than adore.

One of the nicest and sturdiest plush toys is the Vermont Chewman, solidly made of thick fake lambskin and available in catalogs and pet-supply stores.

Fetchies

Fetch is an outstanding way to exercise your dog while reminding him of your role as pack leader. Many people use flying discs for this and, while it's great fun, you should be aware that some dogs have been injured to the point of needing surgery while leaping after flying disks.

Tennis balls are another common toy with built-in risks. *Never* let your dog chew on a tennis ball or play with one unattended. Some dogs have died after a tennis ball, compressed by powerful jaws, popped into the throat and cut off the air supply.

Does that mean you should avoid playing with flying discs or tennis balls? No, but use some common sense. With flying discs, avoid the acrobatics that wow spectators at half-time shows but have your dog leaping, twisting, and landing hard. Work on low throws in front of your dog, to encourage him to run, but not to jump. (I like to use the floppy discs made of fabric, not plastic.) Tennis balls are fine for fetch, but put them away when the game's over.

Tennis balls are a perennial canine favorite, but exercise some caution when using them.

Photo courtesy of Gina Spadafori.

You can, of course, buy solid rubber balls. And for water retrieving — a great exercise for the dog who enjoys swimming — Kong makes a floating variety that's easy to throw a long way.

If you buy a toy that invites tug-of-war games, it's fine to let your pet pull against another dog. But *never* play tug of war with your dog, and make sure that your children don't, either.

What seems like an innocent game could be a set-up for tragedy. That's because tug-of-war can teach your dog to be dominant. Here's how it works: You play with your dog, pulling against him in a battle of dominance, however playful in appearance. You get bored, the phone rings, and you drop your end. You think: Game's over. Your dog thinks: I win.

It's exactly the opposite message your dog should get, and it may lead to other dominance challenges.

More Great Gear

Didn't I tell you you can spend as much on a dog as on a child? Here are a few nice-to-haves that don't fit anywhere else.

Pooper scoopers

It's a nasty job, so wouldn't you rather be handling it from the other end of something designed to pick up the poop quickly and efficiently? A lot of people just use a shovel, but I personally don't want a shovel that has been used for this being used in my vegetable garden. Plus, scoops are easier to use.

What's also easy to use are portable scoops for cleaning up after your dog when you're away from home. (It's the law in some places, and a responsible thing to do in all others.) While you can buy bags designed for that purpose — and scented, to boot! — I find it's easy and economical to use sandwich bags for the small dog and plastic grocery bags for the large one. Put the bag over your hand like a glove, pick up the poop, pull your hand and the poop so the bag inverts, tie or flip the ends and discard. No mess, and you don't touch anything!

Smell and stain removers

Never clean up a pet mess with an ammonia-based product: It makes the area smell even *more* like urine — ammonia being a component of urine — and attracts the dog back to the site for more messing.

Several good products are designed to remove stains and smell through enzyme action; one of these can be a lifesaver, especially when you're house-training.

Another possibility is Petzorb, a product made of absorbent crystals that absorbs the moisture of pet messes and then can be vacuumed up.

Silly stuff

Some stuff that seems silly isn't really so much. Boots and raincoats, for example, can make all-weather excursions a little neater for the owners of city dogs. (The dogs themselves would probably rather get muddy!) And sweaters are a merciful gift to old or arthritic dogs, or chronically cold ones, like whippets.

Other things are definitely just for fun. Does your dog need a leather bomber jacket or a collar and tie for special occasions? No, but as a person with a dog who has his own pair of shades, I'm not in a position to tell you not to buy anything.

I could write a whole separate chapter on dog-themed stuff you can buy for *you*. Bumper stickers and T-shirts. Plates and cups. Calendars and stationery. Windchimes, mailboxes, and tote bags. Jewelry, both kitschy and fine. You're going to find all this on your own, and you're probably going to buy a lot of it.

Should you end up with a *lot* of money to spend, however, you may want to check out the William Secord Gallery in New York City. Secord is one of the world's experts on dog art, especially paintings by 19th and early 20th century masters such as Sir Edwin Henry Landseer and Maud Earl. (Landseer painted so many Newfoundlands that the black-and-white variety are called Landseers.)

For significantly less than the cost of anything in his gallery, you can buy Secord's lavishly illustrated book, *Dog Painting, 1840-1940: A Social History of the Dog in Art*. It's $79.95 from the Dog & Cat Book Catalog, the most complete mail-order source for pet books around (how to reach them is in this book's Appendix).

Even less expensive — and more useful, if you spend as much time at a computer as I do — is a mousepad with your breed on it, for about $11. Reigning Cats and Dogs, a pet boutique in Sacramento, Calif., has them in many of the most popular breeds. You can check out the mousepads and other items by visiting their online store in the Pet Care Forum of America Online (keyword: PETS), or e-mail them at RECATSDOGS@aol.com. For more information, see this book's "Additional Resources" appendix.

Another possibility: T-shirts, mousepads, and other items that can be printed with a computer-generated picture of your actual pet.

Part II

Bringing a Puppy or an Adult Dog into Your Life

The 5th Wave

By Rich Tennant

"When we got him several years ago he was a Golden Retriever. Now, he's more of a Golden Recliner."

In this part . . .

This part explains everything you need to know about choosing that one special puppy or dog who's right for you, plus you find help in getting the relationship started right. Puppy-training tips and puppy veterinary-care plans are in here, too, along with step-by-step strategies for house-training your new pet.

Chapter 5

Choosing and Bringing Home Your Puppy

"*A*cquiring a dog may be the only opportunity a human ever has to choose a relative," author Mordecai Siegal has commented, and that may explain part of the excitement that goes with bringing home a new dog of any description, young or old.

Add to this thrill the natural charm of all puppies — those round bellies, those shining eyes, that wonderful puppy breath — and you've got all the ingredients for a day that ranks up there with the most anticipated events of our lives. The moment you lock eyes with the puppy who will be yours is sweetly perfect, one to remember forever.

I want you to enjoy your perfect puppy moment, really I do, but, because I want you to have a lot more than that, I want you to be sure you're considering your decisions carefully. Don't check your common sense at the breeder's or shelter's door. Take your time and bring a friend to help you if you think you might be too impulsive. Choosing your puppy is just the first step in a lifetime together, remember.

The second step, surviving that long first night, makes you wonder if you've made the right decision even if you have, for sure. It's tough on your puppy, too, but you both get over it.

From the minute you bring your puppy home, keep your eyes open. Puppies are an unending source of wonder and delight, and they grow up so fast! Do your best not to miss one precious minute for, once it's gone, it's gone forever.

Before you pick out your puppy, be sure you get the breed or breed type that's a match with your personality and lifestyle, and be doubly sure you're going to a reputable source. Check out Chapters 1 and 2 for help in considering such things as size, fur, breed type, and trainability, and Chapter 3 for the sources that give you the best shot at acquiring a puppy or dog with good health and a sound temperament.

If you're adopting a "teenage" dog, or an adult dog of any age, tips on choosing a dog and getting that relationship started properly are in Chapter 9.

Puppy Preparations

Is your house ready for the running, jumping, chewing machine that is a healthy, happy puppy? Are you? Before you bring home your special pup, you need to look your home over, and make some purchases.

Puppy-proofing

One of the first rules of making a home safe for a puppy — and keeping a home safe *from* a puppy — is to start him out with a small, safe area. That means keeping the doors closed to the kids' bedrooms for a while, lest pieces of action figures end up in your puppy's stomach, to the horror of your children. That means using *baby gates,* expandable barriers you can put in any doorway or at the top of a stairway to further limit your puppy's options.

In the parts of the house you have left, get down on your hands and knees and take a look at things from a puppy's point of view. Conceal those tasty electrical cords under furniture and carpets, and put away any low decorations or bric-a-brac for now. Think "toddler-proofing" and you're on the right track except, with puppies, you're thinking of things they can chew, not places they can stick their fingers.

Puppy gear

Since you shouldn't let your puppy venture into places where other dogs have been until he's through with all his vaccinations — see Chapters 6 and 7 for more on socialization and vaccinations — you should make your first run to the pet-supply store without him. If you've already chosen your puppy and are just waiting for him to be old enough to come home, you can get everything on the list except his collar and ID tag (the latter because you haven't named him yet!) If you're going to the shelter and don't know for sure who you'll come home with, make your supply run after the day he comes home.

The low-down on all these items, such as the proper kind of brush or comb, and the proper type and size of shipping crate, is in Chapter 4.

Here's your shopping list:

- ✔ Brush and comb
- ✔ Chew toys
- ✔ Dishwasher-safe, nonchewable bowls: one for water, one for food
- ✔ Pet stain cleaner
- ✔ Flat or rolled collar, buckle or snap-together — *not* a slip collar — with an ID tag
- ✔ High-quality puppy food, as recommended by breeder, shelter, or veterinarian
- ✔ Lightweight leash, six foot
- ✔ Nail trimmer and Kwik Stop powder
- ✔ Pooper scooper and plastic bags
- ✔ Properly sized shipping crate, for house-training
- ✔ Puppy shampoo

You might even throw in a couple of extras for yourself, such as an "I love my [breed]" T-shirt, or a coffee cup or mouse pad for work.

Puppy Picking

The day a puppy comes to a new home is one of great promise. You can't wait to get through all the paperwork. You don't want to read the information you've been given. You just want your puppy. Now.

You'll soon have all the time in the world to make a fuss. But now, you should keep your enthusiasm in check just a little while longer.

Before you get down to bringing home the puppy who'll share your life, take a second to confirm that your bases are covered. Go back and read Chapter 3 and be sure you're dealing with a reputable source. You don't want to fall in love with a puppy who has health and temperament problems, after all. Before making your final choice, review these good-puppy criteria:

✔ Be sure you're getting your puppy at the right age — between his seven-week and eight-week birthdays. Some breeders, especially those with toy breeds, insist on holding their puppies longer — because they're small and delicate, primarily, and that's fine, but only if the breeder has continued to socialize the puppy with people. While you want a puppy who can get along with other dogs, you don't want one who's too dog-oriented to bond well with you, and that's what you get when puppies are left with their littermates too long and not socialized. Age is not as big a concern with a shelter puppy: He has probably been handled by staff and volunteers since the time he came in.

✔ Look for a puppy who has been raised as a pet — in the kitchen, ideally. You want a puppy who has heard the normal sounds of living with people from the day he was born — talking, laughter, and even fights, the TV, music, and the sound of the dishwasher. Health screenings and good breeding are *very* important, but so, too, is socialization. Don't buy a puppy from someone who has raised them in a kennel, barn, or basement. If you don't know how he has been raised, check out his temperament with the tests located elsewhere in this chapter.

✔ Check for signs of good health. While your puppy will be seeing a veterinarian within 24 hours — you should make a health check a condition of sale — you should be able to spot any obvious signs of disease on your own. Your puppy should be plump and glossy, with eyes, nose, and ears free of any discharge. He should seem upbeat and happy, not listless.

If you have questions, ask the seller, and make sure you're satisfied with the answers. Above all, don't let your enthusiasm override your common sense. It's hard to say no to a puppy, but you must if the puppy's not the right one for you.

Sometimes a pup is alone in this world, a single pup born to a mother who died. Should you avoid such a puppy? That depends on the breeder. A knowledgeable breeder does his best to make up for the shortcomings, taking over the role of the mother and, later, giving the puppy exposure to other dogs. Single puppies are often sent to be "adopted" by dogs with puppies close to the same age or at least given the opportunity to socialize with other puppies after weaning.

If this socialization has been done, you should have no qualms about adopting such a puppy, but you should continue to look for as many opportunities as you can to expose your puppy to other dogs as he grows up.

TIP

Is a Christmas puppy a good idea?

The image of a beribboned puppy and delighted children on Christmas morning is both endearing and enduring.

Never mind that humane societies, trainers, veterinarians, and reputable breeders say that Christmas morning is just about the worst time to introduce a puppy to the family. To parents with camera at hand, the scene seems worth the trouble of an energetic ball of fluff rolling around on one of the year's most hectic days.

But is it really?

Getting a Christmas puppy is OK — if you get one before Christmas or after. Introducing a puppy on Christmas Day is very stressful for all concerned: The puppy needs your attention — but so does everything else.

Even if you get your pup before or after the actual holiday, you have some challenges. The first may be finding the right puppy. Many shelters and reputable breeders will not place puppies right before Christmas, because they believe the time is just too high-risk. That leaves you with less-than-ideal sources for your pet.

And that's not all: Consider the problem of socializing and training a puppy in the dead of winter, if white winters visit your corner of the universe in December. By the time the snow starts to melt, you could have a half-grown canine terror on your hands.

Giving up that Norman Rockwell moment when your children discover that St. Nick has answered their pleas for a puppy is difficult. But if you want a better chance of still having that pet as a well-loved member of the family at future Christmases, consider this option:

Wrap a collar and leash and a dog book for the children and put that under the tree — promise your children that their puppy had to wait to be born, but will be with them as soon as she can.

As far as holidays go, I like Easter break a lot better for starting a puppy out. Your camera works just as well then, your children will be just as happy, and your puppy has a better chance at getting the attention she needs.

Working with a breeder

If you've found a reputable breeder, you may not have much to do when it comes down to choosing your puppy. You've let the breeder know if you prefer a male or a female, and whether you want that puppy to be more than your pet — you're considering showing, for example, or some other canine competition (more on these in Chapter 16). Maybe the litter has different color puppies, and you have a strong preference for one or the other. All these factors can narrow your choices dramatically (even when considering a very large litter).

The breeder has been narrowing the choices, too. He's talked with you enough to get a feel for the kind of home you offer, whether you'd be too much for a shy puppy or too little for a bossy one. In the end, you may have a choice between two or three puppies — or maybe just one fills the bill.

This is a give-and-take process, of course, and you may decide to broaden your selection criteria a little when faced with a squirmy litter of fat, healthy puppies. Suddenly a black Lab might seem perfect when before only a yellow one would do. The breeder, too, should be open to discussion. Just remember that he has a better idea of the personalities of his puppies — he knows his dogs, after all, and has been living with *these* pups for weeks. If he suggests the bold puppy who's crawling all over your son might not be the best bet for your family, believe him — he has probably learned from a past bad call and ended up with an unhappy family and a dog returned.

While it's a pretty good bet that there'll be plenty of puppies for you to choose from in a litter of Great Danes, that may not be the case if you're dealing with a toy breed, where small litters are the norm. You may want to hedge your bets a little by dealing with more than one reputable breeder. Chances are the breeder you choose already has that in mind: Good breeders are active in their local club and are likely to know who else has a litter that might suit you if theirs does not.

Puppy testing

What if you aren't dealing with a breeder, you're not selective as to gender, and couldn't care less about your puppy's color or markings? What if you're offered the pick of any pup you want, not just from one litter, but from a whole shelter full of them. How can you decide?

By testing the personalities of your prospective pet, that's how.

Remember that while you can potentially find a good puppy anywhere, making the most of any help offered is a good idea. Good breeders and good shelters test their puppies. If you're dealing with one that doesn't, you have to wonder about what else isn't top rate. And you may want to go back to Chapter 3 and take a shot at finding a better source.

Puppy-testing methods vary widely but, in general, the purpose of testing is the same. The goal is to determine the following:

- **A puppy's level of dominance.** How bossy or shy is he? While a lot of people are inclined to pick the boldest pup of a litter — because he seems to pick them — he's probably not the best choice for most homes. He *may* be just the ticket for someone with a great deal of dog-training experience who intends to compete with her dog, but for an average home, a less-dominant dog's a better choice. Avoiding the shyest, least dominant puppy, which some people pick "because he needs us!" is best, too.

- ✔ **A puppy's level of interest in people.** Some puppies are more dog-oriented or really don't care much about anything at all. A puppy who's not curious and interested in people — perhaps because of little or no socialization — isn't a very good prospect as a pet. You want a pup who wants to be with you, because that's the pup who'll be loving — and trainable!

- ✔ **A puppy's trainability.** The goal here is a puppy with the ability to concentrate — as much as any baby can — and absorb information. A puppy who is so busy bouncing off the walls that he can't give you even a moment's attention is going to be one you want to avoid.

Take each of the puppies you're thinking about to a safe, secure area away from littermates. Observe how the puppy reacts to the change — tentative exploration is OK, but beware the puppy who's so terrified she won't move. Look, too, for how busy a puppy is: Playfulness is fine, but full-out go-go-go is maybe a little too much.

Remember, *ideally* your observations should be compared and discussed with the observations of others who have looked at these puppies, such as the volunteers and staff at the shelters or the breeder.

Keep in mind that the puppy who's probably going to be the best for you — after you find the right breed or breed type, the right source, and decide between male and female — is going to be "medium" in personality. She may not be the smartest in the litter, but she may be more interested in your point of view than the one who is the smartest. She's got moxie, but not so much that she'll drive you crazy. She's willing to try new things — she's no shrinking violet — but she'll like them better if you are with her.

Although a particular breeder may *always* test his puppies at a particular age — six weeks, say — you may not have this luxury. Anything in the five-to-twelve week range is OK, but remember if you're testing puppies in their eighth week, they may *all* be a little skittish because they're in a so-called "fear" period, where they're a little leery of new things for a few days. Testing before or after this stage is a better idea.

You can size up a puppy's personality in several ways, but here are a few exercises anyone can do well:

- ✔ **Interest in people.** Put the puppy down facing you. Walk a few steps away, bend over, and call to him. (Bending over makes you less intimidating.) If the puppy seems a little tentative, crouch, and open your arms. You're not "ordering" the pup — he doesn't know what you want, after all. You're trying to see how attracted he is to a nice person. So be nice. Call gently, click your tongue, rattle your keys. The medium puppy you want will probably trot over happily, perhaps after a slight hesitation. The bossy puppy may come over and nip at you, and the shy one may not move except to shiver in terror. The one who doesn't care a bit about people may go investigate a bug in the corner of the room.

A puppy should be interested in you and come over when you beckon.

✔ **Accepting authority.** Gently roll the puppy onto his back and hold him there with your hand. The medium pup you're looking for will fuss a little, settle down, and maybe even lick your hand. Bossy pups usually keep struggling, and the shyest ones generally freeze in terror.

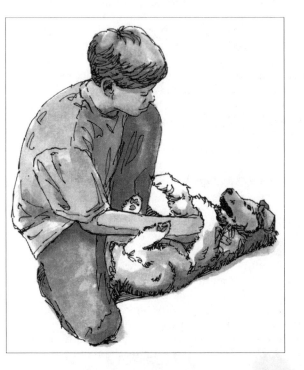

A puppy who bites or fights your authority, or is terrified, is best avoided.

✔ **Praise and petting response.** Praise and petting are integral parts of training and communicating with your dogs, and so finding a puppy who wants affection enough to earn it is important. Talk to the puppy lovingly and stroke him, but let him decide whether he stays with you or not — don't hold him. The medium puppy will probably lick your hands and be glad to stay with you. Rolling over is OK, and don't be surprised if he urinates a little — called *submissive urination,* this gesture is kind of a canine compliment, a recognition that you're "top dog" (More on submissive urination in Chapter 8.) A puppy who bites hard is probably dominant and unsocialized, and the one who wants nothing to do with you probably isn't people-oriented enough. Stay away, too, from the one who's terrified of being touched.

Look for the puppy who wants to be with you and enjoys your attention.

Listen to your head, not your heart. Doing so is really, really hard when you're in a shelter and thinking the puppy you don't pick isn't going to get picked at all. Don't play the guilt game. Pick a puppy with a temperament that's likely to produce a good pet. You're still saving a life in the case of a shelter puppy, still providing a good home in the case of any puppy. Keep that in mind and pick the best puppy you can.

You may be tempted to take two puppies home, with the grand idea that adopting littermates will keep them from being too lonely while you're at work and will give them something to do besides pester you.

Give this idea a lot of thought.

Raising two puppies together means twice the work, twice the craziness, and twice the mess. Most people barely have time to properly socialize and train *one* puppy, much less two. Plus, two puppies raised together may remain more bonded with each other than they are to you.

If you want two dogs, consider waiting until your puppy is grown to add another puppy. Adding a grown dog at the same time you add a puppy may be OK but, still, puppies are such work that you're better off getting your little one squared away before you add to your pack.

One of the best things you can do to get this special relationship started out properly is to take time off work when your first get your puppy. Call it *pupernity leave* if you like, but take the time if at all possible. A week — two is even better— gives you time to get house-training off to a great start and to enjoy your puppy while easing the transition for her between life with her littermates and life with you. For more on early puppy training, see Chapter 6.

Puppy Comes Home

The day your puppy comes home is a big step for both of you. She's leaving her littermates and throwing her lot in with yours. You're taking on the huge responsibility of raising a dog.

You want the transition to be as smooth as possible, and yet you want to make sure that from that very first day you're laying the groundwork for a wonderful life together.

Repeat after me: ***I will never let my puppy do anything I wouldn't want her to do as a grown dog.***

Good! You're ready to be a full-fledged puppy parent now, heaven help you.

When you go to pick up your puppy, bring towels, both old bathroom ones and the paper kind. Chances are your puppy will get carsick. (This doesn't mean she's going to be carsick her whole life.) Don't go alone, either. If you're a single person, have a friend drive so you can hold your puppy. Have a spouse, kids? Take 'em. This moment is one you'll want to remember.

JUST FOR FUN

Watch the birdie, puppy!

Don't forget to load up your camera with film and record the special day your puppy comes home. Even better, buy lots of film, because over the next couple of months you're going to kick yourself for missing some great shots if you don't — and hate yourself later for not having pictures of your wonderful dog as a baby.

Here are a couple of tips for taking great puppy pictures:

Head outdoors. Natural light — early morning is best — avoids the dreaded red-eye shot, where the flash makes your beautiful puppy come out as a monster. Taking pictures outside gives your new pet a more natural, healthy look.

Get down and get close. If you want a good puppy picture, you're going to have to go where your puppy is — on the ground. Shoot at just below your puppy's eye level and zoom in as closely as you can for good detail. If getting down isn't something your back will tolerate, bring the puppy up: Have someone hold him — this has the added benefit of keeping him still — or put him on an elevated surface, such as an outdoor table.

Watch your backgrounds. I have a wonderful picture of Lance, the Original Demo Dog. He's freshly groomed. He's standing perfectly. His ears are up, his mouth smiling, his eyes bright. And he has a telephone pole growing out of his back. Be sure you have an uncluttered background, so your dog can shine!

Be creative. If you want your puppy to kiss your children, do as the pros do: Put a little dab of butter on your children, and let the puppy kiss it off. Another professional's trick: Just before taking the picture, rattle keys, squish a squeaky toy or throw something in the air. Your puppy will come to attention, splendidly.

Get your children involved. This is a special day, so if you have kids, let them make some memories, too. Get them each one of those throwaway cameras and take pictures of their new puppy. You'll be delighted at some of the shots you get back — and they'll be doubly so!

But don't let your children fight over the puppy. She's not a football. *One* person can hold her, on a towel, for the ride. You can draw lots and make it up to the other kids later. Remember that you want to lay the groundwork for your puppy from the beginning. You want to do so with your children, too, by insisting on gentle, respectful handling.

If the puppy throws up, or makes any other kind of mess, don't make a fuss of any kind. Change to a clean towel, and clean it all up when you get home.

TIP

The *first* thing you should do when you get home is take your puppy outside and praise her for relieving herself, if she does. More on house-training in Chapter 8.

The name game

Naming a dog has to be one of the most delightful parts of getting one. It seems not a year goes by without a new book of dog names being published, including ones that specialize, such as a book on Irish names. I have no fewer than six books of names on my bookshelves, including two that were meant for the parents of human babies, not canine ones.

Do you need to keep anything in mind when naming a dog? Yes. Avoid names that sound like common obedience commands. A friend of mine who had worked in Alaska adopted a beautiful husky mix and wanted to name her Sitka, after a place he'd loved visiting. After I pointed out she'd have a hard time telling the difference between "Sitka" and "sit," he named her Juneau instead.

Keep names short, one or two syllables, and easy to pronounce. I tend to use "people" names for my own pets, but you don't have to limit yourself. Name books are a good start, but don't forget atlases or special dictionaries such as those for foreign words or a book of baseball, railroad, gardening, or music terms, if your interests lie in any of those directions.

Make your puppy love his name as much as you do by making sure that it has a positive association. *Never* scream your puppy's name at him or use it in punishment. The late dog trainer Job Michael Evans used to recommend making up a song with your dog's name in it and singing to him. Commercial jingles are wonderful for this, he said, because they're catchy and you can put the pet's name in where the product is mentioned.

Oh, and yes, I do this. "You Are My Sunshine" becomes "You Are My Andy" ("you make me happy/because you're gray") and Benjamin gets regaled with the Monty Python, "Spam" song, with Ben substituted for Spam — "Ben, Ben, Ben, Ben, Ben, Ben, Ben, Ben, Wonderful Ben . . ."

Yes, it's silly. But try it anyway. You'll both smile.

The name your dog hears — his everyday name — is what fanciers call a *call name* as in, it's what you call your dog. If you have a purebred dog, he'll have a *registered name,* too. You get 28 letters and spaces with the American Kennel Club to come up with a registered name for your pet. If you choose a name someone else has already chosen, the AKC issues it along with a number to distinguish your dog's name from the others, so unless you want your collie to be the AKC's 897,042th "Lassie," use all those spaces to come up with something sure to be unique.

Puppy's first night

Your puppy will probably be so overwhelmed by the new sights, sounds, smells, and all the attention that she won't much miss her littermates and her old home. Don't worry, that will come soon enough — and last most of the first few nights.

Keep things nice and easy to start out with. Everyone will want to hold the puppy and play with her, and that's fine, but remember she's still a baby and gets worn out quickly. She needs to sleep, but she may not eat on that first day. She has a lot to get used to; don't worry about it very much. Let her explore.

Puppies aren't stuffed toys, and you must help your children to realize that. Small children — especially those under five — can't really help being a little rough with puppies (and dogs) and must be carefully supervised to ensure that neither hurts the other.

Where should your puppy sleep? I think dogs should sleep in the bedroom always, not on your bed in most cases, but in their own. Allowing the dog to sleep in the bedroom is especially important for households where a dog is left alone for hours at a time when the family is at work and at school. Letting your dog sleep in your bedroom — or in your child's bedroom — counts for time together, even though you're all asleep. It can go a long way toward building and maintaining a strong bond, assuring your pet that she's an important member of the pack.

If you want your dog to sleep in the service porch, though, that's your business. But please don't start on the first couple of nights after you bring your puppy home.

Those first couple of nights are very tough on a puppy. The reassuring warmth of her littermates is gone and everything has changed. She's going to have a lot to say about this, so be prepared. She will fuss less if she's in your presence, if she can be reassured by your smell and the sound of your breathing.

Set up her crate next to your bed, and prepare it with a soft blanket to sleep on and a chew toy or two. Tell her "crate" firmly, put her inside and close the door. And then open a book, because you won't be sleeping for awhile. (For more on the use of crates in puppy-raising, see Chapters 6 and 8.)

Endure the cries and whines as best you can, but don't punish your puppy, and don't take her out when she's carrying on — you'll teach her that all she need do is fuss and she gets what she wants. She'll probably settle down and then wake once or twice in the middle of the night. Take her out to relieve herself — and praise her for doing so — and then put her back in her crate.

In a day or two, the worst of the heartbreaking crying is over.

Puppy-raising tips are in Chapter 6, and house-training schedules are in Chapter 8.

Chapter 6

Early Puppy Training

In This Chapter

▶ Beginning to shape a well-mannered puppy

▶ Teaching your puppy the basics

▶ Dealing with your puppy's shortcomings

*Y*ou can see in your puppy today what our ancestors saw when this astonishing trans-species relationship was just forming. In the eyes of that wolf cub thousands of years ago was the same thing anyone who has ever taken home a puppy since can't help but notice: The beginning of a beautiful friendship.

There's no doubt many of these beautiful beginnings go wrong, however, and people in a lot of different areas — behaviorists, shelter directors, sociologists, and veterinary epidemiologists — spend a great deal of time trying to find out why in hopes of stemming the flow of half-grown dogs into the nation's shelters. Wrong choices, bad timing, and poor planning all play a part, but in many instances "too little" is the sorry epitaph that marks the end of a once-promising relationship. Too little time, too little training.

You don't want this to happen to you. Your concern is for your puppy and making sure she turns out the way you want her to. You don't want to be living with a canine terror a year from now, and you certainly don't want to be finding her another home because you can't handle her anymore.

You can make up a lot of ground with a puppy who wasn't raised under the best of circumstances before you got her, or you can totally undo the careful breeding and handling of your pup by a knowledgeable and reputable breeder. The decision is completely up to you. Ignore your puppy or raise her wrong, and you'll both be sorry.

 Love your puppy, play with your puppy, enjoy your puppy. But you should always — *always* — be thinking of how you're molding this little baby into the confident, obedient dog of your dreams. It takes socialization, and it takes training. And most of all, it takes *time*. Time passes all too quickly in the life a puppy. A couple of critical weeks, once past, are gone forever.

So take the time. Make the effort. Your work in the first few months of your puppy's life will reward you many times over during the lifetime of your dog.

Shaping Good Behavior

Forget everything you ever heard about starting training at six months. Your puppy starts learning the moment he's born and, by the time you get him — seven to ten weeks of age — he's as absorbent as a bath towel, taking in the sights and sounds of his world and trying to figure out his place in it. The answer he arrives at on his own may be quite different from the one you want him to have, which is why you need to be involved in the process.

It's not that complicated, really. Your puppy wants to be part of your family, and he craves loving leadership. Just keep a few things in mind as you enjoy your youngster:

- Bond with your puppy.
- Socialize your puppy.
- Never let your puppy do anything you wouldn't want a grown dog to do.
- Teach your puppy using positive methods; make training fun!
- Realize your puppy will make mistakes, and don't get angry when he does.
- Remember always that *preventing* bad habits is easier than fixing them later.

Every minute you spend with your puppy is not only delightful but also an investment in the future. Do not let your puppy grow up without you. What will happen if you do? A visit to any shelter provides the answer.

You can find step-by-step instructions for training basic commands to both puppies and dogs in Chapter 11, and a guide to puppy house-training in Chapter 8.

Bonding

One of the reasons dogs have adapted so well to being human companions is that the social needs of both species are similar. Dogs and wolves live and work together in social unit called a *pack,* which is really what we would call a family. Because their very survival depends on working together, they have evolved a system of communication emphasizing social order and cooperation. From families to softball teams to corporations, so, too, have we. We count on others of our kind to raise us and help us throughout our lives.

When you take a puppy into your home, you are asking her to accept your family in exchange for a canine one. And she will, quite happily and with amazingly few problems, if you hold down your end of the deal — provide her with companionship and show her her proper place in the social order.

She cannot find her place in your family unless you make your puppy part of your life. Simply put, a puppy cannot bond with people she barely knows.

Bonding isn't hard to accomplish. Spend time with your puppy. Talk to her. Sing to her. Put your hands on her. Use baby gates instead of closed doors if you don't want her in certain parts of the house, so she can hear you and see you and feel part of the crowd.

You are the only family she has from the time you take her home. Make her part of that family, and she'll be a better pet.

One of the easiest ways to promote a fast, tight bond with your puppy is to have her sleep in a crate at the side of your bed. It's almost like cheating: You sleep, she sleeps, but as she sleeps, she bonds. She smells your wonderful smell and hears every sound you make, all night long — and she won't mind your snoring!

When I say *in the bedroom,* I don't mean *on the bed.* Sleeping in your bed gives a dog a rather elevated idea of his station in life, and that can lead to problems. You want your puppy to know from the first that you are the boss in your house. You're a nice boss, however, which is why you've provided a snuggly crate or soft bed for him to sleep on. But you're still the boss. Period.

When your puppy's all grown up and perfectly behaved, you can invite him on your bed. That's where mine sleep. But they understand it's a privilege, not a right. They are not allowed up unless invited, they are not up there every night, and they are never allowed up unless I'm already there.

Socializing

You simply cannot expose a puppy to too many new things — people, places, and other animals. And yet this is one area where puppy owners undo the good work of many reputable breeders. When a puppy is not continually exposed to new things, her social development stops — and in many cases regresses. The goal is a confident, outgoing dog, not a shy or aggressive one. The way to accomplish this is through *socializing.*

We ask a lot from our dogs, a lot more than their wild cousins need for survival. Wild dogs and wolves need to learn to live in harmony with others of their pack and as important members of their ecosystem. They know their own family, and they don't have to get along with members of other packs. No one ever asks them to live in peace with other predators, such as mountain lions, and the only relationship they have with prey animals is when one of them becomes dinner. Wild dogs and wolves know the seasons and the smells of their environment and know that it's prudent to run when anything unfamiliar turns up.

Contrast that picture to what domesticated dogs are expected to endure with good grace. Born of a dog mother and raised among dog siblings, we ask our dogs to form a family relationship with members of another species. We ask them to live peaceably in this strange family, and we expect them to be docile with humans who are outside their pack. We ask, too, that they remain able to get along well with others of their own kind, both in the family and at such events as dog shows. We ask, further, that they abide the presence of a competing predator — the cat — and ignore the presence of what any wolf knows is good eating, although we call them pets: rabbits, birds, and other smaller animals.

Although a wild dog or wolf never gets too far from his home turf — except in cases of human interference — we ask that our dogs be as mobile as we are. We take them when we walk to the store, we put them in our cars when we go on vacation, we place them on airplanes when we move across country.

Dogs are genetically predisposed to have more potential to become part of human society than wolves or coyotes, and some breeds within the family of domesticated dogs find doing so easier still. Compare the easy companionability of a good golden retriever with the suspicious nature of breeds developed to protect livestock, for example.

So part of it's genetics, but the other part is you. Get your puppy out!

The world is full of scary things, especially to a little puppy. At times even the boldest of puppies is paralyzed with uncertainty when faced with something he's never seen before. Your response to his fear is *very* important. Do not soothe him.

Petting him and saying, "It's OK, baby" or something similar gives your puppy the idea that being scared is OK, that you're rewarding him for the behavior.

Be matter-of-fact and encouraging. Let him know that you think there's nothing to be afraid of. Let him work it out and when he takes that step forward, praise him for his courage. And then move on.

Your veterinarian knows what's best for your puppy, and she told you not to take him *anywhere* until the complete course of vaccinations has ended. I'm telling you to socialize him. Are you facing a conflict here?

Yes, and no. Your puppy *is* at risk for contracting diseases from other dogs before his full immunity is in place. This is why you shouldn't go anywhere where dogs you do not know hang out — parks, dog events, or pet stores —

A well-socialized puppy deals gracefully with his other "family members."

Photo courtesy of the HSUS / Joseph R. Spies.

until your veterinarian gives the go-ahead. You *should* take him to places that are probably safe — to see friends and play with their healthy, vaccinated dogs, for example, or to places where humans frequent, such as the outdoor seating area of a sidewalk cafe.

Why take any chances at all? Because doing so is *important*. Behavioral problems present as great or greater a risk to your puppy than do contagious diseases.

So use common sense. Plan safe outings, and carry your puppy if you're not sure. And when that last puppy shot is in — at 14 to 16 weeks — then really pull out all the stops when it comes to socialization.

Be creative when it comes to letting your puppy experience new things. One of my favorite experiences for a puppy is to take him through a drive-through car wash — lots of noise and motion, but absolutely no danger!

Consistency

Puppies are adorable, even when they're naughty. Maybe *especially* when they're naughty. You catch your little fluffball with your slipper in his mouth, or halfway through the destruction of yet *another* roll of toilet paper and, instead of being upset, you smile. And laugh. And head for the camera.

Although this reaction is normal, it's definitely *not* the way to raise a puppy who knows to leave slippers and toilet paper rolls alone. If you want your puppy to learn, you need to be *consistent* about what's acceptable behavior and what's not.

But you know that, which is why sometimes you keep your face as stern as you can for as long as you can, until . . . well, who wouldn't laugh, the way that toilet paper's wrapped around his cute puppy body?

Look. I *know* it's hard. But you're going to be sorry a few months from now if you don't remember this one little rule: *Never let a puppy get away with what you don't want a grown dog to do.*

Developing a consistent approach to naughtiness requires a little thinking and effort on your part.

Puppy classes

Many times when I recommend early socialization and training for puppies, people act surprised. A typical reaction is, "I though you weren't supposed to start training until a dog's six months old!"

What the experts meant was *formal* training, as in a class. And even *that's* not true any more. Almost every trainer offers classes for puppies as young as 12 weeks of age.

I highly recommend them.

Understand this: These are not boot camp classes for problem pooches. The goal here is socialization and lots of fun. Big puppies play with little ones, and everybody gets to pet everyone else's pup. And along the way, puppies pick up a few nice tricks — sometimes all the basic commands, taught in an encouraging, reward-centered way.

Puppy classes are good for your puppy and good for you, too. A puppy class gives you the opportunity to talk to a trainer every week about difficulties you may be having at home and get tips on how to keep puppy problems from becoming dog disasters. For your pup, the class is a megadose of socializing, an ongoing lesson that learning is a pleasure, and the foundation for a lifetime of canine good manners. You can find out more about choosing a trainer in Chapter 11.

The bottom line on puppy classes: Make sure that you're dealing with a trainer who asks for proof of vaccinations — for the protection of *all* the puppies in the class — who trains in a secure place, and who does not use firm corrections or training collars on the puppies. Watching a class or two will give you a better idea of the trainer's skills and philosophies than any phone call or brochure. A good trainer welcomes observers.

First, envision the kind of pet you'd like to live with. Some people are considerably looser with their dogs (and kids) than others. If you think that allowing dogs on the furniture is OK, fine, then let your puppy up on the furniture. But if you think it's only OK for *puppies* to be on the furniture because you want to snuggle yours, then not so fine. You're not being fair.

Second, follow through with the ground rules, every time. No letting things slide because you're tired. No letting him get away with things because he's cute. When he jumps on the couch for the first time — and he will try it, at least once — tell him "off" and set him on the floor. Praise him for being a good puppy on the floor. When he jumps on you, or the kids, tell him "off" and then take his collar and show him what you mean. Praise him for keeping all four paws on the ground.

Consistency also means that every human member of the family is clear on puppy rules and helps the puppy learn and live by them. If you've decided you don't want your dog to beg food, you're going to have a hard time enforcing the rule if your son is slipping the puppy French fries while watching TV.

Loosening the rules is easier than tightening them. A puppy who grows up thinking every obnoxious thing he wants to do is fine is going to grow into a dog you're not going to enjoy living with or be able to take places. Once your puppy is a well-mannered dog, you can invite him up on the couch or teach him to put his paws on your shoulder and give you a big slurpy kiss. The distinction between him doing what he wants and him doing what he wants *with your permission* is a big one.

Praise — and correction

Millions of words have been written in the last couple of decades on the theories of dog training. I'm going to sum it up a little more simply: Dog training is a carrot-and-stick endeavor which in recent years has become a whole lot more carrot and a lot less stick. This evolution has come about because of two things: First, no humane person wants to punish a dog, and second, any intelligent person realizes that rewarding good behavior is more likely to produce a strong, trusting bond than is constant punishment.

Physical correction — but not physical abuse — has a place in dog training. I go into that more in Chapters 11 and 12. Dog training has become more positive than negative recently, and puppy training has become more positive still.

Never strike a puppy: not with your hand, not with a rolled-up newspaper. *Never* scream at your puppy. If you do either to show your puppy "who's boss," you'll end up with a puppy who is both leery of you and convinced you're something of a jerk.

You want your puppy to love you and respect you, to know his place in the family, and feel secure and happy in it. Doing so takes encouragement and lots of loving praise.

Don't be stingy. When you're puppy does something right, let him know it. The first time the little light bulb goes off in his head connecting the word "sit" to the lowering of his rump — if you watch, you can see the workings of his mind in his eyes — be ready to tell him he's the most perfect, smartest, beautiful, and well-loved puppy in the whole history of the world the instant that little puppy-butt hits the ground. Croon at him like Bing Crosby. Pat him and stroke him.

At other times, your puppy won't be perfect, and you need to correct his bratty behavior. Remember: Let the punishment fit the crime. A verbal correction, properly timed and correctly delivered, is the gentlest. Done properly, this type of correction may be all you need in most puppy-raising situations. Here are few more ways to send a clear message of disapproval:

- **The ol' switcheroo.** Especially useful for the young puppy, this technique stops a behavior you don't want and provides the puppy with one that's acceptable. For example, if your young puppy's chewing on your nice leather shoes, make a noise to startle and distract him — slap the counter or clap your hands — and then give him something you *do* want him to chew on, a toy. When he takes it, praise him!

- **Ask for another behavior.** With older puppies, you can stop a bad behavior by asking for a better one. Tell the puppy who's jumping up "no" and then "sit" — and praise him for doing so. Tell him once, and if he does not — to be fair, be sure that he understands what you want — gently push him into a sit, and then praise.

- **The big squirt.** Get an inexpensive plastic squirt bottle and fill it with water and something distasteful — lemon juice or vinegar, a tablespoon or so to a 12-ounce bottle. Tell your puppy "no" and then squirt. Try to hold the bottle close to your side so the stream seems to be coming from nowhere.

- **The time out.** This technique has two levels, and you need to pay attention to your puppy to choose the appropriate correction. Puppies thrive on your attention, even if it's negative. The time out removes this reward and gives him a few minutes to think things over: "Oh, I can't stay with them if I do that!" he'll realize. This technique is especially good for a puppy who doesn't want to keep his mouth to himself, a bad habit for any dog to get into where people are concerned. When the puppy starts nipping, tell him "no," and them *clam up,* pick him up, and put him in his crate for five minutes. Ignore the cries and whimpers. After a few minutes, let him out without much fanfare and let him hang out with you gently for a while.

CAUTION

No, no, no, no, no, no, noooooooo

Almost without fail people use one word too much and incorrectly when raising a puppy. The word? "No." Some puppies hear it so often they think it's part of their name: "JoeNO!" "MeganNO!" Used constantly and especially if used in a whiny, pleading manner, "no" loses its value as a training tool.

"No" should be delivered firmly and sharply, as guttural as a low, barky growl — comparable, in other words, to how a puppy's mother expresses her displeasure. Don't whine your correction: "No, no, no, *no*. Mommy's fluffums is bad, bad, *bad!*" Instead, *throw* the word at the pup.

Because of the overuse of the word, some trainers suggest using another sound especially for correction, something that lends itself more naturally to sounding like a growl, like "arrrggghhh." I use both "no" and a guttural "argh" sounds as a correction words, but I don't use "no" as a warning word. I use "I wouldn't" when a dog is contemplating something like a second assault on something he has been told to leave alone. Again, the delivery is the key: I drop my voice and growl, "I WOULDn't."

They try by their innocent expressions to assure me they were not even thinking about it. But I know better.

If your puppy has been running around for a long time and just seems bratty, he may be tired. If that's the case, put him down for a nap in his crate, along with a chew toy. Again, ignore his fussing. Chances are he'll be asleep in a few minutes.

✔ **The shake-up.** We're talking serious infractions here, such as a growl, show of teeth or, worse, a genuine bite (as opposed to a good-natured puppy nip or nibble). This correction mimics the scruff-shake older dogs use when disciplining recalcitrant youngsters. Take your pup by the loose skin at the neck, lift his front paws off the ground, make eye contact and bark your sternest "no" at him. Then drop him and ignore him for a while — or put him in his crate — to give him time to think about his crime. (More on this correction in Chapter 12.)

If you're finding you need to do a lot of stern corrections, you've probably been sending your puppy mixed signals. You've probably led him to believe he has a chance to be "boss" — or at least go up a notch or two in pack order — and he's trying the higher position on for size. Discuss the situation with a trainer, and soon. You may have some big problems developing if you don't learn how to correct your puppy in an effective way.

Teaching What Every Puppy Should Know

People sometimes tell me they don't believe in dog-training because training will break their puppy's spirit. "I want him to be *free!*" says the person whose dog is running amok. While this attitude was a lot more prevalent during the '60s and '70s, when free-roaming canine nuisances played fetch in the common areas of college campuses, it remains even today, despite the enthusiastic enforcement of leash laws in some areas.

And it's not just running amok that's the problem. The late trainer Job Michael Evans used to say that when your dog jumps in a guest's lap, and that guest says, "Oh, it's OK. I *love* dogs" she's probably just being polite while wondering why you don't teach your dog some manners.

No dog in the world has more freedom than one with good manners. And no dog is easier to live with. These dogs can go in to stores and on vacation. They're welcome at the veterinarian's and the groomer's. Well-mannered dogs are helping to *reverse* the trend of anti-dog laws, including opening the minds in some communities to the possibilities of dog parks where good dogs can be rewarded by running . . . free!

About a million and six good reasons exist to train your puppy, and only one exists not to: foolishness. Do both you and your dog a favor and train. Remember my motto: *It's easier to raise a puppy right than to fix problems later.*

Getting used to a collar and leash

Your puppy can start wearing a buckled collar from the time you bring him home. I like lightweight nylon collars, inexpensive to replace when puppy grows, and they come in oodles of fun colors. Quick-snap collars are fine, too, and easy to adjust to larger sizes. Check the collar frequently to ensure a good fit. (And don't forget to attach a small ID tag!) For more on collars and IDs, see Chapter 4.

By the time your pup's ten weeks old, you can introduce a leash, for a few minutes at a time. Instead of using the leash to get the puppy to go your way, go *his* for a while, and then bend down and call him to you, sweetly. When he turns and heads in your direction, praise him and then get up and keep going, patting your leg and jollying him along. Introduce a command such as "walk on" or "let's go" for him to start associating with the idea of heading in your direction.

A few minutes is enough. Try again later in the day, and maybe change direction once, saying "let's go" and praising when the puppy follows.

The leash can be an important bonding tool for both puppies and grown dogs. After your puppy's comfortable with the feel of the leash, try tethering him to you for a few minutes at a time. With a six-foot leash, slip the leash handle through your belt and then snap it to the puppy. And then go about your business, hands off the leash. Doing so teaches the puppy to keep an eye on you, which in turns reinforces the idea of you as leader.

Puppy's first leash should be six feet long, slender, and light as possible, especially at the clasp. If you've got a heavy leash that you bought for your last dog, save it for later and get something appropriate for a puppy. Even a length of lightweight cord tied to a light snap is better than a leash that's too heavy to start with. See Chapter 4 for more on leashes.

The leash is a symbol of your leadership, and when you let your puppy chew on the leash, you're letting him chew on your authority. Considering the sharp nature of puppy teeth, you'll also be spending money for new leashes pretty regularly. Neither of these is desirable. So *do not* let your puppy chew on the leash. Yank it upward an inch or so out of his mouth while delivering a stern "no."

Grooming

All dogs need to learn to be bathed and brushed, to have their nails trimmed and their ears cleaned out. Some breeds — poodles, for example, as well as terriers and cockers — need to be professionally groomed at regular intervals during their lives.

The time to start introducing your puppy to these experiences is the day you bring him home. Handle his feet and toes, lift and caress his ear flaps, all the time telling him what a wonderful puppy he is. Keep the sessions short and always end on an upbeat note.

For brushing and combing, put a towel on top of a high, solid surface like your dryer — it's easier on your back — and hold him while you brush. He'll wriggle and carry on, but don't let that stop you. Brush for a short period, and end the session with brushing in an area most dogs adore — their tummy. Then call it a day.

Expose your puppy to the concept of electric clippers by running a sweater "de-piller" — or other small humming device — near him. Place the handle of it against him gently so that he can feel the vibration. Don't punish him for being scared: Let him get used to it for a second or two, and praise him afterward for being so brave.

If your puppy is of a breed that needs professional grooming, make his first appointment as soon as he's done with his puppy shots — at 14 to 16 weeks of age — to minimize the risk of exposure to disease. Make sure that the groomer knows you're bringing in a puppy so she can take a little extra time with him.

Nail trimming should be done frequently from the time you bring your puppy home to avoid the fits many older dogs throw when faced with this necessary task. Nail-trimming — and other grooming tips — are in Chapter 10.

Sit for what you want

Teaching a puppy to "sit" is almost effortless. You don't need to lay a hand on him. All you need is his food bowl and the force of gravity. Here's how it works:

Call your puppy's name and hold his food dish over his head, forcing him to raise his muzzle high to keep an eye on it. Soon he'll lose his balance and his back legs will start to fold. The micro-second this starts to occur, say "sit." When his rump hits the ground, praise and give him his dinner. Within a short time — if you're consistent in asking — he'll be sitting automatically for his food.

Test that he understands the command by trying it at different times, pulling up on his collar and pushing his rump down to remind him and them praising grandly for success (even if you helped engineer that success).

Once your puppy knows "sit," expand the situations in which you ask for it. Have him sit before you put the leash on, sit before you go out the door for a walk, sit instead of jumping up (although you'll probably need to correct him for the bad behavior first). My dogs sit for *anything* they want — their dinner, their toys, to leave the house or car, or to be petted by guests. Not only does sitting make them easier to live with — especially the 75-pound retriever — but it also constantly and effortlessly reinforces my role as the boss. And like any gentle and generous leader, I *always* thank them for being good dogs with an ear or chest scratch, a sweet word, or a hug.

Molding good behavior by controlling food is why I don't recommend free-feeding by puppies. When you — and other family members — are the ones who offer the food and make your puppy sit before getting it, you're integrating puppy training into all of your lives seamlessly.

When food is always available, you lose the training tool. And you also lose this chance to reinforce your role as top dog, which can contribute to dominance problems later on. When you give your pup food, and make him earn it, you make it clear that you own the food and are giving it to him. He's eating with your *permission*. This understanding can help prevent food-guarding and growling.

"Sit" isn't the only command you can teach your puppy. "Down," "come," "stay" — puppies can and should learn them all. For step by step instructions on how to teach these obedience basics — and more — see Chapters 11 and 12. And because life's not all work, see the tricks in Chapter 20.

Teaching your puppy to sit for what she wants helps to ensure a well-mannered pet.

Photo courtesy of Richard D. Schmidt.

TIP

Building your puppy's vocabulary

Dogs trained to work with people who use wheelchairs learn to understand more than 60 different commands, performing such tasks as picking up dropped items, turning off light switches, pressing elevator buttons. Are these special dogs? Sure, but so is yours.

Expanding your puppy's vocabulary is a good idea for two reasons. The first is that doing so offers an alternative to the "no, no, no" pattern so many pet-owners fall into. Take jumping up, for example. Instead of constantly correcting your puppy for jumping, correct him with one "no!" and then say "off!" and praise him for obeying when his feet hit the floor. Instead of yelling at him for being on the couch, take him by the collar, say "off!" put him on the floor, and then praise. This strategy turns a negative experience into a positive one and gives you another opportunity to tell your puppy he's brilliant. Go one step farther and say "sit," and then praise again.

The second reason to put names to activities is that living with a dog with a bigger vocabulary is more pleasant. My favorite story about enlarged vocabularies involves Lance, the Original Demo Dog, who had a command of the language that rivaled any service dog. For a short while in college, Lance and I lived with my grandmother, who'd put in new carpeting shortly before we moved in. Gram taught Lance not only to walk over to and stand on the "dog towel" she'd put down when he came in from the yard, but also to pick up each paw *by name* to be wiped off. And if he wasn't paying attention and offered the wrong paw, the left front instead of the right front, she'd say "other paw" — and he'd switch!

So use your imagination and teach your pup as much as you can. Remember, though, to be consistent in your naming — don't say "off" one time and "down" the next. (I prefer "off" for asking for all paws on the floor and "down" for lying down; it's less confusing for your puppy.)

Fixing the Things That Drive Puppy Owners Crazy

All dogs chew, jump up, bark, and nip. It's part of being a dog. Some do more of one than others — some breeds are yappier, some are diggier — but these are all part of the genetic blueprint of the dog. If you aren't prepared to live with a little of these activities — especially in the puppy stages — you're really better off with an iguana.

That's the bad news. The other bad news is puppies do not "grow out" of problem behaviors, so drop that idea right now.

The good news is that you can diminish, redirect, and control — and in the case of nipping, eliminate — these behaviors when raising your puppy. But be fair: You cannot expect a puppy — or dog — to spend boring, empty days without filling the time with activities you may not like. A dog requires a lifelong commitment of time for training and exercise.

Chewing

All puppies chew. So would you if your gums drove you as crazy as theirs do, especially when their adult teeth are coming in, around four months of age. The trick here is to redirect the behavior by keeping things you don't want your puppy to chew on out of reach and by giving her approved chews and praising her for using them.

One of the oldest pieces of pet advice in the world is to not give your puppy things that are *like* the objects you want her to leave alone. In other words, don't give her your old slippers to chew on and expect her to leave your new ones alone.

Some objects — like table legs and, in the case of one puppy I raised, walls — are not capable of being picked up and put away. Discourage chewing on these by applying Bitter Apple (available in pet-supply stores) to favorite spots — the taste is so horrible your puppy won't put a tongue on it again. Tabasco sauce is another petstopper.

Remember that puppies *must* chew. If you catch yours chewing on something you don't want her to, don't make a big deal out of it. Throw a sharp "no" at her to distract her, give her an approved toy, and cue her by giving her a word to associate, like "chewbaby." Then praise her for using it.

Never give a puppy free run of the house, allowing her to make her own decisions on what is and isn't chewable. If you cannot observe her, put her in a safe area — a crate, ideally, but also a small area like a laundry porch with a baby gate across the door. Make sure that you leave a chew toy or two!

Think cool when it comes to puppy's painful gums. I like to take a piece of beef leg bone (trimmed of fat) and put it in the freezer before giving it to a teething puppy. I look for clean shanks and have the butcher cut them into four-inch pieces, so the marrow can be chewed out. Alternately, look for sterilized bones at the pet-supply store, stuff the inside with a little peanut butter, and chill. The indestructible Kong dog toy — truly a pet toy Hall of Famer — can likewise be stuffed with peanut butter and chilled.

Improper greetings: sniffing and jumping

What do dogs do when they meet? They touch noses and then check out each other's privates. Doing so is natural, normal, and unstoppable canine greeting behavior, and yet we *insist* our dogs do not use it on us. We don't want dogs who stick their noses in people's crotches, and we don't want dogs who jump up to touch our noses. The former we consider merely disgusting; the latter could be downright dangerous, with children or people who are unsteady on their feet.

Of course it's not your dog's fault that he was born unprepared to deal with a species who prefers a handshake to a butt-sniff, and whose noses are so far off the ground you just *have* to jump to be friendly!

These problems are fixed by redirection and consistency. When your puppy jumps up, throw a sharp "no" at her, followed by the command "off," and then "sit." If that doesn't do the trick, hold your puppy's paws and squeeze until it's uncomfortable, giving the "off" command just as her paws head for the floor. How much pressure? You'll know the right amount when she drops to the floor — she'll give in before you can hurt her, I promise.

You may find it easier to put your puppy on her leash and invite a guest over. It's a simple matter then to give the correction word "no," the command "off," and pull the puppy sharply off your guest, quickly asking for a "sit" and then praising.

Consistency is the bigger problem here, I've found. People let puppies get away with jumping up and sniffing because they're *puppies,* so cute and so small. But remember they don't stay small for long, and making sure that your 20-pound Lab puppy never gets in the habit of jumping up is a lot easier than convincing your 70-pound, full-grown Lab to knock it off.

Barking

Some breeds and breed types are noisier than others. Terriers and poodles and Shelties can be truly obnoxious yappers, and it doesn't help that even reputable breeders think nothing of breeding the worst barkers if their appearance closely matches the standard for their breed. For hounds, *giving voice* is a thing of beauty to connoisseurs, but not so widely appreciated by neighbors of a suburban beagle whose melodious baying is a constant annoyance.

Still, a lot of barking is trained into by owners who aren't thinking about what they're doing when raising their puppy. Puppy barks for attention, owners pick him up. Puppy barks for toy, or treat, and gets it. A friend of mine "discovered" that the only way to quiet her golden was to give her a dog biscuit — and ended up with a nonstop barking problem and a very fat dog.

Realize that you can never turn a yappy breed into a hush puppy, but you *can* teach him to turn off the noise on command. When he barks, issue a sharp "no," the command "quiet" or "hush," and then praise him for quieting. *Never* yell at a puppy who's barking — he'll think you're joining in, too. A squirt in the kisser — discussed earlier in this chapter — can also be a good correction for barking.

By all means don't teach him to bark by rewarding him for the behavior. If he's barking for attention, to get out of his crate, for a toy, whatever, tell him "no" then "hush" before picking him up, letting him out, or giving him his toy. Better still: "hush" and "sit." A dog who sits for what he wants is a lot nicer to live with than one who barks for it.

More on barking problems and solutions is in Chapter 12.

Nipping and biting

Nipping and biting is serious, serious stuff, and you need to take it that way. Like jumping up and sniffing privates, dogs display this behavior naturally with each other, roughhousing with teeth fully — but gently — in play. That's fine for playing with dogs, but not for playing with people — our skin's a lot more tender, without a protective layer of fur. Puppies need to learn it's *never, ever* appropriate to use teeth on a human being. Not in play. Not ever.

All puppies nip, but some are worse than others. Those who were removed from their litters too young may never have learned how much those little teeth hurt and may be more inclined to use them than a puppy who was allowed to stay with his littermates for at least seven weeks. You can get this point across to the youngest puppies in the same way their littermates do — by crying out sharply and dramatically when those needle teeth touch your skin.

For some puppies, that may be enough. For others, you need to do more. Correctly *sharply* with a "no" for nipping, stop play *immediately,* and put her in her crate to think about it for a while. For more dominant puppies, a scruff-shake may be needed in addition.

If you can't seem to stop your puppy from nipping and biting — and especially if the behavior is accompanied by growling — consult a trainer *right away.* Private consultation early on can prevent a tragedy later.

Keeping puppies from growing up aggressive

Aggression is a complicated problem for dog trainers and behaviorists and a serious public-health threat. Dogs bite because of fear, pain, dominance, and predation.

Despite statements by the owner to the contrary, bites almost never come out of the blue. They are almost always preceded by lots of warning signs that pet owners either overlook, misinterpret, or make excuses for. And sometimes encourage, taking pride in the "macho" behavior of their pet.

Puppies do not outgrow aggression. You must make sure, through training and socializing, that your pup understands every human is above him in the pack order and aggression to other dogs and predation upon smaller animals will *not* be tolerated.

Here are a few tips:

- Never let your puppy chew on you or other family members, even in play. Correct sternly and offer a chew toy, instead, or go to the time out, or scruff shake and time out, for more serious infractions.

- Never let children and puppies play unsupervised, and never let them roughhouse like littermates. Instead of tug-of-war, teach your children to play fetch with your puppy.

- Make sure that every member of the family acts as "leader." Teach your puppy manners such as sitting for his dish and then have everyone practice.

- Teach your puppy that humans control the food. Have every member of the family add food to the puppy's dish while he's eating so he learns to tolerate activity near his food. Correct sternly for growling.

- Practice taking away and returning toys to your puppy. Give the command "give" then take the toy and praise him for obeying.

- Have your puppy neutered. Young, unneutered males are most likely to be involved in a serious bite incident than any other kind of dog.

- Get a trainer's or behaviorist's help if you even *suspect* you have a problem, the sooner the better. A professional can help you see ways in which you are encouraging aggression and help you to reorder pack structure to eliminate it.

Please note: These rules apply to puppies only. If you've got a grown dog with aggression problems, go right to the last step and bring in a trainer to help sort out the situation before a tragedy occurs.

Working through the Rough Spots

Welcome to the canine equivalent of junior high, that oftentimes challenging period between the ages of three and six months, with growing proceeding one spurt after another, hormones raging, and your puppy's brain seemingly rewiring itself before your eyes. Some dogs, like some kids, go through a stage where they seem to be growing in the most awkward of ways — back legs longer than the front, bodies too long or too short. Your dog will emerge from the *puppy uglies,* of course, but at times you may doubt it.

Age three to six months is an awkward but important time in a puppy's life.

Photo courtesy of Randy Pench.

Other times you'll wish an ugly puppy is all you had to worry about. The canine phenomenon who learned to "sit" at 11 weeks — and was *soooo* proud of himself for doing so — may now give you a blank look as if he has never heard the word *sit* before, much less what you expect of him when you say it. Or maybe he recognizes the word just fine, thanks, but has something he'd rather do more than whatever it is *you* want.

Which is not to say your puppy becomes a complete heathen during this period. Sometimes he's just wonderful, sometimes not. This time is difficult for him, too, after all. His adult teeth are coming in, and they're driving him crazy — and you, too, with all the chewing he wants to do to feel better. You may even notice he seems tentative and shy for a week or so at a time — think of your first junior high dance to help you relate.

Your puppy's behavior is perfectly normal, but your behavior can mean the beginning of the end for your relationship. No matter how much he's driving you crazy, you must continue to socialize and train your puppy. Even if nothing seems to be getting through at times. If you give up at the first sign of trouble, you'll have more trouble later: This stage is when bad habits can really settle in.

Remember above all that *this, too, shall pass.* At the end of this period, your pup will reach sexual maturity and become — gasp! — the canine equivalent of a *teenager!*

Chapter 7

Puppy Veterinary Care

- -

In This Chapter

▶ Puppy's first trip to the veterinarian

▶ Shots and wormings

▶ Elective procedures

▶ Puppy birth control

- -

*I*n the years I've been writing about pets and their care, I've gained a great deal of respect for veterinarians. Consider the challenge of diagnosing and treating illnesses for several different species when you can't even ask the patient where it hurts! Fortunately, the majority of other pet lovers appreciate the role of a good veterinarian in ensuring the best possible life for their dogs. (A 1995 study by the American Animal Hospital Association survey revealed that nine of ten dog owners made sure their dogs receive regular checkups and vaccinations.)

When you first get a puppy, you need to become part of the group that gives their dogs regular care — the veterinarian is an important part in any plan to raise a happy, healthy dog.

The veterinary information in this section concerns topics that apply *only* to puppies. For more on health-care issues that pertain to all dogs — as well as on choosing the right veterinarian — see Chapter 10.

Developing a Healthy Relationship

A puppy is a big investment in time and emotion, and often in money as well. That's why you should take your new family member to see the veterinarian within a day or so of adoption to make sure that everything checks out. Better still, make your puppy's passing a health check a condition before you agree to buy or adopt.

What if your pet has already been examined by the seller or shelter's staff? See your veterinarian anyway to be sure of your pup's good health. The price is not much to pay for peace of mind, and the visit could prevent a lot of problems down the road.

Keep your heart in check until your pup gets clearance from your veterinarian. If you've dealt with a reputable source, everything should check out just fine. Be prepared to return your pup if your veterinarian finds something serious enough to warrant doing so. No, doing so is not easy. But the purpose of getting a dog is to have a happy, healthy companion, and if the puppy you've chosen isn't going to be, you need to consider finding another.

Puppy's First Veterinary Exam

Your puppy's first trip to the veterinarian is almost as much about educating you as checking out the puppy. Besides your many questions and concerns, you should bring two things with your puppy to the first exam. The first is whatever health information the seller or shelter provided to you, such as records of vaccinations and wormings. The second is a fresh stool, which is examined for the presence of parasites.

While answering your questions, your veterinarian will likely do the following:

- ✔ Weigh your puppy and check her temperature — 100 to 102.5 degrees Fahrenheit is normal — as well as her pulse and breathing rate.
- ✔ Listen for heart and lung abnormalities and examine other internal organs by *palpating,* or feeling them.
- ✔ Give your puppy's ears a going-over to ensure they not only look right but also *smell* right — no infections or parasites.
- ✔ Check the puppy's genitals to ensure two testicles are present in males and there's no sign of discharge or infection in females.
- ✔ Go over eyes, nose, skin, and the anal region carefully to check for discharge or other signs of disease or parasites.
- ✔ Open the puppy's mouth to see that teeth and gums look as they should.

A puppy exam is one of the best parts of a veterinarian's job, and she works to keep it fun for the puppy as well. She wants to set up a relationship where your puppy accommodates being handled without fear or aggression. You are an important part of this learning process. Do not encourage shyness or aggression in your puppy by soothing her. Be positive and matter-of-fact in all your pup's social interactions in order to raise a confident, secure dog.

My, what big teeth you have!

You will be delighted to see those sharp little puppy teeth replaced by adult teeth by the age of four months — going from 28 deciduous teeth to 42 permanent ones. But problems can occur.

Sometimes baby teeth are retained after the adult ones come in, a situation that can cause many problems, including the misalignment of permanent teeth, incorrect development of the jaw, and infections. Check your puppy's mouth weekly while adult teeth are erupting to ensure the baby teeth aren't being retained — a double row of teeth, especially in the front, tells you they are.

Have your veterinarian check out any suspicious developments. Retained baby teeth need to be surgically removed.

Because your puppy's immunity against disease is not yet like that of an adult dog, be sure to carry your puppy into the veterinary hospital, and don't let her interact with other dogs. Inside the exam room, the veterinary staff takes precautions to protect your pet, such as cleaning off the exam table with disinfectants and washing their hands between patients.

The cheat sheet at the front of this book gives the signs of a veterinary emergency. You're sure to have at least one urgent trip to the veterinarian's while raising your puppy — most people do — so make sure that you know what you should look for.

Well-Puppy Care

After your veterinarian has determined that your puppy is healthy, she offers ways to keep him that way. A good veterinarian schedules enough time to reassure you about every puppy hiccup while explaining preventive care, primarily vaccinations, parasite control, and spaying and neutering.

Ask your veterinarian about *puppy plans* or other packages that save you money over purchasing services individually. Such a plan may include examinations, all shots and necessary wormings, heartworm tests, and even spaying and neutering.

Puppy shots?

Vaccines are one of the most common reasons pets visit a veterinarian, but they're one of the least understood areas of pet health care. Most people don't even know what they're vaccinating their pets against, much less how often those vaccinations are needed. See the cheat sheet at the front of this book for some guidelines.

Puppy shots and boosters — covering five to seven diseases, depending on the part of the country and the individual veterinarian's recommendation — are weakened doses of the very diseases they protect against, and they're placed in an animal to teach the immune system to recognize and destroy a stronger attack of the disease. The system works because of *antibodies,* the body's warrior particles that surround and destroy viral and bacterial intruders.

A healthy immune system gives grown dogs a fighting chance against disease, but even seemingly strong puppies lack that ability.

Puppies are initially protected from disease by antibodies passed to them through their mother's milk. While this protection declines in the first few weeks of a puppy's life, it interferes with the preventive-care benefits provided by vaccinations. Since it's not feasible to pinpoint the moment when a vaccination will be effective, puppies are given a series of shots over the first few weeks of their lives. Most veterinarians now recommend a series of at least four vaccinations at three-week intervals starting at the age of 6 to 8 weeks.

Often the breeder himself gives the puppy her first shot, and your veterinarian administers the rest. Sometimes a veterinarian repeats the first shot, if she feels it has been given too early or is in doubt that the breeder correctly handled the vaccines. For your pup's sake, follow through on your veterinarian's recommendations — if you stop at just one shot, you're leaving your puppy at risk for disease.

More on preventive care, including details on the diseases that vaccinations protect your pet against, is in Chapter 10.

Rabies prevention

The vaccine against rabies stands alone among preventive-care measures in that it is given as much to protect you as to protect your puppy. Once the signs of rabies are evident, the disease is fatal to both humans and animals, which is why pets are required by law to be vaccinated against the disease.

The greatest threat of rabies is from wild animals — bats, skunks, and raccoons, for example. Vaccinating domestic animals serves to create a barrier between wild animals and humans because, without vaccinations, pets are prime candidates to tangle with rabid wild animals and contract the disease.

Puppies receive their first rabies vaccine at 16 weeks of age and a booster one year after that. The vaccines can be good for three years thereafter, depending on the law where you live.

Parasite control

When people use the generic term *worms* in describing puppy parasites, they are usually talking about *roundworms,* or *ascarids*. That's because hardly a single puppy avoids being born infested with the pest. But puppies can also be plagued by other intestinal parasites such as *hookworms, whipworms, tape-worms,* and single-cell parasites such as *coccidia* and *giardia*.

Left untreated, intestinal parasites can stunt growth and weaken young animals. Worms also present a danger to humans — especially to children, who often aren't as careful around pets as adults are. As with most diseases transmitted from animals to humans — rabies being the most deadly exception — sensible sanitary measures such as keeping pet areas picked up and hands clean minimize the risk of transmission.

The cure for intestinal parasites is easy, if a little repetitious. First, the puppy's stools are examined for signs of infestation at the veterinary hospital, and your veterinarian then prescribes the appropriate drug to kill the parasites. Puppies should be wormed every two weeks from birth on, until a fecal examination reveals no sign of parasites.

Worming medication is available over the counter. The problem is, some intestinal worms and other parasite can be treated with medications available by prescription only. Treating your pet for worms he doesn't have is not a good idea; neither is mis-treating him for worms he does — while thinking that the medication you've purchased is doing the job.

The only way to be sure which parasites your puppy is carrying is to have his stool examined by a veterinarian.

The mosquito-transmitted heartworm is an internal parasite that's better prevented than treated, even though recent advances have made eliminating the pest safer for pets.

Puppies whose mothers were on preventive medication can continue on daily or monthly medication starting from about the time of your puppy's first exam. The preventives often contain medications to control intestinal parasites as well. For more information on heartworms, see Chapter 10.

Information on controlling external parasites, such as fleas and ticks, in Chapter 10.

Elective Procedures

Depending on your pup's breed, you may also wish to discuss a few nonessential surgeries to alter your puppy's appearance.

None of these procedures should be an automatic part of your puppy's first year. Consider the facts, and then make your own decision.

Tail docks and dewclaw removals

Many puppy buyers are not aware that breeds such as the Doberman or many of the terriers have their tails shortened (or *docked*) to a length dictated by their breed standard, or that the *dewclaw,* an unnecessary toe that's an evolutionary leftover, is often removed to give the leg a smoother look. If you purchase your puppy from a reputable breeder, either or both of these procedures may have already been done when the puppy was three to five days old. Some breeders are so skilled that they do the work themselves, with no apparent ill effect to the puppies, who recover quickly from the amputations.

While tail docking is sometimes performed for a medical reason, such as an injury to the tail, it is most commonly done to meet the appearance standards for the breed. Some advocates also tout the preventive value of docking, especially for hunting breeds, pointing out that a tail that isn't there is a tail that can't be injured. The logic is flawed, however: If injury prevention were the only issue, then *all* hunting breeds would be docked — and maybe all other dogs as well.

Tail dockings and dewclaw removals cause so little discomfort to three- to five-day-old puppies that they're usually performed without anesthesia. Both procedures are a little more complicated on older dogs, however, requiring anesthesia and post-operative care.

If your want your pup's tail docked and your breeder hasn't done it, be sure that your veterinarian is knowledgeable as to the correct length of tail for the breed. An incorrect dock may need to be done again, and a dock too short can take your pup out of the running if you hope to show him. If you do not intend to show your pup, I suggest that you leave his tail alone if it hasn't already been done.

A slightly stronger case can be made for the removal of dewclaws because injuries to them are common. It won't hurt to leave the dewclaws in place unless and until you do have a problem (these claws can occasionally get caught on objects), however. And if you do have a problem, you can have the dewclaws removed, ideally when your pet is spayed or neutered.

Ear crops

According to reputable veterinary authorities, the *only* purpose of *ear cropping* is to change a folded-over ear to an erect one, for the sake of appearance. Like tail docking, ear cropping is required for the show ring in a handful of breeds. In some other breeds, cropped ears are not mandated, but the lack of them makes winning in the show ring almost impossible.

Ear cropping entails slicing an anesthetized puppy's ear flap to a shape and length preferred for the particular breed and then bandaging what's left on splints or racks to heal. This procedure is not painless by any definition, although untold thousands of dogs have come through it with no apparent long-term psychological damage.

Ear cropping is by far the most controversial of the elected procedures. Many veterinarians who have no problem with tail docks or dewclaw removals do not crop ears, and some are lobbying the American Veterinary Medical Association to condemn the procedure.

In England and Germany, ear cropping is banned as cruel. No such laws exist today in the United States and Canada. As long as the breed clubs that write the standards insist on this practice, many pet owners will follow suit.

I urge you to *not* crop your puppy's ears. Cropping is a matter of tradition and familiarity, and the more uncropped dogs are seen and loved, the more comfortable others will be with leaving their puppy's ears alone. Perhaps in time, even the breed clubs that defend ear cropping so vigorously will relax on the issue — and this senseless tradition will fade away.

While experienced breeders can and do perform tail docks and dewclaw removals on very young puppies, under *no* condition should an ear crop be performed by anyone besides a veterinarian. Your breeder should be able to recommend a veterinarian who is knowledgeable about the look your particular breed requires, so be sure to ask her for a recommendation if you decide to have your puppy's ears cropped. Your veterinarian, too, may be able to refer you if he doesn't perform ear crops.

The Birds, the Bees, and Your Puppy

Male dogs are early bloomers, showing signs of sexual behavior — mounting and thrusting both male and female littermates — almost as soon as they can walk. While female puppies also mount their littermates, this behavior is not as frequent or as common. While it's all perfectly normal, correct your puppy from mounting people, because it's both a nuisance and a dominance challenge.

Females reach sexual maturity at different times, with small breeds attaining it more quickly than the largest ones. A dog's first *season, or heat,* — and the accompanying vaginal bleeding — can occur anytime from about six months to 24 months, although most dogs come into season for the first time before reaching their first birthday.

The point when males become fertile is not so obvious, but they are capable of enthusiastic reproduction from about six months onward.

Every year I get a few phone calls from puppy owners who are worried because their pet isn't lifting his leg. Male puppies start this scent-marking behavior — which some female dogs also do — as early as four months or so, but there are a lot of variables. A puppy who sees other male dogs lift their legs will likely start this behavior sooner, as may the dog who isn't neutered young.

Eventually, almost all male dogs lift their legs to leave their mark, although some are more enthusiastic about it than others. Some dogs stand on all fours to relieve themselves — leaning forward, but not really squatting as females do — and then lift their legs in a couple of places. Other dogs seem to believe that every drop of liquid they have is best deposited on a vertical object. All of this behavior is in the realm of normalcy and is nothing to worry about.

Don't panic if your female pup gets to her first birthday without showing signs of being in heat. You may have missed it. Some dogs bleed very little, or they keep themselves especially clean. Chances are if you have a male dog in your house or nearby you *know* when your dog's in heat, but if that's not the case, you may miss it entirely.

Talk to your breeder about the age when most of her females come in season. If nothing has happened by the time you go in to get your pet's annual vaccinations, make a note to discuss the matter with your veterinarian.

If you don't intend to show your pup, you both are better off if you arrange for spaying or neutering. The surgeries are common, one-day procedures with few risks of complications in young, healthy animals. For more on these routine procedures, see Chapter 13.

Early spaying and neutering

While spaying and neutering has traditionally been performed on puppies between the ages of four and six months, the procedure can be safely done at as early as eight weeks. If you adopt a puppy from an animal shelter, in fact, you may find that the operation has already been done — as a preventive measure to keep pets from reproducing. Some reputable breeders also have their pet-quality puppies spayed or neutered before they go to new homes.

What age should *your* puppy be spayed or neutered? The traditional six months is still fine. Earlier is fine, too; in fact, veterinary organizations have given their full approval to the early procedure. Some veterinarians are not comfortable operating on the youngest puppies, however, and if this is the case, follow your vet's recommendation.

Chapter 8

House-Training Puppies (And Dogs)

Dog training has changed a great deal in the last couple of decades, and in no area is this more true than that of *house-training*.

For generations house-training was done almost by the process of elimination, if you'll pardon the pun. The puppy-owner screamed when she found a mess, dragged the puppy over, shoved his nose in it, and swatted him. "Well! I can't go there!" thought the puppy, who was also thinking that this newspaper-wielding crazy woman was really not the nicest of people. Eventually, the puppy figured out the place where he *wouldn't* get punished for going — by accident, as much as anything else.

Maybe he got over the idea that his owner was dangerous, maybe not, but one thing for certain: House-training was a nasty business for all.

Today's training methods are kinder, faster, and less messy. And for that, you can thank both a shift to training by positive reinforcement and the widespread use of the crate.

Things are so different now that even the vocabulary has started to change. The battle-of-wills sound of the term *housebreaking* is now frequently replaced by trainers with the more positive term, *house-training*. And so it is in this book. You don't want to *break* your puppy or dog, ever. *Training* — consistent and positive — is the key.

A Positive Approach

In recent years, the use of a crate to house-train puppies and dogs has become standard among knowledgeable trainers and breeders. Crate-training allows you to shape your puppy's potty behavior by limiting his options to three. During training he's either

- ✔ "On empty" and playing loose under your supervision
- ✔ Relieving himself, where you choose
- ✔ Confined to his crate

Confined to his crate? Isn't that cruel? For you, maybe, and for me. But you have to look at things from a dog's point of view. Dogs appreciate the idea of a *den,* a small area they can call their own, in which they can feel perfectly safe. Their wild cousins raise their young in dens, and domesticated dogs still instinctively prefer areas that remind them of a den. Like the "cave" behind the sofa. And like a crate.

How much do dogs hate crates? I wish you could ask dogs that question. In my house two crates are set up permanently in the TV room — the larger one functions as an end table. The doors are always open, and there are always dogs inside — by choice. Any experienced dog person will tell you the same story. *Dogs like crates.*

Another instinct is at work in using a crate for house-training. Because a den would quickly become unusable if its inhabitants messed in it, a dog is predisposed to keep his sleeping area clean. His mother teaches him this lesson when he's little by eating — disgusting, but true — the messes her puppies produce. Later, her puppies learn to eliminate outside of their den, as she does. Which is why your puppy will avoid messing in his crate, if he can help it — and you can help make his success possible.

These complementary instincts — the desire to use a den and the wish to keep it clean — form the basis of house-training by using a crate. A crate encourages your puppy to "hold it" until you can take him to the place where you wish him to relieve himself. And once there, you can attach a "command word" to his relieving himself — and then praise him for obeying. Positive reinforcement. Fewer messes. What could be better?

Why would you want a dog to "go on command"? The owners of city dogs are probably ahead of me here: Because if you can communicate to your puppy that it's time to get down to business, you spend a whole lot less time outside. Your pet knows what's expected — and does it! A dog who eliminates on command is also a lot easier to travel with, and walk with, too, because *you* can pick the time and the place for him to relieve himself, pick up his mess, and get on with your lives. "Hurry Up" is the command I use, but you can use anything you aren't embarrassed to say in public. "Do your ootsie-bootsie puppy poo!" isn't something I'd pick, but if you can stand it, that's your business.

I *guarantee* you house-training is faster, neater, and easier with a crate. If you use one for nothing else — for travel, say — buy or borrow one for the first few weeks of puppy-raising. Chances are you'll recover the cost of the crate in things your puppy *doesn't* ruin — but would have ruined without a crate. For information on the size and type of crate that's right for your dog, see Chapter 4.

Puppies naturally want to eliminate away from sleeping and eating areas, but some are raised in ways that make that impossible. Puppies who can't avoid their messes — such as those raised in a puppy mill or other substandard breeding facility — get so used to the sensation of standing in filth that they can be exceptionally difficult to house-train. You may need to hire a trainer or behaviorist to help you with the task. Tips on where to find one are in Chapter 11.

Your puppy naturally wants to "go" away from her sleeping and eating areas — and you can choose the place.

Photo courtesy of Richard D. Schmidt.

Whatever kind of food you end up feeding — a discussion of food is in Chapter 4 — feed a high-quality kibble during house-training and nothing else. Canned foods are high in water, and other foods aren't as efficiently digested, and so don't produce small, neat stools that are easier for a puppy to hold as he learns what's expected of him. (Neat stools are easier to clean up, too.) Changing foods or adding table scraps may give your pet diarrhea, and that is guaranteed to be both a training set-back *and* a mess.

Easy clean-ups

When accidents occur, you must clean them up promptly and thoroughly, and not just because doing so is better for your carpets. Dogs are attracted to sites of past accidents and will keep soiling the area if they can. Even if you clean up all visible signs of the mess, enough smell may remain to keep the area attractive to your dog. Here are a few tips on mess clean-up:

✔ **Don't use ammonia-based cleaners.** They smell like urine to a puppy — ammonia being one of the by-products of decomposing urine. So instead of making the area smell clean, ammonia products make a mess site seem even *more* attractive.

✔ **Use products designed for pet mess clean-up.** These liquid products contain enzymes that break down the waste and neutralize odor. Crystallized products work well, too, by absorbing the liquid in a few minutes so that you can vacuum the mess up.

You can also make a fairly effective cleaner for a fresh urine accident with water, white vinegar, and a gentle soap such as Ivory. Dog-lover Anne Cotton of Massachusetts has a recipe I've used with good results: One quart hot water from the faucet, one teaspoon Ivory, one teaspoon white vinegar (it neutralizes the odor). Shake a bit. Blot the area with paper towels, and then wet with the cleaner to cover — but not enough to soak the area. Let it sit 15 minutes, then blot again. Finally, follow with a disinfectant spray.

✔ **Clean up the area as soon as possible.** Do this before the mess has a chance to soak through to carpet padding, where getting the smell out is very hard. Once the urine soaks through, you have to pull up the carpet to ensure that the area's truly clean.

✔ **Search for and destroy old stains.** Even if you can't smell anything, old stains may still have a lingering odor that can attract your puppy. Pet-supply outlets offer black lights that show old messes you may not be able to see. Veterinarians and trainers sometimes have these available for rent. Enzyme cleaners will do the best on old stains, but you may need to treat the area a couple of times.

When your puppy's completely house-trained, you'll most likely want to have the carpets cleaned; but, if you are diligent during the training period, you'll probably end up with no permanent stains. Keep clean-up supplies on hand, though, because accidents and illnesses occur throughout your dog's life.

A Puppy Potty Strategy

Crate-training limits a puppy's options and sets the stage for training that uses positive reinforcement. Puppies need to relieve themselves after they wake up, eat or drink, or after a period of play. Set up a schedule to accommodate his needs — puppies can't go very long without eating, drinking, sleeping, or relieving themselves — as you work to mold behavior.

You may well end up *free-feeding* your pet when he's a grown dog; that is, leaving food out at all times. I don't recommend it, however, because free-feeding prevents you from spotting some potential health problems and denies you the ability to use food as a tool for enforcing your status as "boss." You do, however, need to have water constantly available to your pet.

When you're house-training a puppy, however, you need to regulate both food *and* water. That's because if your puppy is eating and drinking constantly, he's going to need to relieve himself constantly, and that makes house-training very difficult. For the first couple of months a puppy needs to eat three times a day — before you go to work, at lunch, and as soon as you come home in the evening. By the time the puppy's four months old, he should be nearly house-trained and you can switch to two meals a day and an always-available supply of water.

If at all possible, come home, beg a neighbor, or pay a pet-sitter to come in at lunch during the first couple of months. Your puppy's *social* development will survive without a midday break — assuming you adopt an ideal schedule on the weekends, and make up for the lost opportunities for socialization. He will *not* make it through the day without relieving himself, however, and that will set your training back.

If you have to leave your puppy alone all day, be fair: You'll have to set his crate up with the door open and access to water and food and to a small area covered with newspapers.

When you come home, you'll find a mess. Clean it up without comment, because it's not your puppy's fault.

Here's an idea of what your puppy's ideal schedule should look like:

- **First thing in the morning:** Take your puppy out of the crate and coax him to follow you outside to the spot you have chosen for him to relieve himself. If he starts to relieve himself on the trip outside, give him a firm "no" and take him to the *potty zone* in your yard. Give the command you've chosen — "hurry up," "do it," or whatever — and praise him for going. Take him inside and give him food and water, and then go outside again immediately — a full tummy puts pressure on a puppy's bladder — give the command and praise him when he goes.

  If you're going to work, put him back in the crate. If you're not going to work, let him play for a couple of hours, but don't give him full run of the house. Close doors or use baby gates to keep him where you can see him, such as in a kitchen/family room area. After an hour or two take him outside again, and repeat the command and praise. He'll be ready for a little nap, so put him in his crate until lunchtime.

✔ **The midday break:** Take your puppy out of the crate and head outside for another round of command, relieve, and praise for a job well done. Then back inside for food and water. Then back outside.

- If you're home on your lunch hour, play with him a little before you put him back in his crate.

- If you're going to be home with him, leave him out to play where you are, under your watchful eye. Take him out in mid-afternoon, and then crate him for his afternoon nap.

✔ **Dinnertime:** Same as at midday. Take him out, feed him, take him out, and let him play. Leave him out for play and socializing, in an area where you can watch him. Offer him a little water a couple hours before bedtime, but no more food.

✔ **Bedtime:** One last trip outside. You may be tired and cranky at this point, but don't let your puppy know it. Be *consistent:* Give your command, and after your puppy does what you want, praise like the dickens. Then bring your little genius inside and put him in his crate for the night. If he doesn't relieve himself within a few minutes, put him in his crate anyway. You'll be up again, soon enough.

✔ **Middle of the night:** If it makes you feel better, dealing with a puppy is not as difficult as dealing with a human baby. But for the first week or so, you may also have to add a wee hours outing. Sometimes you have to do that when your puppy's a little older, too, because he is so busy exploring that he doesn't get around to relieving himself. If he sleeps through the night — roughly defined as after the 11 o'clock news until the alarm clock goes off for work at 6:30 the next morning, then fine. But if he wakes up and fusses at 3 a.m., put your shoes on — you're taking him out.

House-training without a crate

Of course house-training without a crate is possible — it's just harder, more time-consuming, and messier. You still should use a positive approach, though.

Keep your puppy where you can keep an eye on him — and keep him in a small, safe area when you cannot. Baby gates are ideal both for keeping a puppy near you and creating an area for him to stay in while you are gone. Unlike a solid door, which isolates and upsets him, a baby gate allows him to see and hear and smell his family.

Use the same schedule (described earlier in this chapter) for going out — first thing in the morning, after play and eating, at lunch, dinner, and last thing at night — give your command and praise, praise, praise for going in the right place.

Because you are keeping a closer eye on your puppy, you can tell when he's making "gotta go" motions — sniffing and circling — and can whisk him outside. Other times you won't be fast enough. If you catch him, say "no" sternly, and then take him outside to finish the job. Clean up the area thoroughly and without comment.

The older a puppy gets, the longer he can "hold it." For the youngest, six to eight weeks, three or fours hours is about the limit. Up until three or fours months, five to six hours is the limit. By the time a puppy has reached six months of age, he should be able to hold out for the same amount of time as an adult dog — up to nine hours while you're at work.

These are all estimates, of course, but they give you an idea of what's reasonable for your puppy.

House-Training the Adult Dog

The first step in turning an adult dog into a reliable house pet is for you to embrace a key concept:

There's no such thing as a "partially" house-trained dog. He either is, or he isn't.

Why is realizing this concept important? Because if you have a dog who is "sometimes" reliable you have a dog who really isn't getting the picture, probably because no one took the time to teach it to him properly in the first place. To do that, you're going to have to go back to square one.

Before you do, though, make sure you're not dealing with two problems that usually aren't a factor when you're house-training a puppy:

- **Illness.** If you have a dog who was perfectly house-trained and is no longer, you *must* be sure that what you have really is a behavior problem and not a physical problem. So check with your veterinarian, first. To be fair, if you've just adopted an adult dog who seems to be urinating several times a day, you should have her checked out, too, before assuming she's not house-trained. She may have a bladder infection or other medical difficulty.

- **Leg-lifting.** If your male dog is marking in the house — but defecating and also doing some urinating outside, your best chance at fixing this problem is to neuter him and put him on a regimen that will help to convince him that he doesn't run the show in your house. See the "Establish a Routine" section in Chapter 9, and start training basic obedience to establish your role as boss. Another must: Aggressively and thoroughly clean any area your dog soils; if you don't, the smell will bring him back.

Leg-lifting in the house can be a very difficult to cure, since it's tied to dominant behavior. If you're getting nowhere with a leg-lifter — and especially if you're having other problems with potentially aggressive behaviors — see Chapter 11 for more on this — call in a trainer or behaviorist.

What about paper-training?

Letting your puppy relieve himself on newspapers is really only practical if your dog is very small, since the volume of waste makes paper-training an unsavory option for large dogs.

Sometimes people make the task of house-training much harder by insisting on using papers as if they were the first step. If you don't need papers, don't start using them. Take your puppy or dog outside from the first day.

If you choose to use newspapers (you have a small dog in a city apartment, for example)

training your pet to relieve himself on newspapers is done the same way as training him to go outside — take him to the newspapers, give your "go" command and praise him when he does the deed. You must remember, however, that once a pet is trained to use newspapers, he has to be *retrained* to go outdoors Retraining is not that big a deal — just follow the directions I give earlier in this chapter — but you can't expect him to figure it out on his own.

If you've ruled out medical problems and you haven't got a leg-lifter, house-training an adult dog uses the same principals as house-training a puppy, except you have to be even more diligent because you need to do some *untraining,* too.

You need to teach your dog what's right, though, before you can correct him for what's wrong. To do this, spend two weeks ensuring that he has nothing but successes by never giving him the opportunity to make a mistake. Here's how:

- ✔ Leash him to you in the house so you can monitor his every move during his training period. If he starts to mess, correct him with a sharp "no," take him outside, give your "go" command and praise him for doing right.

- ✔ Crate him whenever he's not on leash with you. A grown dog can wait a lot longer than a puppy in a crate, and it's not unfair to leave him in one for four or five hours at a stretch — assuming, of course, that he's getting his regular exercise. If you go to work, you can leave him in the crate with a couple of chew toys to keep him busy and a radio playing to keep him company.

- ✔ Take him outside first thing in the morning, as soon as you get home from work, and just before you go to bed (when you put him in his crate for the night). *Always* remember to give your "go" command, and *praise* when he does as you wish.

The most difficult part of house-training an adult dog is your attitude toward limiting his options in such a way as to make success possible. And that means a crate and a leash. People seem able to accept a crate more with puppies —

perhaps because they enjoy the respite they gain when their little terror is confined. You may not like the idea of crating your adult dog as much, but bear in mind that you won't need to do it forever. But you need to do it for now.

If you've been consistent, your dog likely has a good idea of what's expected of him at the end of the two weeks, and so you can start to give him a little freedom. Don't let him have the run of the house yet: Keep his area small and let him earn the house, room by room, as he proves his understanding of the house rules.

Accidents happen. If you catch him, correct him with a sharp "no," take him outside and give him the chance to set things right. Give your "go" command, and praise if he does. Clean up the mess promptly and thoroughly, so he won't feel so inclined to refresh his smell there. If you aren't catching him, you're not keeping close enough tabs on him: Go back to the crate and leash and start over.

Consistency and patience are necessary for house-training an adult dog. If you have both, you're likely to succeed. Without them, you may have a very difficult time getting the results you hope for.

The "mistake" that isn't

Your pet seems to be flaunting his bad behavior. He comes up to you and piddles, right in front of you! Don't lose your temper: Your dog is acting out of fear and trying to placate you with a classic canine show of submission.

Trainers and behaviorists call this behavior *submissive urination,* and it's something another dog would recognize as a show of respect to a more dominant member of the pack. In many cases, this display is offered to the man of the house — usually the biggest member of the family and the one with the deepest voice.

If you punish your pet for this behavior, you're making yourself seem even more powerful — and making matters worse.

A puppy or dog who has this problem is very sensitive and lacks confidence. Recognize that submissive urination is not a house-training problem: It's a relationship problem. This puppy needs gentle obedience training and lots of encouragement to understand that while you're indeed the boss, you're a kind and benevolent one.

Don't punish your pet for submissive urination. As you work to develop a loving and trusting relationship with your puppy, his confidence will grow, and his fear will decrease along with submissive urination.

Chapter 9

Adopting an Adult Dog

- -

In This Chapter

▶ Evalutating the kinds of adult dogs available

▶ Deciding how to pick the right dog for you

▶ Getting the relationship started right

▶ Managing introductions

▶ Forming a sure, tight bond

- -

*W*e tend to be so nostalgic that it's sometimes hard to believe that the "good old days" weren't always so hot. That's certainly true when it comes to dogs. Societal attitudes have changed, in many cases for the better.

Not very long ago, the experts were adamantly against adopting a grown dog. If you adopted a puppy, you could train him the way you wanted to, the thinking went, and the puppy would bond to your family more closely than a fully grown dog.

No doubt a puppy offers more of a clean slate than the sometimes sadder-but-wiser, older dog, but a grown dog offers many advantages, especially for someone who hasn't the time or the experience to raise a puppy properly. And as for bonding, let me assure you that you won't find any difference. If anything, I sometimes believe a dog adopted as an adult seems *more* dedicated, because he knows what being without people who love him is like.

As with puppies, however, you want to learn a little bit about adult dogs, and take your time in selecting one.

Grown dogs, like puppies, come from many sources — shelters, private parties, breeders of all kinds, and breed-rescue groups. Some dogs walk in to your life as strays. To learn more about various sources for finding a dog, see Chapter 3.

The Adult Dog Defined

The break between puppyhood and adulthood is at sexual maturity, which is a far cry, as is true with humans, from emotional and physical maturity. For most dogs, sexual maturity happens somewhere around six months of age, a time when the once roly-poly pup already appears a gangly adolescent. Although different puppies mature at different rates — small ones "grow up" more quickly than large ones — a dog isn't really an adult until sometime between 18 months and two years, the time when the difficult "teen" stage finally ends and your dog settles down — if you've raised him right, that is — into the companion you were dreaming of.

A dog's time at the peak of his abilities varies, too, according to his breeding. Giant breeds such as the Irish Wolfhound start aging as early as four or five, while a small breed like the Chihuahua won't start slowing down until after 10 or even 12 years. Dogs in the medium-to-large size range have six or seven years of prime adult life — but you can greatly extend those years by providing your pet with proper veterinary care, nutrition, and exercise (discussed elsewhere in this book).

While adult dogs of all ages become available for adoption, convincing people to take a dog over two is often difficult. Over five is even harder, and over ten — forget it! And that's unfortunate, because the dog over two is often an easier

Adult dogs can make wonderful pets.

Photo courtesy of the HSUS.

animal to work into your family, and dogs over five — or even ten! — can be wonderful, calm pets with a great deal of high-quality life still ahead of them.

In case you didn't catch my subtle endorsement, let me spell it out: *Don't rule out a dog because of her age.*

When I was volunteering for Sheltie rescue in my area, we often had prospective adopters who initially insisted they didn't want a dog more than a year old. It's almost as if they thought they were dealing with a used car, with newer models being more "valuable" than older ones. This thinking is simply not the case in dogs — or humans, of course. After some convincing, we placed many older dogs into homes that initially wouldn't consider them. Two of these dogs — a 7-year-old named Spencer and a 9-year-old named Major — live in my neighborhood, and I can report that they both blossomed into perfect companions in their respective families and are still going strong years later.

Strike a blow for ageism! You may end up with a better dog as a result.

The canine adolescent

Most adult dogs available for adoption are young ones, for a couple of reasons. One is that shelters with limited space put out the dogs with the greatest chance of being adopted. People want young dogs, so that's what shelters tend to offer. Older dogs too often go straight to the euthanasia room, unless they've charmed the staffers into giving them a chance with their beauty or good manners. (**Note:** This unhappy situation is *not* the shelter's fault. The shelter's staff didn't bring these dogs into the world, and they're not the people making them homeless. They're just coping as best they can. Maybe if adopters were more interested in older dogs, shelters would be, too.)

Adolescent dogs are also in abundance because dogs just beyond puppyhood are the most likely to be dumped for some of the following reasons:

- ✔ **Bad fit.** Because all puppies are adorable, people easily forget to think about what they're going to have when their sweet little fuzzball grows up. About the time a pup reaches physical maturity is when her owners first realize they've taken on more than they can handle and recognize that they ended up with a dog that's too big, too active, or too dominant for them.

- ✔ **Poor upbringing.** Puppies grow up too fast, and too many people put off until tomorrow the socializing and training they should do today. These birds come home to roost during adolescence, when people end up with an out-of-control dog who's a nuisance — and possibly a danger. Lots of these overgrown puppies just need a little work, some basic obedience, and problem-solving, but that's more than many people want to bother with.

✔ **Novelty wears off.** The very cuteness that keeps people from strangling puppies doesn't protect the formerly fuzzy when they get a little older. Gangly and out-of-proportion, with thin coats you can practically see through, these ugly ducklings show little sign of the swans they'll one day become. And that's not the only problem: The kids that begged for a pup and promised to care for him are now more interested in video games, the parents get tired of nagging, and the dog is suddenly shelter-bound.

Does this mean you should avoid an adolescent dog? Not at all. But you should know that they're bound to be a little more high-spirited and distractible than a mature adult of two or more. An adolescent dog still has some growing up to do, and you're going to need to put some extra effort in to help turn a doggie teen into the pet you want.

Young adults

Dogs who have matured into adulthood and are in their prime years are among your better choices when looking for a pet to adopt. If you choose carefully, you can find a nearly flawless dog here, calm and sensible, sometimes with basic obedience training. Of course, you can also find a dog who's settled into some very bad habits, which is why you should take your time and not let love at first sight or a sad story affect your decision.

Reputable breeders or other serious dog-sports competitors sometimes have dogs in this age group, animals they've raised with the highest of hopes and the utmost of effort. At the age of two or three, though, their owners realize some of these dogs aren't the world-beaters they once thought they were. Instead of leaving them to languish in a kennel run while the next crop of hopefuls get the special attention and training, breeders often prefer to spay or neuter them and find a home where they can be the only one, not one of many.

These dogs are the canine equivalent of the cherry red '67 Mustang convertible driven only on Sundays by the proverbial little old lady from Pasadena. A real find, in other words, and at a price usually comparable to a puppy from the same reputable breeder. It's a great deal, all around.

"Senior" dogs

Why take a chance on an older dog? Because it's the right thing to do. And because he may be perfect for you. And because counting a dog out because he may have a couple less years to spend with you is not fair.

My favorite example of why an adult dog should not be counted out comes from some friends of mine who adopted a collie of about eight years old. The collie died a few years later and, when she did, the friend told me she was the most wonderful dog she'd ever owned. Consider this: The five years that family had with that dog were wonderful, perfect, even. Fifteen with another may not have been so special. So consider quality, not just quantity. And figure you get extra points toward an afterlife for giving a special dog a chance.

One group of people older dogs are perfect for is older people! Many seniors would like a dog as a companion, but are afraid of what would happen to their pet should he outlive them. An older, sweet-natured, small dog is a perfect match for such a person, easing his worries and providing him with love and companionship. An added bonus: An older dog is bound to be more docile, less destructive, and require less exercise than a young one.

New Dog Comes Home

While adopting a grown dog often isn't nearly the work that introducing a puppy is, you should still follow some guidelines to ease the transition. Your new dog will be a little disoriented under any circumstances. But if spaying or neutering was done just before adoption, the post-surgical fog may add to the stress and confusion.

Remember the saying: "You never get a second chance to make a first impression"? The idea works with dogs, too. No matter how happy you are to bring him home, no matter how much you want to make up for the shabby way he was treated before you got him, start him off right from the beginning. Decide what the house rules are and stick to them, for the first couple of months, at least. Let him know that even though you're the nicest person on earth and the best human he could ever hope to find, your house does have rules, and he must follow them.

Be what dog trainer Carol Lea Benjamin calls a *benevolent alpha* — a nice boss, but still a boss. Your dog will understand, respect, and love you for being his leader — it's the way dogs are. You can be in charge, or your dog will. No democracies here. I always figure until my dogs pay our mortgage, the person who makes the tough call is me.

It just works better that way. Honest.

Five questions to help you evaluate an adult dog

No matter the age of the dog you're interested in adopting, you must do what you can to find out everything possible about her. While expecting to work on some things as your new dog gets used to you is reasonable, you want to avoid those animals who have too many problems, especially if one of them is aggression. Here are some questions that will help you:

✔ **What do you know of this dog's history?** You may be dealing with a shelter, a rescue volunteer, the dog's original owner or breeder, or a nice person who found a stray. If you discover the dog is well-bred and his parents have been certified free of congenital defects, more's the better! If you find out nothing about him, though, because he was a stray, don't count him out. If he's healthy and friendly and otherwise fits your size, coat, and activity criteria, he's a contender.

✔ **Why is this dog available for adoption?** Dogs become available for lots of reasons, some as frivolous as a change in decor. "Losing our home," "divorce," and "death" are some of the better ones; "bit our daughter" obviously is not (even if you don't have children). Listen, too, for what *isn't* said: "He needs more exercise than we can give him" may mean "He needs more exercise than *anyone* could *possibly* ever give him, and he eats furniture when he doesn't get it."

✔ **What behavior problems does this dog have?** Many things are fixable and worth considering if you honestly believe you'll take the time to work with the dog. "Pulls on the leash" is fixable. "A little aggressive" is not, at least not by the average pet owner's standard, and not to the extent that you should take a chance on a dog like this. Remember, too, that some problems are the *owner's* fault, not the dog's. "Won't stay in the yard," for example, may be easily cured by a decent fence and neutering.

✔ **How is he with children? Other dogs? Cats?** Even if you don't have children, you're going to run into some from time to time. The same is true with other dogs. You can successfully avoid cats if you don't have them, but make *certain* your prospective pet at least tolerates them well if you have a cat in your home. If you're getting an animal from a shelter, the organization should have asked the former owner to fill out a card on such things as problems with children or other animals. If you're adopting from a foster home, ask if the family has other animals and children. If there's no way to determine the dog's attitude toward children and other animals but he seems friendly, he may be OK. If you have doubts, however, hold out for an animal that you're sure fits well with your family.

✔ **What if it doesn't work out?** Obviously you're on your own if the person is moving out of state, but you need to know what your options are up front. You need to know what time frame you're dealing with for returning a dog who's not working out and whether your adoption fees — if any — will be refunded or if you'll be allowed to choose another dog at no charge.

Introductions

Before choosing your dog, remember to ask if she gets along with what you've got. Make sure by arranging introductions with the people in your family before accepting the pet. The dog who seems perfect with a woman may be afraid of men and downright hostile toward children. The time to find out is before your new dog comes home. If you're childless and single, you may consider bringing a friend of the opposite gender along for introductions, just to be sure. Kids, too, if you can manage it. You never know: You may end up with both a spouse and children during your dog's lifetime.

If your new dog shows aggression toward family members after you get him home, take him back. Yes, in some cases you can train a dominant dog to be more tolerant and build self-confidence in the case of fear biters or growlers. What's more likely to happen, though, is that you end up with a dog who is fine most of the time, a dog with whom you'll fall in love. And that dog, the one you love, is going to bite your child someday, when whatever triggers his aggression — taking away a toy, playing too close to the food dish, whatever — finally happens in your house. Don't take a chance. Leave training the aggressive dog to the people who train dogs for a living.

The following sections offer some tips for handling other introductions.

The original dog

If you already have at least one dog in your household, arrange to have the new dog meet him on-leash in neutral territory, such as at a nearby park, and walk them home together. Try not to telegraph your nervousness to the dog at the end of whichever leash you're holding: Be matter-of-fact but alert, and be sure that both leashes are loose. If either dog reacts aggressively, consider another dog — or no second dog at all, if your existing dog is too dog-aggressive to accept another one. Experienced dog handlers and trainers can keep dogs who don't like each other under control, but the average dog lover isn't up to the task.

That said, some jockeying for position is bound to occur in a two-dog household once the new dog comes home. Let them work it out themselves as long as jockeying doesn't escalate to growling — or fighting. If either happens, call in a trainer to help.

One exercise that helps two dogs learn that it is your wish that they get along — and that you won't tolerate anything else — is side-by-side, half-hour "down-stays." The late trainer Job Michael Evans believed this exercise to be a good way to build biddability in a dog from the inside out. Side-by-side "down-stays" say to the dogs, "Look, I don't care *how* you feel about each other, this is my house, and you'll behave yourselves in it."

For tips to teach the "down" and "stay" commands, see Chapter11.

What to do in the event of a dog fight — and how to protect both yourself and your dog — is in Chapter 11.

Cats

Put the dog on a leash when your cat and dog are first introduced, and be prepared for your cat to freak, especially if the presence of a dog in your home is a new experience. Correct the dog for trying to chase — as long as he's good-natured, don't be overly concerned — and ask him to "sit," instead, and praise for proper behavior. If you have any doubts, let the dog drag his leash around in the house so you can quickly step on it and correct him if he starts to chase the cat.

Cats can take a long time to get used to having a dog in the house — a couple of months, in some cases. Be sure that your cat has a place to eat where he can feel secure — such as a tabletop or in a room the dog can't get into — and likewise take steps to make sure that his litterbox is out of bounds. (If you know you're getting a dog, make these changes many weeks beforehand so your cat doesn't have to deal with too many new things at once.)

Again, the long "down-stay" can do wonders. Put your new dog on one while you pet and massage your cat so that your cat knows he's still loved and your dog understands that no matter what *he* thinks, the cat is to be left alone, because you say so.

Small household pets

This one's an easy one. *Never* trust a dog around loose pets of the smaller variety — rats and hamsters, guinea pigs and rabbits, ferrets, birds, and reptiles. After all, some dogs believe smaller pets to be prey, and they can be very efficient at hurting them — or killing them. A fatal accident can happen in the blink of an eye. Don't take the chance.

Indoor livestock

Pot-bellied pigs and miniature horses are probably big enough to look out for themselves, but still, I'd never leave a dog unsupervised with one. As with introducing a new dog to another dog or to a cat, start the introductions out on a leash, and make sure that your dog understands that your pet is a pet, not a pork chop — aggressive behavior won't be tolerated.

Establish a routine

While every dog is an individual, most adult dogs start feeling comfortable in their new homes in about a month. You can do a few things to help him understand that yours is his new home and he is a loved member of his new family, but he also has to understand his place in the family.

Model your leadership in front of him. Doing so is easy and works great as long as you're consistent. Here are a few exercises to try:

✔ **Leash-bonding.** For an hour each night, attach your dog's leash to your belt — or to a cord around your waist — and go about your business with the other end snapped to the dog's collar. Don't call him along with you and keep your hands off the leash. Just move about your house as you normally would — putting dishes in the dishwasher, paying bills, putting in a load of wash. Don't pay the dog much mind — just let your body weight remind him that he'd better go with you. The payoff is that he learns to pay attention to where you are and to think you and what you're doing are significant.

Using a leash helps your new dog bond with you more quickly.

Leash-bonding can also be used to help house-train an adult dog. See Chapter 8 for details.

✔ **Sit for what you want.** Your dog should get in the habit of sitting for the good things. Ask him to "sit" — and praise him when he does — before putting down his food dish, before petting him, or before letting him walk out the door on a walk. He'll start to think all good things come from you, but only when he behaves as you ask.

✔ **People first.** In the dog world the higher ranking animal goes first. You want that higher ranking animal to be you. So your dog should eat after you do, and he should walk out a door after you do. For the latter, have him "sit" and "stay," and then step outside and invite him along. *Never* let him run past you — out of a car, into your yard, or into the park — as if he owns the joint. He doesn't. It's that simple.

✔ **People food, dog food.** Don't share your meals with your dog, and don't add your table scraps to his. Feed a high-quality diet and leave it at that. If you share, you have no one to blame but yourself for his begging. Plus, your food is boss food. Yours and yours alone. For more on choosing a food for your dog, see Chapter 4.

✔ **People bed, dog bed.** Get your dog a comfortable bed or crate and make him sleep in it. Let him sleep in your room so he can be near you. Your bed is the most prime piece of real estate in his world, and it should be yours alone. He should have access with your permission only.

"Oh, c'mon!" you're saying, "who died and made you a drill sergeant? I want to *spoil* my dog!" Sure. Later. When your dog has impeccable house manners and you have nothing to complain about. Do my dogs sleep on the bed? You bet! But they don't come up without permission and they know it's a privilege, not a right. Do I share my carrots sticks with them while I write? Of course! But they sit for them, every one. And when I tell them I'm done sharing and to go to their beds, they do. This statement is true of the 10-year-old dog I raised from a pup and the 2-year-old who has been with me only a couple of months.

Set the ground rules early and stick to them fairly and consistently. You can always loosen up, but tightening up is awfully hard after your dog's out of control.

Separation anxiety is probably the No. 1 problem among adults dogs who have landed in a new home. Your new dog has had his heart broken once, after all, and learning how to trust again is going to take him a long time. Until that happens, the time you are gone is going to make him nervous — so much so that he may destroy things while you're out.

For tips on dealing with destructiveness, as well as house-training and other problems of grown dogs — and puppies — see Chapters 8, 11, and 12.

Lost dog!

While any dog can become lost at any time, sticking around home isn't something that's easy for a newly adopted dog to do. After all, he's still not sure where "home" is, and so he may take off for who-knows-where — at high speed.

The best time to protect your dog — old or new, young or not-so — is before he gets out. Here's a checklist of things to do, just in case:

✔ **Check your fences and gates.** Are there loose or missing boards or enticing gaps at the baseline that could be opened up with a little digging? Are latches secure, with locks in place? Fix them all. If you have children going in and out all the time, invest in a device that pulls the gate closed automatically.

A special summertime hazard in the United States is the Fourth of July. The noise of fireworks can put pets in a panic, so the best you can do is go for a bowl of cool water and complete confinement in a crate, in the house or in the garage, until the festivities are over. The same goes for New Year's Eve or any other event when noisemaking is the norm.

✔ **Check your dog.** Don't waste time before getting him a license and an ID tag. If your pet ends up in the shelter, a license buys him extra time. And if someone finds him when the shelter's closed, an ID tag with your phone number speeds up the reunion.

Instead of your pet's name and your address on the ID tag, use the word "REWARD" and as many phone numbers as you can fit.

Microchip implants, which carry ID numbers, are a great idea. Make sure that your pet's permanent ID is registered so if someone discovers it, a fast reunion is possible. The AKC's Companion Animal Recovery service can help in the United States and Canada — they don't just deal with purebred dogs and not just with the kind of microchip involved in the program. Call (800) 252-7894 or ask your veterinarian for more information.

✔ **Plan for the worst.** Keep current, clear pictures of your pets on hand — you need them to throw together a flyer in an emergency. If you lose your pet, put flyers everywhere you can and place a lost ad in the newspaper right away — don't waste precious time hoping your pet will wander home. Describe your dog as the general public would see him: To most people, a Belgian tervuren looks like a collie-shepherd cross, and a flat-coated retriever looks like a long-haired black Lab. So say that, too.

✔ **Scan the neighborhood, watch "found" ads, and check the shelters every other day in person.** Don't give up too soon — pets have been located weeks after their disappearance.

If you've never lost a pet, being vigilant is sometimes tough — but you must. Make sure that ID tags stay current and readable, and keep an eye on those gates. In this game, you make your own luck.

Part III
Living with Your Dog

The 5th Wave   By Rich Tennant

"WE'VE HAD SOME BEHAVIOR PROBLEMS SINCE GETTING 'SNOWBALL', BUT WITH PATIENCE, REPETITION AND GENTLE DISCIPLINE, I'VE BEEN ABLE TO BREAK ROGER OF MOST OF THEM."

In this part . . .

Keeping your dog happy and healthy is the focus of this part, with information on health care, training, and fixing bad behaviors. If you're thinking of breeding your dog, that's in here, too — along with the reasons why breeding is probably not such a good idea. You also find special care tips for older dogs, along with the facts you need about euthanasia, and resources to help you through a difficult time.

Chapter 10

Maintaining a Happy, Healthy Dog

- -

In This Chapter

▶ Maintaining a well-groomed canine

▶ Deciding when to use a groomer — and where to find one

▶ Dealing with those pesky parasites

▶ Choosing a veterinarian

▶ Providing basic veterinary care

▶ Deciding if your dog needs a specialist

▶ Helping the medicine go down

▶ Detecting signs of illness

- -

*W*hen it comes to your dog's health, preventive care is easier on both your pet and your pocketbook. Regular grooming helps you spot health problems while they're still manageable, and even routine actions such as annual vaccinations provide an amazing service: They protect your pet from infectious diseases that used to be the terror of the dog–lover's world.

Grooming and vaccinations are just the start.

From head (dentistry) to tail (anal sacs) the emphasis today is on care that deals with little problems before they become big ones.

Your partner in this endeavor is your veterinarian, and choosing a good one is essential. Veterinary medicine is on the leading edge of the health sciences, and top veterinarians keep up through journals, continuing education, and online services that are the envy of other professions.

Many dogs, sadly, never see the benefit of this expertise. They go through life plagued by chronic suffering, dragged down by preventable illnesses and parasitic infestations that drain the pleasure from their lives. This shouldn't happen to a dog, and I know you don't want it to happen to yours.

Your dog counts on you to keep him healthy. Be an informed and active pet-owner and your dog's life will likely be longer and certainly be more joyful.

Keeping Up Appearances

Good grooming is about more than keeping your pet looking beautiful and smelling clean — although that's certainly one of the pleasant payoffs. Regular grooming relaxes the dog who's used to it and becomes a special time shared between you both. A coat free of mats, burrs, and tangles, and skin free of fleas and ticks, is as comfortable to your dog as clean clothes fresh from the wash are to you: It just makes you feel good, and the effect is the same for your pet.

Properly trimmed nails make moving more comfortable, and keeping ears clean of wax and excess hair help keep infections at bay — and eliminates another source of dreaded doggy odor.

Some added benefit for you: Giving your dog a tummy rub after every session is sure to lower your blood pressure and ease the stresses of your day. And for allergy sufferers, keeping a dog clean may make having a dog possible. A better deal I never heard, so you're ready to get grooming.

Brushing and combing

With dogs as with anything else, nothing succeeds like excess. Which is why the dogs who win in the show ring are the ones with lots of lovely coat. Breeds such as cockers, collies, and Afghans have lush, glorious coats that would be wholly impractical in their original lines of work, but oh! they're beautiful at the end of a show leash.

They're beautiful at the end of a regular leash, too, which is why many of these spectacular breeds are so popular. But there's a price to be paid for such beauty and if you don't pay, your dog does. Consider a simple mat, so easy to overlook. Have you ever had your hair in a ponytail that was just a little too tight? A mat can feel the same way to your dog, a constant pull on the skin. Try to imagine those all over your body and you have a good idea how uncomfortable an ungroomed coat can be.

Your dog need never know what a mat feels like if you keep him brushed and combed. You should go over him daily, clearing such things as mats and ticks from his coat — more on those later in this chapter — and brush him out completely every week. For short-haired breeds doing so is a cinch: Run your hands over him daily, a brush over him weekly, and that's it.

Information on tools for grooming — and which are best for the coat type your dog has — is in Chapter 4.

One benefit of short-haired (and medium-haired) dogs: You can use a flea comb on them. Flea combs have narrowly-spaced teeth that catch the little blood-suckers where they eat: on your dog. To use one, comb from the skin out, a tiny bit at a time, flicking the pests into a bowl of warm sudsy water as you go. When you're done, flush the fleas — most of them will have drowned by then anyway.

Remember that combing fleas from your pet does *not* solve a flea problem. See the flea section later in this chapter for a total control program.

For other breeds, grooming is a little more involved. Double-coated, long-haired breeds such as collies, chows, Keeshond, and Alaskan malamutes have a downy undercoat that can mat down like a layer of felt against the skin if left untouched. To prevent this, divide the coat into small sections and brush against the grain from the skin outward, working from head to tail, section by section. In the spring and fall — the Big Shed times — you end up with enough of that fluffy undercoat to make a whole new dog. Keep brushing, and think of the benefits: The fur you pull out with a brush doesn't end up on the furniture, and removing the old stuff keeps your pet cooler in the summer and lets new insulation come in for the winter.

Lightly misting the part of the fur you're brushing with water from a spray bottle makes working the brush through the coat easier and helps keep the long outer coat from breaking.

Don't shave a long-haired dog down for summer. Why would you want to make your beautiful dog ugly for half the year? Double-coated dogs carry less coat in the summer than in the winter — they *blow* most of their undercoat in the spring — and keeping the remainder clean and well-brushed provides insulation against the heat as well as the cold. Some of the dogs *most* affected by summer heat, ironically, are short-haired: Dogs with short noses, such as boxers and pugs, and dogs with black coats, such as Rottweilers and some Dobermans. If you own one of these dogs, be especially careful to keep them cool in hot weather.

Silky-coated dogs such as Afghan hounds, cockers, and Maltese also need constant brushing to keep tangles from forming. As with the double-coated dogs, work with small sections at a time, brushing from the skin outward and then comb back into place with the grain for a glossy, finished look. Coats of this type require so much attention that having a groomer keep the dogs trimmed to a medium length is often more practical.

Curly and wiry coats, such those on poodles and terriers, need to be brushed weekly, working against the grain and then with it. Curly coats need to be clipped every six weeks, wiry ones two or three times a year (but clipping every six weeks keeps your terrier looking sharper).

Learning to clip your dog yourself isn't that hard — if you don't mind a few bad hair weeks on your dog's behalf. Dog clippers are widely available in pet-supply and discount stores, and these kits contain basic instructions for keeping your pet shorn.

If your terrier doesn't come back from the groomer's looking like the show dogs you've seen, there's a reason: *hand-stripping.* The proper terrier coat is maintained for the show ring by painstakingly pulling dead hair by hand using a special grooming tool. Most pet groomers clip the coat instead, which presents an appearance just as neat but not as "correct" as hand-stripping. Clipping is a practical compromise for wiry-haired dogs whose job description is "household pet."

Every grooming session should end with a petting session but, to make things even more pleasant, end it with a massage. Work your dog over with your fingers, applying gentle, firm, and even pressure. This treatment is especially nice for older dogs and for calming young ones.

Giving a bath

Why is it that from the instant the first drops of water spill out of the tap, from the second you reach for the bottle of shampoo, your dog starts burrowing his way to the darkest, quietest, and most hidden corner of the house? The dog who doesn't hear you when you scream, "Get off the couch!" is able to pick out the magic word when you whisper, "I think the dog needs a bath."

Your dog disagrees. Like most dogs, he's content to live his life in dog-smell heaven, a place where water is to drink or swim in and never has soap added. Too bad. We make the rules, and dog-smell heaven is no paradise for us.

How often should you bathe your dog? Forget that old saw about "every six months" or even "every year." Who wants to live with a dog like that? House dogs should be bathed monthly, more often still if they need it. Using a high-quality shampoo and conditioner babies the coat and replenishes some of the oils bathing removes. Another plus for frequent bathing: Fleas go down the drain! More on shampoos and conditioners is in Chapter 4.

Your dog should be brushed before bathing because mats and tangles, once wet, can never be removed — you need to cut them out. Let your dog chill for a minute while you set yourself up with the proper equipment:

> ✔ **Bath mat.** Even if your bathtub already has no-slip strips at the bottom, they may not be positioned well to keep your dog from slipping. Nothing makes a dog more nervous than not being able to stand square on all four paws. A full bath mat is ideal, but in a pinch a towel in the bottom of the tub will do. I bought an inexpensive rubber mat just for the dogs; I put it in the tub before the bath and spray it off and put it away after.

✔ **Spray nozzle.** Some people rinse dogs by pouring dirty bath water back over them, but that defeats the purpose of bathing a dog — to get him clean — so use a nozzle. I have one of those hand-held shower massagers, but an inexpensive alternative is the rubber kind that fits over the bathtub tap.

When you have all your equipment in place, turn on the tap, but do so with the door closed. Dogs have a keen sense of hearing and some are upset by the sound of bath water running when they know it's for them. After the tub is full, turn off the tap and let the water sit while you prepare the dog for the big plunge. Put a pinch of cotton just inside your dog's ears and a drop of mineral oil in each eye to help keep the soap out.

TIP

Getting the gunk (or skunk!) out

Many things your dog gets into — or that get onto him — have to be clipped out. Before hauling out the scissors, try some of these techniques:

✔ **Burrs:** Try spraying a little Pam cooking spray on the area, and then gently use your fingers to work the burr free from the now-slicker coat.

✔ **Mats and tangles:** Sprinkle the area with cornstarch and carefully use a *mat-splitter,* a sharp tool that looks like a small sickle, to cut through the area a couple of times. If you're patient — and gentle — you should be able to work the fur free with your fingers. To finish the job, comb through the area with a wide-toothed steel comb and then a brush to remove the dirt and dead hair that caused the problem in the first place.

✔ **Fleas:** A flea comb will catch the pest, but you'll soon see more if you don't launch a flea-control program. More on fleas later in this chapter.

✔ **Ticks:** Never touch a tick with your hands. Use a tick remover or tweezers, grasp the body firmly and pull with a steady motion. More about ticks later in this chapter.

✔ **Paint or tar:** *Never* use solvents to remove paint or tar: They irritate your dog's skin, are toxic if tasted, and they're flammable! Instead, clip the affected area out.

✔ **Gum or other sticky substances:** You can try a little peanut butter to lubricate the fur enough to slide the gum out, but it's rough going. Clipping is usually the answer.

✔ **Skunk and other critter problems:** You can't clip this problem out. The old stand-by, dousing your pet with tomato juice, works well, as does vinegar (although buying enough can be a little embarassing). Commercial preparations are also available from pet-supply stores, and these work the best of all. If your pet chooses to tangle with a porcupine, call your veterinarian instead of trying to pull the quills yourself — which hurts your dog!

A dog who's *covered* in burrs, mats, or dried paint or tar is best sent to a groomer to be clipped short. Not only is this solution easier on you both, it's considerably more attractive than having dozens of short-clipped areas. Don't worry: The hair grows back faster than you think.

Do the dirty deed: Empty the anal sacs

Many dog owners live in blissful ignorance of *anal glands,* two nasty little organs that produce fluid that carries the unique scent by which dogs identify each other (anal glands are one reason why dogs sniff each other's rumps when they meet). This policy is a bad one, though, because should one of the glands or the fluid reservoirs, the *anal sacs,* become impacted or infected, your dog will need veterinary attention.

The best way to prevent trouble is to empty the anal sacs every time you bathe your dog. The least repulsive way is to suds up the area, including your hand, and then place your thumb and forefinger on the outside of each gland, just below the skin on either side of the anus — you'll feel them as small lumps below the surface. Gently squeeze your fingers inward and together, and you should get a noxious mess for your efforts. Suds and rinse a couple of times and it'll be gone.

If your dog cries out when you touch the glands, or the if the area is swollen, call your veterinarian. If you absolutely can't stand to empty your dog's anal glands, your vet or groomer will be happy to do it for you.

As you drag the dog toward the bathroom door, don't spare words of love and encouragement. In working with dogs, I've found that a good attitude can go a long way, but a bad one can go even farther. If your dog knows how much *you* hate bath time, how can he get a positive — or at least tolerable — opinion of the process? Keep your attitude high and don't let up on the praise.

Start shampooing by working a complete ring of lather around the neck, cutting off the fleas' escape route to the ears. Work forward and back from there, and don't forget to work some lather between your dog's toes — another favorite get-away for fleas. Empty the anal sacs (see the sidebar "Do the dirty deed: Empty the anal sacs") and suds the area thoroughly. Rinse thoroughly, and repeat the entire process if need be before conditioning. Then lift your dog out and put a towel over him loosely while he shakes. Your dog can get more water off by shaking than you can by toweling, so let him have at it, and then finish the job by rubbing him dry when he's done.

If the weather is cold, keep your dog inside while he dries. With young or old dogs, especially, set up a blanket or playpen by the heater or fire to make sure that they stay toasty while they dry. You can use a blow-dryer to speed up the process, but your dog would probably just as soon you didn't.

Let your dog dry clean by keeping him out of the yard, and he'll stay cleaner longer. And that would be a bonus for your both.

Trimming toenails

Many dog owners avoid trimming toenails, too, but not for the same reason they ignore emptying anal sacs: Toenail trims can turn into a hard-fought war with bloody casualties on both sides. Because of that, many people leave the task of trimming nails to their groomer or veterinarian — but unless you're seeing these professionals a lot more than most people, your pet's nails aren't being trimmed often enough. Long nails can make walking uncomfortable and can even cause lameness, which is why trimming nails short — they should be just off the ground when your pet is standing — and then trimming them just a pinch every week is a better way to go.

The problem with nails is that each has a blood vessel inside. The trick is to trim to just beyond the end of this vein; if you nick it, the nail will bleed, and your dog will yelp. Everyone hits this vein on occasion, even veterinarians, which is why you should be sure to have blood-stopping powder on hand, such as Kwik Stop (available at any pet-supply store), before you start trimming. If your dog has light-colored toenails, the blood vessel is the pink area. Black nails are harder to figure out, but you should be able to see the vein by shining a flashlight behind the nail. If you can't tell, just clip back a little at a time. If you draw blood, take a pinch of the powder and press it against the exposed bottom of the nail for a few seconds to stop the bleeding.

If your dog's nails are so long that they're forcing her foot out of position, you can take them back to where they should be in two ways. The first is to cut a little off them every few days: The *quick* recedes before you as you go. The second way is to have your veterinarian take them all the way back when your dog is under anesthesia, such as for a dental cleaning and scaling. After the nails are the proper length, in the front and back both, keeping them that way is easy with a weekly trim.

Whatever you do, don't ignore long nails. Long nails are one of the most often overlooked areas of basic dog care, and if you ignore them, you can cause your dog unnecessary discomfort.

If your dog's resistant to having her nails trimmed, work up to the task slowly by touching her feet, then her toes, then the nails, all while praising her for holding still. When she is used to having her feet handled, put the trimmer against the nail and praise more still. Then trim a little off, and so on. Praise and more praise! The process can take several weeks, working at it every night, but if you're patient, consistent, and persistent, you'll get there.

Not all dogs have *dewclaws* — a useless toe that can be found up on the inside of the leg — but for those who do, neglected nails can be a problem. They catch on things such as upholstery and can tear the toe partly off the leg, which is one reason why many breeders have them removed at birth. Keeping the nail on the dewclaw short is important, too. If dewclaws are a constant problem for your dog, discuss their removal with your veterinarian.

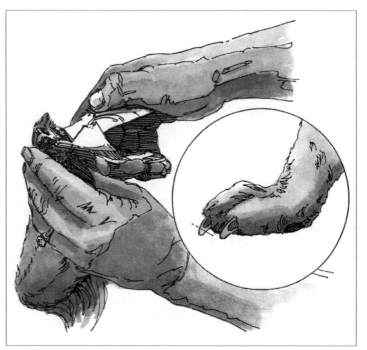

Trim the nail just beyond the quick to avoid any bleeding.

Another way around the Toe-Trim Wrestlerama is to try Karen Peterson's peanut butter trick. Peterson's flat-coated retriever, Ciro, hates nail trims but loves peanut butter. So Peterson puts a big dollop of peanut butter on the door of her refrigerator, at Ciro's nose level. And while the dog's licking up the PB, she does his nails.

Controlling fleas

The experts say the bond with our pets was first formed over food. We had more of it than they did, and they figured if they were nice to us, we'd share. I have an alternative theory, however. Call it the *Rump Theory,* if you will.

See if this one works for you. The ancestors of our dogs figured our ancestors were their only hope to get those itchy places, which they couldn't reach on their own, scratched. Like the rump, see? It's probably no coincidence that fleas seem to prefer the spots dogs can't reach very well — above the tail, primarily. Even the most ardent attention from the sharpest human nails provides only fleeting relief during flea infestations.

Choosing a groomer

For dogs such as poodles, terriers, and cocker spaniels, hiring the services of a groomer is almost a necessity, because the trimming involved with these breeds is beyond the ability or interest of most pet owners. For other dogs, such as long-haired, double-coated Shelties and collies, attention from a professional groomer can make shedding time shorter and keep regular combing and brushing more manageable for you. About the only dogs who don't benefit too much from a groomer's touch are short-haired dogs, who are easy enough for the average person to maintain.

Start your groomer search by asking friends, neighbor's, and coworkers for recommendations. Your dog's breeder and veterinarian, too, may also have some suggestions.

Avoid groomers who use tranquilizers — if your dog needs tranquilizers, consult your veterinarian — and those who hold your pet for much longer than the time it takes to groom him. A good groomer should only need two to four hours, at most, for a routine wash and clip, unless your dog is matted and tangled. If the groomer wants your dog dropped off in the morning and can't say when he'll be done, find another groomer. There's no reason for your dog to hang out all day when he's not being worked on.

You have a role to play, too. Make sure that your pet is current on his vaccinations, especially for canine *tracheobronchitis* ("kennel cough," see Chapter 15 for more details). Do not wait so long between appointments that your dog is full of mats and then expect the groomer to be able to work them out. Listen to your groomer: If she says clipping the coat away is the best way to go, you're better off following her advice than subjecting your dog to hours of fur-pulling. Make sure, too, that the groomer is clear on what you expect your dog to look like when she's done if clipping is involved — and if you don't want bows, nail polish, and perfume, don't forget to speak up.

A good groomer is a real gem, and if you've got one, show your appreciation — with a tip! And speaking of tips: Book early for the end-of-year holidays — a couple *months* in advance, at least. Everyone wants a clean dog when company's coming.

Fortunately, flea control has gotten both safer and more effective in the last few years. Safer, because newer products break the flea's reproductive cycle without containing anything that can harm a dog (or person). More effective, because these products concentrate on keeping new fleas from advancing to the adult stage — the one that bites.

Fleas cause plenty of misery — not to mention annoyance to the owner who has to listen to that scratch, scratch, scratch. Some dogs are so allergic to flea bites they will tear themselves to pieces trying to satisfy the urge to itch, and even ones who aren't *that* sensitive can open up gooey patches called *hot spots* that need veterinary attention.

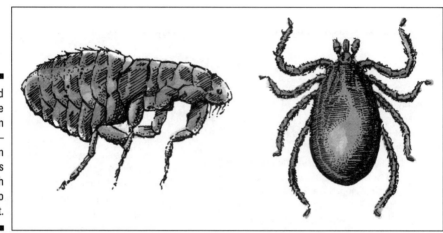

Fleas and ticks are more than annoying — they can pose serious health threats to your pet.

For effective flea control, you have to have a game plan. You have to treat your pet, your yard, and your house. You have to treat to kill biting adult fleas, and you have to treat to keep developing fleas from reaching adulthood. You have to do all you can to keep flea populations manageable with regular vacuuming of pet areas and regular washing of pet bedding.

And you can't let up. Not ever. Flea control is a year-round battle in large parts of the world and, even in the cold areas, fleas can winter inside, just as people and pets do. During peak flea season, control and prevention is a twice-monthly affair.

A few ways exist to accomplish flea-free goals in your home, in your yard, and on your pet. Some possibilities include the following:

- **Your house.** Treat either with a spray or a fogger that contains both a *quick-kill* component, to kill adult fleas, and an *insect growth regulator (IGR)*, which keeps immature fleas from developing. Alternately you can use a borate powder, which kills fleas by dehydrating them. Check with your veterinarian for product recommendations.

- **Your yard.** Treat with a spray that likewise contains an adulticide combined with an IGR, but make sure that the product is designed for outdoor use: Exposure to sunlight and water quickly reduces its usefulness if it isn't.

- **Your pet.** The flea pill, Program, available only through veterinarians, is an effective part of an overall flea-control plan but, because it doesn't kill adult fleas, you likely won't be satisfied with its results on its own. The product works by transmitting a chemical that prevents the eggs laid by the biting flea from developing. Two new products are also available only through veterinarians, Advantage spot-on and Frontline spray, fill the "kill gap" by providing protection against adult fleas for more than a month. Flea collars aren't the most effective form of flea control because they are at one end of your pet — and the fleas are at the other!

The things that don't work — although a great deal of money is spent on them every year — include electronic flea collars and various nutritional supplements such as garlic, brewer's yeast, and Vitamin B. Any evidence as to their efficacy is purely anecdotal and has not stood up to scientific scrutiny. The best "natural" flea-control remedy on the market is already in your house: your washing machine and vacuum cleaner. Weekly washings of pet bedding and daily vacuuming of pet sleeping areas does a great deal to help keep flea populations down.

Flea-control efforts fail when pet owners put only minimal and sporadic effort into them: fogging the house now and then, powdering a pet on occasion, and spraying the yard infrequently, if at all. Such efforts always leave populations of either adult or developing fleas safe to reinfest treated areas.

Flea-control efforts can turn *dangerous* when you use too many and in the wrong combinations. *Always* read directions carefully, making sure the product is safe for the use you intend, as well as around other pets in your home. When in doubt, talk to your veterinarian about your entire flea-control program. If your dog's a puppy, ill, or elderly, talk to your veterinarian first about which products and combinations are appropriate.

Controlling ticks

While ticks have always been disgusting and annoying, they have been considerably more worrisome for dog owners since the discovery of Lyme disease, which affects dogs as well as humans.

While topical flea control solutions such as collars and spot-ons (liquids applied to the skin, usually between the shoulder blades) do have some effect on ticks, you'll likely still be picking them off your dog — favorite spots are behind the ears, and the places where the legs meet the body — whenever you head into tick country.

For your own safety, *never touch a tick with your bare hand.* Instead, use a glove, tweezers, or tick remover. Grasp the body firmly, and pull with a steady motion. Wrap the ticks in tissues and flush, or drop them one by one into a small bowl of rubbing alcohol, and flush the lot when done. Don't worry if a piece of the head remains in your dog: It'll work it's way out in time — just put a little antiseptic on the spot to prevent infection.

If Lyme disease is common in your area, discuss a vaccine against it with your veterinarian.

Doggy breath

Controlling mouth odors is *both* a grooming and veterinary issue. Dental cleanings and scalings are an important part of preventive medicine, and keeping teeth clean between veterinary appointments is something that can — and should — be done by dog owners.

Plaque build-up on teeth causes gums to recede, opening pockets at the root line that are paradise to bacterial infections. Left unchecked, these infections can lead to tooth loss, make eating painful, and put the dog's immune system and internal organs under pressure, causing illness and premature aging. Rotting teeth and gums can become a powerful source of "doggy breath" that some pet owners treat with products that may temporarily fix the smell, but do nothing about the real problem.

While some groomers and dog owners scale plaque themselves, this doesn't address the problem at the root line, so regular cleanings under anesthesia by a veterinarian are essential to ensure dental health. In between, attention two or three times a week with a toothbrush and a toothpaste designed for dogs slows the reformation of plaque and extends the time between dental scalings.

As with nail trimming, the key to getting a pet used to having his teeth cleaned is to take it in small steps over time, be patient, and be encouraging.

Working with Your Veterinarian

This section is called "Working *with* Your Veterinarian" because I have come to realize after years of writing about pets and listening to both pet owners and veterinarians that what should be a cooperative effort to protect and ensure the health of a pet is sometimes anything but that. The relationship between the client (that's you, not your dog) and the veterinarian can become adversarial when neither party respects the contributions of the other and both parties forget the reason that brought them together: To help the patient, in other words, your dog.

Sometimes, the task of figuring out what's wrong with an animal is like walking into a movie in the middle — for one brief moment you have no idea what the story's about and little chance of predicting the outcome. But given the opportunity to see a few more scenes, you start to understand what's going on. For the veterinarian, all too often that one glimpse is all he gets. The client wants an answer, a shot, or a pill to makes things better. He wants the problem fixed, now.

And while the client probably wants an immediate solution to his own health problems, too, he's resigned enough to say "yes" to test after test to find the right answer — as long as his insurance is footing the bill.

And there, of course, is the rub.

In the vast majority of cases, the client is footing the bill for veterinary procedures. And although veterinary costs are a small fraction of comparable procedures in human medicine, the fact that you're spending hundreds instead of thousands (or hundreds of thousands) of dollars isn't all that reassuring when your budget is stretched as far as many families' are today.

The veterinarian has bills to pay, too, and he wants to make you happy, which is why many of them fall into the habit of giving the client exactly what he wants — a shot or a pill that takes care of the symptoms, regardless of whether the problem is fixed for the long term.

Your dog deserves better, and so do you. And so, too, does your veterinarian, who has spent years studying to be able to help your dog. So let him. Listen.

If you've got the right veterinarian, he'll listen, too, to your concerns about treatments and finances. A lot can be accomplished through clear communication, respect, and trust.

Money is the 800-pound gorilla of veterinary medicine, looming over every suggestion a veterinarian makes and every decision a client considers. One way to tame the beast a little is to purchase health insurance for your dog.

Americans have been slow to the concept, which is well-established in Europe: In Sweden, 17 percent of all pets are insured, as are 5 percent of Great Britain's dogs and cats, according to an article in the *Wall Street Journal*. Only one pet-health insurer exists in the United States, VPI Insurance Group of Anaheim, Calif., which covers the health of a mere 75,000 pets (out of more than 100 million estimated pet dogs and cats).

While the insurer doesn't cover preexisting conditions and has both a deductible and an annual limit on claims, the insurance can be the difference between life and death for the pet whose owner is looking at medical bills for something like cancer, which can effortlessly top the $1,000 mark and keep climbing. Another problem: Few veterinarians will let your bill ride while the insurance company processes your claim, which means you usually pay the bill yourself and wait to be reimbursed.

Still, with annual premiums between $100 and $200 — depending on the age of the pet — VPI's coverage could seem a fantastic deal should a health catastrophe strike your dog. For more information in the United States, call 800-USA-PETS. Your veterinarian may offer other health plans that may help your pet.

Choosing a veterinarian

To work effectively with your veterinarian, you need to develop a relationship over time, so she can build a history and become familiar with you and your dog. Group practices are fine, but working primarily with one veterinarian, either alone or in a group, is best.

Your veterinarian should be technically proficient, current on the latest treatments, and willing to seek out more information on your pet's behalf. She should be articulate, able to explain what's going on with your dog in a way that you can understand, and willing to answer your questions so that you can make a responsible decision on your pet's behalf. Above all, you must be able to trust your veterinarian. After all, knowing what goes on in a veterinarian's office after you leave your pet behind is impossible. An animal can never comment on its treatment, and an animal lover must rely on trust to be sure that a pet has been dealt with fairly.

Before you choose a vet, ask friends, coworkers, and neighbors for recommendations. Over the years, animal lovers can tell which veterinarians are knowledgeable, compassionate, and hard-working. Those veterinarians are always talked up by satisfied clients.

Other factors may help you narrow down your list of possibilities:

- ✔ **Is the clinic or hospital conveniently located, with hours you can live with?** If you have a 9-to-5 job, a veterinarian with a 9-to-5 clinic doesn't do your pet much good. Many veterinarians are open late on at least one week night and for at least a half-day on Saturday, or they are willing to make other arrangements.

- ✔ **Does the veterinarian consult with veterinary college staff or independent or in-house specialists, or does she subscribe to an online veterinary service, such as the Veterinary Information Network?** A willingness to discuss tough cases with colleagues is the sign of a veterinarian who's putting in effort on your pet's behalf. Online services are available the world over to assist veterinarians in getting to the bottom of a tough case.

- ✔ **What kind of emergency care is available, if any?** Although emergency veterinary clinics are prepared for any catastrophe, they are not familiar with your pet. If your veterinarian's practice does *not* offer 24-hour care, does it work with one that does?

- ✔ **Do you feel a rapport with this person? Are you comfortable asking questions? Discussing fees?** The final call on whether a particular veterinarian is right for you comes down to intangibles. If you don't feel comfortable, you're less likely to deal with your veterinarian, and the lack of productive communication hurts your pet in the long run.

Preventing illness

While preventive care starts with you, your veterinarian offers medications and procedures that keep your dog safe from some basic pet problems, such as infectious diseases and parasites. Always take your dog in for an annual exam and follow your veterinarian's suggestions for procedures that keep your pet in the best of health.

Vaccinations

"Shots" is what most of us call them, and they've been an important part of preventive care for decades. For adult dogs, an annual combination booster protects your pet, and a rabies shot every one, two, or three years — depending on regulations in your area — protect both your pet *and* the rest of your family from this lethal disease.

Nearly all combination vaccines protect your dog against *distemper, hepatitis, leptospirosis, parainfluenza,* and *parvovirus.* Depending on the risks in your area, your veterinarian may also use a product that protects against *coronavirus* and *Lyme disease.* Your veterinarian can give you information on these diseases, as can any general-interest veterinary manual.

If you board your dog frequently or send him to be groomed or go places where other dogs frequent — such as a dog park or dog-sport competition — ask your veterinarian about additional protection against canine infectious *tracheobronchitis* (more commonly known as "kennel cough"). For more information on this malady, see Chapter 15.

Internal parasites

Dogs can be infected by a range of parasites, and your veterinarian can help you protect your pet against some and rid your pet of others. Here's a pest line-up:

- ✔ **Intestinal parasites.** Try *whipworms, tapeworms, roundworms,* and *hookworms* to start, and throw in some diseases caused by single-celled pests, such as *coccidiosis* and *giardiosis.* Your veterinarian can find signs of these parasites by examining a fresh stool sample and prescribe the appropriate medication to eliminate them from your dog's system.

- ✔ **Heartworms.** Until recently, the cure for a heartworm infestation was so dangerous that prevention was the only safe alternative. A new treatment that kills the parasites more safely is good news, but prevention is still the better route to take. Two choices for prevention exist: A daily pill or a monthly one but, because your dog must be heartworm-free to use either safely, your veterinarian will draw a blood sample to test for the parasite before prescribing either.

Veterinary specialists

While not as many specialists exist in veterinary medicine as in human medicine, you still find quite a few, and there are likely to be more in the future. Your veterinarian should be open to referring you to a specialist, when your pet's condition warrants it, or consulting with one on your behalf.

While many urban areas can support independent specialists or specialty practices, in less populated areas you're more likely to find a full complement of specialists at your closest university with a school or college of veterinary medicine. Current companion-animal specialties include the following:

- ✔ Anesthesiology
- ✔ Behavior
- ✔ Cardiology
- ✔ Dentistry
- ✔ Dermatology
- ✔ Emergency medicine and critical care
- ✔ Internal medicine
- ✔ Neurology
- ✔ Oncology
- ✔ Ophthalmology
- ✔ Radiology
- ✔ Surgery

Each of these specialties require additional study and certification over and above that required to achieve a degree in veterinary medicine.

Recognizing signs of illness

The signs of a healthy puppy or dog are pretty apparent to an observant pet owner: Bright, clear eyes, with no sign of discharge; clean ears, free of build-up or smell; a mouth not overpowering by its odor, with pink gums free of infection; a nose that appears moist, with no discharge; a shiny coat, with unblemished skin below that snaps back easily when pulled away from the shoulders (proof of proper hydration). A healthy outlook, and a healthy appetite and normal thirst are part of the package too, without signs of intestinal upset such as vomiting, diarrhea, or constipation. No lameness, no swelling, and no heavy panting.

Anything to the contrary is reason for concern.

If you know your dog well, you'll probably know when she's a little "off." Taking her temperature is one of the first steps in determining what's wrong — anything below 99 degrees or above 102.5 degrees is worth a call to the veterinarian.

You can buy a pet thermometer, or use a rectal human one — just be sure you label the latter so you never have a mix-up. To take your dog's temperature, put a little water-based lubricating jelly on the tip and insert the thermometer into her rectum. Keep the thermometer in place for about a minute while holding your dog still — it may help if someone else holds her head — and then check the reading.

Anything is worth a call to the veterinarian if you're not sure, but some things require urgent attention. Here are some clinical signs that should have you heading for your veterinarian's — or for the emergency clinic:

- Seizure, fainting, or collapse.

- Eye injury, no matter how mild.

- Vomiting or diarrhea, anything more than two or three times within an hour or so.

- Allergic reactions, such as swelling around the face, or hives, most easily seen on the belly.

- Any suspected poisoning, including antifreeze, rodent or snail bait, or human medication.

- Snake bite.

- Thermal stress, either too cold or too hot, even if the dog seems to be recovered (the internal story could be quite different).

- Any wound or laceration that's open and bleeding, or any animal bite.

- Trauma, such as being hit by a car, even if the dog seems fine.

- Any respiratory problem: Chronic coughing, trouble breathing, or near drowning.

While some problems don't classify as life-threatening, they may be causing your pet irritation and pain, and so should be taken care of without delay. Signs of pain include the following:

- Panting

- Labored breathing

- Increased body temperature

- Lethargy

- Restlessness

- Loss of appetite

Note: Some dogs may seek you out for reassurance; others will draw within themselves.

Giving medication

I once asked readers to send me their best tip for sneaking pills down a pet, and the letters came in for weeks afterward. I can't imagine there's much edible that some dog lover hasn't popped a pill into, including an olive, as I recall.

Giving pills
to your dog
isn't hard
after you
get the
hang of it.

The most popular pill disguisers were hot dogs and peanut butter, but cheese (including canned cheese), liverwurst, and cottage cheese all got lots of votes, too.

Of course, you don't have to resort to such subterfuge if you don't want to. You can gently pry your dog's jaws apart by applying firm pressure from either side with your hand over the bridge of his nose and thumb and forefinger on either side, and then tuck the pill way, way back, at the base of the tongue, hold your dog's muzzle closed and skyward and then blow into his nose while stroking his throat.

Which is why, most likely, most people use hot dogs.

If you're tentative or inexperienced, make medicating a two-person job: One to hold the dog, the other to apply medication. Some other tips include the following:

- ✔ **Liquid medication.** Ask your veterinarian for some large syringes, with the needles removed. These are marked on the sides to make measuring easy, and they're easier, too, at getting liquid medicine in the right place. Raise your dog's muzzle and lift her lip on one side. Ease the tip of the syringe to the back of the throat and then release the liquid in a slow, steady stream.

- ✔ **Ear medication.** Lay a large towel across your lap and coax your dog to put her head on top of it with gentle massage and encouragement. Apply ear drops, massaging the base of the ear gently.

- ✔ **Eye medication.** Have your pet sit between your legs and hold her muzzle up from behind. Gently apply a line of medication from the tube across the length of the eye, being careful not to touch the surface. Try to hit drops squarely in the center. Close the lid for a couple of seconds to let the medication distribute evenly.

As with anything your pet would rather avoid, be patient, gentle, and firm — and follow with praise. If you're having trouble medicating your dog, talk to your veterinarian about alternatives.

A syringe with the needle removed is an easy way to give liquid medication.

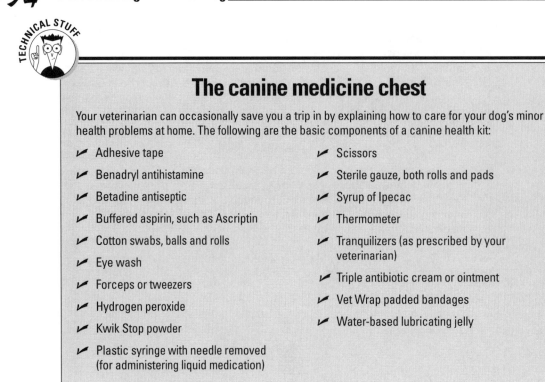

The canine medicine chest

Your veterinarian can occasionally save you a trip in by explaining how to care for your dog's minor health problems at home. The following are the basic components of a canine health kit:

- Adhesive tape
- Benadryl antihistamine
- Betadine antiseptic
- Buffered aspirin, such as Ascriptin
- Cotton swabs, balls and rolls
- Eye wash
- Forceps or tweezers
- Hydrogen peroxide
- Kwik Stop powder
- Plastic syringe with needle removed (for administering liquid medication)

- Scissors
- Sterile gauze, both rolls and pads
- Syrup of Ipecac
- Thermometer
- Tranquilizers (as prescribed by your veterinarian)
- Triple antibiotic cream or ointment
- Vet Wrap padded bandages
- Water-based lubricating jelly

Chapter 11

Basic Training

. . . .

. . . .

*A*n old dog-training adage still applies today: *Every handler gets the dog he deserves.*

In other words, the most important factor in training is not your dog, but *you.* You're the boss — or you should be — and you need to know enough about canine language so you can teach your dog *your* language. You need to show your dog what you want her to do and give her a reason for doing it — and an understanding that not doing the very reasonable things you ask of her is unacceptable.

Your dog is trained, whether you do anything or not. If you don't guide her toward good behaviors, she fills her life with bad ones, instead. If you don't lead, she does. And that's bad news for a dog. Shelters, rescue groups, and newspaper classifieds have plenty of dogs like that: dogs with problems. Their chances of finding happiness — or even staying alive — aren't very good at all.

That's not the way things have to be. First, resolve in your own mind your dog *must* be trained and training is not a one-shot deal, but an intrinsic and ongoing part of the promise you make to your dog when you bring her into your life.

Then, think of the rewards of dog training. The obvious reward is good manners, but the bigger payoff is that as you train your own dog, the bond between you grows stronger, the love deeper.

The special relationship between an owner and a well-mannered dog is the Total Dog Experience, and I don't want either one of you to miss it.

The importance of socializing and early training for puppies is in Chapter 6. House-training solutions are in Chapter 8, and help with fixing other annoying behaviors is in Chapter 12. And because there's more to life than good manners, you'll want to check out Chapter 20 for ten cool tricks you can teach your dog.

A Few Words about Aggression

If you have ever, even for a moment, been afraid of your dog or what he might do, read the rest of this segment carefully and then put the book down, for now. The rest of this chapter and the next is not for you. Not yet, anyway. You need serious one-on-one help, whether you realize it or not.

Aggression in dogs has both genetic factors and learned ones. Some dogs are born with the potential to be aggressive, and that potential can be fully realized in a home that is either encouraging aggressive behavior or ill-equipped to cope with it. Other perfectly nice dogs can become unreliable because of abusive treatment.

Is your dog potentially dangerous? Answer these questions, and be brutally honest:

- ✔ **Has your dog ever "stared you down"?** I'm not talking about a loving gaze — my dogs hold those for minutes at a time. I'm talking about a hard, fixed, glassy-eyed stare that may be accompanied by erect body posture — stiff legs, ears forward, hackles raised.

- ✔ **Do you avoid doing certain things with your dog because they elicit growling or a show of teeth?** Are you unable, for example, to approach your dog while he's eating or ask him to get off the couch?

- ✔ **Do you make excuses for his aggressive behavior, or figure he'll "grow out of it"?**

- ✔ **Do you consider your dog "safe" —** *except* **around a particular group of people, such as children?** When he growls at the veterinarian, do you tell yourself the behavior is reasonable, and a veterinarian should be able to cope with it, after all?

- ✔ **Has your dog ever bitten anyone, even it's "only" once and because "it was an accident," "he was scared," "he's usually so good!" or some other equally inexcusable rationalization?** People often make excuses for the behavior of little dogs, but growling and snapping is no more acceptable from a Pomeranian than from a pit bull.

If, after answering these questions, you suspect that you have a problem, get help. *Now.* You should no more attempt to cure aggression yourself than you should try to treat cancer. The reason is the same: You haven't the training and the expertise to do so. If you suddenly try to eliminate your dog's self-appointed role of leader of your pack, there'll be trouble. If you even attempt to make the eye contact I suggest with such a dog, you may get bitten. So don't.

Ask your veterinarian for a referral to a trainer or behaviorist with experience in aggressive dogs. And realize from the start that just like cancer, aggression is a disease that is sometimes not curable. Have your dog neutered — most dogs involved in attacks are young, unneutered males — and follow the expert's advice. But if, in the end, you have a dog who still cannot be trusted, have him euthanized. I'm sorry if that upsets you, but this is the only responsible thing to do. If your dog is aggressive, he'll probably end up euthanized eventually. The difference is that if you wait, someone will get hurt first.

Finding an aggressive dog a new home — one with no children, perhaps — is not the answer. Children are everywhere, and you may be responsible for one of them being hurt if you pass a problem dog on to someone else. Especially if you do so without admitting the real reason you're finding him a new home, knowing that no one wants to adopt a biter. You do the dog no kindness, and you put the new family at risk.

Maybe you prefer to live in a state of denial, hoping nothing awful involving your dog will ever happen. More than 4.5 million American dog owners are jolted into reality every year — 4.5 million being the number of bites estimated by the U.S. Centers for Disease Control and Prevention. Of those attacks, 800,000 required medical treatment in 1994 — and 15 were fatal. Children were the most frequent victims.

Need more reasons to act? You could lose your homeowners insurance — or more. U.S. insurance companies shelled out more than $1 billion in 1994 to settle dog-bite liability claims. The companies say claims are rising both in number and value — and so, too, are the numbers of lawsuits. Even one "minor" bite claim could cost you your homeowner's insurance — and a vicious attack could cost you a lot more than that.

Aggressive behavior never improves on its own; it only gets worse. So get help. Now.

Developing the Right Attitude toward Training

If you don't have an aggressive dog, consider yourself lucky. Chances are, though, you probably have a dog who's a little out of control. One who drives you just a little bit crazy. A canine adolescent, more often than not. You've given

Dog fight!

Anyone who has ever walked a dog has experienced that terrifying moment when a vicious, unleashed dog is intent on doing harm to your dog. It's a dangerous situation even for owners of big dogs; for small dogs, it could be a fatal encounter.

While the best strategy is to avoid dogs who appear aggressive — those with erect body stances instead of the relaxed, ears back attitude of a dog coming over to play — sometimes there's no escape from a dominant dog.

If the other dog's owner is nearby, *demand* he put his canine terrorist on leash. Should he be clueless enough to say "mine's friendly," yell back "mine's not" and make your demand again.

If a fight starts, *stay out of it.* You could be badly hurt. If you're willing to risk a bite and there's another person to help, pull the dogs apart by their tails — *not* their collars! If you're alone and there's a hose nearby, hitting them in the chops with a high-volume water spray usually stops the action.

If *your* dogs are constantly fighting, call a trainer or behaviorist to help you develop strategies to make it clear you require your dogs to get along. Realize, however, that peace may never be possible, and you may have to find a new home for one of the dogs.

up waiting for her to outgrow her bad behavior — they never do! — and figure it's finally time to . . . (big sigh) . . . train her. You're thinking you can't avoid training; it just has to be done, like cleaning leaves out of the rain gutters.

Stop!

Now, consider the following: If you have a bad attitude toward training, so, too, will your dog. If you think training is a joyless chore, she'll hate it, every minute. If you walk around jerking on her collar and swearing, she'll wonder what she has done to deserve your anger, and she'll be too busy worrying about that to learn anything.

If you tell her she's stupid, she will be.

Expect success from her and be willing to work for it. Praise her not only for succeeding, but for trying. Learning is hard for her, and stressful. Think of your dog as a person who has just moved to your house from a country where the language and customs are different — a transpecies exchange student. She was born, after all, a dog, and you're asking her to live as a member of a human family. You're asking her to learn the language and follow the rules.

The fact that this feat is ever accomplished at all is nothing less than a miracle. So celebrate it. With her.

Consider dog training not as a mechanical thing — if you do X, your dog does Y — but rather as something organic — alive, interconnected, and ever-changing. A well-mannered dog becomes that way from the inside out. "Sit" and "stay" are the least of it, really, and are only the visible manifestations of what that dog is on the inside: A confident, comfortable, and secure member of a loving, human pack. A dog who is, quite simply, a joy to live with.

We all get cranky sometimes. If you've had a horrid day at work, a fight with your spouse, or the mechanic just told you the cost to fix your car is $2,700, you're probably better off skipping any efforts at teaching your dog something new. Instead, use your dog to help you ease out of your funk: Play fetch, or just hang out with her. Pet her while you watch TV — it's good for your blood pressure.

Likewise, if you start out a training session fine and feel yourself getting frustrated and angry, don't push things. End on a positive note. Ask your dog for something you know she knows well and, when she does it, praise her. Then call it a day. If you can't manage even that, just stop before you both get even more frustrated.

In either case, remember: Tomorrow is another day.

Keys to Success

Ask a person who has never owned or trained a dog to teach one to sit and I bet he can come up with a successful plan without any prompting. Hold the front end up, push the back end down while saying the command word of their choice — "sit," "plant it," or even "keyboard." The mechanics of training aren't that hard to understand. But to get your dog to mind you consistently and happily, you're going to need to know a little more.

Dog training is not about eight Thursday-night group classes and the training is over, forever. The training is *never* over. You teach, and then you practice, in ever more challenging circumstances. You correct the behavior you don't want. And you integrate your dog's lessons into everyday life so that the lessons are never, ever lost. Remember the French you learned in high school? How good are you at it now? If you don't use it, you lose it, and the same can be said of skills you teach your dog.

After he knows the language, keep asking him to use it. Following are some tips that will help both of you:

Be on the same team

Don't think of training your dog as a you versus your dog endeavor. Think, instead, about the two of you being on the same team, albeit in different positions. Consider yourself the quarterback, if you like: You call the plays. Maybe you've noticed that the quarterback doesn't get very far without folks to follow those plays. Winning is a team effort.

Of course, your dog has to learn the plays first, and you're the one to teach him. And this relationship is still not an adversarial one. You show your dog the things he needs to learn, and you do so with love and respect, which your dog will return in kind.

To bring your dog onto your team and show him the plays you'll be calling, you need to spend time with him. Bring him into your life. Let him sleep in a crate in your bedroom, practice his "sits" in the kitchen. The more opportunities for interaction and practice you have, the faster and more reliably your dog performs.

Be positive

This tip goes back to having the right attitude, of course, but it's more than that. Praise that's well timed and appropriate is essential to your dog's learning process. If all you ever do is tell your dog "no," your relationship isn't going to be a very good one. How would you like to work with a boss like that?

Praise is cheap — free, in fact! — so use it, lots. Use praise when your dog tries to get it right. Use it more when your dog succeeds. Use it when your dog just pays attention to you, because as you find out in a moment, that's the first step in the training.

You don't have to be some gushing goof, but you *do* need to let your dog know when you're proud of her.

Be fair with corrections

Make sure your dog understands what you want before you correct him for not doing it. And let the punishment fit the crime.

A correction should *not* be a release of anger, a clearing out of pent-up feelings by unloading them on the apparent cause of the problem, your dog. Instead, a correction is another way to communicate with your dog, to foster in him a clear understanding of his place in your human pack. As such, a proper correction is another way to strengthen the bond between you and your pet.

At its mildest level, a correction is the absence of praise. The human equivalent of the mother dog's scruff shake is next up — a quick pull and release on a training collar. Some transactions call for the canine equivalent of reading a dog the riot act. More on when — and how — to correct in a minute. Right now I want you to remember to always ask yourself if you're being fair before you give in to the knee-jerk reaction to leash-jerk.

Be consistent

How would you do in your job if your boss kept changing the names of your tasks or asked you to do two things at once? Or had different rules for different places and times? It would drive you nuts, wouldn't it? And yet, that's exactly what people do to their dogs, all of the time. Here are some things to think about:

- **Training consistency.** Two things to remember: After your dog knows a command, use it the same way each time and never change its meaning. The most common of these is probably saying "sit *down*" to a dog when you really mean "sit." Now, you know when someone says that to you, it's the same thing as "sit." But if you teach your dog "sit" and "down" as two seperate commands, you can understand why it's confusing. Which do you want?

  Same for saying "down" when you really mean "off." I was visiting someone once when her cocker spaniel jumped on the couch beside me. "Down!" commanded her owner, and the dog laid down beside me. "She's so *willful,*" said the woman, who didn't realize the dog had in fact obeyed her perfectly.

  Another kind of inconsistency is when you never expect your dog to mind until you've repeated the command a few times. Instead of teaching your dog to mind, you teach her that she doesn't even have to pay attention until the veins start popping out on your neck. After a dog knows a command, *always insist* that she execute the behavior. Don't repeat the command. She heard you the first time.

- **Situational consistency.** People who compete with their dogs in obedience trials have a word for dogs who know they can get away with disobedience in certain situations — they call them *ringwise*. Because the rules say you can't correct your dog in the competition ring, some dogs realize they can get away with murder. ("Hahaha, and she can't stop me, because that person with the clipboard won't let her!" thinks the dog.)

  Trainers trip up ringwise dogs by *proofing* them: Setting up situations that beg their dogs to test the limits or duplicate the times they actually have. They go to practice matches where they *can* correct, or set up a ring with a "judge" in it, all to present an opportunity to strengthen their dog's training. (See Chapter 16 for more information on canine competitions.)

Like the ringwise obedience-trial competitor, a lot of dogs learn to recognize situations where they can get away with murder. They learn, for example, that you're timid about enforcing the rules in public, lest someone glare at you for correcting your dog. Or maybe that when you're in a hurry you'll shrug off disobedience: You're in a rush to feed your dog, for example, and when you say "sit," he doesn't. And you throw the food down anyway.

If "sit" doesn't always mean "sit," eventually it will never mean "sit." Don't put up with these games.

Build on your successes

Dog training succeeds by degrees and creativity. You continue to expand the length of time and the number of situations in which your dog will execute a command, and you look for new ways to use what he knows so you can continue to develop and strengthen the bond between you.

The half-hour "down-stay," for example, is great for reinforcing your position as leader. With just a couple of words and no more effort than it takes to watch TV — which you can certainly do during that half-hour — your dog will spend a pretty solid chunk of time reflecting on your status as a god. A reasonable and loving god, but still a deity, and don't you forget it, furball. What else does he have to do, after all? He's stuck there until you say otherwise.

Phone call follies

I got a call once from a person who worked as an order-taker for a catalog company, and he wanted the answer to something that had been driving him crazy: Why do dogs bark when their owners are on the phone?

Because they know they can, that's why.

The problem starts when a dog tests the water by barking at you once. If he did that while you were home, by yourself, watching TV, you'd probably correct him. But you don't want to do that when you're on the phone — you're busy, after all, and you don't want the person on the other end to think a) you have a bad dog or b)

you're a mean person. So instead, you either do nothing or you pet your dog to shut him up.

Before too long, you have a dog who starts yapping every time you pick up the phone. Because you've not only been inconsistent, but you've also rewarded the behavior.

On behalf of catalog order-takers everywhere, fix this problem. Arrange to have some friends call you expressly for the purpose of convincing your dog he's expected to behave no matter what you're doing. Show him the meaning of consistency while you chat.

"Half-hour down-stay!" you say. "My dog would *never* do that." Not today, he won't. First he has to learn "down." Then he has to learn "stay." Then he has to learn to do both for one minute, then five, then fifteen, and so on. And he has to learn that if the phone rings he can't move. If you leave and return, he can't move. If you sing, he can't move. This behavior is taught step-by-step, over time.

So build. A little bit at a time, celebrating every step along the way. Living is learning, and learning is good.

What good is the half-hour "down-stay"? Think of it not as some draconian measure but instead as canine meditation. Your dog will *not* be uncomfortable, and you are *not* being unreasonable. During that time you've asked him to "stay," the one topic he's meditating about is your status as leader of his pack, and that's exactly what you want him to be thinking — that you're the boss. A nice boss, a reasonable boss, but a boss nonetheless. The half-hour "down-stay" helps to build an obedient dog from the inside out, and complements all your other efforts to teach your dog good manners.

Tools for Teaching

Dog training isn't expensive, or it needn't be. You need a leash and a properly fitted collar, but the other things you need are free for the asking. The trick is knowing what they are, how they work, and when to use them.

A six-foot lead you can handle easily — leather or nylon, and neither too wide nor too thin — is a must, as is a slip training collar that is properly fitted and put on. For help in choosing and using both, see Chapter 4. Another thing to remember: Slip collars should *never* be used on puppies. Use a flat collar, instead.

Never, ever use a slip collar as your dog's regular collar. The slip collar should be used only for training and walking and must be removed when you are not working with your dog. Otherwise you risk your dog's getting the collar caught and choking to death. A buckled or snap-connect nonadjustable collar should be your dog's regular collar — and don't forget those ID tags!

You can transmit your authority to your dog in many wordless ways, and before you start a formal training program you should be using these, including leash-bonding and "people first" rules. See the "Establish a routine" section in Chapter 9.

Getting your dog's attention

You're not going to be able to teach your dog anything if you can't get his attention. One of the best ways to do so is to teach him to give you eye contact on demand.

Eye contact is one of the most important areas of communication for dogs, and mastering eye contact, dog-style, immediately strengthens your relationship. Catch your dog's eye by swooping your hand under his chin, bringing your fingers back up near your eyes while you make a clucking noise, and say his name, followed by "look," or "watch." The motion upward and the sound orients your dog's eyes up so that he's looking right into your own. When they lock in, hold for a split second, smile and praise. This command may take time to learn, because dogs avoid eye contact to show respect. Build up your time until your dog gives and holds eye contact until you release him. Practice this several times a day and always be loving and encouraging.

As your dog learns to respect and trust you more, you find that he looks at you more. He wants to see what you're doing, because you're where the action is.

Teaching your dog to make eye contact.

Some dogs get a little bit carried away with this devotion thing, to the point where it becomes a way of controlling *you*. The "phone follies" dogs are like that (see the sidebar "Phone call follies"). If your dog is becoming an attention addict, give him something to do to earn your praise — ideally, a half-hour down-stay on the other side of the room. Think of this activity as tough love, if you will, but it's better than spending the rest of your life unable to read your newspaper because your love-junkie dog is sticking his nose through it.

Your dog should know his name not as a command to go to you or as a swear word but as a request for his attention. Praise him for looking at you when you use his name, and then build on that to help get his attention before giving a command. If you're doing your eye-contact exercises, he'll start looking at you at the sound of his name, before he even hears "look." Praise him! Eventually you won't even have to say look. The sequence will be: "Bosco (not yelled, but clear and encouraging) . . ." and then a slight pause, and then the command. Immediate praise for success, or correction for lollygagging (after he knows the command, of course).

Giving praise

All praise is good, but praise specially tailored to connect with the dog's way of reacting is ten times as effective. Here are some tips to follow:

- ✔ **Use the right tone of voice.** Dogs communicate with one another through sounds easily duplicated by humans. If you're angry with your dog, for example, dropping your voice to a low rumble closely approximates the growling of a dog. For praise, use a sweet, high-pitched crooning voice: "Gooooooooood, dooooggggg. Aaaren't youuuu a gooood doooog?"

- ✔ **Tailor your petting style to your dog.** Some dogs go crazy when petted; others hardly notice. Use a little chest pat or scratch for those who tend to be overly enthusiastic, and be a little more boisterous for the ones who really warm to being jollied. Don't let the dog use petting as an excuse to go crazy — lighten up on the pats, but don't correct him — and let your voice do most of the praising.

- ✔ **Smile!** Dogs understand many of our facial expressions because they use similar ones to communicate with each other. A smiling face is understood in both species, but if you really want to get through, make the smile as wide open as you can. You're trying to approximate that big panting grin a happy dog has. Panting is optional (but kind of fun).

What about using treats to train your dog? They can be a quick way to train, and a lot of trainers have their clients use them for that reason. Unfortunately, many people take away the wrong lesson: They come to believe in the treat not as a way to shape behavior, step by step — for which treats can work *very* well — but rather as the wages for obedience. Dog sits, dog gets a treat. Dog sits, dog gets a treat. And guess what happens? You end up with a dog who won't pay attention to you if you aren't in a position to pay the edible going rate.

And what about the relationship that's supposed to be developing from the inside out, that special bond? It doesn't. To your dog, you're a vending machine, not a leader.

I have nothing against using treats for training — they're especially useful for trick training, or for teaching any behavior that requires your dog to be in precise positions, such as those demanded of top-level competitors in obedience trials. But if you're not at the same time showing your dog his proper place in your "pack" by using the commands *without* food after he learns them, you're not really teaching him much of anything.

Maintaining control and giving correction

During training, control and correction are both handled by a collar and leash, which are used both to guide your pet into correct position and to keep him from getting into wrong ones — such as a full-out gallop, heading away from you.

You also correct your dog with your voice, and you need to be sure that you're using both your voice and your vocabulary properly. I don't use the word "no" much because it's so overused. Instead, I use my "bad dog" sound, kind of a honking "Augh," often preceded by a very loud and dramatic intake of air, like the gasp you make involuntarily when you find your dog has chewed your favorite shoes. The word or sound you use should be sharp, guttural, and dramatic. You should throw the sound at your dog, like a rock. Put the emphasis on the correction word, not on your dog's name, to which there should never be any negative connotations.

Using a release word

The last thing you need is a word to let your dog know he is through with the command you gave him. Probably the most common in use is "OK" — regrettably, it's the one I use — but a real obvious reason exists to choose another: Some of us say "OK" practically every other word, like, OK, you know what I mean, OK?

If this is you, pick another word. "Release" is a fine one. I also like the one the sheep dog people use at trials: "That'll do." It sounds very gracious!

Whatever you use, though, just be sure that you're consistent in the use of it.

Your release word can mean more than the end of an exercise, such as "stay." This word is also a sort of all-purpose "at ease" word. If your dog is heeling along at your side, staying out of trouble on a crowded sidewalk, say, you can use your release word to let him know doing a little sniffing is fine, and maybe a little leg-lifting, too.

TECHNICAL STUFF

Using a slip collar and leash correctly

To train your dog, you have to know how to use a slip collar and leash. With your dog at your left, put the loop of the leash over your right thumb, and let the leash drape across your palm and in front of your body. Measure out enough leash so that it's loose, but not drooping, fold the extra into your palm and close your fist. Now put your left hand on the leash, too. When you correct, use a fast, sideways pop-and-release motion. The collar tightens, the collar makes noise, the collar loosens, all in a second or two. This pop-and-release action is the key. A dog can't learn if a dog can't breathe, and if the collar's always cinched down, you're being cruel, inadvertently or not.

Which brings up a point people wonder about: Should you use a slip collar at all? Used properly, with a quick pop-and-release motion, this kind of collar is perfectly fine. (If the collar doesn't release, you probably have it on upside-down, see Chapter 4 for an illustration on putting a collar on correctly.) If you absolutely can't manage working with it without keeping the collar tight, enroll in a group class or get private lessons so that you can get a little one-on-one coaching.

Remember, if you have to correct a dog who knows something well and is choosing not to mind, you should still praise him for his compliance — even though you had to force it.

Basic Things Every Dog Should Know

In the preceding sections I explain *how* to train; in this section I tell a little bit about *what* to train. The basics are the ones taught in every obedience class and done to high-gloss perfection in obedience competitions.

Deliver commands in a sensible, no-nonsense tone loudly and clearly enough for your dog to hear — but never yell. Don't whine a command — "Tiiiigerrrrr, ssiiillliiiiitttttttt, baayaaabbbyyy" — and don't say it angrily or rough. Give the command as if you expect and are confident it will be obeyed.

How often should you train your dog? When you're trying to introduce something new, short lessons twice a day are ideal. You don't have to teach everything at once just because you're in a five- or six-week obedience class. Just do the "sit," twice a day for a week, if that's all you have time for. Then train the down, and so on. Just be — oh here's that word again — consistent. If you take up the same lesson for a day or two and then drop it for two weeks, you'll never get anywhere. After your dog knows the command, look for every opportunity to practice — and praise.

Sit

Two variations exist on this theme. In both, you take the slack out of the leash with your right hand, but don't tighten it. Then, spread the index finger and thumb of your left hand and place them on either side of your dog, just in front of his hip bone, the underside of your finger and thumb resting on his back. Say "sit" and exert gentle pressure inward and down. He should fold up into a sit to avoid the pressure, and when he does, even if only for a minute, praise.

Some trainers prefer to tuck, and that's fine, too, if this method works for your dog. Slide your hand over his rump and apply pressure to the back of his legs right at the "bend," tucking his legs and tail comfortably beneath him.

You can teach a puppy to sit without putting a hand or leash on him. All you need is gravity and a bowl of food. If you hold his dish above and slightly behind your pup's head, he'll look up, lose his balance and . . . sit! Just remember to fit the word in there, and you have it made!

For more tips on raising puppies right, see Chapters 6 and 8.

Down

You can teach the "down" in at least two ways as well. It builds on "sit," though, so make sure your dog is cool with that first. Both methods start with the dog sitting at your left side with the slack taken out of the leash.

The *magic spot* method involves bunching your first three fingers and making them as rigid as you can (for smaller dogs, you may only need two, or one). Between and just in front of your dog's shoulder blades is an indentation. If you slide your fingers in there and press gently down after giving the command "down," your dog's legs buckle and down he goes.

The spot can be hard to find without someone showing you, however, and hard to hit on a small dog. So if you're not getting anywhere with pressing the "magic spot," lift your dogs front legs and slide them forward.

In either case, don't forget praise when the chest hits the ground.

A dominant dog won't like this command much because, in the dog world, "down" is a sign of submission. If your dog passes the aggression test elsewhere in this chapter and "rumbles" when you start to teach the down, stop. If you're truly amazed because your dog is a major wimp, have your veterinarian take a look. Your dog may have a problem that's causing him pain when you attempt to place him into either a down or sit position. If you're *not* that surprised, call a trainer for advice and admit you probably fibbed on the aggression test.

Either way, stop. Doing so could save you a nasty bite.

Stay

"Stay" is a command used in conjunction with another, a request of your dog to hold whatever position you put him in, whether it's "sit," "down," or "rest on the couch." After your dog learns stay in relation to one position, applying the command to the other positions is pretty easy.

Start with the "sit," with the dog at your side, hold the leash in a straight line up from his head with all the slack out. Flash an open palm in front of your dog's nose — you can use hand signals in conjunction with any and all commands, but they work especially well here — and then say "stay." Step out in front of your dog so you can block his forward motion. If he moves, pop the collar, flash your hand, and repeat the "stay" command. If he stays, return to your position alongside him, and after a second or two, give him your release word and praise.

From there, you want to build up time and distances in slow increments. When you're working at the end of the six-foot leash and your dog is "staying" reliably, tug on the leash a little without making a sound. If he moves, go back and correct him with a leash-pop, repeat the command sequence, and try it again. When he resists the tug, return to position alongside him, release, and praise.

The books of Job

Many trainers are fine with dogs but not so hot when it comes to getting a point across to *people*. Sometimes I suspect they don't really want to: If you see how the magic trick works, you're not so impressed.

Trainer and author Job Michael Evans, who died in 1994, never had that problem. He was a funny and generous man, among the very best at explaining things in a way people could understand. My favorite example of his innovative seminar demonstrations involved the hand signal for "stay," which I used to have a hard time getting folks to do with the proper amount of emphasis and style.

Evans likened the signal to the move Diana Ross and the Supremes made on the word "stop" while performing "Stop, in the Name of Love" : a quick opening of the hand with fingers together and stiff, then closed. Every time I tell my dogs to "stay," I flash the Evans/Ross signal, and it not only works, but it also makes me smile.

Many of Evans' training books are still in print. I highly recommend them for both their entertaining style and their thoughtful and straightforward approach. Another trainer and author with a similar people-friendly style is Carol Lea Benjamin, who has been helping people to understand their dogs for more than 20 years.

Heel

Two kinds of "heels" are floating around, and most people only want one of them. In competitive obedience circles, heeling has been raised to an art form as demanding as ballroom dancing, where one false step on the part of handler or dog ruins the performance. The dogs prance at their trainers' sides, practically wrapped around their legs, head turned in, muzzle raised, eyes up. Handler and dog aren't much more than a hair's breath apart, and they glide together so gracefully.

Lovely, you say, but I just want my dog not to drag me down the street. Don't worry, there's that, too. To teach it, your dog should be sitting on your left. Call his name, say "heel" and step off on your left leg so he can see that you're leaving. Praise him for leaving and for staying alongside. If he darts forward, however, pop and correct with the leash, repeating "heel," and praising him for responding. Give the command and then do an about-face, praising him for following, pop-and-release for not, followed by praise. Keep your dog focused on you and keep praising for trying. When you stop, ask your dog to sit at your side. Eventually, that "sit" becomes automatic.

To watch a professional trainer teach the "heel" is impressive: She works quickly, dazzling the dog to the point where he has no choice but to pay attention and stay close. And that's what you should try for: Keep the dog moving on *your* terms, focused on you. Pop-release and praise. Keep it fast, keep it upbeat, *keep it going*.

Keep the leash loose, and corrections smart and fast. Pop! and release, good dog! Pop! and release, good dog! Remember if your dog can't breath, he can't learn, and if the collar's tight, you're hurting him and losing your leverage to boot.

Of all the basic commands, this one probably demands the most coordination on your part. It you can't walk and chew gum at the same time, you're probably going to have trouble saying, "Stanley, heel!," remembering to step out on your left foot, making your pop-and-release corrections suitably brisk, praising, and keeping the proper amount slack in the leash so the collar stays loose. If your head spins just thinking about it, you'll probably do better with the help of a trainer, in a group class, or private session.

Why is "heel position" on your left? Because you'll be carrying your shotgun on your right, of course! The heel exercise is derived from gun-dog training: The dogs would walk "at heel" on the left so they would not be shot when their owners raised their weapons to their right shoulders to shoot birds. The dogs would then be sent to retrieve the downed game, give it to their owners and return to heel. Now, heeling on the left is just tradition. Can you teach your dog to "heel" on your right side? You bet. But if you ever walk with friends and their dogs, go to an obedience class, or try to compete in obedience, you're going to get tangled.

"Heel position" is on your left, with your dog's shoulder even with the seam in your pants leg.

Come

Teaching the "come" is easy. Put your dog on a "sit-stay" on leash, call his name, say "come," reel him in with praise, and give more praise when he gets to you. So how come the majority of dog owners have to cross their fingers when they call their dogs? Here are a few reasons:

- ✔ **Your dog is afraid to come to you.** Recognize this scenario? Your dog slips past your 10-year-old daughter as she comes in the front door and takes off. You run after him, screaming "come" in all it's variations — "SANDYCOME!" "HERE! Sandy, I said HERE! NOW!" "YOU'RE DEAD! COME!" and so on. Sandy's running, but you finally corner him. He knows you're hot, so to try to appease you maybe he rolls over or takes a step forward. You grab him by the collar and scream at him — or worse — for not coming to you. You tell me: What is he going to do the next time? Keep running? You got it.

  The trick here is to be welcoming. Kneel down. Spread your arms. And when he moves in your direction praise; when he gets there, praise more. Even if you want to ring his neck. *Never correct a dog for coming to you.*

- ✔ **Your dog doesn't really know the command.** Sandy probably didn't. Few people practice this one. You probably use "sit" a half-dozen times a day, just around the house, but you probably never say "come" when you want your dog to come to you in the house. You probably just use his name. Or maybe not even that, since the opening of the refrigerator door gets you a canine appearance at the speed of light. But the dog doesn't know "come"; he knows if he's sitting in *just the right* place you may drop something. Big difference.

- ✔ **Your dog doesn't see why he should.** "Come" is where all that work in developing the relationship from within really pays off. A dog who knows what's expected of him and respects you is going to mind. A dog who knows you're not a deity but a flat-footed slow-poke who couldn't catch a bus is going to treat you like the fool he thinks you are.

How to fix this? Train your dog to "come" in increments, on-leash and on longer leashes and lighter lines still. Never let him get into a position where he learns you really can't do much about it when he bolts. Practice, not just in formal training but in everyday life. Build on your successes.

If your untrained dog slips out and takes off, try to use a command he knows well — like "sit" — instead of "come." This is an emergency after all — a wrong move and he could be road pizza. Most dogs know "sit" so well they'll plant their rumps and, once they're planted, you can praise and take their collars. Another possibility is to run *away* from your dog, enticing him to follow you — the chase instinct is very strong in dogs.

Remember, a loose-dog situation is not about dog training, but about dog *saving.* A near-disaster such as this one should convince you it's time to train your dog. If you don't, next time he slips out you may not be so lucky.

Great Things They Don't Teach in Obedience Class

The things you can teach your dog have no end, and you needn't stop with the five basic commands described in the preceding section. My friend Gay Currier, who started thinking and learning about dog training when she worked at the service-dog organization Canine Companions for Independence, got me thinking years ago about expanding my dogs' vocabulary. Gay's wonderful Dobie, Laramie, is quite old — 14 as I write this — but in her prime she knew dozens of useful commands. Here are a few I like so much I've taught them to my dogs and have recommended to my readers for years.

Don't let your mind stop because a trainer's — or author's — suggestions do. After reading this chapter you know how to train a dog, so build on your *own* success. If you have something you want to teach your dog, give the behavior a name and do so!

Wait

This is different from "stay" because the dog is not required to hold a position, just not cross an imaginary line of your choosing. To teach this command, position your dog in a doorway, call his name, say "wait," and draw your hand from frame to frame in front of his eyes. Walk back into the room and allow him to move around, and then step back out. If he follows across the imaginary line, give a voice correction, repeat the command and hand signal. When you're done, give your release word, let him cross the line, and praise.

This command has many uses. I tell my dogs "wait" when I open the car door, so they don't jump out into traffic. They "wait" before entering people's homes or leaving our own.

The "wait" command can help keep your landscaping from taking a beating. See dogs and gardens tips in Chapter 18.

Go to your bed

This one builds on "down," but is not so formal. It means "go there and plant it, pal" and is a great command for getting your dog out from underfoot. Call your dog's name, tell him to "go to your bed," lead him there, and tell him "down." With practice — and consistency, the "down" becomes automatic.

My friend Laura taught this one in reverse: Instead of teaching her border collie, Pancha, where she *should* be, she taught her where she *couldn't* be. The command: "Out of the kitchen," which meant: "Anywhere else but in this room."

The "wait" command is different from "stay" in that it teaches your dog not to cross an imaginary line of your choosing.

Paws up

Super for giving pills — or smooches — to big dogs. Call her name, pat the counter, say "paws up," and then lift her paws into position.

Off

What people often mean when they say "down": "I want all four of your paws on the floor, *now.*" This is not a punishment: It's a command. If your dog's on the couch or the bed without an invitation, take her by the collar, say "off," and then lead her down and praise. Likewise with the jumping dog, though then the command is best taught with a leash and slip collar. "Off," then pop-and-release in a downward motion until those feet hit the ground, ask for a "sit," and then praise.

Don't touch or leave it

Gay uses "don't touch"; I use "leave it." You can use "apple juice," as long as you're — what's that word? — consistent! Teach this command with a physical correction from the get-go. With your dog in a "sit-stay" and your hand in a fist,

Teaching your dog the "don't touch" command has many useful applications.

flat surface up, offer your dog a biscuit with the other. As she reaches for the biscuit, say "don't touch," and bop her under the chin, enough to close her jaw but not lift her off her feet. Offer the biscuit again, repeating the "don't touch" command and, if she hesitates or turns away, praise her. Few dogs need this demonstrated more than twice.

This command is another with many useful applications. A dog leads with his nose, after all, and a dog who knows "don't touch" isn't going to head in a direction you don't want him to go in. Use this command when you're walking and he dives for some dreadful leftover in a fast-food bag. Use it to keep him from lifting his leg where you don't want him to on walks — since the sniff is the prelude to the leg-lift, this command works well. If you drop your sandwich in front of him, "don't touch" assures you get to finish it — assuming you still want to, of course.

Getting Help

Learning dog-training from a book is hard, although millions try. If you're doing pretty well, but could use a little coaching, try a group class. The added benefits: Your dog gets socialized and tested under some distracting conditions.

Considering protection training

One of the reasons people get big dogs is for protection. Should you go the extra step and have yours trained to respond to a threat with aggression? For the overwhelming majority of people this is a frighteningly bad idea.

After a dog learns to be aggressive, putting the genie back in the bottle is hard. The best you can do is work to keep your dog under tight control. That's what people do who compete in the sport of Schutzhund (see Chapter 16 for more on this), and it's among the most demanding of dog sports, requiring constant practice and training by knowledgeable, experienced dog folks.

So you're willing to practice, and your dog respects you as leader. What about the rest of your family? What about your guests? Your dog is never "off" and must be put in a run or crate when not under your control. If someone else trains your dog and you haven't the time or personality to keep the training current, you can have a real time bomb on your hand.

Want another opinion? Ask your insurance agent. A dog who has been trained to attack and does may be seen in a vastly different light than one who attacks "accidentally" as far as your carrier is concerned when that lawsuit is eventually filed for the bite that's nearly inevitable.

Better to get a security system. You get discounts for those, not lawsuits.

As mentioned elsewhere in this chapter, you *need* help if your dog's aggressive. But you can also *use* help if you're just struggling. Sometimes a private lesson or two with a good trainer can save you weeks of misery that may lead to you even considering giving up on your dog. A good trainer can see what you're doing wrong and give you steps to fix the problem.

Some people send their dogs away to be trained and, for some, this option can be a good one. Be sure that the trainer shows you how to handle the dog when he returns, though, or soon, you're right back where you started.

Whatever kind of training help you choose, start with your veterinarian when looking for a trainer. Ask for references, and check them. The trainer you choose should spend the first lesson listening and watching, tailoring an approach to you and your dog.

Chapter 12
Problem-Solving

*O*ne of the things that has surprised me most in the years I've been writing about dogs and listening to dog lovers is not how many times problems, even some minor ones, put dogs in the shelters — to that, I've quite sadly become accustomed — but how many times they *don't*. I've heard some amazing stories over the years of what people have put up with — dogs who've eaten thousands of dollars worth of furniture, dogs who lift their legs on their owners, dogs who bark a thousand times a day in staccato bursts that would outpace a machine gun.

Do people like living with beastly dogs like this? I doubt it. But they hang in there, sometimes for years, hoping the problems will end before the dog does and just getting by as best they can in the meantime.

Others aren't anywhere near so tolerant. Some try a little, some try a lot but, in the end, these people throw up their hands and figure someone else — someone with "more time," "more space," "no children," or whatever — will fall in love with their dog behind the chain-link of a shelter run and everything will work out fine.

Neither approach to dog problems is a good one.

I'm not going to tell you all your dog problems can be fixed. Some can't. Sometimes the best you can do is make adjustments that make life with your dog easier. Sometimes you have the wrong breed type for your lifestyle (see Chapter 2 for more on breed choices) or a dog with problems caused by bad breeding, a lack of early socialization, or a history of abuse before you got her. All of which is why I put such emphasis elsewhere in this book on choosing the right dog from the right source and then putting some real effort into raising her. The time to decide that the hyperactive, unsocialized terriers produced by a clueless or careless breeder aren't the best match with your expensively and intricately landscaped yard is *before* you get the dog, not after.

Still, you *can* do a great deal, no matter your past mistakes or your dog's unfortunate history. And that's what this chapter is all about.

As with basic training, though, you first have to be willing to work with your dog, and you *must* realize that you're in for a long haul. Altering a problem behavior often has more to do with changing your relationship with your dog than with addressing that which is driving you crazy. Such things as digging and barking are often only symptoms, and treating the symptoms don't get you a cure.

If your dog has become a delinquent, working with him can help you to solve the problems.

Photo courtesy of Kerry Drager.

If your dog's showing aggressive behavior, you haven't got a problem, you've got a potential disaster. Stop here and turn to "Basic Training," Chapter 11. Read the section "A Few Words About Aggression." Take the test. And make a phone call to a trainer or behaviorist.

Problems from the Inside Out

As with teaching basic obedience to your dog, you have to look at the big picture when approaching problem behaviors. That's because problems are often a symptom of something larger — most commonly, a dog who's not having his needs met, physically, socially, or mentally.

Remember, dogs are social animals whose ancestors, long ago, lived as part of a pack, working together to hunt and raise young. More recent history has seen the development of dogs who work to serve humans, as hunting dogs, sled dogs, or sheep dogs. Is it any surprise that an intelligent breed such as the border collie, developed to work closely and diligently with a human companion, isn't going to be happy left alone for hours without a job to do? Should it shock you that an Alaskan malamute whose relatives pulled sleds across the tundra has so much energy that the only way he can release it alone in a barren backyard is to reduce a picnic table to splinters? And what about that Lab-shepherd cross, whose parents both come from long lines of intelligent, active, and hard-working dogs? Do you expect her to just hang out every day waiting for a few minutes of your time?

Be fair! While human-dog comparisons don't always work, this one does: How would *you* feel if you never went anywhere and no one ever expected much out of you? What would *you* do to relieve your boredom and anxiety? After a few weeks, you'd be ready to chew a picnic table, too.

 What if you *do* catch your dog in the act? Then he has a correction coming. Read him the riot act with verbal correction that's mostly verbal and a lot theatrical: Take the loose skin at either side of his neck in your hands, and lift him off his front paws just a little. Give him a little shake (commonly called a *scruff shake*), make eye contact, and verbally correct him, loudly and dramatically, but *not* angrily.

Although really letting him have it may feel good, remember that revenge should not be on your motive list, either. Use the minimal correction to get the point across. If a verbal correction is enough for your dog — especially a well-timed one just as he's reaching for that chicken on the table — then that's all you need. Let the correction fit the crime — and the dog.

A simple scruff shake, coupled with a verbal correction, can help to put your dog on the right track.

Recipe for Fixing Behavior Problems

Although I *do* give you some pointers on dealing with specific behavior problems in the upcoming sections, learning some of the things common to many of the problems and developing a strategy for addressing bad behavior from the inside out is more valuable. I once listed some of the behavior problems people have asked me about over the years and I came up with more than a hundred — many simply variations of some very common themes.

If you learn what goes into behavior problems, you're better equipped to deal with anything that comes up. It's like that old saying: *Give a man a fish and he eats for a day; teach him to fish, and he eats for the rest of his life.* I want you to develop the problem-solving skills you need to live happily with your dog forever.

Besides, if all I did here was tell you how to stop one problem behavior without telling you to fix the underlying cause, your dog may simply start another. He may trade barking for digging, or digging for chewing.

What dogs don't know — and what people should

Dogs don't know guilt, they don't know a be-havior is bad until you teach them so, and they don't know how to be spiteful. They're just be-ing dogs. They live in the now, and revenge is not in their gene pool. Barking, chewing, and digging are another story: They're natural, nor-mal behaviors, part of every dog's DNA.

Which means a lot of the motives some people attribute to dogs for their behavior just can't be. They don't chew because they're mad at you for leaving them; they chew because they're stressed about being alone; chewing fills the time and makes them feel better.

"Aha!" you say, "if that's true, how come when I come home and find a mess my dog looks guilty and tries to find a place to hide?"

Look at this scenario through his eyes. Your owner comes home, and you're trotting happily down the hall to meet him when you hear . . . swearing. You pause, uncertain. Then . . . yelling, and *you hear your name* in the middle of that diatribe. And you realize: He's mad at *me!* Why, you have no idea — you've long forgotten chewing all his underwear — but you're scared and fairly certain the most prudent plan of action would be to take off.

When he finds you, he's so angry it scares you, and so you do your best to appease him, dog style. You roll over and show your belly, or maybe you release a little urine. A dog would see both as efforts to say, "I'm sorry, I'm sorry, I don't know what's making you angry but I apologize, any-way," but instead . . . more yelling, and maybe a smack.

Get the point? A display like this one doesn't teach your dog anything except that you're an unpredictable lunatic. And that doesn't get you any closer to solving that chewing problem.

Some dogs have problems because they don't feel their place in the household is secure. For some tips on giving your dog the help he needs, start using the leash-bonding and "people first" rules in the "Establish a routine" section in Chapter 9. Going back to these basics is a good refresher course in "me person, you dog" for any dog.

Ensure good health, inside and out

The first step to solving a behavior problem is to make sure that it's not a health problem, *especially* if nothing has changed in your life except suddenly you have a dog problem. For example, a dog who starts throwing fits when you try to brush out the mats that form in the feathery hair behind his ears may have a painful ear infection. Two more examples: Some kinds of chewing can be attributed to nutritional deficiencies, and some house-soiling problems can be the result of a urinary-tract infection.

Don't guess at the problem and throw a home remedy at it. S*ee your veterinarian.* You'll probably save money in the long run, and you'll certainly spare your pet some misery.

After your dog checks out OK on the medical front, you need to start addressing the other necessities of his life:

- ✔ **Mental exercise.** Training is for life. Your dog needs to keep learning, and keep using all he has been taught. That doesn't mean, however, that you have to make formal obedience sessions a permanent part of your life. Think, instead, of creative ways to expand your dog's working vocabulary and integrate the skills he has learned into your life together. When you play fetch, vary the routine: Make him do a "sit" or "down" before you take the ball from him. Put him on "stay," throw the ball, and then send him. Have two family members play recall games with him in the house: One calls and praises, and then the other does. These games keep him engaged, and they also help enforce his place in your family, which makes him feel confident and secure.

- ✔ **Physical exercise.** Probably one of the biggest contributors to dog behavior problems is that dogs don't get nearly enough exercise. (Lack of exercise is also a big contributor to health problems: Too much food and not enough exercise make dogs fat.) By enough exercise I don't mean a walk around the block, stopping and sniffing at every shrub, street light, and fire hydrant. These outings are important, too, for your dog's mental health, not his physical one.

    Your dog needs 30 to 40 minutes of aerobic exercise that gets his heart pumping, and he needs it three or more times a week to stay fit, burn excess energy, and alleviate the stresses of modern life, which for many dogs starts with being a latchkey pup. This kind of exercise is especially important for dogs with a working heritage such as sporting or herding breeds. They need to *move!*

    The good news is that you don't need to live in the country to keep your dog well exercised. Folks in Manhattan manage it as well as anyone around, arranging doggy play groups and visiting dog runs. You just need some time and some creativity.

Fetch is a fantastic way to give your dog aerobic exercise. ***Tip:*** Get an old tennis racket to get some real distance on those tennis balls. Jogging is another way to get canine hearts pumping. If you don't jog and your dog is well-behaved on-leash, you may have a friend or neighbor who'd welcome the company and the added security. Swimming is a natural for retriever types, and if you're lucky enough to be near an off-leash dog park, play with other dogs is a first-rate exercise option.

A gentle stroll is important for your dog, but so, too, is regular exercise that gets the heart pumping.

Photo courtesy of Gay Currier.

Bicycling is another great exercise, and three products are on the market designed to help you bicycle safely. They attach to the bicycle and so allow you to keep both of your hands on the handlebars — a much safer plan than holding onto a leash with one hand and the bike with the other. The three products on the market are the Springer, the Bicycle Dog Leash, and the K9 Cruiser. Check out this book's "Additional Resources" appendix for contact numbers.

Roadwork such as jogging or tagging alongside a bicycle can be good for dogs, but remember to pace your dog properly: A brisk trot is ideal.

Thinking of inventing an indoor dog exerciser? A treadmill for dogs? Don't bother: They've been around for years. One such product is The Trotter, a variable-speed treadmill used by show-dog handlers to keep dogs in top condition for the ring. The Trotter can be yours for a mere $1,795 and, if you want one, the contact for that, too, is in the "Additional Resources" appendix.

A few caveats about exercise, especially roadwork. Have your veterinarian sign off on any exercise program, making sure that your dog hasn't any joint problems that rule out any particular kind of exercise. Make sure that you build up slowly, especially if your dog is overweight. Let your dog set the pace, and check the bottoms of his feet (the smooth parts are called *pads*) often for tears or cuts.

A handful of manufacturers make it easy to exercise your dog while riding a bike.

Exercise when the weather is cool — dogs aren't as efficient at lowering their body temperature as we are — carry water, always, and know the signs of heat stress: glassy eyes, frantic panting. If your dog gets in trouble, get him wet and call your veterinarian *immediately*.

Do *not* force puppies to sustain a pounding pace, especially on pavement, lest you injure their developing bones. That means no jogging or bicycling until they're through adolescence — two years old is a good ballpark figure, but check with your veterinarian.

Minimize mischief opportunities

As with any relationship, you're going to have to make some adjustments for living with your dog. One of those is that you're probably not going to be able to put meat scraps in an open-topped kitchen trash can that just happens to be at perfect nose height for your dog. Yes, you can correct your dog when you catch her in the trash and, yes, you can booby-trap the garbage to make it less appealing (see the upcoming section "Let the situation teach the dog"), but sometimes the best answer is to get a trash can with a lid, or one that fits under the sink or behind a door you can close.

Sometimes doing things a little differently just makes sense with a dog in the house. Not that I want to add even more to the toilet seat wars that rage in some households, but if you want to know how to keep your dog from drinking out of the toilet, how about looking for the obvious answer: Close the lid. (Come to think about it, that solves the human gender war over this issue, too.)

Another problem where an adjustment is in order: Dogs who love to snack from the litter box (which is most of them, really). Put your cat's litter box in a place where the cat has access and the dog does not.

Some adjustments are forever, some not. When you have a dog who goes nuts when you leave her alone, the answer — while you're building up her confidence and taking care of her exercise needs, of course — is not to give her more choices, but less. That may mean putting her in a crate with a chew toy while you're gone and then slowly building up the space available to her, room by room.

Again, the crate comes to the rescue as one of the best ways to deal with dog problems. For more on choosing a crate for your dog, read the section on them in Chapter 4.

Substitute other behaviors

Instead of jumping on your dog for what he *can't* chew, show him what he's allowed to chew and praise him for doing so. Make his toys more appealing than your shoes or the remote control: One tactic is to take a destruction-proof Kong toy — more on this marvel and other top toys in Chapter 4 — and put peanut butter inside it. Your dog stays busy for hours.

For a special discussion on puppy chewing — a normal part of the teething process — see Chapter 6.

Another kind of substitution is to put an activity you approve of in the place of one you do not. For example: Teach the dog who jumps up on people that sitting, not jumping, gets her the attention she's looking for. And be consistent: If you don't want your dog to jump up in greeting, don't ever let her. No fair saying that jumping is OK when you're in jeans but not when you're dressed for an evening out.

Let the situation teach the dog

You can help steer your dog away from inappropriate behavior by making the objects you want to protect do their part to discourage your dog. You can do so in three ways:

✔ **Make the object taste bad.** Coat the object with something dogs find hateful, such as Bitter Apple, available in any pet-supply store. Tabasco sauce is another disagreeable taste to dogs. No matter what you choose, remember to test it on a small area first, in case the product you use causes a staining problem.

✔ **Make the object startle him.** Balloons and mousetraps make sharp noises that startle your dog and help him decide that maybe he'd better leave the booby-trapped area alone. Some products give off a piercing noise when motion is detected near them, and these can work, too. (The mousetrap won't hurt your pet: It's the noise of it snapping shut and the motion that scares them.)

✔ **Make the object shocking.** Vinyl mats and strips that give off a tiny static shock can be very effective in teaching dogs to stay off furniture and countertops.

Mousetraps don't hurt dogs, but the noise they make when triggered can startle them into leaving trash alone.

Problems That Often Put Dogs in the Shelter (And Their Solutions)

Ready to problem-solve? Let's see how your new skills apply to some of the things that really endanger dog's lives by putting them at risk for needing a new home.

Two problems that belong on this list are covered elsewhere. House-soiling is in Chapter 8, and biting, or any sign of aggression, is in Chapter 11.

Barking

This one puts your dog at risk from the people in your neighborhood: The poisoning of a nuisance barker is all too common. Even if your neighbors aren't the kind to take things into their own hands, a barking dog can run you afoul of the law, and not dealing with the situation marks you as an irresponsible and inconsiderate dog owner.

Vicious dogs may be what you read about in the papers, but the barking dog is truly the bane of urban and suburban life.

Dogs bark to express a variety of emotions: anxiety, boredom, territoriality, aggression, playfulness, and hunger, to name a few. In addition, barking sessions can be triggered by certain conditions in the dog's environment. For example, a dog who barks a warning when strangers are near will bark constantly and frantically if one side of the fence in his yard separates his area from a well-traveled, public sidewalk. Likewise, an intelligent, high-energy dog, neglected and bored in a lonely back yard, often rids himself of that excess energy by indulging in barking sessions that can last for hours, day or night.

Breed characteristics factor in, as well. Expecting an arctic breed or mix not to engage in an occasional howl — or a hound not to give voice when on the trail of a squirrel or rabbit — is unrealistic. Some herding dogs drive livestock by nipping and barking at their heels, and even their suburban relations many generations removed from the farm may still yap joyfully at the heels of the family's children at play.

Figure out the kind of barking your dog indulges in. Is he a fence-runner, trading insults with the dog on the other side of the back fence? Consider reworking the yard to deny him access to that activity. Is he a bored outside dog? Make him a part of your life, bring him in to the house, and make sure that the needs for physical and mental stimulation are being met. Another advantage of having him in the house: Many of the sounds that trigger barking are masked inside. (You can help this masking even further by leaving a radio on when you leave.)

Train him not to bark by teaching him the "quiet" or "enough" command. Allow him a bark or two — let him get his point across — and then say (don't yell) "enough" and put your hand over his muzzle. Praise him for stopping. If he's loose, you can also get the point across with a shot from a spray bottle: Allow him a bark or two, say "enough," squirt, and then praise him for stopping.

For tricks that use barking, see Chapter 22.

Problems people produce

Sometimes dog owners teach their pets bad habits.

Do you think your dog would ever have learned to beg if the first time he tried it he got nothing for his efforts? After this habit starts, some dogs can be very persuasive, either by being cute or annoying. How to stop this behavior? Stop giving in, and substitute a "down-stay"— see Chapter 11 for tips on training one — for begging at the table. As your dog gradually becomes convinced that he will never again see another piece of food delivered from under or over the table, he'll stop asking.

Another people-produced problem results from inconsistency. Say you're replacing an old couch with a new one, and while there wasn't much your dog could do to hurt the old one, you'd rather he stay off the new one. If you work with him, he'll eventually get the idea, but it isn't really very fair of you. If you don't want your dog on the furniture, ever, don't let him up on the furniture, ever.

And what about nervousness? Many people train their dogs to be afraid by soothing them when they show shyness. When a dog is acting shy, don't pet him and say, "There, there, it's OK," because doing so just reinforces the behavior. Instead, be-matter-of-fact with him: Jolly him along and keep moving. Show him he has nothing to be worried about.

Remember, preventing problems is *always* easier than fixing them later.

Photo courtesy of the HSUS/Hartrum.

It's not a quick fix — you still have to address the underlying problems of boredom, stress, and inactivity — but one kind of training collar offers real promise in fighting the battle of the bark. The ABS Anti-Barking System is a collar that releases a mist of harmless yet annoying citronella spray when the dog barks. The collar made a huge splash when a trainer recommended it on *Oprah* and has been in demand ever since.

The distributor, ImmunoVet of Tampa, FL, markets the product through veterinarians, trainers, and behaviorists, but it's starting to show up in catalogs aimed at the general public (see the "Addition Resources" appendix for more information). This device is a good alternative to an electric collar, which is really not a product that should be used without the guidance of a trainer or behaviorist.

The biggest problem with the citronella collar is the price — around $140 — but some trainers have set up programs for leasing them as part of an overall behavior modification program.

Digging

Filling up the holes and putting the dog's own stools inside is one oft-toted solution that can help — assuming your dog's not into eating stools; many are — but digging is a classic case where looking at the bigger picture is essential. If your dog is left outdoors while you're gone — or all the time — and never gets worked or exercised, he'll destroy your yard. Add to that the fact that some dogs — such as terrier types — simply live to dig and the fact that your yard is as holey as Swiss cheese is no surprise.

Three things that can help: Work and exercise your dog. Limit his unchaperoned access to the parts of the yard you'd like preserved. And give him an area where digging is OK — and tell him so!

More hints on having a nice yard and a dog are in Chapter 18.

Destructiveness when left alone

This is *the* classic problem with the dog you adopt as an adult. He's had his heart broken once and his hopes rekindled, by you. And then you leave him and he copes with his anxiety — will you ever return? — by going nuts, chewing, most typically.

You help build his confidence by getting him into a routine — more on this in Chapter 10 — and by training him. You relieve some of that excess energy by exercising him. And finally, while the cure is working from the inside out, you minimize the damage potential by confining him to a crate or small space.

The surgical option for barkers

Call it the "final solution before the final solution," if you will, but one method of controlling barking that works well in almost all cases is available: Debarking. The procedure is, however, as controversial as it is successful.

Debarking is the surgical altering under anesthesia of the vocal cords, changing them so that the dog can still bark, but at a greatly reduced volume. The "debarked" dog ends up with a bark that sounds like a harsh whisper, although the unpredictable final outcome, in terms of tone and volume, will vary from dog to dog.

While other options should be explored first, debarking is certainly better than euthanasia. It can be a good call in some cases, especially with dogs who simply like to yap. The dog still gets to bark, but the owner — and the neighbors — can live with it.

Talk to your veterinarian about this bark-control option.

A couple of other tips for dealing with separation anxiety:

- ✔ **Feed your dog his biggest meal before he's about to spend his biggest chunk of time alone.** What dogs do after they eat is sleep and, if you're lucky, he'll sleep most of the time you're gone.

- ✔ **Give him something special to chew on just as you leave.** Have a really good chewy that's just for his alone time, and hand it to him as you leave. He may even become a little glad to see you go!

- ✔ **Leave a radio on to mask outside noises.** Something soothing, please. Classical music. Your dog's anxious enough without having to listen to talk radio.

- ✔ **Practice no-fuss comings and goings.** Some people unwittingly make matters worse by staging hellos and good-byes that look like scenes from *Gone With the Wind,* and I'm thinking of the ones where Ashley leaves Melanie in Atlanta and then reappears after the war. Emotional stuff, and your dog doesn't need it. New rule: No pats. When you leave, tell your dog "guard the house" and give him his special chewy — it makes him feel important. When you return, tell him to "sit," and then praise slightly — I mean *very* slightly — and ignore him for the next ten minutes. Read your mail, check your answering machine, visit the bathroom. And then sit down, call him to you, and tell him how your day went. The message here is that all this in-and-out is *no big deal,* so chill already.

"Disobedient"

You say your dog's a holy terror, doesn't mind you when you say "sit" and drags you down the street? He needs exercise and training and lots and lots of practice. See Chapter 11 for the basics.

If your dog's an adolescent, he'll calm down some as he matures, but not enough to making living with him tolerable if you *don't* train him. So do.

New baby worries

Some people in this world — and maybe you're related to them — consider a dog as kind of a "parenting trial run," and suggest that when you're ready to try parenting "for real" you should find your dog another home. Because of this mentality, some dogs end up in shelters in kind of a preemptive strike against any potential problem interactions of dog and baby.

Sometimes those worries are justified. If you have a dog who has aggression problem — and I hate to keep harping on aggression, but I must in hopes of saving even one child from a bite, or worse — get help from a trainer or behaviorist with experience in dealing with these problems. And realize that a chance exists that you may *not* be able to trust your dog around children, which means you have some very difficult decisions to make.

More likely, though, you've just got a dog whose exuberance worries you. The best exercise for this is a solid "down-stay." Practice 30 minute "down-stays" in the couple of months before the baby arrives, especially in the nursery. When the baby comes home, practice them while you're nursing.

Want your dog to love your baby? Give him positive attention — praise and treats — only in the baby's presence for several weeks. He'll soon make the connection that the baby's a cool thing. If you pay attention to your dog only when you're away from the baby and ignore him when the baby's around, he never makes the connection between "cool thing" and "baby."

Aside from that, the usual rules apply: exercise and training. Managing both an infant and a dog in the first few months is hard, so maybe a neighbor kid can help you out with walks or you can find another creative solution.

Some parasites and contagious diseases can be passed from a dog to a child, but the risk of these is minimal if your veterinarian checks out your dog and you make sure that proper sanitary conditions are met in your home and yard.

Help your dog love your baby by letting him know he's special in your new child's presence.

Photo courtesy of Gay Currier.

Puppy Prozac and other "miracles"

Three times more dogs die because of behavior problems than because of cancer in the United States, and that sobering figure has caused a boom in the study of behavior in veterinary schools. One thing to come out of all that work — or at least the one that has caught the public's fancy — is the use of human psychiatric drugs such as Prozac and Valium in treating some canine behavior problems.

These findings are promising, no doubt, but there's still no quick fix. Whether an expert learned about dogs from years in academia or the School of Hard Knocks, you find very similar recommendations for proper health, exercise, and training.

For a thoughtful read on canine behavior problems and the use of medications to treat them, pick up Dr. Nicholas Dodman's *The Dog Who Loved Too Much: Tales, Treatments and the Psychology of Dogs.*

You're more likely to be able to find a veterinary behaviorist if you live in an urban area or near a veterinary college; ask your veterinarian for a referral. Whether you choose a veterinary behaviorist or a trainer, though, get help if you feel you're getting nowhere with your dog's problems. Sometimes a dog's owner isn't able to see what the real heart of the problem is and needs assistance in setting up a program that works.

Chapter 13

To Breed or Not To Breed

Somebody has to breed dogs, or there wouldn't be any. And I certainly want dogs to be in my life — and yours — for a long, long time. As there always have been, I hope, there will always be, good breeders. They care about their breed and the dogs they produce. They put years of study and effort into breeding dogs who are healthy and temperamentally sound—dogs who closely match the standards for their breed.

These breeders, unfortunately, are the minority. All is not right in the dog world, and it hasn't been for a long, long time. The reason: too many. Too many what?

✔ **Too many dogs** dying for the want of a home. Not just mixed breeds, either: Shelters and rescue groups deal with plenty of purebreds.

✔ **Too many dogs** with health problems that could be eliminated through conscientious breeding.

✔ **Too many dogs** with inherited personality problems, such as aggression or shyness or even yappiness.

✔ **Too many dogs** with personality problems caused by improper handling in the first weeks of their lives.

Too many dog problems are caused by people who shouldn't be breeding dogs. If you care about dogs — your dog, the dogs you're thinking of producing, and all dogs — you need to consider breeding very carefully. You need to educate yourself about your breed and the congenital health and temperament problems within your breed. You need to have a plan for breeding, and a plan — as well as a fund — for dealing with emergencies. You need time to help the puppies be born, to care for them, and socialize them. You need to know how to find good homes for those babies, and you need to be prepared to deal with the puppies you can't sell, or the ones who come back, for they are your responsibility, forever. These are all the things that typify a reputable breeder. You can be one, but you have to work at it, for there are no shortcuts.

If you cannot honestly say you can do all of those things a reputable breeder does, you need, finally, to spay or neuter your dog.

A Case Against Breeding

According to a 1995 survey by the American Animal Hospital Association, nearly 80 percent of all U.S. pets are spayed or neutered. The Amercian Kennel Club's findings back this up — most AKC-registered puppies are never bred.

What do these people know that you don't? Spayed and neutered dogs make happier, healthier, safer, and less expensive pets.

Health and behavior

Spaying and neutering have benefits that extend greatly beyond the subject of birth control.

A neutered male

- Is less likely to roam, less likely to fight, less likely to leg-lift in the house, and less likely to bite. The latter is especially significant: The profile of a dog involved in an attack on a human is typically a young, unneutered male.

- Is less likely be involved in a dog fight. Aggressive dogs find the presence of another unneutered male a challenge they take very seriously. If yours is a large dog he may escape such an attack with only a bite or two; a small dog could be killed.

- Is spared from testicular or prostate cancer.

For females, the behavior benefits aren't as remarkable, but the health benefits are more so. A spayed female

- Is safe from breast cancer if you spay her before her first season.

- Is protected from other cancers of the reproductive system.

TECHNICAL STUFF

Spaying and neutering: What's involved?

Spaying and *neutering* are the everyday terms for the surgical sterilization of a pet — spaying for the female, neutering for the male. Neutering — or *altering* — is also used to describe both procedures. The clinical terms for the two operations are *ovariohysterectomy*, for the female, and *castration*, for the male.

Both spaying and neutering must be done only by a veterinarian, and both require general anesthesia. The procedures have traditionally been performed starting at the age of six months but, in recent years, *early spay-neuter* on puppies as young as 8 weeks has been widely approved by veterinary groups and is gaining favor.

Spaying involves the removal of the female's entire reproduction system: The uterus, Fallopian tubes, and ovaries are taken out through an incision in the abdomen. Your veterinarian may require you to return to have your dog's stitches removed in about 10 days, time, or he may use stitches that are absorbed into the body. Recovery is fast, taking just a few days, during which you should limit your dog's activities — no jumping or boisterous play. Most owners notice very little difference in their female's personality.

In neutering, the male dog's testicles are removed through an incision just in front of the *scrotum,* the pouch holding the testicles. Self-absorbing stitches are the norm in this relatively minor procedure; your veterinarian will inform you if your dog needs any post-operative care.

Many dog owners are surprised to see that their dog doesn't "look" neutered at first, since the scrotum remains in place and may be somewhat swollen. The loose skin will shrink gradually away over a few weeks' time.

Behavioral changes can be dramatic in some neutered males. Such hormone-linked behaviors as mounting and dominance-related aggression will diminish in a good percentage of young adult males. In older ones, there may be little behavior change at all, and in dogs neutered before sexual maturity — before six months or so — sex-linked behaviors will likely never develop.

Spaying and neutering are among the most common medical procedures in the United States and Canada, and carry very little risk for your dog. Your veterinarian will discuss your role to ensure that any complications that *do* develop are dealt with promptly.

✔ Will not develop *pyometra,* a life-threatening infection of the uterus.

✔ Will not spot your carpets with the twice-yearly mess caused by the vaginal bleeding of a dog in season.

✔ Will not attract male callers.

Time and money

Breeding a dog takes time and money, especially for the owner of the female. Your dog, and the dog you breed her to, needs to be certified clear of inherited problems such as hip dysplasia, deafness, and inherited eye diseases. Both dogs need to be tested for venereal disease, and they need to be current on their vaccinations, free of parasites, and on heartworm preventive. This all costs money, a figure that could easily reach into the hundreds of dollars.

After the male dog has all his health clearances, his job is easy. He gets to the party early and leaves the scene before long. Not so for the female. Most of the costs are borne by her owner, starting with the stud fee. But even before you can pay that, you'll have to find a stud dog. You're not likely to find a suitable mate around the corner, or even in your town, which means you have spend more money to drive or ship your female.

Your dog will need high-quality food in greatly larger amounts than usual and possibly supplements, if your veterinarian recommends them, for the last few weeks of her pregnancy and the entire time she's nursing. If the litter is too much for her, you'll be hand-raising at least some of the puppies, and maybe all of them if she becomes unable to nurse. Above all, you have to be prepared to deal with a long list of medical emergencies that can threaten the life of both mother and puppies and can result in very large veterinary bills.

If your breed requires tail docking and dewclaw removals, you'll need to pay for that, along with vaccinations and other health needs, not to mention puppy food for the last three or four weeks you have the puppies after they've been weaned, assuming you can sell them promptly — sometimes you can't.

You have to take time off work when your dog's *whelping*, or giving birth, and you should take more time to socialize your pups to ensure that they become good pets for the people you sell them to. You need to expose your puppies to children, men, women, cats, and the normal noises of a human household. A litter of puppies is a constant mess-making machine: Your washing machine will be going around the clock and you'll be begging your neighbors for their old newspapers and towels within a week. You need more than free newspapers, though: You need a whelping box and hot-water bottles or a special heating element or lamp to keep puppies warm when they're young, because they can't regulate their own temperature well. When they're up on those pudgy little legs, you need an exercise pen to keep them safe and away from the many, many things those puppy teeth can decimate.

What if you can't get the price you want for your puppies? The popularity of fad breeds means that before long, too many puppies are around, and prices fall accordingly. You may be playing *Let's Make a Deal* with the last couple, or even giving them away. It's not unheard of for desperate first-time breeders to drop the remains of a litter off at a shelter, either.

Ask a reputable breeder to show you just what producing a high-quality litter costs. Chances are you'll find even more items in the expenses column than I've listed here, things such as ultrasounds to verify pregnancies, or cesareans. Litter announcements and advertising costs money, too, and hardly a breeder alive hasn't dealt with a disaster such as an illness that has wiped out an entire litter of dreams and left nothing but huge veterinary expenses behind.

What if you meant to spay your dog and come home to find her mating with the dog from three doors down? She doesn't have to carry the litter to term. Your veterinarian will outline your options.

A Dog-Breeding Primer

The business of dog breeding hasn't changed much over the years: You breed the best to the best, and hope for the best. The ways of determining quality have changed a great deal, though, and will change even more as health screenings move to the chromosome level in the future.

The whole thing would likely make the owner of a working sheep or hunting dog shake his head. In the old days, if a dog didn't earn its keep, it didn't live long enough to breed. In some circles today that's still the bottom line, although more — but not all — of the less-gifted career dogs today find homes as pets, be they greyhounds, beagles, or border collies.

Because few breeders work their dogs as a shepherd does his, they rely on other factors to determine which animals they should breed. They show them to have judges evaluate their *conformation* — a measure of how closely they conform to the blueprint for the breed, called the *standard* (more on standards is in Chapter 2). They may test their working instincts or put hunting or other working titles on them in competitions that emulate the real thing. They certainly have them tested for hereditary defects and consider temperament before breeding. High-quality dogs are produced through this selective process.

For more on canine competitions, see Chapter 16.

If you're thinking of breeding your dog, you want to go to the best stud dog you can, and that means the best stud dog for *your particular dog,* one who is a good match for her pedigree, her conformation, and her temperament. The person who can best help you find such a dog is an experienced, reputable breeder with knowledge of your dog's breed in general and her pedigree lines in particular. A better deal still is if you can convince this person to mentor you through the mating, pregnancy, delivery, raising, and placing of the puppies — everyone has to start somewhere, and good breeders know this.

If your dog's neither titled nor of reasonable conformation, such a person may not want to work with you or allow her stud dog to breed your female. It doesn't hurt to ask, though, because this is a much better way to go than breeding your dog to one that your neighbor, cousin, or coworker owns. The latter may be your only option, however, if your dog is not of a quality that should be bred. Which means, of course, you shouldn't breed her.

Mating, gestation, and whelping

Your dog should be two years old before you consider breeding her, because she needs to be more than a puppy herself to be a good mother to her babies. She should be fit and in good health to withstand the rigors of pregnancy, whelping, and nursing. Her vaccinations should be updated, and she should be clear of parasites and on heartworm preventive. Test for genetic defects in her breed should have come back clear, as should a test for *brucellosis,* a disease passed through mating that causes sterility in dogs.

All of which means, of course, that you need to be see your veterinarian.

The stud dog, too, must meet this criteria and should be chosen before your dog is ready for breeding. Females are usually sent to the stud for breeding, and some are shipped thousands of miles for just the right match.

Some breedings take place without either dog ever interacting with as much as a sniff, thanks to frozen semen and artificial insemination. Some stud dogs have even sired litters after their demise! If the stud dog that suits your dog is too far away, discuss this option with the owner of the dog and with your veterinarian. This procedure is increasingly common, and the puppies are eligible for full registration with the AKC and other organizations.

Females *come into season* (or *heat*) for approximately 21 to 30 days every five to seven months. Her heat begins at the first sign of bleeding and ends when she loses interest in breeding. The female does not become interested in breeding until a week or so after her season begins. While your veterinarian can pinpoint when she is most likely to be successfully bred, the dog has a pretty good idea herself, flirting with the males and standing with her tail up in her best canine come-hither behavior.

The males don't need that much encouragement. Her smell from the first day of her season has been driving them wild, and the only thing that has kept them from mating with her sooner has been her refusal to allow it.

As soon as the first signs of season appear, you should finalize arrangements with the stud dog and send your dog to him so she can be there when she's ready to breed.

An experienced breeder can best handle your dog at this point. She allows the dogs to become comfortable with one another and, after the female is interested, the breeder does what it takes to get the job done, including holding the female for the male and even inserting the male's penis into the female if the stud is inexperienced. Far from being embarrassed about such things, the experienced breeder considers it just another job that must be done to produce puppies.

The male starts to ejaculate soon after he starts thrusting, but the most sperm-rich semen is released after the action appears to have stopped and the so-called *tie* begins. The base of the canine penis swells while inside the female, locking the dogs together to give the sperm a chance to impregnate — and keeping competitors at bay. After the tie begins, the male turns away from the female so that the two are positioned rump to rump. This stage can last for more than a half-hour before the swelling goes down and the dogs break apart. If it lasts for more than two hours, call your veterinarian.

After mating, the dogs are "tied" for more than a half-hour to better the odds of fertilization.

Pregnancy ranges from 58 to 70 days, during which you should follow your veterinarian's instructions on prenatal care. A couple of weeks before her due date, you should prepare a *whelping box,* a place for her to have her puppies, in an out-of-the-way corner of your home. For large breeds, a plastic kiddy pool lined with layers and layers of newsprint works well; smaller breeds may use the bottom half of a shipping crate. The most important characteristic in a whelping box is that it can be easily cleaned.

Printed newspapers are messy, so try to get unprinted newsprint. Your local newspaper may sell — or give away — the ends of the giant newsprint rolls that go onto the presses.

Final preparations for long-coated breeds include clipping the hair on her hind end very short, to keep puppies from getting caught, and on her belly to make the nipple area neater. Don't worry about how awful she looks; she'll lose even more fur on her own before it's all over and look even more dreadful!

Talk to your veterinarian one last time about what to expect. Ideally, if you've been working with an experienced breeder, she'll be there to help you as your dog starts labor. He may suggest an ultrasound or X-ray to aid in predicting the size of the litter and any potential problems with the delivery.

Birthing emergencies

Most dogs are natural whelpers and may not need your help at all. Many a pet owner has fallen asleep waiting for the big event only to wake up to a box full of puppies born, cleaned up, and nursing. If your dog isn't quite so efficient, you have to release the puppies from their amniotic sacs within 30 seconds or so and help them to breathe on their own. Clean the fluid from their mouths and noses by supporting their heads and swinging them between your legs, stopping sharply. You can also remove fluid with a bulb syringe. Rub the puppy with a clean towel and put her on a nipple. Above all, keep the puppies warm.

If the mother doesn't sever the umbilical cord, you may need to do that, too: Tie it off about an inch from the puppy with a thread soaked in alcohol and then snip with clean scissors. Dab the end with Betadine to combat infection.

While many experienced breeders are sometimes as capable as any veterinarian when it comes to saving puppies, the novice breeder should not hesitate to get veterinary help quickly. You *must* take your dog to the veterinarian when:

✔ She fails to enter labor 24 to 36 hours after her temperature dips to 99 degrees.

✔ She's in labor and more than four hours lapse with no puppy being born, especially if a dark green fluid passes.

✔ She seems very uncomfortable and is panting heavily.

✔ A puppy gets stuck while being delivered.

✔ She has a puppy, and 30 minutes pass without another puppy being born yet she's having strong contractions.

✔ If she doesn't expel an afterbirth, or *placenta*, for each puppy. Retained afterbirths can trigger infections.

If in doubt about anything, call! She may need more help than you can give her, including a cesarean section.

If everything goes well, clean the mother up with Betadine while *she* cleans up the nest — eating the afterbirths is a normal part of the process.

An important after-birth problem to look out for: If your nursing mom becomes restless, agitated, and trembling, call the veterinarian's and tell them you're on the way. She may need calcium treatments for a condition called *eclampsia*.

A day before the big date your dog will probably lose her appetite and become more restless. She may dig in laundry piles; show her to her whelping box, instead — you may need to be persistent, but she should have her litter where *you* can care for them best. Take her temperature: A dip to 99 degrees shows that labor is near. ***Make sure that you know where your veterinarian is — or the closest emergency clinic — and cancel all your plans, because the time is near.***

Take the puppies and their mother to the veterinarian's within the first day after the birth to make sure that everything's OK with them all. If dewclaws are to be removed and tails docked, discuss these procedures with your veterinarian right away — these minor surgeries (both elective, neither necessary) need to be done before the age of three days. While experienced breeders often complete these procedures themselves, a novice breeder should not even attempt it — have your veterinarian take care of it. (For more on cosmetic surgeries, see Chapter 7.)

Another job in those first few days: Paperwork! Send in litter registration so that you get individual registration forms back in plenty of time to provide to puppy buyers. Contact the registry for more information on what's required. Addresses are in this book's "Additional Resources" appendix.

Mother and puppies should visit the veterinarian within the first 24 hours after birth.

Raising Good Puppies — and Finding Good Homes

If you want to increase the chances of raising your puppies right — and be reassured that your puppies are "normal" — knowing a little about how puppies mature is helpful. As with children, these stages each have their wonders and their challenges. *Tip:* These stages pass too quickly, so to get the most out of the *puppy experience* clear your calendar of nondog activities and keep your eyes open.

All puppies look much the same when they're born. You find size and marking differences, but they come into this world looking something like a sausage, with tiny ears, tiny legs, and tightly closed eyes. Things start to change before long.

Although people have raised puppies for thousands of years, most of what we now know about how people can influence a puppy's development — and about developmental stages in puppies — goes back only about four decades, starting with the work of John Paul Scott and John L. Fuller in the '50s. From their "school for dogs" in Bar Harbor, Maine, came the basis of what trainers and breeders have been using to get the most out of dogs ever since.

Animal Behavior, (Paul Scott, University of Chicago Press) is a fascinating place to start a study of dog behavior. Fuller and Scott teamed on *Genetics and the Social Behavior of Dogs,* also from the University of Chicago Press. Although out of print, these books are in many libraries, and a good second-hand bookseller should be able to find copies without too much trouble.

A more recent — and less academic — treatment of the subject can be found in many subsequent books. Three I like to recommend are Carol Lea Benjamin's *Mother Knows Best: The Natural Way To Train Your Dog* (Howell/Macmillan); *How To Raise a Puppy You Can Live With,* by Clarice Rutherford and veterinarian David H. Neil (Alpine Press); and *The Art of Raising a Puppy* by the monks of the New Skete Monastery (Little, Brown).

Birth to 3 weeks

Puppies are pretty helpless at birth. They can't see or hear and need their mother for everything. She is their source for food, warmth, and protection; they cannot even eliminate waste without her gentle licking to stimulate the process.

Newborn pups can crawl and right themselves when turned over, and they can seek out food by smell. They can also seek out the warmth of their littermates — they are unable at this stage to regulate their own body temperature.

On the outside, this time seems quiet — puppies at this age sleep almost constantly — but a lot of development is going inside their brains and central nervous system. Leave them alone, except for one thing: Handle them briefly on a daily basis, so they are subjected to the tiniest amount of stress in the process. Puppy-raising experts believe this stress — such as the cool feel of a scale — is as important as handling in the development of a confident dog.

Even this early in a puppy's life, some temperament patterns are set. If you watch, you can already see which puppies will later become dominant with their siblings. These are the ones who push others out of the way at nursing time — an impression confirmed during frequent weighings: The pushier pups are growing faster. Other pups are more wiggly, nervous, or cry during handling. You should note all these things.

Towards the end of the second week, the puppies start to open their eyes, although they see little more than light at this point. In the third week, the first teeth appear and puppies start to hear. By the end of the third week, the sausages look like puppies, and they're ready to start exploring the world.

What if you have a litter of black Labrador puppies? How can you possibly tell one from another enough to follow and record changes in the early weeks when personalities are not so obvious? Use this trick: Make little collars of *rickrack,* a decorative zigzag trim material available in fabric stores, a different color for each puppy. You won't have to resort to this tactic, of course, if you can note the puppies' markings to keep things straight.

3 to 5 weeks

During this stage puppies start relying less on their mother and start to learn from each other. They learn to play and to eat solid food.

Even as all of this activity is happening — a wealth of new experiences, overwhelming their new senses of vision and hearing — the puppies are learning the rudiments of canine communication and social structure. Puppies start to learn to use those teeth and, more importantly, when they cannot use them. Their mother teaches them some of this behavior, using her teeth to correct, but not hurt, them. In play with each other, an observer hears plenty of cries and squeals as bites are delivered just a little too hard, and puppies learn to *inhibit* their biting, delivering them with a force that matches the situation. (When puppies don't learn to inhibit biting from their mother and littermates, problems are bound to occur when they're in their new homes. More on this in Chapters 6 and 12.)

While the puppies are most interested in each other at this stage, you should be busy reminding them that there are people in the world, too. Make sure their environment is always changing, and continue to handle the puppies, making sure that each gets individual attention. Expose the puppies to both genders and to children as well as adults. If a cat lives in the house, even better — although do your cat a favor and let him choose his interactions. His mere presence is enough to expose the puppies to the existence of felines.

Start weaning the puppies after three weeks. Discuss with your veterinarian or mentor breeder the soft food you'll offer the puppies and help the pups get the idea by putting the food on your finger and helping it into their mouths. Puppy pans — doughnut-shaped dishes with a low outer rim — are ideal for giving every pup a place at the "table."

After puppies are eating semisolid food, the mother will quit cleaning up the nest by eating their waste — so the task of keeping puppies clean falls to you entirely now. About this time the mother will start helping the weaning process by spending more time away from her babies — she's getting a little sick of them!

Watching a litter is a wonderful way to spend some time. Although I've seen many, many litters, one in particular seems special to me: My dog Andy's. I saw Andy at least twice before he came home with me — the first time he was two days old. He wriggled a little in my hands and settled down as I stroked the tan patches on the sides of his face. It was as if he recognized me and, years later, he still sighs in happiness when I run my hands along the sides of his face.

5 to 7 weeks

The biggest mistake you can make in this period is to remove a puppy from the litter and send him to a new home. This practice is probably based on the idea that weaning is the logical time for puppies to be sold — puppies can start on hard kibble around six weeks — but the research emphatically insists that this "logic" is wrong.

Puppies have a lot more learning to do during these two weeks, and they need to be with their littermates to do it.

Think of this period as the *time of more*. Puppies can see more, hear more, and play more at this stage. They are starting to become more interested in the world beyond their enclosure. They are especially attracted to those funny, two-legged dogs who have spent the last few weeks picking them up, talking to them, and petting them. Suddenly, they think humans are pretty cool.

This stage is when humans think puppies are pretty cool, too. They are absolutely adorable now, with the softest fur and the cutest faces. They run with a rolling, bouncing, puppy gait, tripping over their big paws at times. They roughhouse with each other and stalk their toys. They drive their mother crazy — she is interested in spending as little time with them as possible now.

They are still learning, but what a fun time they're having.

You should spend a lot of time with them at this stage, for socializing is in full swing. Keep exposing them to the sights and sounds of life all the way up until they go to their new homes, ideally, after their seventh week.

Finding proper homes

If you've done your job right, you have something truly remarkable to offer puppy buyers: Fat, friendly, well-socialized puppies who promise a lifetime of good health and companionship. You want to be sure that the people who take them are worthy of such wonderful pups.

Which means you need to be extra-careful in screening homes and not just accept money from the first half-dozen people who walk through your door. If you've been working with a reputable breeder, ask for her help in placing the puppies.

Some questions you should ask:

- ✔ **What is your living arrangement?** You don't need a house with a yard — some dogs, even large ones, do just fine in apartments — but you do need a person who's aware of what a dog needs and is prepared to deliver it. Just say no to anyone who plans to stick one of your pups on a chain in the yard.

- ✔ **Have you had dogs before? What kinds, and what happened to them?** Wrong answers include "lots" and "they ran away," "we moved," or "he got hit." Accidents happen to even the most conscientious of dog lovers, but a pattern of mishaps says a great deal about the way the prospective buyer treats dogs — and it's not well.

- ✔ **Do you have any experience with this breed? What do you expect of it?** You want to educate — and possibly eliminate from contention — anyone who isn't prepared to deal with the reality of living with a dog like yours. A person who isn't prepared for the shedding of a long-haired dog or the activity level of a terrier, for example. Be honest with buyers about the drawbacks of the breed, and you're much more likely to put your puppies in homes that will keep them, because they know what to expect.

- ✔ **Do you have children? What ages?** Some dogs, such as delicate toys, just don't work out well with children. Still, be flexible. A thoughtful, gentle child could work out fine. Discuss your concerns and see what answers you get.

- ✔ **Do you intend to breed your dog? Show your dog? Train your dog?** Your pet-quality puppies — ones with obvious show faults, such as wrong markings — should be sold on contracts that require them to be spayed or neutered. (Some breeders have the surgery taken care of before their puppies go to their new homes!) People who are interested in training and competing with their dogs plan to be involved in their pup's life, and that's the kind of thing you like to see. Look, too, for people who travel with their pets or obviously treat them like the family they are — or should be.

Be cordial and informative, but be persistent. Check references, including calling their veterinarian. A person who has had numerous pets and *doesn't* have a veterinary reference is another to cross off your list. Don't be afraid to turn people down. While it may not be pleasant, you must do what's best for your puppies. You've put a lot of effort into them, and you want them to live with someone who will continue to love and care for them as you have.

Remember, always, that you want your puppies to go to good homes, and the only one who has a chance at making that happen is you. So do your best.

If you are considering breeding your dog again, you need to skip at least a season to give her time to recover. In any case, one or two litters are about all you should ask of her if she's to enjoy just being a member of your family. As soon as her motherhood days are behind her, arrange for her to be spayed to give her the best chance at a healthy life.

Another reason to spay her quickly: If you keep a puppy, you may be positively shocked to find your girl pregnant again — thanks to her own son. I once got a call from a woman who wanted me to convince her husband their dog could not possibly be pregnant, because the only male she'd been around was a pup from her last litter. "But that's incest!" yelled the woman when I gave her the bad news. "Don't they know better?"

Unfortunately, they don't.

If such a thing happens to your dog, call your veterinarian right away.

Homes for older dogs, too

Puppies aren't the only dogs who need responsible, loving homes. Oftentimes older dogs do, too. If a stray follows your son home from school and you can't find an owner, you inherit an older dog from a sick relative, or you end up with an extra dog for any other reason, you want to find the best home for the dog you can. Here are some tips:

✔ **Do everything you can to make the animal more adoptable.** The pet has a better chance if she has current shots, is house-trained, and neutered. It also helps if she's socialized and friendly with children, with other dogs, and with cats. Try to fix behavior problems before placement, or you may see a quick return. (For more on problem-solving, see Chapter 12.)

✔ **Ask a price.** People show more respect for something they've paid for, and a price tag dampens the interest of profiteers, such as those who collect "free to a good home" pets for sale to research labs or to dog fighters.

A good rule of thumb: Charge an amount to cover the cost of the spaying/neutering and vaccinations. That makes sense to prospective adopters, because it's money they would have had to spend anyway.

✔ **Don't lie about the pet's problems, or why he's being placed.** Although finding a new home for a pet with behavior problems takes longer, it can be done. But the person who gets such a pet without warning is likely to bring him back or place him somewhere without your knowledge, maybe into a horrible situation.

✔ **Ask lots of questions and verify that the answers are true.** Ask for a telephone number and call back to check it. Ask to see a driver's license. Check out the home in person, and bring along a friend. Don't forget to ask prospective adopters if they've had pets before and what happened to them. Make sure that you're dealing with people who realize owning a pet is a long-term commitment.

Chapter 14

Caring for an Aging Dog

● ●

In This Chapter

▶ Easing the aging process

▶ Dealing with older-dog health concerns

▶ Letting go

▶ Getting help when you're grieving

▶ Preparing for your pet in your will

● ●

*P*eople flip over puppies but, to me, a well-loved older dog is one of the most beautiful beings on earth. An older dog has a nobleness about him, a look in the eyes that speaks of years of the special love only a pet can give — trusting, nonjudgmental, and unwaveringly true.

Your dog's health as he ages is not entirely in your control, but you can have a real impact on his attitude. When you see those first gray hairs appearing on his muzzle, getting a little upset about them is natural. The normal lifespan of a dog isn't even remotely close to ours, after all, and those first signs of aging remind us that the years between a puppy's first gasp and the last sighing breath of a dying dog are not really that far apart.

But consider the following: Your dog doesn't know he's getting older. His gray hairs concern him not, nor does he worry about the other visible effects of time, the thickening of his body, the thinning of his limbs. He doesn't count the number of times he can fetch a ball before tiring and compare that to his performance when he was a young dog in his prime.

A dog lives in the now. Just as he doesn't reflect on his past, he can't imagine his future. He doesn't know his time is growing shorter, and that he'll get weaker, grow blind, perhaps, or deaf. He doesn't know that he'll die someday.

You know all of that, but this information is a secret best kept to yourself. Your dog takes his cues from you, and when you're upbeat, encouraging, and loving, he'll be at his best no matter his age. Keep your aging dog fit and healthy, and don't exclude him from your activities.

This time can be a special one for both of you, and it's up to you to make the most of it.

Dogs need love and special care to stay happy into their golden years.

Photo courtesy of Gay Currier.

Special Care for Seniors

Next to you, your dog's best friend as he ages should be his veterinarian. Preventive care is not only more cost-effective than crisis care, but it's also the only way to ensure that problems are caught *before* they lessen the quality of your dog's life.

I don't care if you've had a healthy dog, if you've rarely taken him to the veterinarian, if you given your shots yourself. Take him in for a thorough "senior dog" physical when your dog hits eight or so, including whatever tests your veterinarian recommends — blood, urine, and so on. The information these "extra yard" tests provide can spot treatable problems early and provide baseline information against which your veterinarian can compare as problems develop with your dog's increasing age.

I have nothing against group practices — in fact, the discussions within them can be beneficial to your pet's care overall — but for my dogs, I prefer to work with one veterinarian. Ours is in a top-notch specialty group, but he is the one we always see, because he is most familiar with my dogs, their needs, and their idiosyncrasies. This information and rapport is never more important than when you're guiding your pet through his senior years.

Nutrition

Your pet's nutritional needs change as he gets older and so, in most cases, should his food. If you have been satisfied with a particular food, you may be able to switch to the brand's formulation for older dogs. If not, your dog's breeder or veterinarian may be able to suggest something suitable.

The biggest food-related problem for older dogs is obesity, which puts pressure on joints and internal organs that aren't able to withstand the pressure. If your pet is portly, talk to your veterinarian about safe ways to thin him down slowly. Remember that unlike us, dogs have no control over how much they eat: Your dog's weight is dependent on *your* self-control, not his.

Dogs with heart, kidney, or other chronic health problems may end up on a prescription diet available only through your veterinarian. These diets — which come in both canned and dry varieties — are carefully formulated to address your pet's particular health needs. Some pets may not like them, especially compared to the fat- and treat-based diet they were on before, but don't sabotage your pet's care by adding goodies to the mix. A simple strained broth made from boiling chicken bones with a crushed garlic clove or two — no added salt — may make the diet more palatable. Check with your veterinarian, though, before adding even this mixture to a prescription diet.

Exercise

"If you don't use it, you lose it" is true for both humans and dogs. Exercise keeps your dog's body in good condition and brightens his outlook.

The secret here is increasing the frequency and diminishing the intensity. Instead of taking your dog to the park once a week to chase tennis balls until he's exhausted, take him for a walk daily. If you are going to throw a tennis ball, keep it low to avoid leaps, twists, and hard landings, and consider walking to the park and back. Warm-ups and cool-downs are important for older dogs, whose bodies aren't as able to withstand the pounding a younger dog endures without pause. Inactivity punctuated by bouts of overexertion isn't good for any dog, but for the older dog it can be painful, or even dangerous.

Despite your best intentions, sometimes an older pet is going to make like a puppy and play hard. The next morning, she'll surely feel it. Give her a buffered aspirin, 5 mg. per pound of body weight every 12 hours. If the stiffness lasts for more than a day, consult your veterinarian. If she's on other drugs, check with your veterinarian first.

Putting junior in his place

If you have an older dog and a younger one, the competition between them can be frustrating to the older dog. Here's an exercise that lets the older dog win and improves the obedience of the younger:

After your younger dog has chased a few balls, put him on a "down-stay" (see Chapter 11). If you've never tried this exercise before under such tempting conditions, leave his leash on and then stand on it. Repeat the "stay" command and then throw the ball — a short throw — for your senior dog. Let him get the ball a few times, and then release the younger dog and praise him. Then tell them both they're wonderful.

Walking is a good exercise for older pets; swimming is another, if you have a dog who enjoys it. (Choose a lake or pool rather than a river, and keep her close to the bank.) Whatever you choose, just keep her moving, every day. Push her a little on the distance and the time, or at least try to maintain what you've got going, but don't overextend her — let her set the pace.

Think about games she can do just as well — or better! — than when she was younger. In my house, senior dog Andy no longer chases tennis balls until he drops. Instead, I put him on "stay," show him a toy and *hide* it for him to sniff out. He's so good at this game that I'm thinking of loaning him to the government to sniff out contraband. And he's so *proud* of his cleverness that watching him strut about makes me smile.

While few dogs, even young ones, get enough exercise to keep their nails short without trimming, old dogs rarely do. Arthritis and muscle stiffness makes moving around hard enough for older dogs; overgrown nails make things worse, and they're something that you have the power to fix — so do!

INFO SNIFF

See Chapter 10 for tips on how to keep nails short.

Dentistry

One of the most important recent advances in the care of older dogs regards their mouths: Canine dentistry is an area of preventive care you ignore at your pet's peril.

Preventive care involves brushing your dog's teeth — two or three times a week is fine — using gauze wrapped around your finger or a toothbrush, whichever your pet tolerates best. Toothpastes made just for dogs are available, with flavors that appeal to the canine palate and ingredients that can be swallowed. (Because dogs can't spit and rinse, people toothpaste and baking soda, which is high in sodium, aren't recommended.)

Anesthesia and the older dog

As common as anesthesia is in veterinary medicine, many misconceptions exist about its use where older animals are concerned. The idea that the risk of anesthesia outweighs the importance of preventive veterinary care such as dentistry is no longer supported by veterinary findings.

The risks can be greatly minimized by a few basic tests, including a laboratory evaluation of blood and urine, a chest x-ray, and possibly an electrocardiogram. While these tests admittedly add to the cost of a procedure, they allow your veterinarian to provide the life-enhancing and life-extending benefits of preventive care to the pets who need them most.

Your veterinarian may also recommend IV or subcutaneus fluids while your pet is under anesthesia, and, for dental procedures, pre- and post-surgical antibiotics.

No discussion of anesthetic danger can be complete without a few words on your responsibilities where anesthesia is concerned:

✔ **Follow your veterinarian's instructions on preparing your pet for surgery.** If no food is specified, then make sure that you deliver a pet with an empty stomach. Following this one piece of advice is one of the easiest and most basic ways to reduce risk. During anesthesia, the contents of a full stomach can be inhaled into the lungs.

✔ **Be prepared to provide special home care for your pet after surgery.** Releasing animals before the preanesthetic sedation wears off is common practice. Such animals must be kept safe from hot or cold environments, because their reflexes are reduced. If you do not feel comfortable caring for a sedated pet, arrange for your veterinarian to extend the care.

✔ **Don't hesitate to ask questions.** Make sure that you understand what the procedures are, and what to expect. For example, pets commonly have a cough after anesthesia, because the tube used to deliver the gas may cause some irritation. If the cough does not clear in a couple of days, call your veterinarian.

No matter what the age of the pet, chances are very high that the anesthetic will present no problem if both you and your veterinarian work to minimize the risks.

Before you start your at-home regimen, your pet will likely need some help from your veterinarian. A complete dentistry under anesthesia takes 45 minutes to an hour, and involves not only cleaning and polishing the teeth, but also checking for and treating broken or rotting teeth, cavities, abscesses, and periodontal disease. This procedure is especially important if you've neglected your pet's mouth: Brushing prevents plaque from forming, but it won't help much with the muck that has already built up — and it won't fix bad teeth or infections.

Why is dental care so important in older dogs? Neglected mouths can make eating painful. Infections are a problem, too, and the adverse effect of bacteria from chronic mouth infections take their toll on your pet's internal organs and can overwhelm her immune system. Bacteria can even travel through the blood stream from your dog's mouth to her heart and infect her heart valves.

The benefits of such care extend to more than the elimination of bad breath in an older dog: Once your pet is no longer fighting infections and pain, his spirits will lift along with his health — all of which can spark his appetite.

Some Common Problems

While every dog is an individual, a few age-related maladies seem to strike many of them. You should of course discuss how they affect your dog — and the best approach to treating them — with your veterinarian, but knowing a little bit about what you're dealing with before you go in is helpful.

Here are a few old-dog problems, along with some things you can do to help:

✔ **Decline of the senses.** Deaf and blind dogs do just fine, as long as you do your part to keep them out of any danger their disabilities may cause. Blindness, in particular, is a problem dogs adjust to with an ease that stuns their owners. But consider the following: Dogs don't have to read the newspaper, they don't care about TV, and they count on you to read the ingredients label on a bag of kibble. Sight isn't their primary sense anyway; they put much greater stock in their sense of smell. After they learn the layout of the land, they rarely bump into things (as long as *you* don't keep moving the furniture). Handicapped pets should *never* be allowed off-leash on walks, because they can't see danger and cannot hear your warnings.

One time I had a foster dog who I suspected was totally blind, and I took her in to the veterinarian to be sure. "Wait here," he said after examining her. "I have to get a special piece of equipment." He came back with . . . a Nerf ball! He bounced it off her nose and those eyes didn't even blink. We had our answer.

Even if your older dog *is* blind (or deaf — check by clapping your hands behind his head), there *may* be something that you can do. Ask your veterinarian for a referral to a specialist like a veterinary ophthalmologist. Problems such as cataracts may be treatable with medications and surgery.

✔ **Incontinence.** I get letters all the time from frustrated owners wondering why their older dogs are no longer house-trained — and how they can get them back on track. The first rule of any sudden-onset behavior problem is to make sure that it's not a health problem, and I can think of no case where this rule is more true than with an older dog who's suddenly urinating in the house. Your pet could have an infection or, if she's an older spayed female, she may be suffering from the loss of muscle tone related to a decrease in her hormone levels. Both are treatable; see your veterinarian.

At a certain age, a little dribbling of urine is practically inevitable, especially while your older dog is sleeping. With my old dogs, I've placed old rubber-backed bathmats in their favorite sleeping areas. They catch the dribble and are easily washable, keeping odor, dampness — and flea eggs! — under control.

Living with pets, like living with children, can be one big mess — literally. For tips on removing pet-specific stains from carpets and furniture, see Chapter 4.

✔ **Lumps and bumps.** Benign fatty tumors are common in older dogs, and the vast majority are nothing to worry about. Benign tumors are round and soft, with well-defined edges. You can usually get your fingers nearly around them, and they don't seem well-anchored. Showing them to your veterinarian for a more complete evaluation is important, and you should inform her of any changes in size or shape, especially if they happen rapidly. Your veterinarian may be concerned enough about the size, appearance, or location of a mass to suggest its removal and a biopsy; most bumps, however, are left alone. The best time to check for lumps and bumps? During regular grooming, weekly, at least. Run your hand over every inch of your dog, and don't forget to talk sweetly — she'll think it's petting.

✔ **Stiffness.** Your veterinarian can help you determine if the stiffness is because of temporary muscle soreness — say from overdoing it — or the onset of arthritis. Many dogs are worse in cold weather and first thing in the morning. Arthritis is common in older dogs, and while no cure exists, treatments are available that can make your pet's life comfortable. Your veterinarian may prescribe buffered aspirin, food supplements, or anti-inflammatory medications, all of which your pet may need to take for the rest of her life. For your part, you need to be sure that your pet is not overweight and is kept consistently, but not strenuously, active.

Some dogs lose strength in their hindquarters as they age or become paralyzed because of a spinal injury. This condition need not mean euthanasia. A company called K-9 Carts manufactures wheeled devices that support a pet's weight and allow him to be mobile again. For information, write to the company at P.O. Box 160639, Big Sky, MT 59716, or call 406-995-3111.

Reasonable Accommodations

Your dog has no real sense of shame or embarrassment, so she has no loss of face if you come up with some ideas to make her life a little easier. I once bought a wagon so that an older dog with bad legs could go to the park — the best part was the harness that let the younger dog pull the load! Truly, the number of ways you can give your oldster a break is limited only by your imagination. Here are a few tips to get you thinking:

- ✔ **Beds.** Think soft. Think cushioned. Think low. Think heated. Your dog will thank you for all of these thoughts, especially in cold weather.

- ✔ **Clothes.** Canine clothing isn't just for poodles anymore. Older dogs, like older people, have a harder time maintaining their body temperature. This problem is even more pronounced in slender, short-coated breeds like the greyhound or whippet. So check out the sweater selection at your local pet-supply store, or consider altering one of your own for the task.

My favorite of these custom-designed dog-warmers was the brainchild of my friend Judy Harper, who put a worn-out sweater with the sleeves hacked off on her old Irish setter, Shannon. "It's a fashionable Capri length," she observed. Shannon thought it was swell.

- ✔ **Dishes.** Raised food and water dishes are a kindness to tall dogs of any age, but they are especially easy on the back of an oldster. You can find them at pet-supply stores or you can make your own.

- ✔ **Ramps and steps.** If your dogs are allowed on the couch and the bed — and mine are — you should be able to find or build something to help out the dog who can no longer make it in one jump. You wouldn't want to watch TV without your dog at your side, would you? I thought not.

Older dog versus new puppy

All the trials of old age can make a dog downright cranky and make some people long to have a puppy in the house. Of course, you want to be sure that your older dog enjoys the change, or at least tolerates it. So should you add a puppy to an older dog's life?

That depends. For some older dogs, a puppy is a big boost to the senior's enthusiasm for life. For others, a puppy's energy and attention are enough to make an older dog want to leave home. You must determine which of these attitudes your older dog has.

In general, older dogs who are still fit and full of life probably get the most out of an addition to the household; elderly or severely debilitated dogs enjoy it least. No matter your dog's age, however, try to keep tabs on the interaction until you're sure how things are progressing. Don't let your older dog overextend himself, and put the puppy in his crate to give your oldster a break from time to time. Finally, save some energy and time for dog No. 1: Spend time together, just the two of you, so he realizes he is still very much loved.

Knowing When It's "Time"

Euthanasia, the technical term for "putting a dog to sleep," is one of the hardest decisions you will ever make, and it doesn't get any easier, no matter how many times over the years you face it. Your veterinarian can offer you advice and your friends can offer you support, but no one can make the decision for you. When you live with an elderly or terminally ill pet, you look in her eyes every morning and ask yourself: Is this the day?

To know for sure is impossible.

Some owners do not wait until their pet's discomfort becomes pain and choose euthanasia much sooner than many people would. Some owners use an animal's appetite as the guide — when an old or ill animal is no longer interested in eating, they reason, he's not interested in anything at all. And some owners wait until there's no doubt the time is at hand.

Each guideline is the right one, for some dogs and some owners at some times. You do the best you can, and then you try to put the decision behind you and deal with the grief.

Ironically, the incredible advances in veterinary medicine in the past couple of decades have made the decisions even more difficult for many people. Not too long ago, the best you could do for a seriously ill pet was to make her comfortable until that wasn't possible anymore. Nowadays, nearly every advantage of human medicine — from chemotherapy to pacemakers — is available to our pets.

If you can afford such care and have a realistic expectation that it will improve your pet's life — rather than simply prolong it — then it is an option that should be pursued. But let nothing push you into making a decision based on guilt or wishful thinking.

Euthanasia is a kindness extended to a treasured pet, a decision we make at a great cost to ourselves. It is a final act of love, nothing less.

Euthanasia options

Should you be with your pet at the end? What should you have done with the remains? The questions are all difficult, but no answers are wrong.

As performed by a veterinarian, euthanasia is a quick and peaceful process. The animal is unconscious within seconds and dead within less than a minute; the euphemism "put to sleep" is a perfect description. Those who attend the procedure come away reassured that their pet felt no fear or pain.

Some people say staying with a pet at the end is the final gift of love, but no decision you make regarding the last few minutes of an animal's life will change the love you shared for the years before those final moments. If you wish to be there, then by all means stay. But leaving euthanasia to your veterinarian is no less a humane and loving gesture.

Call ahead to set the appointment, and make it clear to the receptionist what you're coming for. That way, the practice can ensure that you don't have to sit in the waiting room but instead be immediately ushered into an exam room, if you choose to remain with your dog. Your veterinarian will do his best to be sure that all your questions are answered and that you are comfortable with everything before proceeding. He may clip the fur on your dog's foreleg to have easier and quicker access to the vein for the injection of the euthanizing agent; he may also choose to presedate your pet. Remember: Crying is normal, and your veterinarian will understand. So, too, I believe, will your pet. I always hold my hand near my dog's nose, so the last breath will have my scent in it; I don't know if it eases my pet's mind, but I do know it eases mine.

You may wish to spend a few minutes with your pet afterward, and your veterinarian understands that, as well, and will give you all the time you need alone to begin the process of coming to grips with your loss.

You may be more comfortable with having your pet euthanized at home. If this is your wish, discuss the matter with your veterinarian directly. Many vets extend this special service to long-time clients. If yours doesn't, you may alternately consider making arrangements with a mobile veterinarian.

You can handle your pet's remains in many ways, and doing so is easier on you overall if you make this decision beforehand. The choices include having your municipal animal-control department pick up the body, burying the pet in your back yard (where local regulations permit) or at another site (with the land owner's permission, of course), arranging for cremation, or contracting with a pet cemetery for full services and burial. Again, no choice is "wrong": Whatever feels right to you and comforts you best is what you should do.

Several manufacturers offer markers for your yard to memorialize your pet; they are often advertised in the back of magazines like *Dog Fancy*. Other choices include large rocks or slabs of stone, or a tree or rose bush. Even if you choose not to have your pet's body or ashes returned, placing a memorial in a special spot may soothe you.

Another way to celebrate the memory of your dog is to make a donation to your local humane society, regional school of veterinary medicine, or other favorite animal charity. A donation in a beloved pet's name is a wonderful thing to do for a friend who has lost a pet as well.

Dealing with loss

Many people are surprised at the powerful emotions that erupt after a pet's death, and they are embarrassed by their grief. Remembering that pets have meaning in our lives beyond the love we feel for the animal alone may help. Often, we don't realize that we are grieving not only for the pet we loved, but also for the special time the animal represented. When a friend of mine lost her very special German shepherd, her grief was a double-whammy: The dog had been given to her as a puppy by her father, not long before he died of cancer. Suddenly, she was grieving for them both.

Taking care of yourself is important at this difficult time. Some people — the "it's just an animal" crowd — will not understand your feelings and will shrug off your grief as foolish. The company of other animal lovers is very important. Seek them out to share your feelings. The commercial online services — America Online, CompuServe, and Prodigy — encourage animal lovers to share memories of special animals with one another, and the outpouring of support in these virtual communities is heartfelt. So,too, is it in the canine areas of the Internet (see Chapter 1 for more on canine cyberspace).

A difficult time, no doubt, but remember: In time the memories become a source of pleasure, not pain. There is no set timetable, but it happens. I promise.

What if YOU Go First?

First things first: You can't leave your estate to your dog, because in the eyes of the law, an animal is an "it," with little more legal status than a chair. Nor can you set up a trust for your dog, for the same reason. The beneficiary of a trust has to be a bona fide human being, and the fact that you think of your dog as a person doesn't really matter, because the courts don't.

While you should discuss this matter with your attorney, talking it over with your friends and family is even more important, because finding one of them whom you trust to care for your pet when you're gone is what you must do. You will leave your canine "property" to that person, along with enough money to provide for that animal's care for life. You have no real control over the outcome, which is why you have to choose someone you trust and hope, for your dog's sake, that things turn out OK.

Another option is offered by two veterinary schools, at Texas A&M and Purdue, both of which offer programs that accept pets when owners pass on. They also accept money — $25,000 is Purdue's suggested "donation" per pet — so you need to a) have some money; and b) work out all the details in advance.

You're not alone

You may find talking to others about your pet's death helpful. Ask your veterinarian about pet-loss support groups. Almost unheard of a couple decades of ago, many communities have these groups now. You may also wish to see a counselor; this, too, can be helpful.

Veterinary schools and colleges have been among the leaders in creating programs to help pet lovers deal with loss. A handful now operate pet-loss hot lines staffed by veterinary students trained to answer questions, offer materials that may help you, and just plain listen. (A piece I wrote in 1988 when Lance, the Original Demo Dog, died is one of the handouts used at UC Davis.) These are wonderful programs, and they are free for the cost of the call. (If you call during off hours, they will call you back, collect.)

Locations, operating hours, and phone numbers of pet-loss hot lines:

- **University of California, Davis, School of Veterinary Medicine,** Davis, CA; (916) 752-4200. Operates Monday through Friday, 6:30 to 9:30 p.m. PST.

- **Virginia-Maryland Regional College of Veterinary Medicine,** Blacksburg, VA; (540) 231-8038. Operates Tuesdays and Thursdays, excluding holidays, 6 to 9 p.m. EST.

- **Tufts University New England Veterinary Medical Center,** North Grafton, MA; (508) 839-7966. Operates Tuesdays and Thursdays, excluding holidays, 6 to 9 p.m. EST.

- **Michigan State College of Veterinary Medicine,** Lansing, MI; (517) 432-2696. Operates Tuesdays, Wednesdays, and Thursdays, 6:30 to 9:30 p.m. EST.

- **Ohio State University Veterinary Teaching Hospital,** Columbus, OH; (614) 292-1823. Operates Mondays, Wednesdays, and Fridays, 6:30 to 9:30 p.m. EST.

An excellent reference on providing for your pet in your will and other canine legal niceties from dog bites to veterinary malpractice is Mary Randolph's *Dog Law: A Legal Guide for Dog Owners and Their Neighbors* (Nolo Press).

Part IV
Finding Cool Things to Do with Your Dog

The 5th Wave   By Rich Tennant

In this part . . .

Get moving! You can do more things with your dog than ever before, and this section gives you the information you need to start enjoying these activities. Traveling with your pet has never been easier, with everything from campgrounds to swanky hotels open to dogs on the road. Canine competitions from agility to sled-racing offer active enjoyment to every dog — and every dog owner.

Chapter 15

Traveling with Your Dog

- -

- -

*F*or some folks, a beachside vacation isn't complete without a big stick and a wet, smelly dog to chase it.

These are the people who travel with water dishes, leashes, and plenty of towels. People who trade information on good dog beaches and pet-friendly inns the way gourmands talk about new restaurants. People who would no more think of leaving the dog at home during vacation than leaving the children with neighbors.

Their numbers, travel industry watchers say, are growing. And you and your dog can be among their happy ranks.

Still, traveling with a dog is no picnic sometimes. Finding lodging is harder; luxurious inside dining is largely sacrificed in favor of eating takeout in the car or a park; and hours spent tripping through quaint shops becomes a thing of the past when a dog is waiting in the car. Traveling with dogs offers some challenges, nearly all surmountable with common sense and creativity.

Traveling with dogs is not new, of course. The unique combination of companionship and protection that dogs offer has made them welcome on trips from the very beginning of our centuries-old partnership with them. They've gone along with every mode of transportation we've invented — accompanying us on foot or alongside our horses, trotting under carriages, riding in our planes, trains, ships, and automobiles. They've even been in space.

Although most dog-related travel is strictly for pleasure now, such was not always the case. Breed historians tell us that dogs such as the Rottweiler once helped their human partners take goods to market and carried the profits home in a pouch attached to their collars to deter thieves. While the idea still has appeal, not that many dogs are so intimately involved in business travel today.

Recreational travel for dogs, however, has never been more popular. Dogs can be seen at the roughest campsites and the swankiest hotels. Several books cover traveling with dogs, and some travel agents have carved out a niche booking canine-centered vacations. People in the travel industry have learned that many travelers with dogs are exceptionally grateful for pleasant accommodations and return to the places that treat them well year after year. As a result, some entrepreneurs have gone to great lengths to attract dog lovers: You can even find canine camps where people do nothing but share a slice of "dog heaven" with their pet for a week or more at a time.

Should Your Dog Travel?

A pet who is very old, not in good health, or is nervous or untrustworthy in new situations is probably best left behind with a sitter, in a kennel, or at your veterinarian's (see the upcoming section "What to Do if Your Dog Can't Go with You" for more information).

The best canine travelers are reasonably well-mannered — more than can be said for many human tourists — and in good health. That said, don't count your pet out without a little consideration and a trip to your veterinarian. Your pet may be in better shape than you think, after all, and any behavior problems she has may be fixable.

Health concerns

Before you hit the road, make sure that your pet is fit for travel. If your dog's last check-up was a few years ago, this is a good time to schedule one. You have to, anyway, if you're shipping your pet by air or going to another country, because you need a health certificate. But even if you're only driving to a state park four hours away, you want to know your pet is in good health, and you need to know he's current on his vaccinations, especially rabies.

Because you'll be picking up after your pet on vacation — more on that coming up — you also want to make sure that he has been wormed so clean up's not a total gross-out (just a partial one).

Car travel is pretty easy on a dog; air travel, however, is another matter. Because of the stresses of traveling in an airline cargo hold, some experts suggest dogs who are not designed for easy breathing — pug-nosed breeds such as the boxer, bulldog, and of course, the pug — should never travel by air. Old dogs and those in marginal health are likewise not good candidates. Your veterinarian can help you make an honest appraisal of your pet's condition.

If your pet doesn't have a regular veterinarian, tips on how to find a good one are in Chapter 10.

Travel manners

The *minimum* requirements for canine travelers is that they be able to behave themselves on-leash in some very exciting circumstances — around strange people, strange dogs, and strange scenery, sounds, and smells. If you plan to let your dog off-leash, you'd better be sure that she'll come when called and leave something — like a dead fish on the beach — alone when you ask her to. She should also be trained to stop barking on command.

"Sit?" "Down?" "Stay?" Are these foreign concepts to your dog? All you need to know to make your dog a well-mannered companion is in Chapters 11 and 12.

How training saved a life

The biggest near-disaster I ever had proved that one of the best things you can teach your dog is a reliable down-stay from a distance, known in competitive obedience circles as the *drop on recall.*

I was camping with some friends along with the Original Demo Dog, Lance, an obedience-titled dog of no small accomplishments and, by far, the best-trained dog I've ever owned (which is my own lazy fault, really, not the fault of the dogs I have now). Lance had wandered across a small dirt road in the campground to put his mark on some shrubbery and was ambling back when some idiot in a pickup truck came blasting down the road. Three more steps and Lance would have been toast but, instead of calling him, I shouted "down!" and he dropped where he stood. It was five full minutes before my heart started beating normally again, but Lance was safe.

A better testimony for the importance of training I have yet to run across.

The AKC Canine Good Citizen program

One of best things to happen in the dog world in recent years is the growth of the AKC Canine Good Citizen program, which gives formal recognition to dogs of all ages, sizes, and backgrounds who prove themselves — and their owners — to be ambassadors of good will to those among us who wish dogs would stay home or simply go away.

The certification program was designed to duplicate the everyday challenges a well-mannered dog should be able to handle in good grace. In order to be granted the Canine Good Citizen (CGC) title, the dog must accept the attention and handling of a friendly stranger, sit politely for petting, walk on a loose leash, walk through a crowd, demonstrate an understanding of the commands "sit," "down," "stay" and "come," and behave politely around other dogs, distractions, and when separated briefly from his owner.

Some owners have used this program to prepare their dogs for therapy work in hospitals and nursing homes, and the program is one more tool in helping to keep lodgings, parks, and other areas open to canine travelers.

For a free information kit on the Canine Good Citizen program, write to The American Kennel Club, Attention: CGC, 5580 Centerview Drive, Suite 200, Raleigh, NC 27606, call (919) 233-9780, or send e-mail to: info@akc.org.

What to Do if Your Dog Can't Go with You

You need to know what to do if you can't take your dog — even if you end up taking him most of the time. Business travel is necessary, after all, as is that emergency trip cross-country to handle the estate of the relative you haven't heard from in 15 years (but who you hope left you money).

You may even decide to go someplace where canine tourists aren't welcome, such as Hawaii or England, both of which have months-long quarantine requirements to keep rabies off their shores. Another place you may go where your dog can't — and I hope you don't, because I've been there and didn't like it much — is the hospital.

In any case, you're better off checking out your options ahead of time.

Ask your friends, neighbors, and coworkers what they do with their pets when they're gone. Ask your veterinarian, too, for referrals to pet sitters or kennels. Remember, the people you ask may have different criteria for selecting a service than you do. I find that for some people, the closest or cheapest kennel (or veterinarian) is the one that always gets the nod, while I would drive to the next city — and have — for the *right* trainer, kennel, or veterinary specialist for my pet.

When you have a service in mind, whether a kennel or sitter, call and ask for references, and then check them out — a step few people take. Ask about professional affiliations, such as the American Boarding Kennel Association or National Association of Pet Sitters, both of which offer materials and training to U.S. and Canadian members to encourage a higher degree of performance from their members.

No matter what kind of care you choose for your pet while you're gone, make your arrangements early. Pet sitters and boarding kennels are booked weeks and sometimes months in advance for peak travel times such as summer or the winter holidays.

A friend of mine found this out firsthand when he and his family flew from California to Minnesota on Christmas Day, planning to take their basset hound with them. Problem was, the temperature in Minnesota was below the federal regulations for shipping animals — more on that soon — so the dog could not fly. A frantic phone call turned up a friend willing to leave gift-opening with *his* family to pick up the dog at the airport, but all the begging and pleading in the world failed to turn up a boarding kennel for three days. The friend, fortunately, was a *good* one, and the dog was OK.

Prepare for emergencies

One of the easiest things to overlook when leaving your pet behind — whether with a friend, a pet sitter, or kennel — is how you want him cared for should he become ill. Discuss care options with your veterinarian in advance, and then clue in the person who'll be caring for your dog.

Setting up emergency-care arrangements work best if you have a good relationship with your veterinarian — but then, so does everything else concerning your pet's health. My veterinarian knows the kind of health care I expect for my pets, and I trust his judgment if he cannot get in touch with me. In my dogs' records is a note from him saying that no matter who shows up with my dogs, his hospital is to provide care, and my credit card number is on file to handle the charges. Every so often I touch base with my veterinarian on this topic so no misunderstandings come up.

For the ultimate in preparing for a trip where you can't take your pet, see the information in Chapter 14 on providing for your pet in your will.

Consider pet sitters

A wide range of services is lumped under this general title, covering everything from a reciprocal agreement between friends to care for each other's dogs, to paying a neighbor kid to look in on your dog, to hiring a professional pet-sitting service to care for your pet either in your own home or, less commonly, in theirs.

The benefits of having your pet stay in your own home is that she's familiar with the surroundings and gets to sleep in her own bed — or, because you're not looking, on yours. Additionally, if your pet is not well-socialized, she won't be stressed by the presence of other dogs in a boarding kennel. And pet sitters can do more than just look in on your pet: They can take in your mail and newspaper, water your houseplants, and turn lights on and off.

Make sure that you discuss services and prices beforehand and, if you're dealing with a service, make sure that they are bonded and insured.

The biggest drawback is that your pet is left alone a great deal of the time, because most professional pet sitters have a list of clients to drop in on every day and are probably not able to spend all that much time giving your pet individual attention. (An arrangement with a young person — or a house sitter to stay in your home while you're gone — may get your pet more time being walked or played with.) If your pet becomes ill or manages to escape, it may be a while before a pet sitter comes back to notice. And finally, some people just aren't comfortable with having people in their home when they're gone.

Informal arrangements for house-sitting (having the person move in) or pet sitting (having them drop in) can be even trickier than hiring a professional service. Just ask the friend of mine who left her house and pets in the care of a friend's college-aged daughter, only to find the young woman had been anything but a quiet resident. She'd had guests and even parties. The house was a bit worse for wear, but the pets were fine.

If you're going to go with a young person — and many people do, with no regrets — be sure that parental oversight is part of the picture.

One of the best solutions is to *trade* dog care. If your dog is socialized, well-mannered, and gets along well with other animals, he may be able to stay with friends while you are gone — as long as you reciprocate when your friends need help. If your pet won't be comfortable in another's house, then trade in-home care, with your friend looking after your house and pets in your house while you're gone, and you doing the same for them when they are gone.

Although I have, on occasion, used both professional pet sitters and boarding kennels with no complaints, trading care is the solution I prefer for my own dogs. My two are familiar with the people and pets with whom they stay, and they love having another playful dog around in their own house from time to time. Having dog-loving friends who knew my dogs and upon whom I could rely was crucial to me at one point, when I unexpectedly ended up in a hospital for a week. The friends with whom I share dog care had the homefront secured within hours, and I never worried about my pets during my recovery.

Trading care is a solution that's both reassuring — I know my friends care for my dogs as I do — and inexpensive.

Boarding kennels

Boarding kennels are another option, ideal for friendly, well-adjusted pets. Despite all the recommendations in the world, don't, on short notice, leave your pet at a kennel you haven't inspected yourself. You should see clean, comfortable, and well-maintained facilities; if you don't, go elsewhere.

Ask where your pet will stay. Some kennels leave pets in crates for most of their stay, so as to maximize the number of animals they can take in, especially during peak vacation periods. While I have nothing against keeping a pet in a crate for a short while, I would not want my pet spending a couple of weeks so confined. Make sure that your pet has a comfortable run of his own — your own pets can share a run, but bunking with strangers is not recommended. You pet should also get individual attention such as walks or time in a securely fenced play area. Areas for cats or other animals should be separate — for the good of all!

The kennel operators should seem sincerely interested in tailoring their facility to make your dog's stay more comfortable. They should be prepared to feed your dog as you do, especially if he's on a special diet, and they should be willing to allow you to leave toys or articles with your smell — like a dirty sock — behind to reassure your pet.

Boarding your pet at a kennel has a few advantages. Boarding kennels are usually very secure — more than most people's backyards! — and the best ones always have someone onsite to check in on your dog. Some kennels make up for the fact they're out in the sticks by picking up and delivering your pet.

If you don't have a home yet in a city you're moving to, a reputable kennel may meet your pet at the airport in advance of your arrival and care for her until you get there. Alternately, you can often leave your pet while you're house-hunting and arrange for the kennel to ship her after you find proper lodgings.

Many veterinarians have boarding facilities, and if yours is among them, this option may well be the best kennel choice for your pet. The biggest advantage is that the staff is already familiar with your pet and her medical background — a real plus if your dog is elderly or has a chronic health condition.

Boarding with a trainer is another possibility, if you want your dog to learn something while you're gone. The cost is higher — training plus boarding — but you return to a dog who has a much firmer understanding of basic obedience than when you left him.

"Kennel cough"

Boarding kennels take some heat over *kennel cough*, an upper-respiratory infection that's as contagious as sniffles in a daycare center. In fact, some kennel operators even find the name a little pejorative, insisting that the ailment be called by its proper name, *canine infectious tracheobronchitis*, or even *bordetella,* after its most common causative agent.

And maybe that's fair, because dogs can pick up kennel cough any place they come into contact with a dog who has it — and that means anywhere. Parks, dog shows, the waiting room of your veterinarian's office, or the fund-raising dog walk thrown by your local humane society — these are all possibilities for infection.

Fortunately, the ailment is not usually serious, even though the dry, bellowing cough can sound simply awful. For most dogs, the disease runs its course in a couple of weeks; others, especially yappy dogs who keep the airways irritated, may develop an infection requiring antibiotics. See your veterinarian for advice; he may recommend nothing more than Robutussin and rest.

Although not completely effective against the disease, a vaccine is available against the ailment. A boarding kennel should demand proof of it. The rub: It requires two doses a couple of weeks apart, which means you need to call your veterinarian at least three weeks before a kennel stay — or a trip to a dog-dense area.

Do not patronize a kennel that does not ask you for proof of up-to-date vaccinations. If they do not insist that *your* pet be healthy and well-protected from disease, they are not asking these questions of other boarders, either, and that puts your pet at risk.

No matter what, I would not recommend boarding a puppy who hasn't had all his vaccinations — which means no boarding before 16 weeks. The increased possibility for disease isn't worth the risk.

Many boarding kennels also have a grooming shop, and even those that do not are usually equipped to groom their boarders. Arrange to have your dog freshly groomed when you pick him up. The extra cost is well worth the price, because even in the most fastidious of facilities a dog can get a little rank during his stay.

Travel Preparations

Enough of this stay-at-home talk! You're ready to think about hitting the road. Although dogs aren't as complicated to travel with as, say, babies, you do have to pick up and work out a few things in advance of any trip.

The well-equipped travel dog

You can really go crazy packing things to ensure your dog's safety and comfort. My friend Maria Goodavage, who has written a couple of books on traveling with dogs, even packs her dogs' *beds* in the camper shell of her battered pickup truck. I don't have as much room in my little sedan, but I don't bring along all that much less. Whenever I've thought "I really don't need that," I've been wrong on the very next trip.

What should *you* bring? First, some basics.

✔ Your dog should be wearing a sturdy collar with a license and an up-to- date ID tag with at least one number, area code included, that's not yours — someone who'll be there to answer the phone should you lose your dog miles from home.

If your dog is more comfortable in a harness, put the tag on that, but remember, a harness isn't a good option for a dog who doesn't behave well on-leash, because you have less control with a harness.

Ideally, your pet should also be carrying an imbedded microchip for unshakable, permanent ID. (See Chapter 4 for more information on microchipping.)

My friend Judy Jordan got me started carrying paper key tags for disposable IDs while traveling. You can buy a bag of a hundred of them at any hardware store for not a lot of money and throw a couple dozen in a baggie in your glove box. Every time you change location on a vacation, write the day's information on the tag, for example: "Russian Gulch Campsite No. 15," or "Sea Dog Inn, Room 32, 707-555-DOGS."

✔ Bring along a six-foot leash. A longer leash is handy, too, especially a reel type leash such as the Flexi, which is great for giving your dog a little room to stretch his legs in areas such as rest stops.

I always bring an extra leash, as well as a nylon, one-piece slip lead like those veterinary hospitals and kennel operators use. (The one-piece lead, which is like a very long choke collar with a handle on the end, is in permanent residence in my glove box, for coping with the occasional stray or dog in trouble.)

✔ Two bowls, one for food, one for water.

Water bowls that either collapse for easy storage or don't spill are perfect for travel. I take the spill-proof one on all my trips and keep a collapsible bowl in the trunk, along with a bottle of water, always, because you just never know when you're going to run across a thirsty animal.

- ✔ If your dog's on a widely available brand of food, just pack enough to get you started and pick up the rest on the road, if you're going to an area with a market or pet-supplies store. Prescription food or anything out of the ordinary you'll have to bring along, enough for the trip. If your pet eats canned food, you need a can opener and a spoon.

- ✔ Don't forget some treats!

- ✔ A comb, brush, and tweezers or ready-made device for pulling ticks come in handy, especially on back-country trips.

- ✔ Some basic first-aid supplies — scissors, gauze, tape, and Pepto Bismal, for diarrhea — are handy to have around. Your veterinarian can prescribe some motion-sickness medication, if need be, and you certainly want to pack that.

- ✔ Don't forget to pack any regular medication your pet takes.

- ✔ Bring along cloth towels, for drying off wet, dirty dogs, and paper towels, for cleaning up more things than you can imagine before you go.

  I also pack an old sheet and blanket, for covering bedspreads, furniture, and carpets in motel rooms, and a multipurpose cleaner in a spray bottle.

- ✔ Plastic bags are a must-bring, too.

- ✔ I've purchased dog shampoo on a couple of trips; now I just bring it along.

- ✔ For the owners of little dogs only: A shoulder bag for carrying your pet. With this — or any oversized bag — you can slip your dog into areas the big dogs can only dream of, and most of the people around you will never notice.

- ✔ Last, but certainly not least, from your dog's point of view: A couple of his favorite toys!

The standard travel advice has been to bring water from home, but that's just unfeasible for a trip of any decent length. Your dog will be fine drinking the same water you do in unfamiliar places. That said, I always travel with a couple gallons of bottled water, either from the tap or the store, because I often stop to water and walk my dogs in areas where a source of safe drinking water isn't readily available.

More on first-aid kits is in Chapter 10, as are tips on basic dog care, including tick-removal.

The well-prepared dog lover

As with anything else, the goal for traveling with a dog is "prepare for the worst, hope for the best." Carry some ready-made "LOST DOG!" flyers with your dog's picture on them and a place to write a phone number with a big marker, which you should also pack. (More on preparing these flyers is in Chapter 19.) Don't forget your pet's health records, including microchip number, and especially proof of rabies vaccination. The latter is absolutely imperative should the unthinkable happen: Your dog bites someone or tangles with a rabid creature in the wild.

I also travel with a directory of pet-friendly lodgings. Some travel guides, such as AAA, mention whether pets are accepted, but calling ahead is always a good idea: Policies and ownership can change, after all.

My favorite dog travel book is Maria Goodavage's *The California Dog Lover's Companion,* the better of two offerings on canine outings in the Golden State. If you live in or are planning to visit California, this book is a must buy. Better still, the publisher, Foghorn Press, is going forward with a series of "Dog Lover's Companion" guides that promises to be fantastic.

Another good resource is *DogGone,* a newsletter highlighting the best and most interesting places in the United States and Canada for dogs and their people to visit. *DogGone* is $24 for six issues a year from P.O. Box 65155, Vero Beach, FL 32965-1155. You can also e-mail publisher Wendy Ballard for information at DogGone@aol.com.

Finally, the TravelDog site on the Web, http://www.traveldog.com/ shows great promise. This page offers travel tips, stories, destination ideas, and products for the canine on the go.

Travel by Car

Given the worries most pet lovers have about air travel, it's no wonder that most doggie vacations are conducted in the family car. After they understand car rides end up in exciting places like the beach, most dogs greet the prospect of a car ride with unabashed enthusiasm — a little too much, for some drivers.

Making car rides safer

As with all other training, ending up with a good car rider starts with molding correct behavior when your dog is a puppy. No matter how cute or how small, do not allow your pup to ride in your lap, and don't make a fuss over him while you're driving. On short neighborhood trips, ask your pup to sit quietly, and praise him for proper behavior.

Traveling with your dog in a crate is often easier and definitely safer. Depending on the size of your dog and the size and shape of your car, a crate may not be feasible. Crates should always be considered, though, especially for those dogs who are so active they distract the driver. Collapsible crates are available for easy storage in the trunk when not in use.

Another safety tool is a doggy seat belt, which fits into a standard seat-belt buckle and then attaches to a harness on the dog. Also good for keeping a pet in her place, if you have a station wagon or similar vehicle, are widely available metal barriers that fit between the passenger and cargo areas.

Uneasy riders

If your dog's only exposure to riding in a car is an occasional trip to the veterinarian's, don't be surprised if he's not the most easy of riders. Try to build up his enthusiasm by increasing his time in the car and praising him for his good behavior. The first short trips should be to pleasant locations, such as parks.

Dramamine prevents car-sickness in dogs as well as people, but other remedies are available — talk to your veterinarian. A dog-handlers trick: Your dog should travel on little or no food, and the dog should get a jelly bean — or any other piece of sugar candy, except chocolate — before hitting the road.

Because most of the problems come from fear, not motion sickness, building up your pet's tolerance for riding in a car is a better long-term cure than anything you can give him.

Although fresh air is a wonderful thing, don't let your pet hang his head out of the window. Small debris kicked up by other cars can strike him in the eye or nose and injure him. Roll the window down enough for a sniff, if you like — but no more.

On the road, remember to stop a regular intervals — about as often as you need to for yourself — for your dog to relieve himself and get a drink of fresh water. Remember to always to keep your dog on-leash for his own safety.

For information on heat stroke and other canine emergencies, see Chapter 10.

The Humane Society of the United States offers free *Hot Car* flyers to slip under windshield wipers to inform others of the risks of leaving a dog in a car. Send a self-addressed, business-sized envelope to "Hot Car," HSUS, 2100 L Street, N.W., Washington, D.C. 20037. If you see a dog in danger, contact local police or animal-control officers immediately.

If, when you're on the road, you want to spend a few hours kicking around an area where dogs are not welcome, a local veterinary clinic is a safe place to leave your dog. I've always managed to find one amenable to a short-term boarder within a couple of calls, and I know my dogs are in safe and secure surroundings while I'm not with them. The price for this service is negotiable — a half-day's boarding is a good starting point — and on a couple of occasions I wasn't charged at all.

Another possibility is your motel room. Although leaving a dog loose in a strange room is not a good idea — most places forbid doing so, in fact — you

Hot dog!

Just about everyone understands that dogs shouldn't be left inside a car on a hot day, but fewer realize the danger is just as great on a warm one.

It's a horrible way to die.

A car functions similar to a greenhouse, and heat can build up to lethal levels in minutes, even on a pleasant day in the 70s or low 80s. Even with the windows rolled down, a dog can show signs of heat stress — heavy panting, glazed eyes, rapid pulse, dizziness or vomiting, or a deep red or purple tongue — in the time it takes you to get a six-pack through the Ten Items or Less line. Brain damage and death can follow within minutes.

Another danger to the unattended dog is theft, which, when combined with heat dangers, means a few minutes looking through that cute little shop really isn't worth the risk that is posed to your pet.

can leave a *crated* dog alone, provided he's not a barker. Just another reason why a crate is one of the most versatile pieces of canine equipment your dog can have.

Travel by Air

If you don't take your dog by car in the United States, air is your only other option. The major bus lines and Amtrak don't allow any animals except those serving the disabled. Other countries are far more liberal on this point — dogs are welcome in restaurants, too, in some places — but it's still hit and miss.

Although horror stories make the news, the truth is that airline travel is relatively safe for most dogs, and it will be for yours if you play by the rules, plan carefully, and are prepared to be a little pushy on your pet's behalf.

Animals move through the airline system in two ways: As cargo or as accompanied baggage. Either way, almost all of these animals will travel in a pressurized cargo hold beneath the passenger compartment. Although the accommodations aren't any nicer, it's better for your pet if he is traveling as your "baggage," so you can ask about him in person.

Some airlines allow small dogs in the cabin, if their carriers can fit in the space beneath the seat. This way is by far the best that your dog can fly, because he never leaves your care during the course of the trip. Not all airlines allow dogs to travel in the cabin, however, and others put a limit on the number of dogs in the cabin, so making your arrangements far in advance pays.

The only larger dogs allowed in the cabin are service dogs traveling with a disabled person.

The Air Transport Association estimates more than a half a million dogs and cats are transported on commercial airlines in the United States each year, and the industry group insists 99 percent reach their destination without incident.

To make sure that your dog is one of them, pay careful attention to the following:

- ✔ **Talk to the airline.** Some carriers — especially the new no-frills companies — don't take animals at all. Even those that do have limits to the number of animals on a flight because a set amount of air is available in the sealed cargo holds. You also need to know where and when your dog has to be presented, and what papers — health certificate, and so on — you need to bring.

- ✔ **Be sure that your dog is in good health, and isn't one of the pug-nosed breeds.** These dogs find breathing a little difficult under the best of circumstances, and the stress of airline travel may be more than they can handle.

- ✔ **Be sure that your dog is traveling in a proper carrier that has contact phone numbers at both ends of the journey.** (Your home number won't help if you're not home.) The crate should be just big enough for your dog to stand up and turn around in.

Be sure that all the bolts securing the halves of the carriers are in place and tightened.

While he cannot wear a collar in his crate — it's not safe, because it can get caught on other objects — put an ID tag on a piece of elastic around his neck; in addition, you may want to consider having him microchipped before travel. (See Chapter 4 for more on microchipping.)

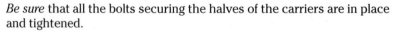

✔ **Don't ship your pet when the weather is bad, or when air traffic is heaviest.** Avoid peak travel days such as around the Christmas holidays, and be sure to choose flights that are on the ground when the temperature is neither too hot nor too cold, not only at the departure airport but also at the connecting and arriving airports. In summer, a night flight is likely better, while the reverse is true in the winter.

✔ **Fly with your dog whenever possible.** Keeping on top of things is easier when you're on the same flight.

✔ **Choose a direct flight; if that's not possible, try for a route with a short layover.** Most canine fatalities occur on the ground, when dogs are left in their crates on the hot tarmack or in stifling cargo holds. Direct flights eliminate layovers, and short layovers reduce the time on the ground.

✔ **Remember, your dog's life relies on the attentiveness of airline personnel.** Most of these employees are excellent and caring, but mistakes do happen. You should be prepared to pester airline personnel to confirm your dog has been loaded and has made the same connections you have. If your pet is flying unaccompanied, talk to freight-handling personnel at every airport your dog will visit. Be polite but persistent; don't take "I'm sure he's fine, have some delicious honey-roasted peanuts" as an answer from a flight attendant. Make the staff *check* and report back.

Contrary to popular belief, it's generally better that your dog *not* be tranquilized before flying. The combination of high altitude and limited oxygen is a challenge your pet's body is better prepared to meet if she's not sedated. Still, your pet may be an exception. In the end, you and your veterinarian should decide on this issue.

The Air Transport Association has a free booklet, *Air Travel for Your Dog or Cat.* The booklet is available by sending a self-addressed, stamped, business-sized envelope to: ATA, 1301 Pennsylvania Blvd. NW, Suite 1100, Washington, DC 20004.

Dog-Friendly Vacations

Just as vacations with children are different from adults-only trips, traveling with your dog works out better if you plan the journey with an eye to finding places where dogs are not only welcome but also able to enjoy the surroundings.

In general, that means an emphasis on the outdoors. But as you'll soon find in traveling with your dog, all parks and beaches are not the same. In some cities and towns, dogs aren't even *allowed* in municipal facilities; in other open areas, human popularity may make things tough for dogs.

Dogs are versatile travel companions: They just want to be where you are!

Photo courtesy of Gina Spadafori.

Even camping can be a disappointment. The U.S.'s national parks aren't much fun for dogs, but national forests are. The difference: The crowded national parks — such as Yosemite — have strict leash laws and require dogs to stay off most trails. National forests, on the other hand, have wide open spaces with few people and fewer leashing requirements — although that doesn't relieve you of the responsibility for your dog's poor behavior. The requirements in other parks vary, so check them out in advance.

I prefer to head for a generally pet-friendly area and stay in lodgings where dogs aren't just tolerated — they're welcomed. The owners of dog-friendly inns and motels are often dog lovers, and they're happy to give you clues on the best things to do in the area. A less-popular resort area is almost always more laid back and tolerant where dogs are concerned.

Don't forget to make the most of online resources: Posting a note on a bulletin board may net you all kinds of suggestions for lodgings and activities.

Whatever you do: *Call ahead!* Even the most dog-friendly places may have only a couple of rooms available for dog-lovers, and if these are in popular resorts areas, they can be booked months in advance for prime vacation weekends. Better still, plan for an off-season vacation (and still call ahead).

It's no longer the only, but it's probably the first, certainly the best-known, and possibly the best ever. Camp Gone To The Dogs is a celebration of all things dog on a leashes-optional piece of heaven in Vermont. Honey Loring puts the camp together every year, offering sessions on dog sports, guest speakers on training and health, and games and contests to keep human and animal guests deliriously happy. For information, write to Loring at RR 1, Box 958, Putney, VT 05346.

Getting Past "No Dogs" — It's Possible!

If you travel with your dog a lot, a time will come when you're going to be stranded somewhere you weren't counting on — because of a car problem, perhaps — and you're going to be trying to find a place to stay. This has happened to me more than once, and although I've gotten plenty of definitive "no's" at registration desks, I've also managed to convince some motels to let the rules slide. Here are some tips:

JUST FOR FUN

To leash, or not to leash

My favorite travel story regarding dogs and leash laws happened in a state campground on the drop-dead gorgeous northern coast of California, where my dogs and I go as often as we can. As we pulled next to the ranger station to check in, one of the two rangers leaned out and started explaining the rules in a loud voice.

"No dogs on trails. No dogs on these two beaches, marked on this map. Dogs must be in the car or in the tent at night. And remember: We *absolutely, positively* will not tolerate any off-leash dogs. It is *expressly* forbidden in California state parks."

And then she leaned out a little more, and dropped her tone so the other ranger couldn't hear her. "Two miles up the road is the beach where I take my dogs," she said. "We never, ever patrol there." And then she smiled and waved us through.

She was one of us!

At this point, a confession is in order: I am a chronic breaker of canine leash laws, like probably three-quarters of the nation's dog lovers. I am very careful about where and when they're

allowed off-leash: Early in the morning or late at night, far from people, traffic, and wildlife. They are under voice control, and leashed at the first sign of trouble.

Should you let your dog off-leash? I'm not going to tell you to break the law. Just be careful out there. And be considerate.

One of the best things for us habitual offenders is the creation of *dog parks,* special areas, often fenced, where dogs can legally run free and play with other dogs. The first dog parks were in the San Francisco Bay Area, but they're scattered across the U.S. and Canada now. They're great places to visit if you're on the road and to lobby for in your own home town. The most winning argument: People with dogs have recreational needs that should be addressed just as those of tennis players, boaters, and soccer teams are. My recreation is throwing a ball for my retriever until my arm drops off, and I need a place to do so.

Dog parks are a way to keep dog lovers and dog haters safely out of each others' way. Support them!

✔ **Offer a deposit.** If you're confident your dog isn't going to cause any damage — and if you aren't, you shouldn't be traveling with her — put your money where your mouth is and offer to guarantee your pet's good behavior.

✔ **Show off your dog's good manners and well-groomed appearance.** Obviously not a plan for someone with a muddy, out-of-control , 125-pound shedding machine. But if your dog is clean and well-behaved, show him off!

✔ **Show the manager a crate.** A dog who's going to sleep in a crate and not be left to his own devices is a much better risk.

I would never, never, encourage anyone to sneak a dog into a motel room, but I've heard doing so works better if your room is far from the office and you're prepared to sleep in your car, just in case. If you're planning to have your *dog* sleep in your car, you'd better be with him: Leaving your pet unattended is *never* a good idea.

Even a casual reader of this chapter will get the idea that crates are a very useful item, and indeed, they are. They're good for training, good for travel, and indispensable in disasters. For more on choosing a crate, see Chapter 4.

Ruffing it!

Some people spend their vacation not in some fancy resort, but in the great outdoors — and they want to take their dogs with them. Fortunately, sturdy, well-designed packs are on the market designed to let your dog carry his share of the load, and even some of yours. An adult dog in top condition can carry up to a quarter of his weight, evenly distributed in a properly fitting pack. Get your dog used to the feel of the pack on short walks and trips and gradually build up the weight and distance.

Dogs aren't welcome everywhere, and the biggest danger to the future of canine backpacking is other hikers more than wild beasts. Don't give the dog haters any ammunition: Keep your dog under control, and that means on-leash in areas with other people or animals. Take something to bury waste, or supplies to pack it back out.

You won't take much into the back country — food and water are the basics — but you will need a few extra things. Grooming tools — a brush or comb, and tweezers or a tick remover — keep your pet healthy and comfortable. Basic first aid supplies for human and canine packers should be included, as should a light rope for tethering your dog when necessary.

Charlene G. LaBelle's *A Guide to Backpacking With Your Dog* (Alpine) is an outstanding little book offering invaluable tips on how to train and equip your dog, and where to take him.

Keeping the World Safe for Canine Travelers

Even though more people than ever are traveling with their dogs, plenty of people are still out there who don't like sharing their space with the four-legged tourist. Some of them, unfortunately, own motels, and others are politicians like those in my home town, who allow drug dealers to work the margins of an outdoor street fair but absolutely forbid the presence of dogs there.

Still, you can see how the decisions to ban dogs get made. There are the liability concerns over dog bites and the sanitation worries over dog mess. But our job as caring, responsible dog lovers is to make sure that people realize more good dogs are around than bad ones. Here are a few things to do on the road:

- ✔ **Keep 'em clean.** Your dog should always be well-groomed and clean-smelling. Always dry off wet dogs and wipe off muddy feet — using *your* towels, not the motel's — before allowing your dog inside. Cover furniture, carpets, and bedspreads with your old sheets and towels, and if you need to bathe your dog, be sure, again, to use *your* towels and to clean up all the fur.

- ✔ **Keep 'em under control.** Your dog should be obedient, friendly but not annoying, and *never* aggressive, not to people, not to pets, and not to wildlife. Do *not* allow your dog to bark uncontrolled in a car, camper, or motel room. Use your best judgment on when to let a dog off-leash — even in areas where doing so is allowed, and be sure that your dog isn't annoying other people or dogs.

- ✔ **Pick up after 'em.** I am always astonished that well-mannered people who would never consider tossing a soft-drink cup on the ground will look the other way when their dog deposits something 5,000 times more vile. Don't give me that "it's biodegradable" excuse, either. Pick up after your dog. Did you get that? No? Then let me repeat it: *Pick up after your dog.* Dog mess is the single biggest complaint dog haters have against our being in public areas, so don't give them any ammunition. When you check into a motel, stress that you intend to pick up after your dog, and inquire if they have a place where they prefer you take him to relieve himself. Don't let a male dog lift his leg on the shrubs while you're walking there, either: Teach the "Leave it" command — see Chapter 11 — to get his nose up. No sniff, no lift.

Easy ways to scoop the poop

In the couple of decades since urban areas started fining people for failing to pick up after their dogs, a zillion products have come and gone in an effort to make the task easier and less disgusting. The latter is just not possible. The only thing that helps is time, over which you get so used to the feel of warm dog poop that your stomach doesn't even shimmy anymore.

Forget the long-handle gizmos. The easiest way to get the job done is with a plastic bag. Fold-over sandwich bags are fine for small dogs, but for larger ones I prefer to use plastic grocery bags, which tie off nicely at the top. In either case, here's how it works:

Pull the bag over your hand like a loose mitten, then pick up the poop. Pull the outer edges of the bag over your hand while still holding the poop, until your hand ends up on the outside of the bag and the mess is inside. Then close, either by flipping the flap or tying the tie, and drop in the closest garbage can.

Clean-up bags become one of those signs of a real dog lover, as in "You know you're a real dog lover when there are plastic bags in the pockets of every coat and jacket you own."

They are in mine. They should be in yours, too.

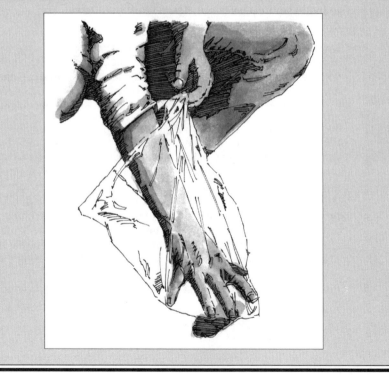

Chapter 16

Canine Competitions

● ●

In This Chapter

▶ The benefits of organized dog play

▶ What's it all about?

▶ Dog shows and obedience trials

▶ Games for working dogs

▶ Hot new sports

▶ Getting involved

● ●

*N*early all sports have their origins in some real-life activity, be it war or farming, and dog sports are no exception. Likely not a minute had passed between the time our ancestors figured they could get a hound to hunt for them and the instant one ancestor turned to the other and said, "Yeah, well I bet *my* hound is faster!"

The races haven't stopped since.

The game today is for more than the swift, however. In some competitions, looks take the day and in others agility — literally — is the point of it all. Some sports are meant to show off a breed's original function, such as hunting, sledding, and herding tests, and others stress precise teamwork the likes of which a ballroom dancing pair would be proud. Some sports are for a particular breed or handful of related breeds only, others are only for purebreds, and a few are open to every dog. Some are as old as the relationship between humans and dogs, and others are taking shape even as you read this chapter.

Although some canine sports require top physical performances from both dog and handler, others are within the abilities of people slowed by age or disabilities. I have seen people in wheelchairs compete, and at a recent national obedience competition, the oldest competitor was nearing 90. And speaking of age: In no other collection of sports would a 12-year-old win over adult professionals at a top-level event — a feat that happened at a recent Westminster Kennel Club dog show.

There is, truly, a competition for every one — and every dog.

To the uninitiated, dog sports can be a little hard to follow, which is why learning a little bit before you go is a good idea. Whether you're planning to attend with an eye to compete someday or you're just looking for a pleasant family outing, this chapter contains plenty of information to get you started.

Be careful: Dog sports can be addictive. For some, a casual introduction to canine competitions ends up as a whole lot more. Before they know what's happening, they're buying air-conditioned motorhomes for the comfort of their dogs on the road and homes in the country so the ever-growing canine family can practice on agility or obedience equipment that's permanently set up. They have dog classes and club meetings nearly every night of the week, and they plan their vacations around such events as the national specialty show.

All this activity costs money, and the entry fees — which start at around $10 for a match and climb from there — are the least of it. Equipment and travel are expensive, and if you hire a professional handler to *campaign* your dog for you, you're looking at thousands of dollars.

Go to the dogs if you must; these folks have no complaints. Just don't say I didn't warn you.

The Benefits of Organized Activities

Ribbons and trophies are all well and good, and I wouldn't suggest you ever turn one down should you and your dog get to such a level of proficiency that you start earning them. But I find the true benefits of canine competition are in the way they encourage a tighter bond between humans and dogs, and a camaraderie among the human participants, united as they are by the common thread of enjoying the company of dogs.

Preparing a dog for competition takes time, and time is the greatest gift you can give your dog. Training, practicing, grooming, traveling to events, and hanging out while waiting for your turn to compete all take time. While your closest humans may find all this hanging out decidedly less than entertaining, your dog could not be happier. After all, she's with *you*.

At times, you'll be particularly happy to have her around, too, for like any competitive endeavor, all is not supportive good sportsmanship in the world of canine competitions. One of the best things about these competitions is the competitions themselves: In canine sports, the beginners compete against the experienced, the young against the old, the amateurs against the professionals. While the whole thing works a lot better than seems possible, these differences are a source of grousing, at the very least, and shouting, on more than a few occasions.

Dog events are happening nearly every weekend, but they can be a little hard to find. Calendars of events are listed in the general-interest dog magazines like *Dog Fancy;* the American Kennel Club and Canadian Kennel Club offer complete lists of their sanctioned events in their respective magazines, *The AKC Gazette* and *Dogs in Canada.* You may even keep an eye out in the events calendar of your local newspaper.

If you get involved with a particular sport, you'll land on mailing lists event organizers use to keep entry forms constantly in prospective competitors' mailboxes.

Making Sense of It All

Although the point of some dog sports is rather obvious — you chase it, you pull it, you find it, or you bring it back — others aren't so easy to follow. The most popular dog sport of all — a conformation show (see the section "Dog Shows" later in this chapter) — is one of the hardest to follow. Sometimes determining who won in a given class is hard enough, much less understanding where that dog goes from there.

A dog show is surely the only sporting event in the world where the overwhelming majority of spectators — and even competitors — neither know nor care who won the final round (with the exception of the Westminster Kennel Club dog show and Crufts in England, both of which function as national championships). Most competitors go to show their own dogs and then leave, and most spectators go just to look at the dogs and maybe buy a few canine accessories.

Still, if you get the basics down, you soon start understanding the nuances. And even if you don't stay for the finale, you will better enjoy the time you spend at the event.

No matter what kind of canine competition you attend, you need to take your comfort into your own hands. Dog shows are held both indoors and out, in all weather. Wear casual clothes and shoes you can walk in, and bring a lawn chair and shade if you plan to spend the day. (For indoor shows, just the lawn chair will do.) Although big shows have concessions, smaller events don't, so pack a lunch and make sure you've plenty of drinks.

Unentered dogs are not allowed on the grounds of events where dogs are competing for titles or points, so leave them at home until they're ready to enter. They are allowed at practice events, called *matches,* and these events are where exhibitors first expose their young dogs to the sights and sounds of competition.

An excellent resource on canine competitions is Ellie Milon's *201 Ways to Enjoy Your Dog: A Complete Guide to Organized U.S. and Canadian Activities for Dog Lovers* (Alpine). Milon's book provides the rules and regulations for virtually all dog sports, along with tips to get you going.

Dog Shows

Although the registries such as the AKC and CKC sanction field and obedience trials, most of the action is in *conformation competitions,* what most people think of when they think "dog show."

A dog show is at its heart a single-elimination tournament, with quarter- and semifinal rounds leading up to the selection of one winner — *the best in show.* The competition starts in the breed ring, where dogs of the same breed and similar characteristics square off against one another.

Dog shows are the most well-known canine competition.

Each dog is judged against a *breed standard,* a set of rules and guidelines that define an ideal specimen of that breed. Parts of the standard may be quite specific — eliminating dogs over a certain size, for example — or quite vague, as in standards that ask that the dog have "dignity." The breed clubs set the standards, although they are available from breed registry; the AKC's are all listed in *The Complete Dog Book* (Howell Book House Macmillan General Reference).

On the breed level, dogs are divided by sex and then again into smaller classes such a *puppy, bred-by-exhibitor,* and *open.* Some of these classes may be further divided by such factors as coat color.

The judge chooses a winner from each of these classes and then the best male and female from those winners. This pair then competes against established champions for best-in-breed honors. The best dog from each breed goes on to the semifinal round, against other dogs in the *group.* The best dog in each group — seven dogs in all — are all that remain at the end of the show, and one of those seven will be the top dog — best in show. (Groups are *sporting, hounds* and so on; for more on the groups, see Chapter 2.) The judging procedure is the same from puppy classes to the best-in-show finale, as dogs are judged not against each other but against that mythical standard of perfection for their breed.

Although the tables at ringside are heaped with ribbons, very few dogs go home with what their owners really want: points toward a championship. This separate competition is conducted and completed in the first stages of the dog show, in the breed ring. While accumulating the 15 cumulative lifetime points necessary to win an AKC championship may seem a simple thing, it is an expensive and time-consuming quest that may take show after show and for many dogs is never completed. (This is what a breeder means when she says a dog is *pointed* — the animal has some points toward his championship, but didn't end up with enough to complete it.)

Championship points are awarded on a sliding scale that takes into account the popularity of the breed: The more popular the breed, the more dogs are needed to increase the point value of the total breed entry. A popular breed such as a Golden retriever may need more than 50 dogs to qualify for the same amount of points a vastly less popular breed, such as the flat-coated retriever, can attain with ten dogs.

At any one show, from one to five points can be awarded, with wins of three points or more called a *major* win. The 15 points necessary to earn a championship must be awarded by at least three different judges, and must include two majors won under different judges. In every breed ring, only one female and one male dog get the points: the best of each gender, excluding established champions.

Just for kids

The AKC and CKC offer separate handling competitions just for youngsters where the conformation of the dog doesn't matter as much as the handler's ability to present them to their best advantage. Called *Junior Showmanship* in the United States and *Junior Handling* in Canada, these events give youngsters a chance to compete — and to learn.

For some, these competitions are the start of a career in show handling: Many professional handlers get their start in the junior ranks, and more than a couple of them have shown in the junior championships at Westminster and years later turned up again — in the Best in Show ring.

Dog shows aren't the only child-friendly canine sport. Youngsters have done well in obedience, too, and no regular dog sport puts any limit on the age of a competitor. For some, dog sports are truly a family affair.

Other organizations, such as the Canadian Kennel Club and the United States' smaller canine registry, the United Kennel Club, have somewhat different procedures for awarding championships, as does the Kennel Club in England. Write to the clubs for their rules and regulations; the addresses are in this book's "Additional Resources" appendix.

Obedience Trials

The sport of *obedience* started out as little more than a traveling exhibition more than 50 years ago, as its early proponents struggled to establish a friendly competition that challenged the intelligence and promoted the companionship ability of purebred dogs. They succeeded, but only just. For years the sport languished in the shadows at dog shows, its classes small, its top dog-handler teams overlooked.

There were three levels of competition, three titles to attain, and when a team reached the top level, there was little incentive to stay involved. But then the AKC tossed the top trainers a meaty bone: a championship of their own. The addition of this obedience-trial championship, along with an ambitious series of national competitions and awards, shook up the sport.

Today, at the highest levels of obedience competition, the scores of the top dog-handler teams are often separated from each other and from perfection by the smallest of margins, sometimes by as little as one-half a point, the penalty for a crooked sit.

But unlike the breed ring, where the difference between a first- and second-place finisher is difficult for the casual observer to spot, the difference between top-performing dogs and the others in the class are easy to see. Top-performing dogs work happily, willingly, and speedily, tearing through exercises that include jumping, retrieving, and heeling with the polish and panache of a true performer. These dogs are always "on," eyes glued to their handlers, muscles tensed in anticipation of a word or hand signal. The work is fast and exacting, but it's also apparent that the dogs are having fun.

The top dogs come from a relatively small handful of breeds — golden retrievers, Shetland sheepdogs, border collies, poodles, and Dobermans, for the most part — but almost all breeds are represented in the sport as a whole. They're all trying for the same thing — a perfect score of 200 on the road to an obedience title.

To attain an *AKC obedience title,* a dog-handler team must receive a qualifying score, at least 170 points out of a possible 200, under three different judges on different days.

At all three levels — called *novice, open,* and *utility* — the dogs start with a perfect score, from which points are deducted for such violations as slowness, inattention, or whining. Some offenses are more serious than others: If a handler is forced to repeat a command, the team is disqualified.

After a dog has attained a degree at each of the three levels (a goal that can take two or three years to attain, and many never reach it) comes the hardest test of all — the pursuit of an obedience trial championship. The dogs are awarded points for first- and second-place finishes in the two highest classes, with the value of the win determined by the number of dogs in each class.

The Canadian Kennel Club and United Kennel Club also award obedience titles, as does the Kennel Club of England, although their rules are a little different.

You can write to these organizations for guidance in competing in their events. You can find their addresses in the "Additional Resources" appendix in the back of this book.

Obedience competitions used to be for purebreds only, but that's no longer true. While AKC-sanctioned events are still purebreds only, some events — including the prestigious Cycle Classic series — are open to all dogs. The American Mixed Breed Obedience Registry (AMBOR) is the governing body for non-purebreds in the sport. For more information, see this book's "Additional Resources" appendix. The United Kennel Club also accepts mixed breeds for obedience competition.

Working Events

While dog shows and obedience trials attract the majority of competitors every year, several more sports are available to you and your dog. Most of these fall into the category of working events — competitions designed to prove a purebred dog still possesses the ability to do the job for which his breed was developed.

Some of these sports are governed by a major registry such as the AKC, UKC, or CKC, while others have their own governing body. Each sport is involved enough to warrant its own book — and most have them. In this book, though, I just give you a brief overview to get you thinking.

Hundreds of books are available on training for and competing in every kind of canine sport — you can find more than a dozen books on agility alone. One of the best sources finding a dog-sports book is the *Dog & Cat Book Catalog* of the Direct Book Service. For a copy, send an e-mail to dgctbook@cascade.net or call 800-776-2665.

The ability to compete successfully at a working event has been virtually lost in some breeds. As a result, some breeds, such as the cocker spaniel, have nearly abandoned their hunting heritage, while other breeds have split into *field* and *show* lines, with the dogs in each quite different in appearance. This split is perhaps most obvious in the Labrador retriever, where show dogs are heavier in appearance than their leaner cousins in the working events.

Field trials

These competitions are designed to duplicate situations that would face hunting dogs at work. They break down by breed type:

- **Trials for scent hounds.** Beagles are the most popular entrants in these events, designed to show that a dog is capable of trailing game. Basset hounds, dachshunds, and coonhounds have their own events, too.

- **Trials for sight hounds.** Coursing events — usually using an artificial lure, not live game — test the enthusiasm of these most ancient of breeds to hunt using their awesome speed. Sight hound breeds as small as the whippet and as large as the Irish Wolfhound find these events a blissful way to accomplish what many don't get the chance to do in more developed areas: Run like the wind.

- **Trials for pointing breeds.** Here the point is to search for and find a bird, indicate its location with a classic point, and hold that position while the handler fires to prove that the dog isn't gun-shy.

✔ **Trials for retrieving breeds and spaniels.** These events test the ability and endurance of these hunting breeds to retrieve game under a variety of conditions. Spaniels, usually English springers, must additionally find and flush the game.

✔ **Trials for terriers.** The courage and tenacity of these "earth dogs" — that's where the name *terrier* comes from, *terra* for *earth* — is tested in a covered trench where they must race through the darkness to attack a caged and protected quarry, usually a rat.

Sled dog events

The International Sled Dog Racing Association serves as the primary governing body of this sport, which offers a variety of events for teams of all sizes and breeding. (Collies, hounds, and even poodles have competed in these events.) Races of different lengths are usually run over a groomed snow course — although some are run in snowless areas, using a *gig* — a sled on wheels. Freight- and weight-pulling events are also run, as are long-distance races such as the Iditarod and those of lesser fame.

Protection dog events

Schutzhund — German for *protection dog* — is an international sport that tests the intelligence, endurance, and courage of dogs trained for police work. Competitors work their dogs through progressively harder levels of competition including tests of tracking, obedience, and protection. German shepherds, Belgian malinois, Rottweilers, and Dobermans are among the breeds most popular in this sport.

Herding dog events

These range from trials of real working sheep dogs to events that test the ability of a herding breed dog to move instinctively toward sheep or ducks as if herding. In the United Kingdom, sheepdog trials are so popular they're televised, and the movie *Babe* gave millions of people a taste of the intensity and grace demonstrated by working sheep dogs.

New Sports for the '90s — and Beyond

Some of the fastest-growing dog sports around are less than 20 years old, and some are even more recent. What they have in common is that they're *fun,* for dogs, for handlers, and even for spectators.

Even better, they're open to all breeds, purebreds and mixes alike.

Agility

In agility competitions, the dogs race the clock over a course that includes a variety of obstacles to go through or jump over. The teams are penalized for missing or knocking down obstacles or not completing the course within the designated time.

Both dogs and handlers have to be in decent shape for this one, because the handlers run the course while directing their dogs over the obstacles.

Flyball

At the heart of the flyball competition is a launcher that releases a flying tennis ball when the dog steps on a board at the front of the device. Picture two such devices, side by side, at the end of a series of low jumps, and a relay team of dogs and handlers, and you can imagine just how fast and exciting flyball can get.

The dogs leap over the series of jumps, trigger the launcher, grab the ball, and jump, jump, jump back to the beginning of the course — all in a few seconds. After these actions are complete, the dogs must cross the finish line, which allows the team's next dog to be released. The team that gets all its dogs up and back the fastest wins.

The flyball competition is exciting to dog and owner — and spectators, too.

Photo courtesy of Gay Currier.

Freestyle obedience

The latest competition to be developed, freestyle obedience, consists of dog-handler pairs performing original and intricately choreographed routines set to music. Think dancing with your dog or figure skating. The latter comparison makes sense if you think of traditional obedience as the compulsory figures and freestyle as the creative program, complete with costumes!

Flying disk competitions

This competition is probably the only dog sport that started because of a single dog — Ashley Whippet, who in the '70s became a media superstar performing gravity-defying leaps at nationally televised sporting events. Today, hundreds of dogs compete in regional events leading up to a world invitational tournament — where style, height, and daring in the art of the retrieve separate the winners from the other competitors.

Getting Started

So maybe now you want to quit watching and get out there and *compete* with your dog. Good move, but where do you begin?

Some dog sports — or events, anyway — are clearly not for beginners (the Iditarod comes to mind here). Others aren't open to all breeds, and some rely much more on your dog's natural attributes than anything you can contribute to make him more competitive. So the first step in getting involved in canine competitions is to take a look at what you've got, and by that I mean your dog.

Choose a sport

No dog can compete in all sports, so the first step in deciding what canine competition suits you both is to take a good look at your dog. First, is he purebred or mixed? The majority of dog sports are for registered purebreds. If your dog is truly an original in appearance — the result of some illicit dalliance between a golden retriever and a basset hound, say — you're going to have to stick to those events open to all.

If your dog *is* a registered purebred, is he a good representative of his breed? If so, you may decide to go the dog-show route. Be warned, however, that what a lot of puppy sellers call *show quality* isn't really *show winning*: What they're guaranteeing is a dog who has no disqualifying faults, such as being too tall or the wrong color.

You need only a few minutes with the breed standard — available from a governing registry such as the American Kennel Club or Canadian Kennel Club — to get an idea of how your pet stacks up. A person with experience breeding and showing dogs like yours should also be able to explain the good and bad points of your pup and assess his chances in the show ring.

No matter how lovely your dog, he or she can't be a show dog if you've arranged for spaying or neutering already. Because a dog show is supposed to be about evaluating breeding stock, animals who have been altered aren't eligible.

The dog-show game is a hard one to break into, a super-competitive blend of big money, professional handlers, and some very hot dogs. But beginners can do well now and then. A few years ago, a couple's very first show dog, a lovely Doberman, had a spectacular show career capped by a win in Madison Square Garden, where she was named Best In Show of the prestigious Westminster Kennel Club dog show.

For more on breed standards and researching a breed, see Chapter 2.

So maybe your dog's markings aren't right, or one of his ears sticks up when it should fold over, or maybe you've already done the responsible thing and neutered him. Although he isn't going to be a show champion, he has plenty of titles left to work for. If he's one of a working breed, a group is probably around that's prepared to honor him for showing he can still do the job for which he was bred.

Some of the best competitions for beginners — open to all dogs, purebred, mixed, or neutered — are sports of a more modern development, such as obedience, agility, or flyball. The latter two would get many a dog's vote as "best," too, for they are full of high-flying canine competitors who can barely stand to wait their turn to compete.

Although you cannot enter your pet in a dog show if he hasn't full registration with a governing body such as the AKC, you may be able to make him eligible for other canine competitions run by the same group. The AKC has a designation called *Indefinite Listing Privilege (ILP),* and this designation is a way into competition for dogs who aren't eligible for full registration. Although the ILP was meant to limit the competition to otherwise unregisterable purebreds, many a dog of unknown parentage has passed for a papered pup and so been made eligible to compete, for obedience competitions, for example. For more information on ILP registration, contact the American Kennel Club (see the "Additional Resources" appendix for more information).

Take a class, join a club

After you decide on a sport for you and your dog to try, you need to find other people who are interested in it and willing to share their expertise with you. You find those people in dog clubs and in training classes.

Dog clubs come in several varieties, and plenty of them are available. The AKC, which is itself a club made up of smaller breed and activity clubs, reports that more than 4,000 clubs are holding shows and other competitions around the United States.

You can find all-breed kennel clubs, such as the Louisville Kennel Club or the Kennel Club of Northern New Jersey. Every breed has a national club, such as the Afghan Hound of America Club or the American Bouvier des Flanders Club, and hundreds of local or regional single-breed clubs, such as the Greater Atlanta Fox Terrier Club or the Papillon Association of Puget Sound, exist as well. Some clubs exist because of a particular sport, such as the Fresno Dog Training Club, the Snake River Retriever Trial Club, or the Haute Dawgs Agility Group. Such groupings of fanciers exist all over the world.

Clubs exist to put on competitions, provide training facilities and advice, and to share information between club members. These are the folks with whom you need to be associating if you're going to get started in competition.

 Classes are another good opportunity to get started. Group or individual classes exist to teach dog-show handling, competitive obedience, agility, or nearly every other canine endeavor. Some of these classes are sponsored by clubs, others by top individuals who make their living competing in canine sports.

Making the connections

So where do you find these clubs and classes? Following are a few ideas:

- ✔ **Breeder.** If you bought your dog from a reputable breeder, chances are she's already involved in her local and national breed club and has attended plenty of classes and seminars. She should be happy to mentor you or point you in the direction of people who can.

- ✔ **Registry.** You can also work your way from the top down, by asking the AKC, CKC, or UKC (or other dog registry or governing body) to provide you with a contact name and address in your area, or at the very least, a contact for the national breed club.

- ✔ **World Wide Web.** A little Web crawling should turn up some contacts, too. Feed the name of your breed (such as Vizsla) or sport (such as Schutzhund) to a search engine like Yahoo! (http://www.yahoo.com) and take a look around! (See Chapter 1 for tips on navigating canine cyberspace.)

✔ **Publications.** Hundreds of national, regional, and local canine publications are available, from the simple newsletter for a small local breed club to slick magazines dedicated to a single breed or sport. Such publications can quickly increase your knowledge and competitive edge, and I highly recommend them. Internet e-mail lists such as Obedience-L for obedience trial competitors are an unending flow of useful information and tips.

Keeping Things in Perspective

Whatever you do, try to keep in mind the original purpose of getting involved was for you and your dog to have something fun to do *together*. Sometimes people lose sight of that, constantly replacing one dog in favor of another who they hope will be better. And while it's true that to be truly competitive you're going to need a very special dog — and a large dedication of time and money — it's also true you can pick up many titles with the dog you have now, if you work with her.

Your dog will be happier if you keep the love of dogs primary in your mind, not the love of competition. With that in mind, you'll both have a better time.

Paws for a cause

Not everyone who likes to get out and about with a dog is chasing ribbons; a great many people gauge their success in smiles, and you and your dog can be among them.

Animal-assisted therapy is a growing field of volunteerism that uses friendly, well-mannered dogs to make a difference in the lives of people in institutional settings. Children in hospital wards, residents of nursing homes, people in hospices — all of these and more have benefited from the visits of these marvelous dogs and their caring owners.

Therapy work is not for every dog — or every person. Although breed and breeding don't matter, therapy dogs do share the ability to behave calmly and predictably in all surroundings. For their handlers, perhaps the most important trait is commitment, because people come to depend on the visiting dogs.

If you think animal-assisted therapy is something you'd like to do, find out more. The rewards of making a difference in the lives of others are truly breathtaking.

The Delta Society is an excellent resource for information on animal-assisted therapy, service dogs, or any other expression of the human-animal bond. Contact the organization at P.O. Box 1080, Renton, WA 98057; 800-869-6898 or 206-226-7357. Their e-mail address is 74403.1730@compuserve.com.

Part V

The Part of Tens

In this part . . .

So many fun and important things don't fit anywhere else, but are just too important to leave out. Things like tricks you can teach your dog, so he's always amusing. Or some ideas on how to have a nice yard *and* a dog — yes, it's possible! And what about all those things people "know" about dogs. Which ones are true and which are not? The answers are in here!

Chapter 17
Ten Dog Myths — Debunked!

Some of those old wives were pretty smart cookies, because more than a few old wives' tales aren't that far off the mark. Of the ones still floating around about dogs, however, the accuracy rate isn't all that high.

In an attempt to set the record straight, here are some of the most popular old wives' tales and their truths.

One Dog Year Is Equal to Seven Human Years

You can see how this one started. Something in the neighborhood of 70 is a decent life span for a human being, while 10 is probably average for a lot of dogs — although some, especially small ones, live far longer. Divide 70 by 10 and what do you get? You got it: 7.

But if you look at a year-old dog you can see that he's an adult — physically, mentally, and sexually mature, or nearly so. These characteristics don't compare with the attributes of a seven-year-old human child. So the rule of thumb has been changed, but it's nowhere as easy to remember.

According to the American Animal Hospital Association, the first eight months of a dog's life equals 13 years in human terms — birth to puberty, in other words. At a year, a dog's a teenager, equivalent to a 16-year-old human, with a little filling out still to do, After the age of two, when a dog's about 21, every dog year equals approximately five human ones.

Photo courtesy of Gina Spadafori.

Exercise
and good
nutrition
keep dogs
healthy and
happy
longer.

These are ballpark estimates, because the fact is dogs age at very different rates. Small dogs may hit puberty at five months, while some large ones may be more than a year and a half old before a female comes into heat for the first time.

So when is a dog "old"? Giant breeds such as Great Danes are senior citizens at six; a Lab may be considered old at eight. A little dog like the Pomeranian, however, could behave like a healthy adult well into her teens.

Two things go a long way to keep your pet acting young longer, and they should come as no surprise, because they have the same effect on human longevity. Proper nutrition and regular exercise keep dogs active and happy for as many years as possible. The biggest risk to an older dog? Obesity. Not only does obesity shorten lives, but it makes the years that remain miserable, especially for older dogs with arthritis.

To give your pet the best shot at a healthy, long, and happy life, keep him svelte and keep him moving. It's good for you both!

A Hot, Dry Nose Means a Fever

A dog has a fever when a thermometer properly inserted into his fanny exceeds 102.5 degrees. His nose has nothing to do with it.

Thermometers for dogs and cats are available at any good pet-supply store, or through mail order (see the "Additional Resources" appendix for catalog sources). A thermometer is an essential element of a home-care kit for your pet, along with a tube of lubricating jelly to make the task of temperature-taking easier for you both. (For more on temperature-taking, see Chapter 10.)

A Dog Should Go through One Season before Being Spayed

Wrong. You don't need to wait. In fact, the opposite is true: Spaying *before* your puppy comes into season reaps health benefits. Veterinary experts are now saying you can have your puppy spayed at the age of eight weeks, and an increasing number of shelters do just that!

Spaying before the first season reduces to almost nothing the chances of your pet getting mammary tumors — breast cancer — later. And of course, without the uterus and ovaries, your pet is also safe from cancer in those parts of the body, as well as life-threatening infections. (See Chapter 13 for more on spaying — and neutering.)

Spaying and Neutering Makes Dogs Fat

Too much food and too little exercise make dogs fat. You may need to adjust the levels of both after your dog has recovered from surgery to make sure that he or she stays in shape. The activity level of male dogs, in particular, may decrease after neutering because they are not so anxious to get out and roam after the alluring scents of females in season.

Grown dogs are less active than puppies, and if you do not adjust your feeding routine when your puppy nears maturity — about the same time as neutering — he will put on weight.

Obesity is a completely human-driven problem for dogs who, after all, are incapable of opening the refrigerator, getting a second serving of kibble, or taking the dog cookies out of the cupboard.

Spaying and neutering offer important health benefits to your pet. Don't offset those by allowing your pet to get fat. Feed an appropriate diet in the proper amounts, use treats sparingly — substitute rice cakes and carrots, even better — and don't share your meals with your dog.

Look no further than canine competitions (discussed in Chapter 16) such as agility and obedience and dogs who work for a living (such as service dogs) to see examples of properly fed, well-exercised, neutered dogs without a touch of fat on them!

If a Dog Scoots on His Rear, He Has Worms

This one has a little truth to it. A dog scoots on his rear in an attempt to relieve irritation — and worms can be one source of that discomfort.

They aren't the *only* potential problem, however. Impacted or infected anal sacs can be a problem, too, and so can a piece of something a dog has chewed that hasn't been completely expelled in the stool. For long-haired dogs, fecal material can cause a nasty, itchy, and oh-so-smelly mess that needs to be cut out prior to bathing.

You need to keep an eye on this area, whether or not your pet is scooting. Express the anal sacs when you bathe your dog (see Chapter 10 for instructions) and keep the hair clipped short and clean around the anus. (Your groomer or veterinarian can take care of the job for you if you'd rather leave this task to someone else.) Be observant for signs of worms on your pet's rear, such as the squirming segments of a live tapeworm or the rice-like appearance of dried segments.

If you think your pet has intestinal worms — because you've seen them on his rump or in his stools — have your veterinarian confirm your guess and prescribe appropriate treatment. Be on alert, too, for swollen areas on either side of the base of your dog's tail, which indicates infected anal glands, a condition that also demands your veterinarian's attention.

A Dog's Mouth Is Cleaner than a Human's

Some folks have taken this idea so far as to say that letting your dog lick *your* cuts as they lick their own is a good idea to aid your healing.

Whoever thought this one up apparently never observed the things a dog takes into his mouth, some of which are quite disgusting, as any dog lover knows. A slurpy dog kiss isn't going to hurt you, but the good it does you isn't anything more than psychological.

Dogs Eat Grass When Their Stomachs Are Upset

The common wisdom on this one is that grass makes dogs throw up, so they seek it out when they've got a tummy ache. But many dogs eat grass constantly, with no after effects.

One theory as to why dogs seek out grass is it fulfills some nutritional deficiency caused by a diet too heavy on meat. In the wild, the thinking goes, wild dogs and wolves consume vegetable matter when they devour the stomach contents of prey animals.

The reasoning may be this simple: Some dogs eat grass because they like to, nothing more.

Unlike cats, dogs are not pure carnivores. They can live on a vegetarian diet — although given their druthers, they'd rather not — and commercial dog foods have high percentages of vegetable matter. Advocates of freshly prepared diets, such as veterinarian Richard Pitcairn, author, along with Susan Hubble Pitcairn, of the immensely popular *Dr. Pitcairn's Complete Guide to Natural Health for Dogs & Cats* (Rodale Press), recommends putting fresh raw vegetables such as carrots, parsley, and zucchini in the mix. If you'd like to try cooking for your pet, with fresh meats, grains, and vegetables, Pitcairn's book, now in its second edition, is a wonderful resource.

Adding Oil to a Dog's Diet Solves Skin Problems

Some people have what I call "add-in-itis" — they aren't happy unless they've added something to even a top-quality commercial dog food. And it's true that some skin and coat problems can be helped by oils — including some oil supplements veterinary dermatologists prescribe.

Making sure that skin problems are correctly diagnosed is important before treating with a blanket cure-all like oil, which, after all, adds fat to the diet of a pet who may not need more. Skin problems caused by fleas or allergies are not magically cured by the addition of oil, nor are those problems produced by intestinal parasites or hormonal imbalances.

Before adding anything to your dog's diet, check with your veterinarian to make sure that the supplement is doing what it's supposed to and is not causing any other problems for your pet.

Brewer's Yeast and Garlic Control Fleas

If only controlling fleas could be so easy! Adding garlic gloves and brewer's yeast to your dog's food fall into the can't-hurt-might-help category of flea control — no solid evidence exists that either deter fleas when taken internally. Some believe brewer's yeast makes an effective flea powder, although the evidence on that, too, is largely anecdotal.

Many dogs love the taste of garlic and brewer's yeast, though, so adding some to your pet's food if you want to won't hurt anything — and if you don't mind a little garlic breath! Check with your veterinarian first, of course.

Everyone's looking for a "magic bullet" when it comes to fleas, but none exists — and probably never will. Still, safe, effective strategies for flea control are available. To check them out, see Chapter 12.

A Barking Dog Won't Bite

A really, really dangerous idea, this one. Barking or growling can both telegraph the intention to attack, which is why watching a dog's *body language* for signs of aggression is important.

Some of the warning signs of a dangerous dog include standing tall on his toes, leaning forward a little. His ears are forward, too, and his eyes have taken on a steely glazed expression. The fur over his shoulder — his *hackles* — stands on end. He may be barking or growling — or neither — but if he is barking, the sound is low, no-nonsense, and guttural.

Leave this dog alone — as well as any others you don't know, just to be safe.

CAUTION

Keeping children safe around strange dogs

Even if your family dog is a cupcake, your child may still be at risk for a bite. The Humane Society of the United States suggests teaching your children how to behave around strange dogs and how to react if attacked. Make sure that your children know

✔ **To never approach a loose dog, even if he seems friendly.** Dogs that are confined in yards and especially on chains should also be avoided — many are very serious about protecting their turf. If the dog is with her owner, children should always ask permission before petting and then begin by offering the back of the hand for a sniff. Pat on the neck or chest — the dog may interpret a pat from above as a dominant gesture. Teach your children to avoid fast or jerky movements.

✔ **To *be a tree* when a dog approaches, standing straight with feet together, fists under the neck and elbows into the chest.** Teach them to make no eye contact: Some dogs view eye contact as a challenge. Running is a normal response to danger, but it's the worst possible thing to do around a dog, because it triggers the animal's instinct to chase and bite. Many dogs just sniff and leave; teach your children to stay still until the animal walks away, and then back away slowly out of the area.

✔ **To "feed" the dog a jacket or backpack if attacked, or use a bike to block the dog.** These strategies may keep an attacking dog's teeth from connecting on flesh.

✔ **To *act like a log* if knocked down — face down, legs together, curled into a ball with fists covering the back of the neck and forearms over the ears.** This position protects vital areas and can keep an attack from turning fatal.

Role-play these lessons with your child until they are ingrained. Knowing how to act around dogs may spare your child a bite — and can save his life.

Chapter 18

Ten Ways to Have Both a Dog *and* a Nice Yard

*1*s having both a dog and a nice backyard possible? Nancy Dyson says you can, and she's living proof.

Dyson is a University of California-trained master gardener and a dog trainer of considerable accomplishments. One of her four dogs, Flora, is an AKC Obedience Trial Champion, and the pair have competed successfully at the highest levels of competition.

Her retrievers, three Labradors and one flat-coated, are models of canine decorum. But they're still dogs, quite oblivious to their owner's desire to have plants left unmolested.

The key, says Dyson, is being realistic about the needs of the garden — and of the dogs. Following, from Dyson and others, are a few tips.

Give Your Dog Lots of Exercise

A dog with too much energy isn't one you want to leave alone all day in a nice yard — and yet, that's exactly what many people do. If you don't take care of your dog's exercise requirements, he's going to take care of them on his own — by digging a hole to China or removing the shrubs in your yard.

Exercise is the missing element in most owners' attempts to fix behavior problems such as digging. Dogs, like people, need a half-hour of aerobic exercise three or four times a week — jogging, playing fetch, or swimming, for example.

Dogs who don't get this exercise are likely to expend that energy and cure boredom doing things people don't like — digging, chewing, and barking. Dogs who are well exercised are more likely to sleep while you are gone.

Give Your Dog Mental Stimulation

A tired dog is a happy dog, and that means more than physical exhaustion. Dogs need to exercise their minds as well as their bodies, which means working on basic training regularly — teaching new commands and practicing those your dog already knows. It's good for your dog's overall manners, and it wears your dog out mentally so he's more likely to snooze when you leave him.

When you leave, you should also offer your dog alternatives to choosing his own amusements: Provide him with chew toys. You can make them more appealing by praising him for using them and, also, by stuffing hollow toys — such as a Kong — with something delicious, such as peanut butter.

Giving your dog plenty of exercise is a good way to ensure that she doesn't take up annoying or destructive habits.

Photo courtesy of the HSUS/ Carmony.

Keep Potty Areas Separate from Ornamental Gardens

In Dyson's yard, the dogs aren't allowed to get into much trouble. They are turned out to relieve themselves in an area separated from the ornamental garden, and they are allowed in the rest of the yard under supervision only. She says keeping dogs out of elaborately landscaped areas is key to protecting plants from being pulled up, wet on, squished, or otherwise tortured.

As long as your dogs get their regular exercise, their potty area can be quite small. Although the Dyson retrievers live on acreage now, they once used part of a concrete driveway for a potty zone — they were let into the area not to play, but to get down to business. If you have a small area for your dogs to potty in, be especially diligent about keeping the area picked up. Control odors and disinfect the potty area frequently by using commercial kennel-cleaning products.

Don't Leave Dogs Unsupervised in the Yard

Dogs don't know a wisteria plant from a weed, and they never will. That's why it's up to you not to leave them unattended around plants you want left alone. When you leave for work, limit your dog's space for his safety, as well as your plants'. Most of a dog's time alone is spent sleeping, anyway, so he doesn't need to have the entire run of the house and yard. Outings — for jogging, walking, fetch, or swimming — should be done with your supervision.

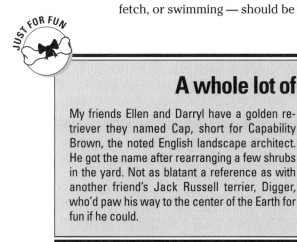

A whole lot of diggin' goin' on

My friends Ellen and Darryl have a golden retriever they named Cap, short for Capability Brown, the noted English landscape architect. He got the name after rearranging a few shrubs in the yard. Not as blatant a reference as with another friend's Jack Russell terrier, Digger, who'd paw his way to the center of the Earth for fun if he could.

One of my readers named his Labrador retriever Cat, an unusual name for a dog to be sure. The name, though, was really short for Caterpillar, as in the giant manufacturer of earth-moving equipment.

If your dog is allowed in your yard under your supervision only, the chance of him digging or chewing is just about nil — you can stop him before the damage is done and tell him what he did wrong.

Put Special Plants in Safer Places

Raised beds and hanging planters are the place to put your most precious plants, says Dyson. In borders, she adds, put the plants that can take being stepped on in front.

What are some dog-friendly plants? Mint is a good one. This plant is nearly indestructible and greets each assault with a wave of cool mint smell. Some lilies are tough enough to be stomped or sat on, as well, and your gardening center may have suggestions for others that are dependable growers in your region.

Raised beds and low border fencing keep small breeds out, but larger breeds or agile jumpers need to be trained in what's off-limits. Be consistent. If you *never* want your dog in certain areas, never allow him in.

Vegetable gardens are one kind of garden that should always be off-limits, for both health and aesthetic reasons. (No amount of washing will clear your mind of the sight of your dog lifting his leg on your zucchini plants.) The best way to prevent entry is to fence the area off completely.

The compost pile is another part of the garden that *must* be off-limits to your dog. Dogs have a much higher tolerance for decaying food than we do and will rummage through the muck gleefully given half a chance.

My dog Andy will kill for carrots and cherry tomatoes, even half-rotted ones. Having seen more than a couple of compost-covered dogs pop through the pet door in my time, I can assure you this smell experience is one you do *not* need.

Another note about compost piles: Never put your dog's feces in the pile. While the waste of herbivores — chickens, rabbits, guinea pigs and so on — is just fine in the compost pile, using the waste from dogs (or cats or any carnivore) puts you at risk for disease.

Discourage Digging

Some breeds were developed to dig, and expecting them not to is unfair. You can find most of these digging dogs in the terrier group — the word terrier comes from *terra,* for "earth."

Dogs love to dig, a fact well-known by many gardeners.

Photo courtesy of Richard D. Schmidt.

You can keep many dogs from digging if you keep them exercised, limit their access to dirt, and make the digging experience unpleasant. Sometimes putting the dog's own stools in the hole and covering them with dirt deters them. Many dogs won't dig if their own mess is under the surface.

If you don't mind the mess, you may think about giving your dog a *dig zone*. While hardly clean fun, it is good fun, especially for dogs who are happiest with their noses in the dirt and their paws flying.

If your dog is digging not for pleasure, but for escape — along the fence line, for example — the habit may be hard to break. The first step is to reduce the desire for roaming by neutering and by making sure that he's kept well-exercised. For persistent problems, you may need to bury wire fencing beneath the ground, pour a concrete curb or run a hot wire — available at farming-supply stores — around the base of the fence. None of these solutions are inexpensive or easy, but they could save your escape-artist pet's life.

Teach the Wait Command

Living with your dog is all about communication; after all, how *else* is she going to know you don't want her jumping up into the raised beds if you don't tell her? Instead of yelling at her to get out of the garden, teach her the "wait" command to keep her from going in.

Wait is different from *stay.* "Stay" means "don't move until I tell you to," while "wait" means "you can move anywhere you want except across this line." The line can be the edge of a flower garden, or it can be the open gate of a vegetable garden while you're inside picking tomatoes. It's anywhere you deem to be off-limits for your dog.

For information on teaching the "wait" command, see Chapter 12.

Boundary training such as "wait" is not to be relied on when your dog is alone. "Wait" is a command to be used in your presence so you can correct transgressions if you need to.

Give Your Dog Space of His Own

If you have space, take the "potty zone" concept a bit further and give your dog a yard of his own. Dyson advocates a place where dogs can run and play and not hurt anything.

This play area can be worked into the landscaping of your yard in clever ways. The dog area can wrap around the ornamental garden, or be along one side of it. A low fence to separate the play area from the rest of the yard can be made of attractive wood or chain link and covered with vines.

Ideally, a dog space is not one that isolates your pet, but is instead a place to share. A place for fetch or other games. The area should be designed for your pet's enjoyment, with things to jump on and to play with, and a kiddie pool for water-loving dogs, perhaps. Trees for shade, and sunny spots for resting in the warmth are also important. Provide access to your house through a dog door, and you're talking pet paradise.

Small trees and big dogs often are not a good combination, but large trees are important to make the dog space more pleasant. Which is why you need to protect the trees as they grow. They should be staked to get a head start on growing straight and tall, and Dyson suggests putting wire cages around them to protect them from being knocked over or dug up.

What kind of grass works best in a dog area? I've had the best luck with weeds, kept watered and mowed. They look fine from a distance and are well-nigh indestructible. If you want the perfect lawn, you're going to have to be perfectly resolute about keeping your dog — and your kids — off it.

Work with the Patterns in Your Yard

If you must share yard space with your dog, put paths in high traffic areas and plants in low ones. If you have a dog who runs along the fence line, for example, don't put plants in the area in front of the fence — dogs will run right through them — even the thorny ones. Dyson suggests leaving a *running track* along the fence line, with plants along the edge of it.

Fence-running is one of the things that can trigger unacceptable barking. If your dog is *just* running — and you don't mind the wear on the area near the fence — then it's fine, fun, and good exercise. But if every step is matched with a bark, you may need to close that area off to keep the peace.

For more strategies to keep barking to a minimum, see Chapter 12.

Keep Things in Perspective

Remember the secret to having a nice yard and dogs is planning and training. Still, keep in mind that tolerance is a must, too. Accidents *do* happen. Few love a nice yard as much as Nancy Dyson, but her final words of advice: Plant are just plants, and you can always replace them.

You can't say the same about your dog.

Seeing spots — yellow ones!

Dick Tracy, the garden writer at the *Sacramento Bee* newspaper, has long kidded me about how we can retire rich on the money we'll earn when we come up with the "cure" for urine burns on the lawn. (Or for cat mess in the flower beds, but that goes in another book!)

We aren't going to be retiring anytime soon. Trust me.

The best way to keep urine from ruining your lawn is to make sure that your pet puts it somewhere else — like in a potty area. But you can reduce the potential damage to your lawn by flushing the piddled-on area immediately with water. But I *do not* recommend — as I've seen some do — giving your pet extra salt to encourage her to drink more water and so produce a more diluted urine.

A friend of mine used to use another trick. She kept a roll of sod growing in a side yard, and every weekend she'd cut out the yellow patches and replace them with fresh sod.

Toxic plants

Dogs can be deadly to plants, but more than a few plants are quite capable of getting revenge. Here are some bad seeds. Most "just" make your pet sick, but a few of them can kill. If your pet has tangled with any of these, call your veterinarian.

- American yew
- Angel's trumpet
- Apricot, almond
- Arrowgrass
- Azalea
- Bird of paradise
- Bittersweet
- Black locust
- Buttercup
- Castor bean
- Cherry tree
- China berry
- Coriara
- Daffodil
- Delphinium
- Elderberry
- English holly
- English yew
- Foxglove
- Hemlock
- Jasmine

- Jimsonweed
- Larkspur
- Lily of the valley
- Locoweed
- Lupine
- Mescal bean
- Mistletoe
- Mock orange
- Moonweed
- Mushrooms and toadstools
- Oleander
- Peach tree
- Pokeweed
- Privit
- Rhododendron
- Rhubarb
- Skunk Cabbage
- Soapberry
- Spinach
- Tomato vine
- Wisteria

Chapter 19

Ten Things You Need to Know to Prepare Your Dog for a Disaster

*F*or pet owners faced with a flood, fire, hurricane, earthquake, or other crisis, disaster experts are all of one mind on what to do:

Take your pets with you.

While animals are not allowed in disaster-relief shelters, an increasing number of animal shelters and veterinarians are better prepared now than ever before to take in animals during an emergency.

In fact, a model program started by the California Veterinary Medical Association has a veterinarian in place in each county to help coordinate animal-relief efforts. Other states are starting to see the light, too, with veterinarians, shelter groups, and specially trained disaster teams from the Sacramento, CA based United Animal Nations are prepared to do for animals what the Red Cross does for people.

Why all the changes? A growing realization that animals need help, too, and that some people choose to put their lives in danger rather than abandon their pets.

So take your pets. Also take their food, leashes, medicines, blankets, and carriers if told to evacuate.

You do can do better, still, if you plan ahead. Here are some tips from disaster-planning experts.

Have a Plan

Prepare for all possibilities, including the possibility that you may be away from home when disaster strikes. Make sure that everyone in your family — children, too! — is prepared in the event of an emergency. Make a plan and go over it until everyone knows what to do.

People need to rely on each other during emergencies, and this is just as true when it comes to your pets. Get to know your neighbors, and put a plan in place to help each other out. Find out from local shelters and veterinary organizations what their emergency response plans are and how you fit into them in case of a disaster.

Planning ahead for a possible disaster can save your dog's life.

Photo courtesy of Richard D. Schmidt.

Know What Your Veterinarian's Plans Are

Ask your veterinarian if he has a disaster plan, and how he plans to fit in with other veterinarians in an emergency. If he has never thought of it, pushing him a little on the subject won't hurt. If he has no interest, consider changing vets or exploring back-up care for your dog from someone who is more tapped in.

Maintain Your Pet's Permanent and Temporary ID

Most animals will survive a disaster. But too many will never see their families again without a way to determine which pet belongs to which family. That's why pets should always wear a collar and identification tags. Better still is permanent identification that can't slip off, such as a tattoo or imbedded microchip.

Keep temporary ID tags at hand, too, to put on your pet if you're forced to evacuate.(Your pet's permanent ID isn't of much use if you can't be home to answer the phone.) One of the easiest: Key tags on which you can jot a current number, slip into a plastic housing, and then attach to your pet's collar.

Keep Vaccinations — and Records — Current

Infectious diseases can be spread from dog to dog through floodwaters, which is why keeping pets' vaccinations up-to-date is essential. Kennel cough, although not serious, is common in sheltering situations and also preventable through vaccinations.

Prepare a file with up-to-date medical and vaccination records, your pets' microchip or tattoo numbers, your veterinarian's phone number and address, feeding and medication instructions, and recent pictures of your animals. Trade copies of emergency files with another pet-loving friend — it's a good idea for someone else to know about your pet should *anything* happen to you.

Have Restraints Ready

Even normally obedient dogs can behave rather strangely when stressed by an emergency. Consequently, you should be prepared to restrain your pet — for his safety and the safety of others.

Keep leashes and carriers ready for emergencies. *Ready* means *at hand* — the means to transport your pet shouldn't be something you have to find and pull from the rafters. Harnesses work better than collars at keeping panicky pets safe.

Shipping crates are probably the least-thought-of pieces of emergency equipment for pet owners — but are among the most important. Sturdy crates keep pets safe and give rescuers more options in housing pets. They give *you* more options, too, in the homes of friends or relatives, or in shelters outside of the area. Depending on weather conditions, crated pets may also be safely left overnight in vehicles.

Another item to keep on hand is a muzzle, because frightened and injured dogs are more likely to bite.

Rotate a Supply of Food, Water, and Medications

Keep several days' worth of food and safe drinking water as well as any necessary medicines packed and ready to go in the event of a disaster. Rotate your supplies so they do not get stale. If your pet eats canned food, be sure to keep an extra can opener and spoon tucked in among the emergency supplies.

Keep First Aid Supplies on Hand — with Directions

Pet-supply stores sell ready-made first aid kits, or you can put your own together fairly easily. You can find the ingredients of a good basic kit in Chapter 10.

Keep a first aid book with your supplies, but give the book a quick read before you store it. Veterinarian Michelle Bamberger's *Help! The Quick Guide to First Aid for Your Dog* (Howell/Macmillan) is one that's well organized and easy to follow.

Pet-Pak, Inc., manufactures animal first-aid kits in five sizes, all neatly packed in a plastic container (the four largest have handles). The kit contains the basics for emergency care, along with a pamphlet on using the supplies. For information, contact the company at P.O. Box 982, Edison, NJ 08818-0982; (908) 906-9200.

Know the Locations of Other Veterinary Hospitals — and Animal Shelters

Your veterinary hospital may be damaged in the disaster, which is why having some back-up plans for boarding and care is good. Know where other veterinary hospitals are, as well as animal shelters and animal-control facilities in your area.

Keep a "Lost Dog" Kit Ready

In case of a disaster, you probably won't be able to get flyers printed up, so make up some generic ones and keep them with your emergency supplies. In the biggest type size you can, center the words: "LOST DOG," along with a clear picture of your dog. Then below, provide a description of your dog, including any identifying marks, and a space to add the phone number where you can be reached, along with any back-up contacts, friends, relatives, neighbors, or your veterinarian. Print a hundred copies and keep them in a safe place.

A staple-gun allows you to post your notices; keep one loaded and with your supplies along with thumbtacks and electrical tape.

If your dog becomes lost, post flyers in your neighborhood and beyond, and distribute them at veterinary hospitals and shelters. While relying on the kindness of strangers is nice, offering a reward makes many strangers just a little bit kinder.

Be Prepared to Help Others

You may be lucky to survive a disaster nearly untouched, but others in your community won't be so fortunate. Contact your local humane society and veterinary organization now to train as a volunteer so you can help out in a pinch. Disaster-relief workers do everything from distributing food to stranded animals to helping reunite pets with their families — and helping find new homes for those who need them.

Volunteering in a pinch is not only a good thing to do — it's the right thing for anyone who cares about animals and people.

Chapter 20

Ten Silly Tricks to Teach Your Dog

*O*ne of the biggest shames in all of dogdom is how few things most people teach their dogs. A handful of basic obedience commands, at best — "sit" and "down," usually, and maybe "stay" and "come" — is all most dogs know. What many people don't realize is that training is a way of communicating with your dog, of sharing a common language. The more words you both know the meaning of, the more you are sharing your lives.

How many words can your dog know? A lot more than you can imagine, I'm guessing. Consider that dogs who help wheelchair users are routinely trained to perform dozens of different tasks — more than a hundred in some cases. And if you argue that your dog's not as smart as a service dog, I'll argue back that even if he's only half as smart, he can learn a couple of dozen more things than he knows now.

Besides, tricks are *fun!* You *can* teach old dogs new tricks — and young ones, too. While canine whiz kids such as poodles and border collies pick things up quickly, any dog catches on eventually if you're patient, consistent, and encouraging. You can teach tricks one at a time or a couple at once, as long as you've time to practice each a couple times a day.

Some dogs are better at some tricks than others. A small, agile terrier may find jumping through hoops easier than a bulldog would. And a retriever is probably more willing to hold things in his mouth than is a Pekinese. A basset hound can probably roll over but may find begging difficult, being a little top-heavy. So think about your dog's form and aptitudes before you start. The tricks in this chapter are just starting points, and many more possibilities exist. You may notice something special *your* dog does that would be entertaining if you can get him to do it on command. You can. Give it a name, use that word when he's most likely to do his thing and praise him for "obeying." He'll make the connection soon enough.

The following tricks are built on three of the basic commands your dog *must* know — "sit," "down," and "stay." For information on how to teach these, see Chapter 11.

Tricks are a wonderful way for children to learn more about dog training and enjoy the experience of owning a pet more. Involve your children in the training and everyone will have a better time.

Shake Hands

Have your dog "sit," "down," and "stay" and then say "shake hands" or "give me your paw" — one or the other, your choice, but not both — and then tap the back of his leg or tickle it a little, whichever seems to work best. When he picks up his paw, take it in your hand and praise. Build on the skill through repetition until he's lifting his paw reliably and then higher and higher. Some dogs get to the point of practically giving a high five.

A second step to this trick is to teach him the "other paw" command. Always ask for the same paw for "shake hands" and then, when he's reliable, teach "other paw" in the same way, but this time tap on the back of the opposite leg. He'll get the idea quickly, and soon will be giving you one paw at the command "shake" and the opposite one for the command "other paw."

This trick is probably the one most commonly taught, but it also has a practical application. You can teach your dog to stop on a mat just inside the front door and wait for you to wipe off his muddy paws before he comes all the way into the house. Ask him to give you his paw and then wipe it, then the other paw and wipe it. Teach him to offer his back paws in the same way, using the command "back paw" for one, and "other back" for the last paw. As always, don't forget to tell him he's wonderful when you're done!

Roll Over

Another all-time favorite. Have your dog lay down, ask him to "roll over," and then roll him and praise. A variation on the theme is "dead dog."

Dead dog is a partial roll, if you think about it. From "down," give the "dead dog" command and then put him on his side, holding him flat for a couple of seconds, and then saying "OK" to end the trick. When he understands and is doing the trick reliably — I don't have a cure for the tail-wagging "dead dog" so just let it slide — you can substitute a hand signal for the command. Make sure that you have your dog's attention and start pairing the dead dog command with a hand signal that looks like a pistol being aimed and shot. Over time, you should be able to use the hand signal only, and drop your dog from a standing position.

Beg

This trick practically teaches itself. If your dog already sits up for food, put a name to the trick and you're done. If not, the trick is pretty easy to teach.

Sit your dog with his butt in the corner of the room. Show him the treat, and with your other hand, raise him into position so he's aligned above his hindquarters and able to balance. Hold him for a second or two, release, praise, and give him the treat. Practice a couple of times a day in the corner, and when you're sure that he both understands the command and is capable of performing it without support, move away from the wall. But don't be in such a big hurry that he falls over backwards and scares himself, otherwise getting this one right could take a long time.

Think a little about the possibility of your creating a monster here. If you *do not* want your dog to beg for your food or pester your guests for their hors d'ouevres, don't teach this command, or limit it strictly to when you ask for the trick and reward with a dog treat, not a human goody. Do not reward the behavior any other time, no matter how pleading those big brown eyes get.

Jump Through (Or Over)

To teach this one, you can use a long dowel, a broomstick, a children's plastic hoop, or a specially made stick for dogs to jump, available from those pet suppliers who carry equipment for obedience trainers.

With your dog on-leash, hold the stick or hoop an inch or two off the ground and say "hup" or "over," and then draw the dog over the stick by his leash and praise. After the command is understood, work at gradually raising the height of the jump.

You can also teach your dog to jump *into* something, be it your car or your arms — the latter *not* recommend if your dog's a 60-pound Airedale!

Don't get carried away, even if your dog really, really enjoys jumping. Some dogs have been injured by jumping too high. A good rule of thumb is to never ask your dog to jump much more than his height at the shoulders, more for small, agile breeds, like Shelties, less for ones who aren't really built for jumping, like basset hounds.

The games dogs play

Writing a book is dull work sometimes, for the writer and especially for the writer's dogs. Mine keep themselves amused in various ways — bringing me balls to throw (Ben) and stalking the neighbor's marmalade tabby (Andy). Then came the day when even that wasn't enough, and I taught Benjamin to jump out the office window. He already knew "hup," so teaching him wasn't hard. I let him look out the window, made him step back, tapped the sill, and said "hup." And

out he went. This game is one of his favorites now. Sometimes I throw things out the window first; other times I just have him jump. He has to run all the way around the house to get back in through the dog door, so he gets good exercise, too.

The game *has* limited me a little bit, though: I don't think buying a two-story house would ever be a good idea during Benjamin's lifetime.

Carry and Fetch

I don't care if your golden is the best retriever on the face of the earth: In order to reliably build a collection of carry and fetch tricks, you have to teach your dog to take something at your command and hold it until you ask for its release. Otherwise, no matter how enthusiastic your pet is about retrieving, he's always doing so at his discretion, not yours.

The best piece of equipment to start with is a properly-sized obedience dumbbell, widely available through catalogs and some pet-supply stores. The obedience dumbbell is a key piece of equipment at advanced obedience competitions and comes in either wood or plastic. The center piece should be the width of your dog's mouth so that when he's holding it the wide end pieces lie closely and comfortably against his cheeks.

Put your leash on your dog and sit him beside you, to your left in the *heel* position. Put your thumb and forefinger on either side of his jaw and apply a gentle downward pressure, keeping the dumbbell close in your other hand. As soon as you feel his jaw opening, give the command "take it," slide the dumbbell inside, and then hold his jaw closed for a few seconds, praising gently and stroking under his jaw. Then give the command "give" and let him spit it into your hand. Praise. Repeat this process three or four times a session, a couple of times a day. Within a few days, he should be opening his mouth at the "take it" command.

The next step is to have him reach for the dumbbell. Hold it an inch or so in front of him, slightly above his nose so he can see it. You should again have him in heel position on your left, but now you should be holding his collar and his ear in your left hand. Give the "take it" command, and push his head forward until he can take the dumbbell in his mouth. If he opens his mouth and takes it, praise him. If he doesn't, apply a little pressure to his ear and when his mouth opens in protest, push it over the dumbbell and praise. Have him hold it a second or so, and then tell him to "give."

From that point, the process is a slow build-up. You can't rush the training if you want to develop a reliable, happy retriever. Reach six inches, and then a foot, and then from the floor. Always work on a leash, always with your hand ready to correct by applying pressure to the ear. You should soon be able to have him go out to the end of the leash, pick up the object and return it to you.

Putting a little pressure on your dog's ear will help you teach him to take an object.

If your dog won't bring the dumbbell back or won't release it, it's because you haven't trained him to do so. If he's dancing around outside of your reach, put him on-leash, draw him in, and have him sit in front of you. Don't bother wrestling the dumbbell from him, either. Say "give" — *once* — and if he doesn't, blow in his ear or his nose. He'll drop it like a hot coal.

Reliable off-leash retrieving — like the off-leash recall — is one of the hard ones to teach, and if you find that you're having trouble at a certain step, then you shouldn't be at that step yet. So go back.

The training is worth all the effort, though, because once your dog reliably carries what you give him and retrieves what you tell him to, the possibilities are endless. Tricks aside, fetch is a wonderfully efficient and enjoyable way to exercise your dog while enforcing your role as boss.

But the tricks! One dog can "walk" the other, if you tell him to hold the leash of the other. Your dog can hold a basket and serve guests or take a message from you to your spouse. Admittedly, I lead a fairly dog-centric life, so I doubt most people have been to even *one* wedding where a dog was the ring bearer — I've been to two. The ring was in a basket, which the dog carried, both times.

The possibilities are limited only by your imagination.

After your dog can hold a basket, you can set up a lovely portrait. Arrange flowers in the basket, put your dog on "sit-stay" in front of an uncluttered background, and then ask him to hold the basket. The picture will be a keeper, I promise.

Speak

"Speak" is another trick that's really about you putting a name on a normal canine behavior and controlling it. Think of the situations in which your dog barks — when begging for food or at a knock on the door — and then prepare to replicate it, but under a controlled situation. Your dog should be on-leash, at your side, and you should give the command "speak" just before the bark-triggering situation begins, then repeat it again and praise her for "obeying." Then tell her "hush" or "quiet" and put your hand gently around her muzzle to silence her, and praise again.

You've probably already figured out the *true* beauty of this command — a dog who not only *starts* barking on command, but also *stops*. Remember, dog training is really about communication. This trick is a good example. When you name a behavior, you add a word to the vocabulary that you both share. And in so doing, develop a way to ask for something your dog can understand. Which is why all the "shut up, you stupid mutt"s you can scream in your dog's life will not have as much impact as teaching her to bark — and stop barking — on command.

More strategies for dealing with barking problems can be found in Chapter 12.

Barking isn't the only sound you can teach your pet to make on command. If you've got a Nordic breed — such as an Alaskan Malamute or Siberian husky — you can probably teach a howl pretty easily. Some dogs howl if you do — try it, it's fun! — and others howl if you play a musical instrument, anything from a harmonica to a flute.

Some dogs make a playful rumbling noise that sounds like a little like growl — a rrrrrrrr, but with the dog's eyes smiling and body relaxed — and you can certainly call it one if you want. The same rules apply: Connect the word to the behavior, and praise for the association.

In the don't-try-this-at-home category: Don't put your pet in a situation where the growling is real, in hopes of getting a scarier dog. Trained, controlled aggression is best left to experienced protection-dog trainers. For more on this topic, see Chapter 11.

Find

"Find" builds on the skills your dog learned if you taught him to carry and fetch. First, you teach him to associate a word with a person, animal, or object — "bigbone," "Stanley," or "kittycat." The word can be as silly as you like, just as long as you're consistent. Pick a toy he really, really likes, hide it just slightly while he's on "stay" — the toy should still be in view — and then tell him to "Find [object]." Slowly work on increasing the degree of difficulty, and remember to be enthusiastic during the searches and full of praise when the object is found.

If you have more than one dog, you can put one on "stay" and work the other, and then reverse. Doing so is a great exercise both for sharpening your pets' attentiveness and making you all feel good and proud of yourselves.

Again, the only limits are your imagination. You can teach your dog to bring you the phone, a box of tissues, or a roll of toilet paper if you're in the bathroom and realize you're without. Now *that's* a useful trick!

Dogs love to find various objects — especially if it's a toy they really like.

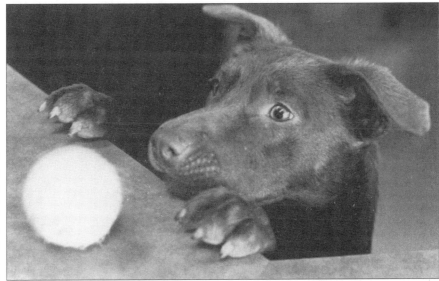

Photo courtesy of the Marin County HS.

By combining "take it" and "find" you can develop a canine messenger system that would be the marvel of UPS. Give your dog a note and ask her to find your spouse. This "game" became more than that for a deaf man I once wrote about: He and his deaf wife used his service dog to locate each other in the house or deliver messages.

Spin

I've given you a couple of hard ones, so let me give you an easy one. Take a treat and show it to your dog, and then move your hand toward his tail and around in a circle. His nose will follow, and when he starts to spin, give him the command "spin." After a couple of rotations, give him the treat and praise. Repeat a few times, a couple times a day.

The advanced version is "spin right" and "spin left," taught in the same way. If your dog starts in the wrong direction, say "no" and repeat the command, "spin left (or right)." If he doesn't seem to get it, keep training.

Dance

This trick is another with an unexpectedly useful flip side. Put a word to your dog's habit of putting his paws up on you — "paws up" is the command I use — and another word for getting off you, as in *now*. I use "Off," not "down," which can confuse your dog, because "down" to him may mean "lie down," not "put all four paws on the ground."

If he doesn't jump already, pick his paws up and put them on a low surface — such as a coffee table, for a large dog — while giving the "paws up" command, and praise. Slowly build until he'll put his paws up on any surface you indicate. For "dance," take those paws in your hands and boogie.

I use "paws up" for a lot of different things, including giving dogs their monthly heartworm pill. They put their paws on the counter at my command, and I pill 'em. (More on this in Chapter 11.)

Say Your Prayers

A fitting end to the list. Take a treat in your hand and ask your dog to "paws up" into your lap. Hold the treat between his forelegs, and say "say your prayers." When he drops his head between his legs trying to get the treat, give it to him, and praise.

Chapter 21

Ten Questions to Ask When Buying a Purebred Puppy

*Y*ou can find many poor-quality purebreds around. Vicious golden retrievers, crippled German shepherds, and deaf Dalmatians — virtually every breed has some kind of genetic problem that reputable, knowledgeable breeders work to eliminate. Defective dogs most often come from two kinds of breeders: The clueless and the careless. The first group is blissfully ignorant of the potential for congenital problems, the second group knows full well and could not care less.

Weeding out poor breeders doesn't take much, if you know what to ask. Following are ten questions, along with the answers you want to hear.

You should ask lots of other questions, of course, that are more breed-specific, involving shedding, drooling, aggressive tendencies, size, or life span. Make a list and ask them all. A reputable breeder is reassured by your interest. Also, if you want to know some questions to ask when considering an adult dog, see Chapter 9.

Remember, finally, that one sure sign of a reputable breeder is that she asks you more questions than you ask her. Don't be put off by this questioning: Someone who cares about her dogs is just the kind of person from whom you want to buy a puppy.

See Chapter 5 for more on how puppies develop and temperament tests you can do when looking at litters.

How Long Have You Been in This Breed, and What Others Have You Bred?

You're looking for someone who has worked with one or two breeds at the most and studied them for years or, possibly, someone who has bred a litter with help from a mentor in the breed. (Everyone has to start somewhere!) Someone who has jumped from popular breed to popular breed is more likely in the business to turn a fast buck and certainly isn't going to have the expertise you're looking for in a breeder.

What Are the Congenital Defects in This Breed?

Every breed has some problems, be it *hip dysplasia* (a painful malformation of the hip socket), *progressive retinal atrophy* (an eye disease), increased cancer susceptibility, epilepsy, or a dozen others.

The breeder who says "none" or "I don't know" is to be avoided. She's not screening for what she doesn't know about, and you don't want to pay the price for her ignorance.

A good breeder tells you every possible problem in the breed, from droopy eyelids to ear infections.

What Steps Have You Taken to Decrease Congenital Defects in Your Dogs?

You want to hear words like "screened" and "tested" and "certified." You want to see documentation. You want to go elsewhere when you hear, "The mother's plenty healthy. We've never had to take her to the vet!"

In breeds with the potential for hip dysplasia — almost every large breed — look for PennHIP or Orthopedic Foundation of America certification. These are expert, unbiased evaluators who know exactly what to look for. Don't take: "My vet X-rayed her, and he says she's fine." Insist on documentation on both parents. And their parents, too.

Do You Have the Parents on Site? May I See Them?

This is a bit of a trick question. You should *always* be able to see the mother — unless she died giving birth — but reputable breeders usually don't have the father on hand, too. That's because the best match for any particular dog may be owned by another breeder, and the female is sent to the stud for breeding.

As for the mother, she may be a little anxious with strangers around her puppies, but on her own you want to see a well-socialized, calm, and well-mannered dog. So, too, should be the rest of the breeder's dogs. If you don't like the temperaments of a breeder's grown dogs, what makes you think you'll get a good temperament in one of her puppies?

What Are the Good and Bad Points of the Parents, and What Titles Do They Have? Will You Explain Their Pedigrees?

You may be looking for a pet-quality purebred, but you want to buy him from someone who knows what top-quality examples of the breed are — and uses them in her breeding program. The only way for a breeder to maintain top-quality dogs is to constantly be testing breeding stock — in the show ring, in the field, and in public. Look for titles, titles, titles. Show titles like "Ch.," for champion. Titles for working dogs, such as field trial titles for hunting dogs. Obedience titles, agility titles, whatever. CGC, for Canine Good Citizen, is nice to see, too; this certification shows a breeder who cares about the impression her dogs make in public. (For more on titles — and competitions to earn them, see Chapter 16.)

It doesn't matter if you never compete with your dog, or if you go home and throw that fine pedigree in a drawer. Recent titles on both sides of a pedigree show a breeder who's making a good-faith effort to produce healthy dogs who conform to the breed standard.

A couple of "champions" two or three generations back proves nothing. Especially if they're only on one side of the pedigree — either the mother's or father's side.

There's more to a dog than paper, however, and the breeder should be able to go over the mother and the other dogs in the house, explaining where their good and bad points lay — too thick a backskull, for example, too short a tail, or a near-perfect gait when trotting. Again, a breeder who cannot explain the good and bad points about her dogs is someone you should avoid.

Where Were These Puppies Raised?

"Underfoot" is the best answer. "In the basement," "in the garage," "in the kennel," or "in the barn" are not great indicators. You want a puppy who knows what the dishwasher sounds like, who you don't have to peel off the ceiling when a pan drops, who has set a paw on linoleum, carpet, and tile.

Raising a litter of puppies in the house is a massive undertaking, and doing so shows not only commitment on the part of the breeder but also a knowledge of the importance of socialization.

How Have You Socialized These Puppies?

Environmental socialization is important, but so, too, is the intentional kind. The best breeders make sure that their puppies have been handled by adults of both genders and by children, even if they have to borrow children to accomplish the task. They expose the puppies to all kinds of noises and all kinds of objects.

You want to deal with a breeder who clearly demonstrates in her discussions that she knows the importance of socialization and has taken steps to provide the puppies with many experiences during the first extremely important weeks of their lives.

How Have You Evaluated These Puppies?

You're looking for someone who not only knows the difference between *show* and *pet* pups — and can explain the difference — but also has a feel for the temperament of each pup as an individual. Within each litter are shy pups, bold pups, and some in-betweens. Depending on the breed and your family, the wrong pup chosen from the litter can be just as big a mistake as choosing the wrong breed.

Let the breeder help you choose. Too many puppy buyers buy a pup "because he chose us," when in fact that puppy would have chosen anyone — he's the most outgoing in the bunch. For most people, one of the "middle" pups — not too pushy, and certainly not too shy — is the best choice. You can find more on evaluating pups in Chapter 5.

What Guarantees Do You Provide?

Bad breeders forget your name after your check clears. You want to buy a puppy from someone who provides you with a health record on the puppies to date — vaccinations and wormings — as well as a contract laying out her responsibilities to you should the puppy develop a congenital ailment such as hip dysplasia. In most cases, such contracts state either replacement with a new puppy or refunding of your purchase price.

The contract also states *your* responsibilities, mind you, such as neutering your pet. You may also be required to return the dog to the breeder if you can no longer keep him.

Read and discuss the paperwork with the breeder. The best breeders offer contracts that protect not only the buyer and seller, but the most vulnerable part of the transaction: the puppy.

When Can I Take My Puppy Home?

Some poor-quality breeders start selling puppies when they're weaned, at five or six weeks of age. But puppies still have lessons to learn from their mother and littermates and should not go to new homes until seven weeks at the earliest.

Some reputable breeders don't let puppies go until they're a week or so older than seven weeks, but a few weeks more than that and you may end up with a puppy who's more dog-oriented than people-oriented, unless the breeder's been careful to continue socialization.

Chapter 22

Ten Must-See Dog Sites on the World Wide Web

- -

In This Chapter

▶ Visit a dog beach

▶ Celebrate bulldogs

▶ Talk dogs with Dave

- -

The hardest thing about compiling this list was limiting it to ten (or so, but don't point that out to my editors!). The looking was the best part, jumping around from site to site and pointing out the dog pictures to my extremely unimpressed canine office mates, who would much rather me take them to the dog park than Web surf.

How hard is this topic to narrow down? Try putting the word "dog" in the AltaVista search engine (http://www.altavista.com) and see what you come up with. When I did it, I got something close to a half-million hits. Add those sites that say "retriever" or "hound" instead of "dog" and the total is . . . more than I can figure. I'm a writer, not a mathematician. Let's just leave it at . . . a lot. Even figuring that many sites aren't about dogs at all — like the one about some golf thingy called a Golden Retriever — the numbers are still a lot more than I can deal with, although I tried. I really did.

Following are some sites that are definitely worth checking out (but feel free to surf around awhile, because lots of other cool dog sites are out there).

Blue Dog Can Count

My esteemed colleague, Dr. Stuart Turner, D.V.M., of the Veterinary Information Network, thinks this site is a hoot, and I sort of agree, but please don't tell him. I don't want to encourage him to spend even *more* time bouncing around on the Web than he does already.

Surf's up for
a tour of
canine
cyberspace!

Photo courtesy of Richard D. Schmidt.

Blue Dog is a Web site for elementary school children — or like-minded adults — designed to encourage them about math and to help improve their math skills. (Hmmmmm. I wonder if Stuart mentioned this site to me because he thinks some hope still exists for me and those math skills? Nahhhhhh. No hope. Trust me.)

So what's the deal? The screen shows a full-color reproduction of the painting *Blue Dog*, by George Rodrigue, which you will recognize the minute you see it. She's darn cute, this dog, endearing as all-get-out. You enter a simple math problem on the page, such as 1 + 4 = ?, and Blue Dog barks out the answer. No animation, but hey, I'm easily amused.

The site offers some other links worth exploring, although most are not dog-related. Check out the indigo pup at `http://kao.ini.cmu.edu:5550/bdf.html` to sharpen those math skills.

Dog Term Glossary

I tried to print this sucker out for my files and hit cancel as fast as I could — the text is 45 pages long! But what a great site — everything from A ("Abdomen") to Y ("Yorkshire terrier"), with lots of great information and dozens of links to other places in between. Want to know what a *stop* is? First dog in the AKC stud book? The information is in here, along with great stuff about greyhounds, AKC breeds, and rare breeds.

Kyler B. Laird of Indiana pulled this one together, and it should be good for hours of entertaining and informative net cruising. Save your visit to this site for a winter's day, though, so as not to cut into prime dog-walking weather. (My dogs make me type these things.)

Laird's page is at `http://www.ecn.purdue.edu:80/~laird/Dogs/glossary.html`. Check out the picture of him and his dogs. If he looks familiar, maybe it's because you went to high school with him. You can find out where that was in his biography. (It's *his* Web page, folks, he can put anything he wants to on it!)

And a *stop,* by the way, is that area where most dogs' skulls "step down," right where the eyes hit the nose.

Dave's and Other Dog Lists

Almost as much fun as a video of the all-time best Stupid Pet Tricks are David Letterman's Top 10 Lists, at least three of which pertain to dogs. The searchable Top Ten site is at `http://www.late-show.com/ttref/topten.htm`. Search for "dogs," and you'll get the collection.

My favorite of these is "Ways the U.S. Would Be Different if the Next President Were a Dog," from the July 8, 1994, show. Best of the lot: No. 3 and No. 6. Sorry, but the lawyers — Dave's and *...For Dummies'* — won't let me tell you more.

That's just a teaser. You have to check out the rest on your own. Okay, one more, No. 8 on the "Signs You Have a Dumb Dog" list from October 19, 1993. Andy, my smart dog, thinks it applies to my other dog, Ben.

JUST FOR FUN

My dog says, "Cheese!"

Figuring out the No. 1 reason why people put a Web page together is impossible but, based on my travels, I have to guess that putting pictures of your dog in cyberspace has to be in the top ten. Doubt me? Go to AltaVista and enter "dog" or "puppy" and "picture." When your computer stops smoking, you'll have enough canine snapshots to look at for the rest of the decade.

Not that I'm making fun of that, certainly. In my Pet Connection area on AOL are pictures of *my* dogs, Andy and Benjamin (keyword: PET). I think they're the cutest pups in cyberspace, but I figure a few people out there would strongly disagree.

When you're through laughing at your dog, laugh a little at yourself. Check out the "You Know You've Gone to the Dogs When . . ." list at http://www.dogpatch.org/dogs.html.

No mere list of ten here: Here are more than 60 reality checks for dog lovers, such as "Your voice is recognized by your vet's receptionist," "Dog crates double as chairs and/or tables in your family room," and "The No. 1 priority when buying a new house is the size and landscape of the backyard."

Youch! The truth hurts, doesn't it? I'd like to add one of my own: "When you shop for a wagon, van, or sport utility vehicle — what good is a sedan? — your most important concerns are how the seats fold down and if the air conditioning reaches into the cargo area."

She Ate WHAT?

It's pretty well been proven by now that dog lovers have a great sense of humor, but the folks behind the *It's a Dogs Eat Amazing Things World* page are pushing the edge of the envelope. This wonderfully wry page is a tribute to destructiveness, starting with the prodigious chewing exploits of the creators' own dogs, Keppie and Shayna.

Keppie, their "incessantly hungry blonde Lab," sets the tone for the page. The list of items she has destroyed includes: a cooler, a bicycle seat, a trampoline, three pounds of frozen chicken, Christmas ornaments, a two-pound bag of prunes, glasses, three remote controls, a box of chocolate doughnuts, and a package of vacuum-cleaner bags.

Not bad, but some of the other dogs "celebrated" here have done even better. How much "better"? Like peeling siding off the house. Like eating the only copy of a wedding video. A shepherd-Lab cross named Tabitha has eaten the homework of the children in her family — honestly, dogs *do* eat homework!

Some nice links make this page even better. Visit the site at http://www.weblink.com/dog-bite/.

The Mother of All Canine Web Sites

I've sung her praises before, but Cindy Tittle Moore really does deserve some kind of medal for the work she has done to make the Internet a friendly place for dog lovers. Her library of *FAQs* (Frequently Asked Questions) has some of the best information available anywhere on all aspects of choosing and living with a dog. You'll find no sugarcoating here: The breed FAQs are full of detailed descriptions of what living with each breed is like, written by experienced fanciers who are just as keen on sharing the problems as they are the good.

Rawhide remote control

Reading the stories on the *It's a Dogs Eat Amazing Things World* pages confirmed what I'd suspected all along from my own mail: Dogs love remote controls. Think about it: They're the perfect size to carry around. They're just enough of a challenge to chew to bits. And they smell as much like you as does your underwear (another canine favorite).

Which means if you can't find the remote, it may not be because you put it somewhere you don't remember or because your spouse let it slip between the cushions on the couch or because your kids lost it. Your dog may have slipped away with it.

So check your pet's favorite hiding place. If you're lucky, the remote's still in one piece. Mine is, except for some chew marks at one end.

Want a tip? Forget about trying to train your dog to leave the remote alone. Training *yourself* to put it out of harm's way when it's not in your hand is far easier.

And remember: You have to lose at least a half-dozen of them before the folks at the *Dogs Eat Amazing Things* Web site will be the least bit impressed.

Breed descriptions aren't all you'll find either. Also included are FAQs on raising a puppy and on health care, on canine organizations and publications, on dog breeding and canine competitions. Truly remarkable, all told.

The jumping-off site for all this information is the rec.pet.dogs FAQ homepage, at `http://www/zmall.com/pet/dog-faqs/`. This site is an absolute must-see.

Cutting-Edge Net Vets

I have to say up front that I'm associated with the Veterinary Information Network, Inc., because my syndicated columns appear in the Pet Care Forum of America Online, which is a VIN-run enterprise. But that doesn't stop me from being impressed with what they've got going.

VIN is the undisputed pioneer in online resources for veterinarians. With more than 3,000 online veterinarians, including some of the nation's top specialists in every imaginable field, this group is the world's largest group practice, offering consulting, continuing education, searchable databases of the latest from the journals, and a special service for veterinary support staff.

Get a preview of this brave new veterinary world by visiting the VIN Web site at `http://www.vin.com/vinpromo/index.htm`.

As with all professions, online communications in the veterinary industry are an important way to keep up-to-date on the latest trends. Services like VIN are a great equalizer, keeping the lone country veterinarian as current as the sharpest new grad in the largest big-city group practice.

Ask your veterinarian what she is doing to keep her knowledge and skills sharp. An online specialty service like VIN — or the American Veterinary Medical Association's service, NOAH — should be part of the answer.

For Purebreds Only . . . Mostly

Not much on the American Kennel Club's Web site will interest the owner of a mixed-breed dog, and the AKC isn't shy about saying so. Consider the mission statement of this breed registry, founded in 1884:

- ✔ "Maintain a registry for purebred dogs and preserve its integrity."
- ✔ "Sanction dog events that promote interest in, and sustain the process of, breeding for type and function of purebred dogs."
- ✔ "Take whatever actions are necessary to protect and assure the continuation of the sport of purebred dogs."

See any themes here? Women once weren't all that welcome either, if it's any consolation.

Still, the AKC isn't half as snooty as it seems, and their Web site is proof of that. The organization is a tireless fighter against antidog legislation and promotes responsible care of *all* dogs (including mixed breeds) through its Canine Good Citizenship program. Their Companion Animal Recovery service, a registry of microchips and tattoos, is open not only to all dogs, but also to other animals — cats, sure, but also exotic pets such as pot-bellied pigs. So see? They're not so bad.

If you're looking for a purebred dog or puppy, this site is one of the best places to start finding that reputable breeder or breed-rescue group. Information on every AKC-registered breed is available, as well as links to many breed Web sites. During the Westminster Kennel Club dog show, the de facto national championship for show dogs, the AKC site offers same-day results from the breed classes.

This site is worth a good look at `http://www.akc.org`.

And Now a Word from a Shelter . . .

The American Kennel Club and other registries group breeds in a logical fashion, according to their purpose, or lack of the same. The San Diego County Department of Animal Control has a different way of looking at things, on its Ranger's Realtime Rescue page, promoting shelter adoptions and better care and information on dogs.

Instead of the AKC's Sporting group, how about "A Face Only a Mother Could Love," a category which includes Basset hounds, Bloodhounds, Chinese shar-peis and Chinese cresteds. Or "Wolfy Dogs," in which you find akitas, Alaskan malamutes, Samoyeds, and Siberian huskies. Don't expect real serious canine information here, though. Border collies really don't belong under "Furballs," and a kuvasz is more of a guarding dog than a hunting dog.

But the Animal Shelter Success Stories are inspiring, and if you just happen to be in the neighborhood of San Diego, you may find the dog of your dreams on the page of available pets. This page is certainly worth a look at http://merkury.saic.com/ranger/.

More and more shelter organizations and rescue groups are putting up Web sites to put out the word about adoptable dogs. Put "shelter" or "rescue" in your Web search engine, add your city, and see what pops up. You may see the dog of your dreams!

JUST FOR FUN

Sit . . . Assis . . . Zit . . . Oh, just do it!

Now here's something that will impress all your friends: Teach your dog commands in another language. With the help of Mark Plonsky, a psychology professor at the University of Wisconsin, Stevens Point, you can start today.

The good Dr. Plonsky is a dog-lover who has put together terrific site at http://www.uwsp.edu/acad/psych/dog/dog.htm, with articles on a variety of dog-related topics as well as some excellent links. (Check out the link to the Dog Park/Dog Run Reporter at http://www.mindspring.com/~patmar/.) Dr. P's overall site is a solid and throught-provoking resource, but his dog

commands page is what really caught my eye, at http://www.uwsp.edu/acad/psych/dog/languag.htm.

I had a lot of fun with this page, especially the translations for "good dog!" I tried them on my two, and got tail wags for every one. Before I give them credit for being multilingual and oh-so-smart, though, I should confess my crooning voice probably tipped them off. Try them on your dog, and be sweet: "So brav" (German); "bon garcon" (French); "hodny' (Czech); "okos" (Hungarian); "dobry pies" (Polish); or "kelev-tov" (Hebrew).

Good Dog (-e-zine)!

The Dog-e-zine site bills itself as "The Premier Site for Dog Lovers," which takes a fair amount of chutzpah considering the competition, but I have to admit they've got a fair claim. This site is one of the best-looking and best-organized around, with a nice, light touch in dispensing information and linking to other sites. Dog-e-zine does most sites one better by ranking the pages to which it links (on a "bone scale" of one to four). The people who run the site are not the least bit shy about telling you the places to skip, either.

Check it out at http://www.dog-e-zine.com/.

Bully!

For the purposes of this list, I stayed clear of single-breed sites, although hundreds of them out are there, and many are very impressive. I could not resist Bulldog dot Org, however, which was a four-bone pick on the Dog-e-zine site, and rightfully so.

Bulldog dot Org is *not* a single-breed site, so I'm letting them slide in here. Besides, talk about faces only a mother could love: How *can* you resist these guys? You find pictures of bull terriers, bulldogs, American pit bull terriers, French bulldogs, and other related breeds. Tough dogs, some. Dogs that only look tough, others. Snoring dogs, drooling dogs, almost all, with hearts as big as their heads.

Bulldog dot Org has its own Official Policy ("This page is intentionally left blank") and anthem, "Oh Bulldog, eh?" sung to the tune of *Oh Canada*: "... Bullies keep our domain, goldenless and free/Bulldog dot Org we http for free!"

My retriever's feelings were hurt some by the antigolden bias, but when I pointed out that he only *looks* like a black golden, he recovered. Or maybe he was just at the end of his short attention span, hard to tell. Not that those bullies care a bit what some goofy goldens — or any other dogs — think.

Check it out at http://www.bulldog.org.

Oh, What an Exciting Web We Weave

If you have a site you'd like to bring to my attention, let me know at Giori@aol.com. Readers are always asking me for new dog-friendly rest stops on the information superhighway.

Appendix
Additional Resources

Breed Registries

United States and Canada

American Kennel Club
5580 Centerview Drive
Raleigh, NC 27606-3390

American Mixed Breed Obedience
Registry (AMBOR)
205 1st Street S.W.
New Prague, MN 56071

American Rare Breed Association
100 Nicholson Street NW
Washington, DC 20011

Canadian Kennel Club
Commerce Park
89 Skyway Avenue, Suite 100
Etobicoke, ON M9W 6R4

Mixed Breed Dog Club of America
1937 Seven Pines Drive
St. Louis, MO 63146-3717

States Kennel Club
P.O. Box 389
Hattiesburg, MS 39403-0389

United Kennel Club
100 East Kilgore Road
Kalamazoo, MI 49001-5598

Other countries

Australian National Kennel Council
Royal Showgrounds
Ascot Vale 3032
Victoria 3032
Australia

The Kennel Club
1-5 Clarges Street
Piccadilly
London W1Y 8AB
United Kingdom

Kennel Union of Southern Africa
P.O. Box 2659
Cape Town 8000
South Africa

New Zealand Kennel Club
Private Bag 50903
Porirua 6220
New Zealand

International Organizations

Federation Cynologique Internationale
13 Place Albert I
B6530 Thin
Belgium

General-Interest Canine Publications

Annuals

Dogs in Canada Annual
Canadian Kennel Club
89 Skyway Ave., Suite 200
Etobicoke, ON M9Q 6R4

DOGS USA
Fancy Publications
P.O. Box 6050
Mission Viejo, CA 92690

Magazines and newspapers

AKC Gazette
American Kennel Club
51 Madison Avenue
New York, NY 10010

Dogs in Africa
Sixth Floor, Bree Castle
68 Bree Street
Cape Town 8001
South Africa

Dogs in Canada
Canadian Kennel Club
89 Skyway Ave., Suite 200
Etobicoke, ON M9Q 6R4

Dog Fancy
Fancy Publications
P.O. Box 6050
Mission Viejo, CA 92690

Dog World
9 Tufton Street
Ashford, Kent TN23 1QN
United Kingdom

Dog World
PO Box 6500
Chicago, IL 60680

Dogs Monthly/Our Dogs
5 Oxford RoadStation Approach
Manchester M60 1SX
United Kingdom

Kennel Gazette
1-5 Clarges Street
Piccadilly
London W1Y 8AB
United Kingdom

National Dog
P.O. Box 670
Seven Hills NSW 2147
Australia

New Zealand Kennel Gazette
Private Bag 50903
Porirua 6220
New Zealand

Pet-Supply Sources

Bicycle Dog Leash
(Bicycle dog exerciser)
9181 Gaylord Street
Thorton, CO 80229
303-289-4699

Cherrybrook
(General pet supplies)
Route 57, P.O. Box 15
Broadway, NJ 08808
908-689-7979
800-524-0820

Direct Book Service
Dog & Cat Book Catalog
(Pet books, including rare and hard-to-find)
P.O. Box 2778
Wenatchee, WA 98807-2778
509-663-9115
800-776-2665
dgctbook@cascade.net

Doctors Foster & Smith
(General pet supplies)
2253 Air Park Road
P.O. Box 100
Rhinelander, WI 54501-0100
800-826-7206

In the Company of Dogs
(Gift items for dog lovers)
P.O. Box 7071
Dover, DE 19903
800-924-5050

ImmunoVet
(Citronella anti-bark collar)
5910 Breckenridge Parkway
Tampa, FL 33610-4253

J-B Wholesale Pet Supplies
(General pet supplies)
5 Raritan Road
Oakland, NJ 07436
800-526-0388

K9Cruiser
(Bicycle dog exerciser)
4940 DeSoto Street
San Diego, CA 92109
800-592-7847

Oaken Shaw Grange
(General pet supplies)
Doncaster Road
Crofton, Wakefield
West Yorkshire, WF4 1SD
United Kingdom

Pet-Pak Inc.
(Pet first aid kits)
P.O. Box 982
Edison, NJ 08818-0982
908-906-9200
800-217-PETS (7387)

Pet Supply House Ltd.
(General pet supplies)
373 Wyecroft Road
Oakville, ON L6K 2H2
Canada

PF. magic
(Dogz software)
501 Second Street, Suite 400
San Francisco, CA 94107

PTP Marketing
(Canine collectibles)
32 Church Drive East
Keswick, Leeds LS1 79EP
United Kingdom

R.C. Steele
(General pet supplies)
P.O. Box 910
Brockport, NY 14420-0910
800-872-3773
800-424-2205 in Canada
716-637-1408

Reigning Cats and Dogs
(Gift items for dog lovers)
5617 H Street
Sacramento, CA 95819
916-455-5619
RECATDOG@aol.com

San Francisco SPCA
("Digital Dog" poster)
2500 16th Street
San Francisco, CA 94103

Springer
(Bicycle dog exerciser)
1627 Union Street
Bangor, ME 04401
800-BIKE-K9s

Sugargum Dog Centre
(General pet supplies)
20 Boronia Drive
Hillside, Victoria 3037
Australia

The Trotter
(Motorized treadmill)
P.O. Box 256
Massapequa, NY 11758
516-798-5973

Index